PSYCHIC ACADEMY

VOLUME 11

BY
KATSU AKI

TOKYOPOP®

HAMBURG // LONDON // LOS ANGELES // TOKYO

Psychic Academy Vol. 11
Created by Katsu Aki

Translation - Yuki N. Johnson
English Adaptation - Nathan Johnson
Retouch and Lettering - Alyson Stetz
Production Artist - Lucas Rivera
Cover Design - Seth Cable

Editor - Aaron Suhr
Digital Imaging Manager - Chris Buford
Production Managers - Jennifer Miller and Mutsumi Miyazaki
Managing Editor - Lindsey Johnston
VP of Production - Ron Klamert
Publisher and E.I.C. - Mike Kiley
President and C.O.O. - John Parker
C.E.O. and Chief Creative Officer - Stuart Levy

A  Manga

TOKYOPOP Inc.
5900 Wilshire Blvd. Suite 2000
Los Angeles, CA 90036

E-mail: info@TOKYOPOP.com
Come visit us online at www.TOKYOPOP.com

ISBN: 1-59532-430-5
First TOKYOPOP printing: March 2006
10 9 8 7 6 5 4 3 2 1
Printed in Canada

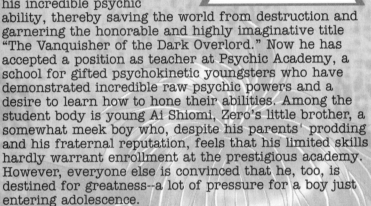

Story Thus Far...

PSYCHIC ACADEMY

Zerodyme Kyupura Pa Azalraku Vairu Rua Darogu (a.k.a. Zero) stopped the evil demon lord with his incredible psychic ability, thereby saving the world from destruction and garnering the honorable and highly imaginative title "The Vanquisher of the Dark Overlord." Now he has accepted a position as teacher at Psychic Academy, a school for gifted psychokinetic youngsters who have demonstrated incredible raw psychic powers and a desire to learn how to hone their abilities. Among the student body is young Ai Shiomi, Zero's little brother, a somewhat meek boy who, despite his parents' prodding and his fraternal reputation, feels that his limited skills hardly warrant enrollment at the prestigious academy. However, everyone else is convinced that he, too, is destined for greatness--a lot of pressure for a boy just entering adolescence.

As Ai's thoughts and dreams are preoccupied with Mew--and the kiss he planted on her--he and Orina start to drift apart. And with new roommate assignments, life at the Academy may be undergoing a bit of change. Meanwhile, three new freshmen at the school challenge the upper-class to an Aura battle at lunch. But when Ai tries to stop the fighting, Orina gets caught in the crossfire! Will the danger bring them closer together?

CONTENTS

煌羅万象
ψchic academy

Chapter 36: The Goodbye Club

φchic acad

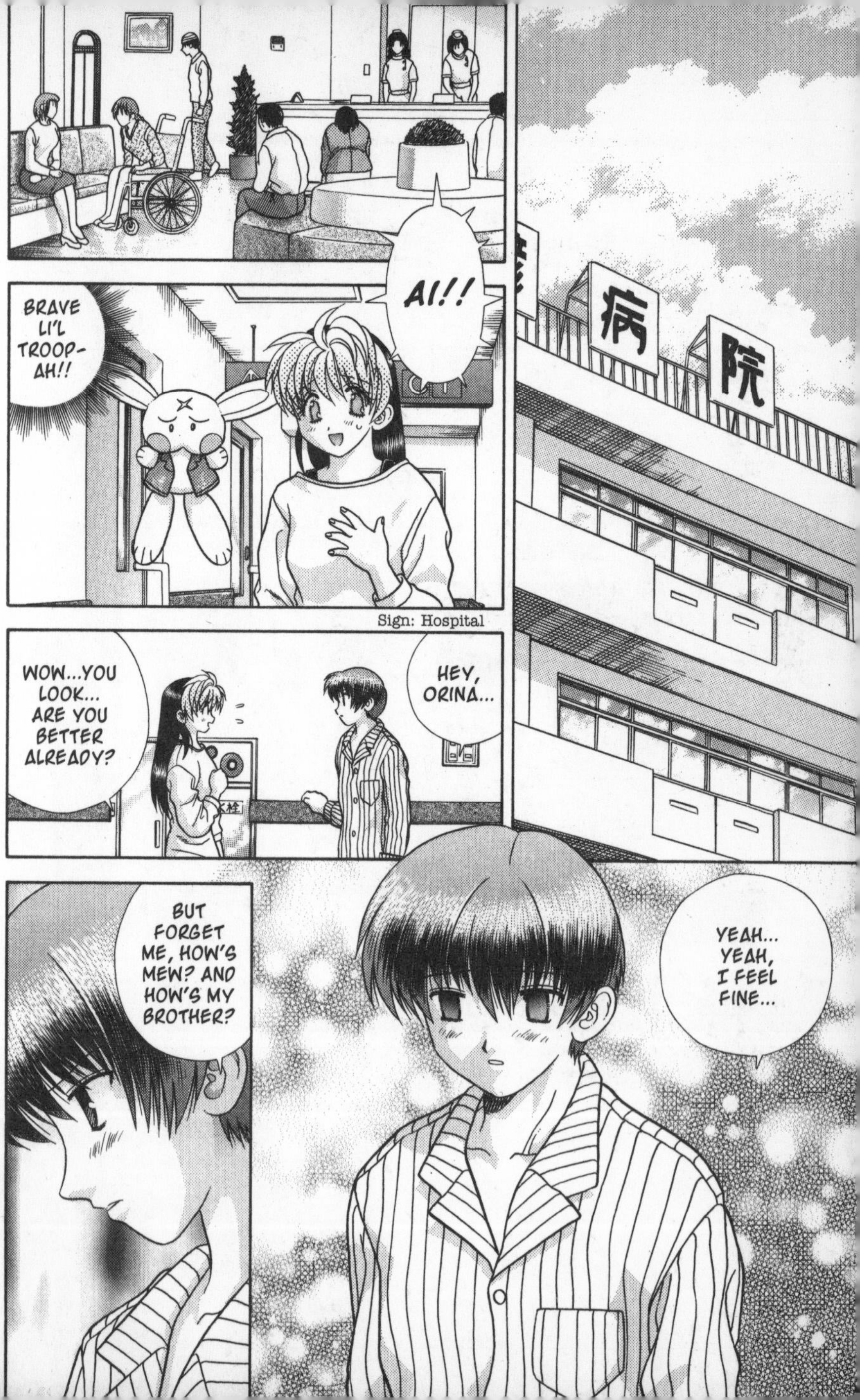
病院
Sign: Hospital
AI!!
BRAVE LI'L TROOP-AH!!
HEY, ORINA...
WOW...YOU LOOK... ARE YOU BETTER ALREADY?
YEAH... YEAH, I FEEL FINE...
BUT FORGET ME, HOW'S MEW? AND HOW'S MY BROTHER?

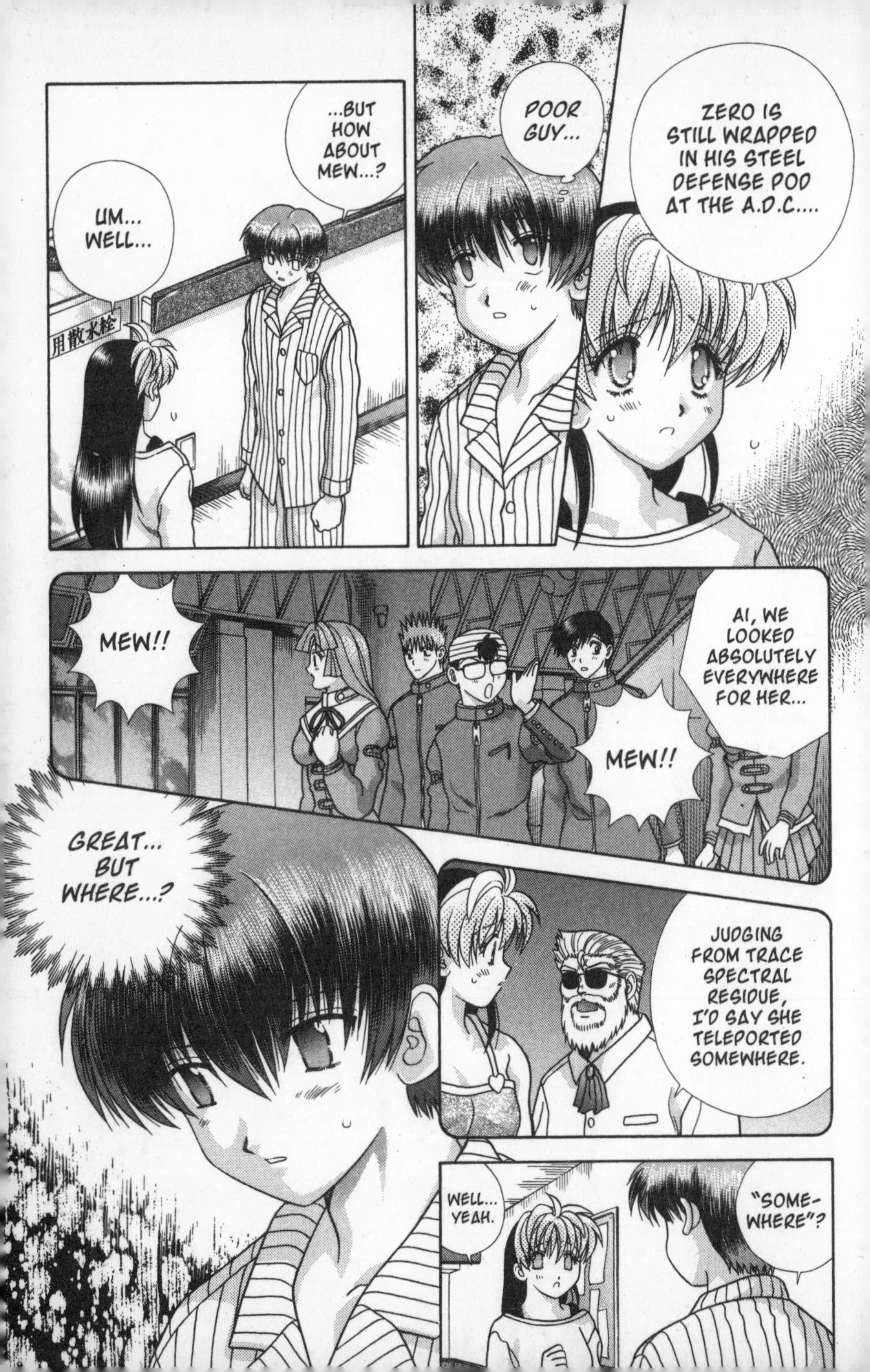
ZERO IS STILL WRAPPED IN HIS STEEL DEFENSE POD AT THE A.D.C....
POOR GUY...
...BUT HOW ABOUT MEW...?
UM... WELL...
用散水栓
AI, WE LOOKED ABSOLUTELY EVERYWHERE FOR HER...
MEW!!
MEW!!
JUDGING FROM TRACE SPECTRAL RESIDUE, I'D SAY SHE TELEPORTED SOMEWHERE.
GREAT... BUT WHERE...?
"SOME-WHERE"?
WELL... YEAH.

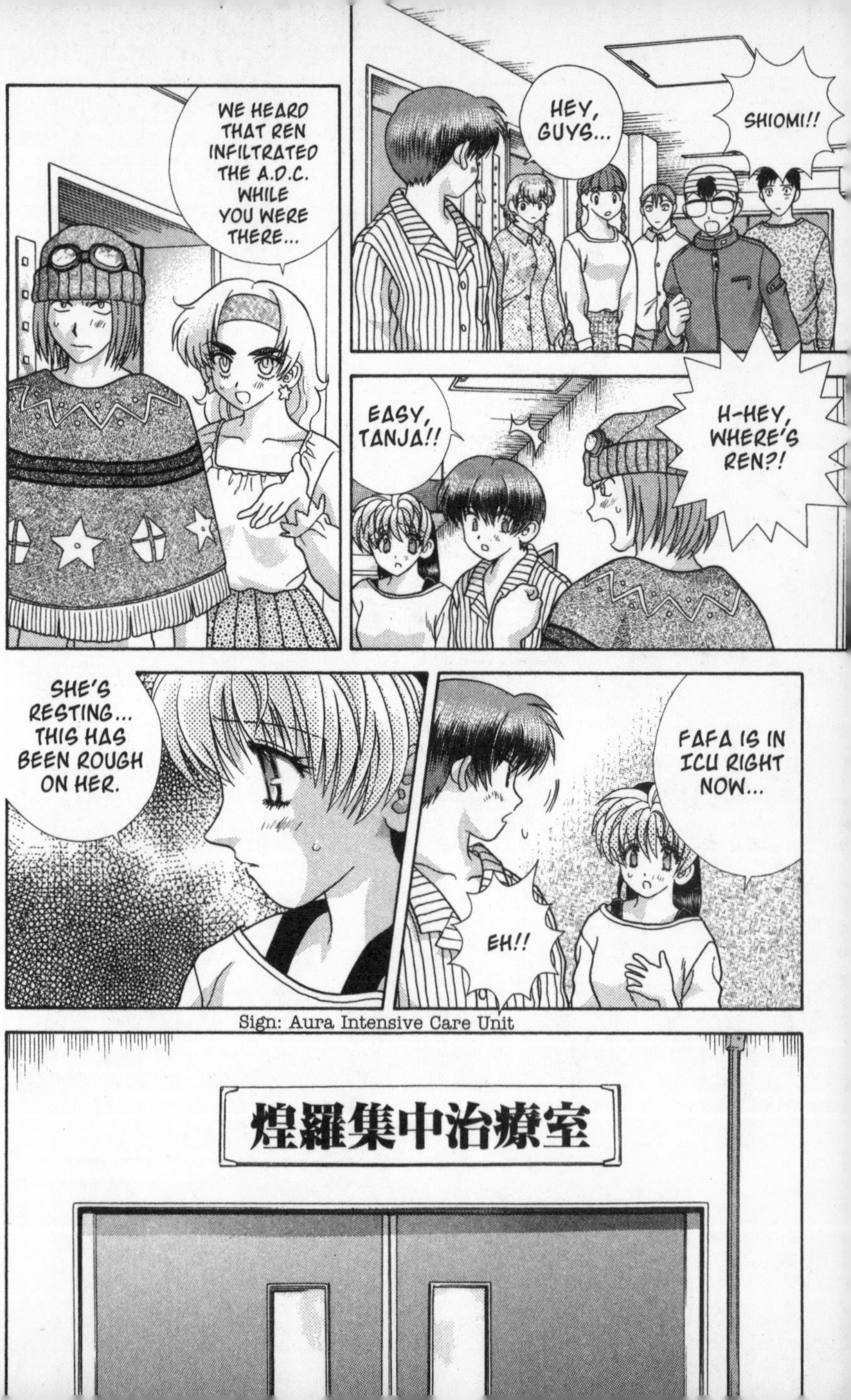
SHIOMI!!
HEY, GUYS...
H-HEY, WHERE'S REN?!
EASY, TANJA!!
WE HEARD THAT REN INFILTRATED THE A.D.C. WHILE YOU WERE THERE...
FAFA IS IN ICU RIGHT NOW...
EH!!
SHE'S RESTING... THIS HAS BEEN ROUGH ON HER.
Sign: Aura Intensive Care Unit
煌羅集中治療室

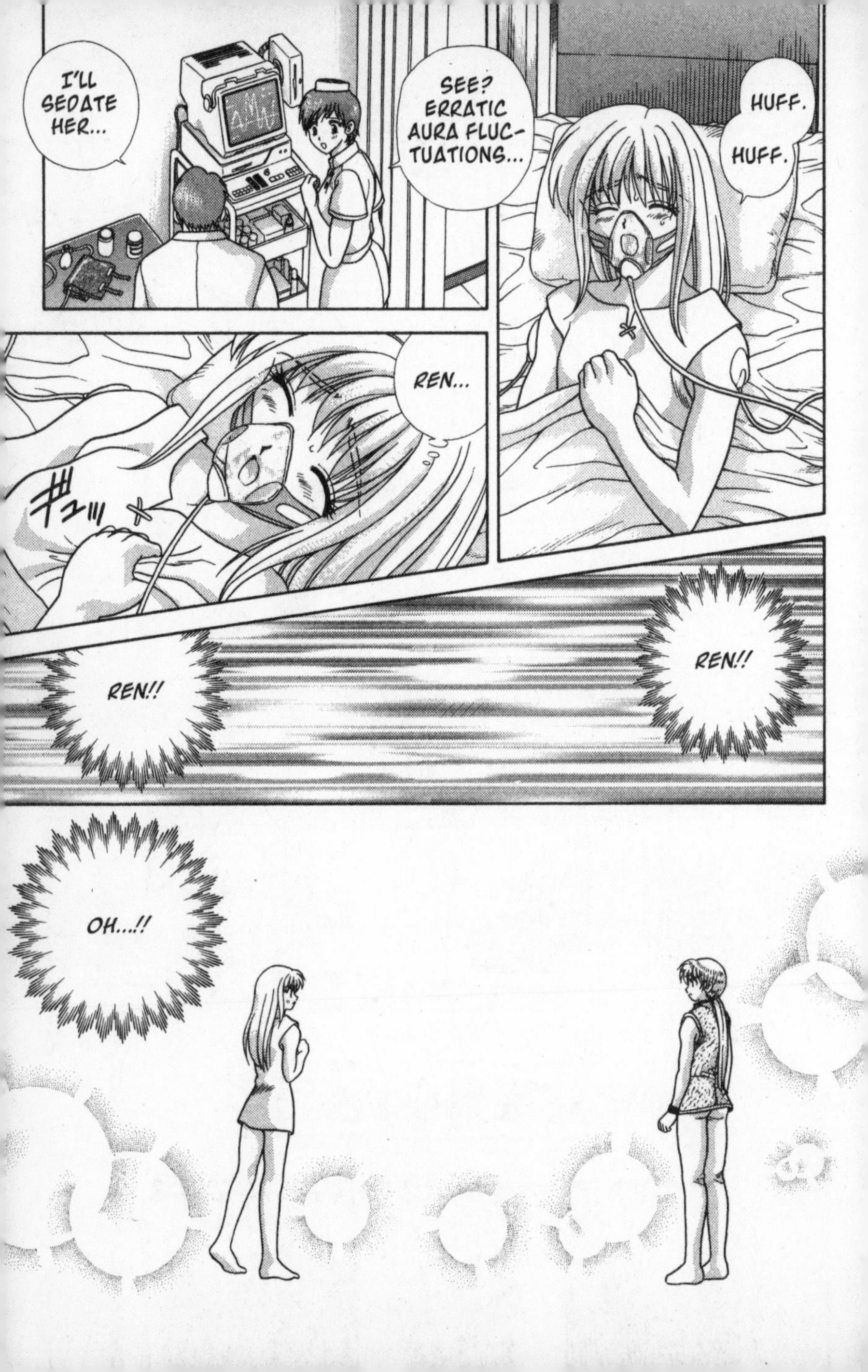
HUFF.
HUFF.
SEE? ERRATIC AURA FLUC-TUATIONS...
I'LL SEDATE HER...
REN...
REN!!
REN!!
OH...!!

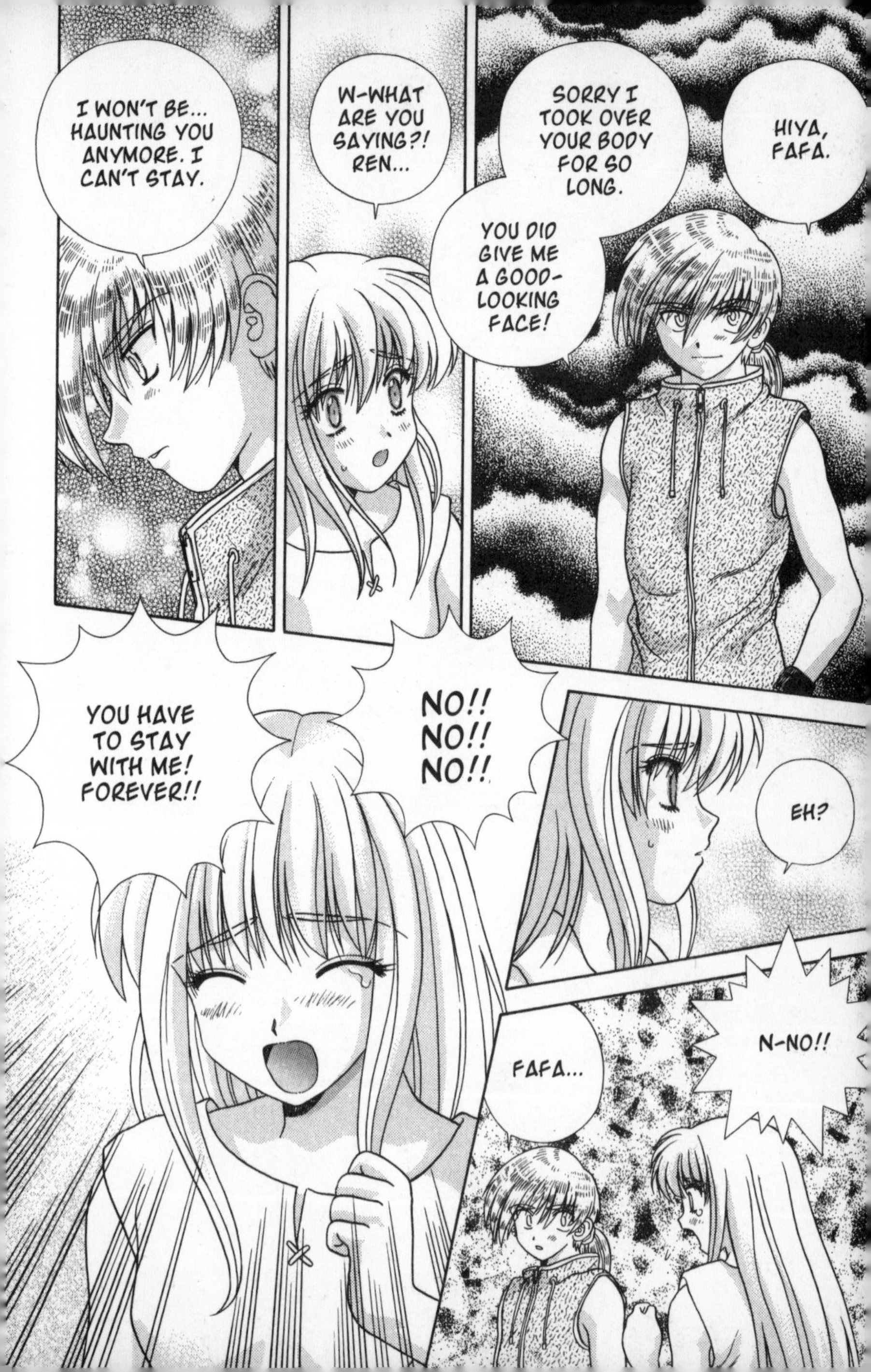
HIYA, FAFA.
SORRY I TOOK OVER YOUR BODY FOR SO LONG.
YOU DID GIVE ME A GOOD-LOOKING FACE!
W-WHAT ARE YOU SAYING?! REN...
I WON'T BE... HAUNTING YOU ANYMORE. I CAN'T STAY.
EH?
N-NO!!
FAFA...
NO!! NO!! NO!!
YOU HAVE TO STAY WITH ME! FOREVER!!

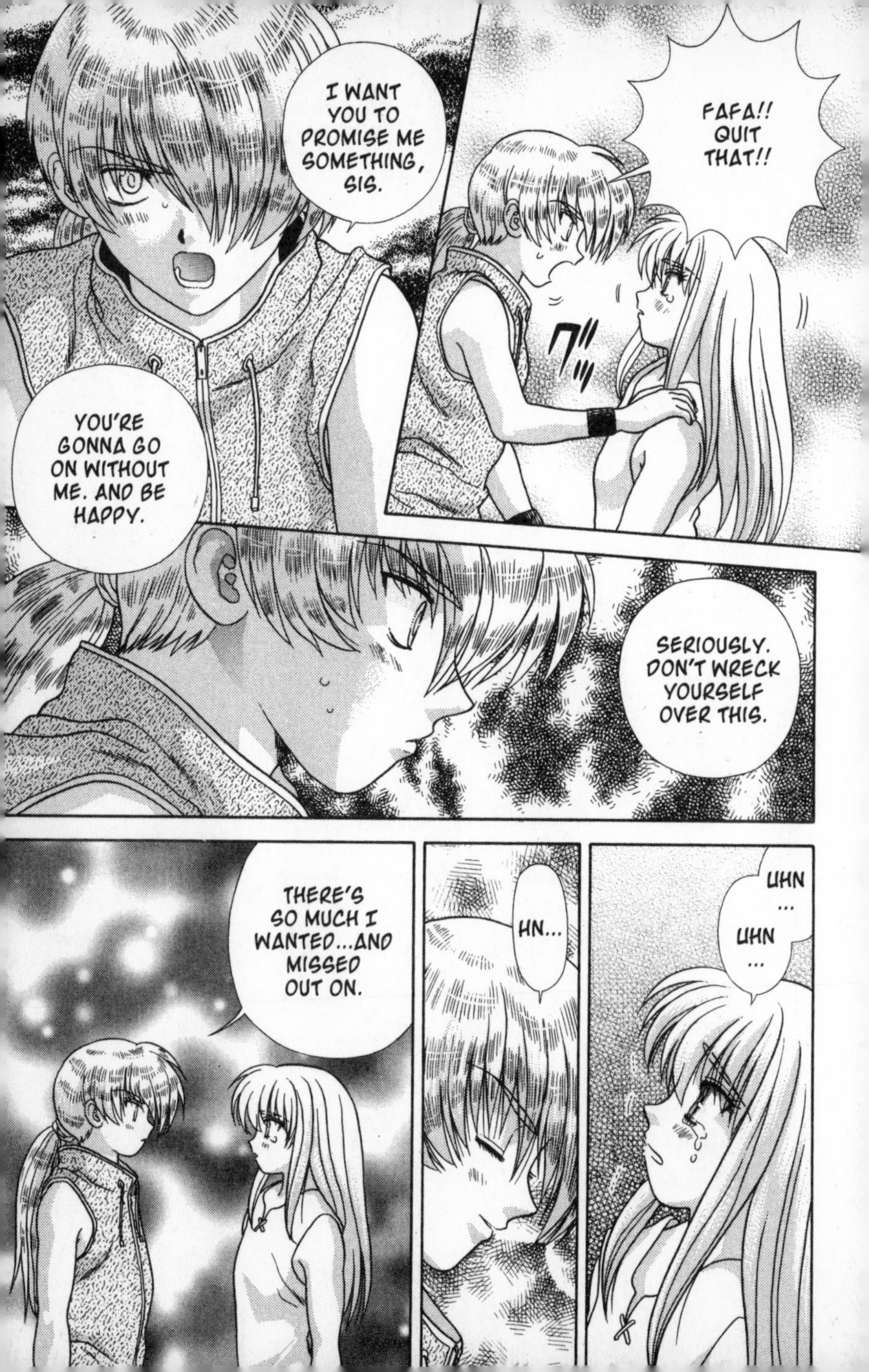
FAFA!! QUIT THAT!!
I WANT YOU TO PROMISE ME SOMETHING, SIS.
YOU'RE GONNA GO ON WITHOUT ME. AND BE HAPPY.
SERIOUSLY. DON'T WRECK YOURSELF OVER THIS.
UHN ... UHN ...
HN...
THERE'S SO MUCH I WANTED...AND MISSED OUT ON.

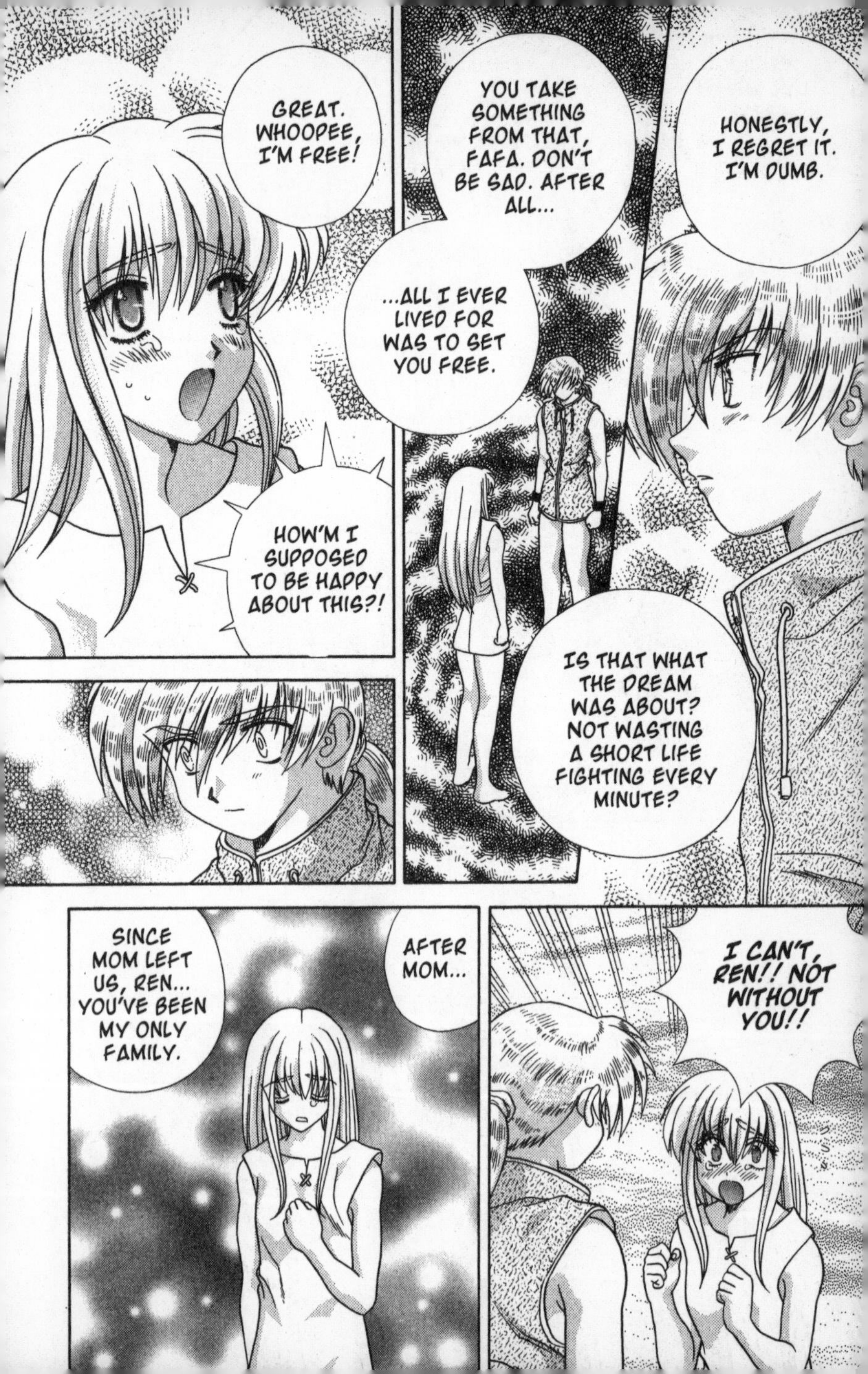
HONESTLY, I REGRET IT. I'M DUMB.
IS THAT WHAT THE DREAM WAS ABOUT? NOT WASTING A SHORT LIFE FIGHTING EVERY MINUTE?
YOU TAKE SOMETHING FROM THAT, FAFA. DON'T BE SAD. AFTER ALL...
...ALL I EVER LIVED FOR WAS TO SET YOU FREE.
GREAT. WHOOPEE, I'M FREE!
HOW'M I SUPPOSED TO BE HAPPY ABOUT THIS?!
I CAN'T, REN!! NOT WITHOUT YOU!!
AFTER MOM...
SINCE MOM LEFT US, REN... YOU'VE BEEN MY ONLY FAMILY.

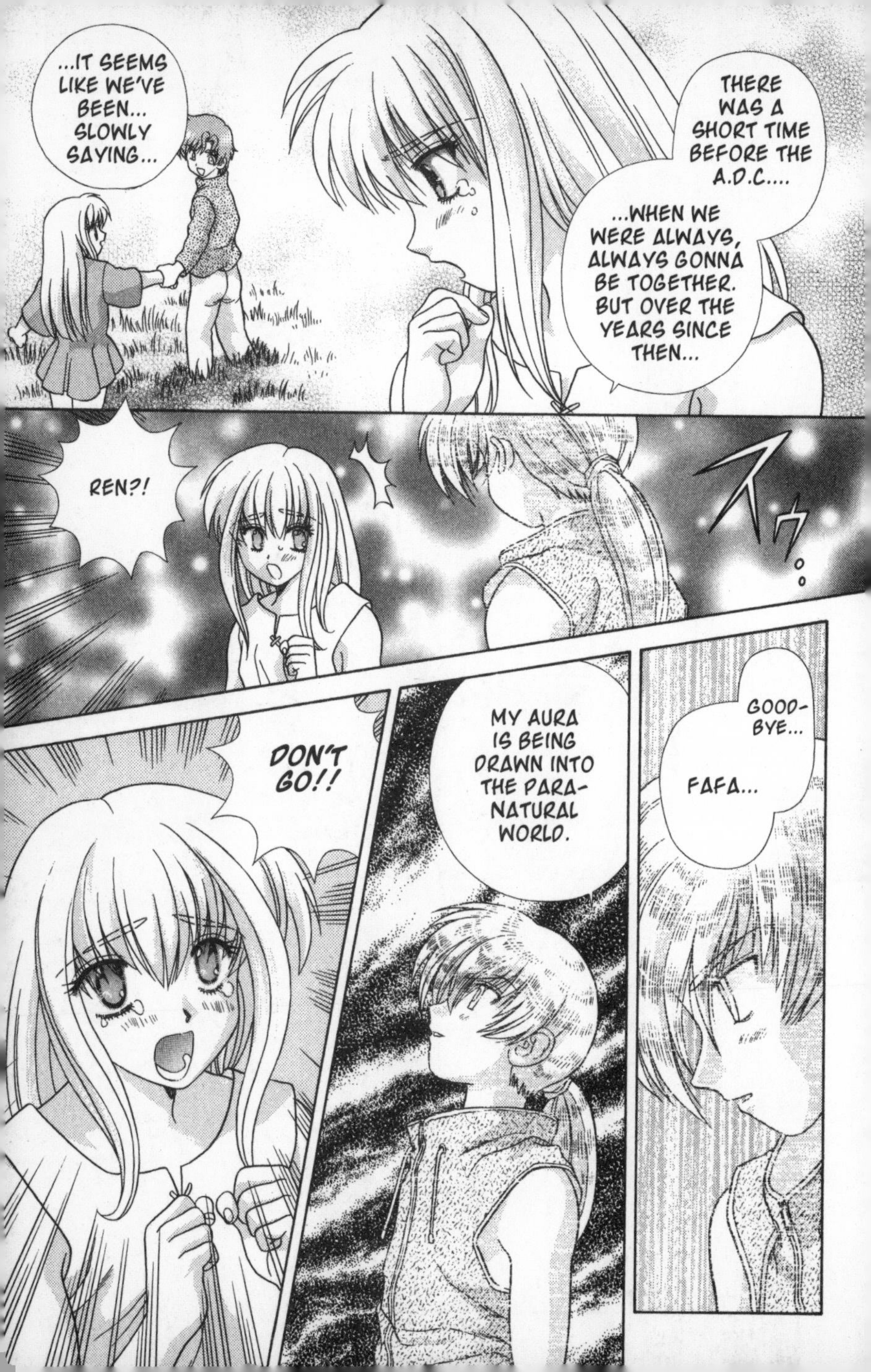
THERE WAS A SHORT TIME BEFORE THE A.D.C....
...WHEN WE WERE ALWAYS, ALWAYS GONNA BE TOGETHER. BUT OVER THE YEARS SINCE THEN...
...IT SEEMS LIKE WE'VE BEEN... SLOWLY SAYING...
スゥ
REN?!
GOOD-BYE...
FAFA...
MY AURA IS BEING DRAWN INTO THE PARA-NATURAL WORLD.
DON'T GO!!

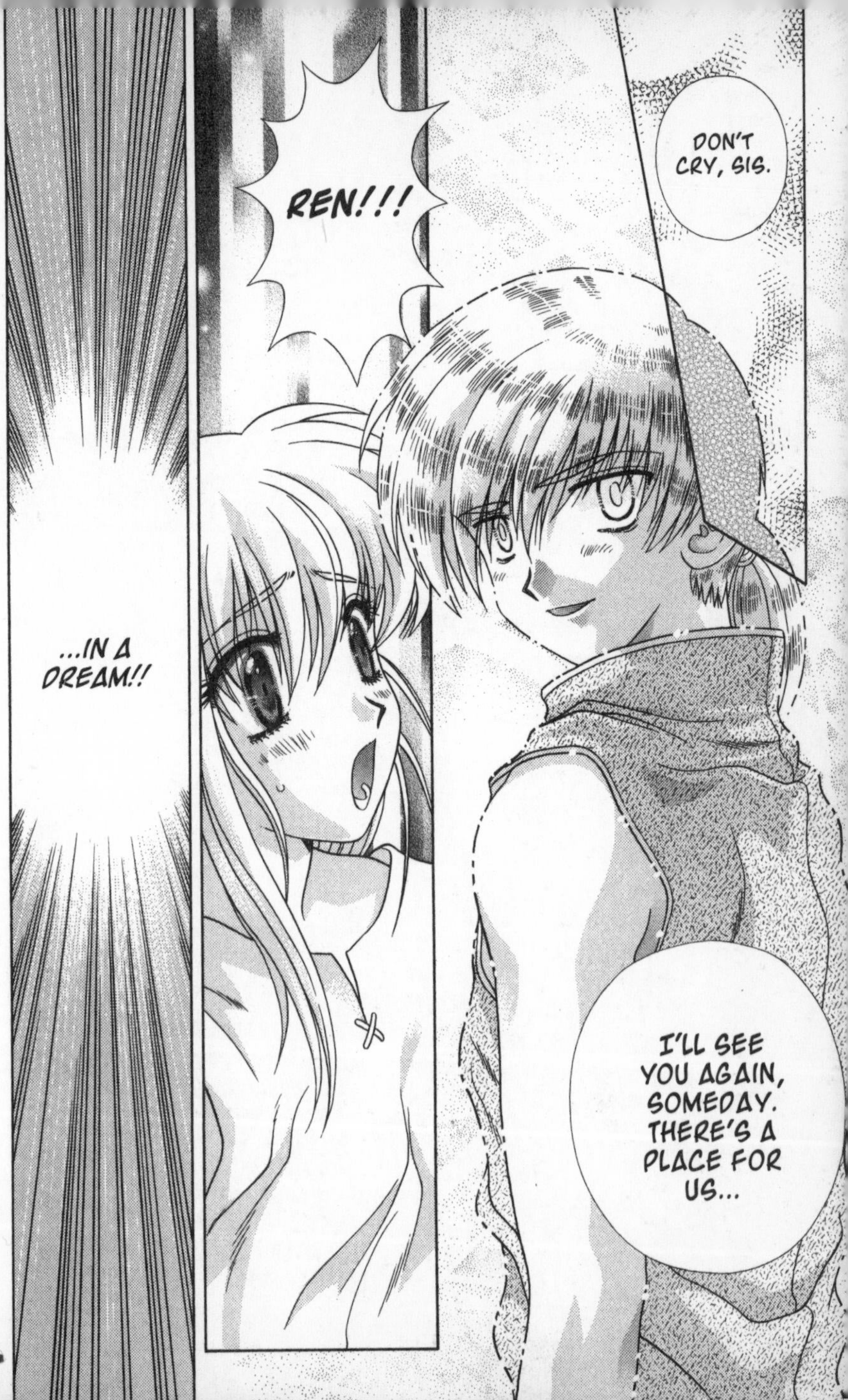
DON'T CRY, SIS.
I'LL SEE YOU AGAIN, SOMEDAY. THERE'S A PLACE FOR US...
REN!!!
...IN A DREAM!!

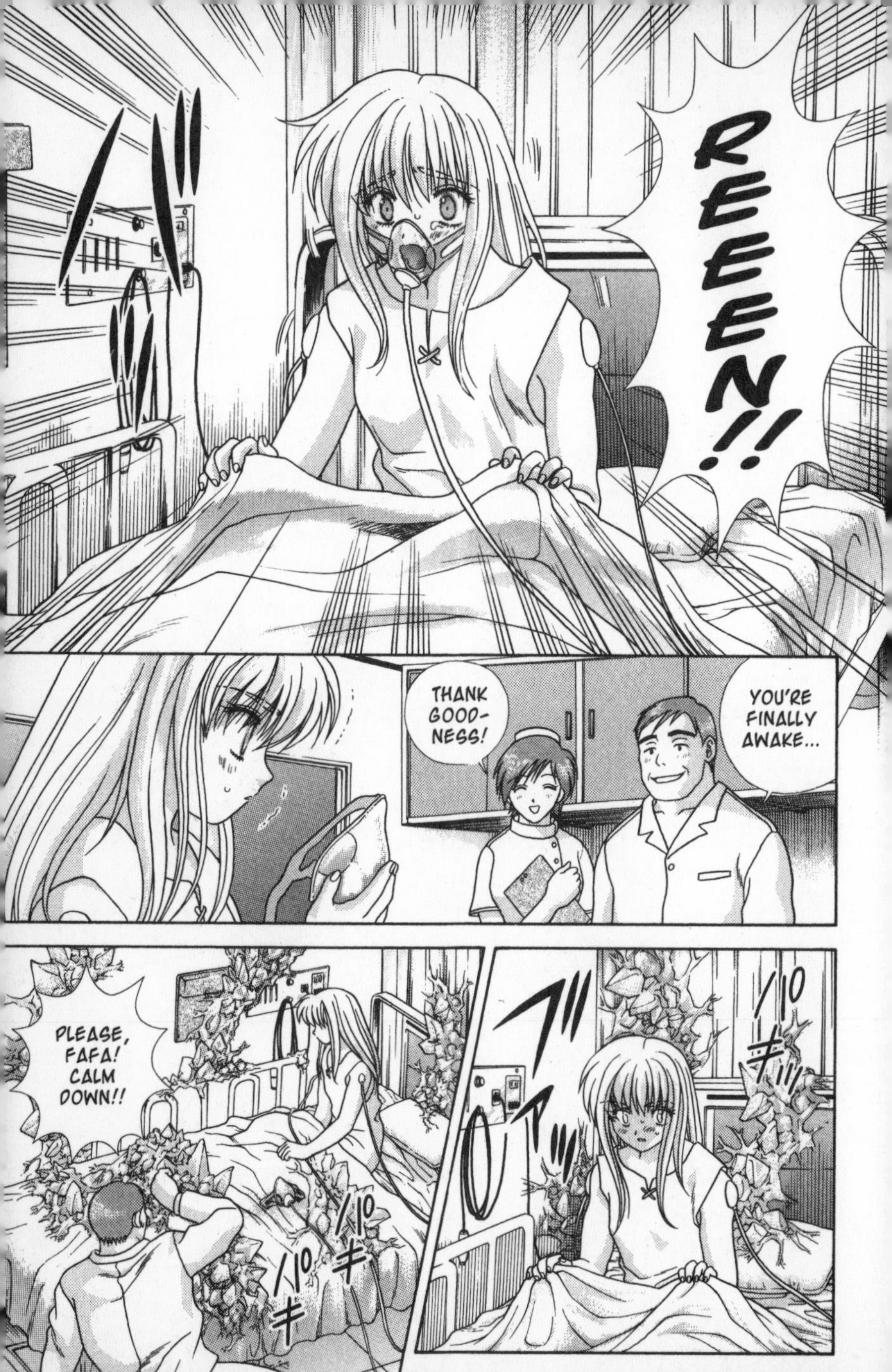
REEEEN!!
YOU'RE FINALLY AWAKE...
THANK GOODNESS!
PLEASE, FAFA! CALM DOWN!!

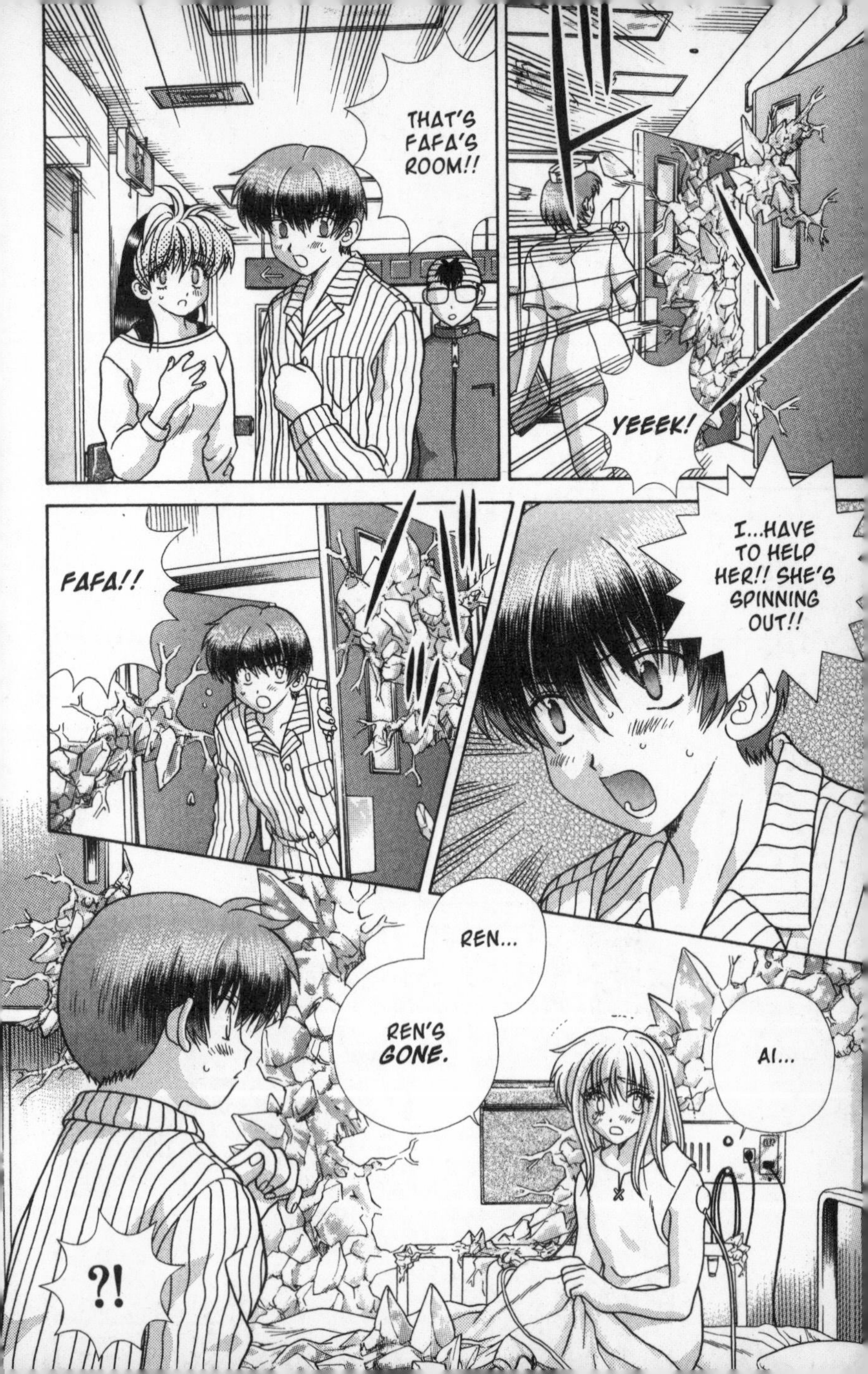
YEEEK!
THAT'S FAFA'S ROOM!!
I...HAVE TO HELP HER!! SHE'S SPINNING OUT!!
FAFA!!
AI...
REN...
REN'S GONE.
?!

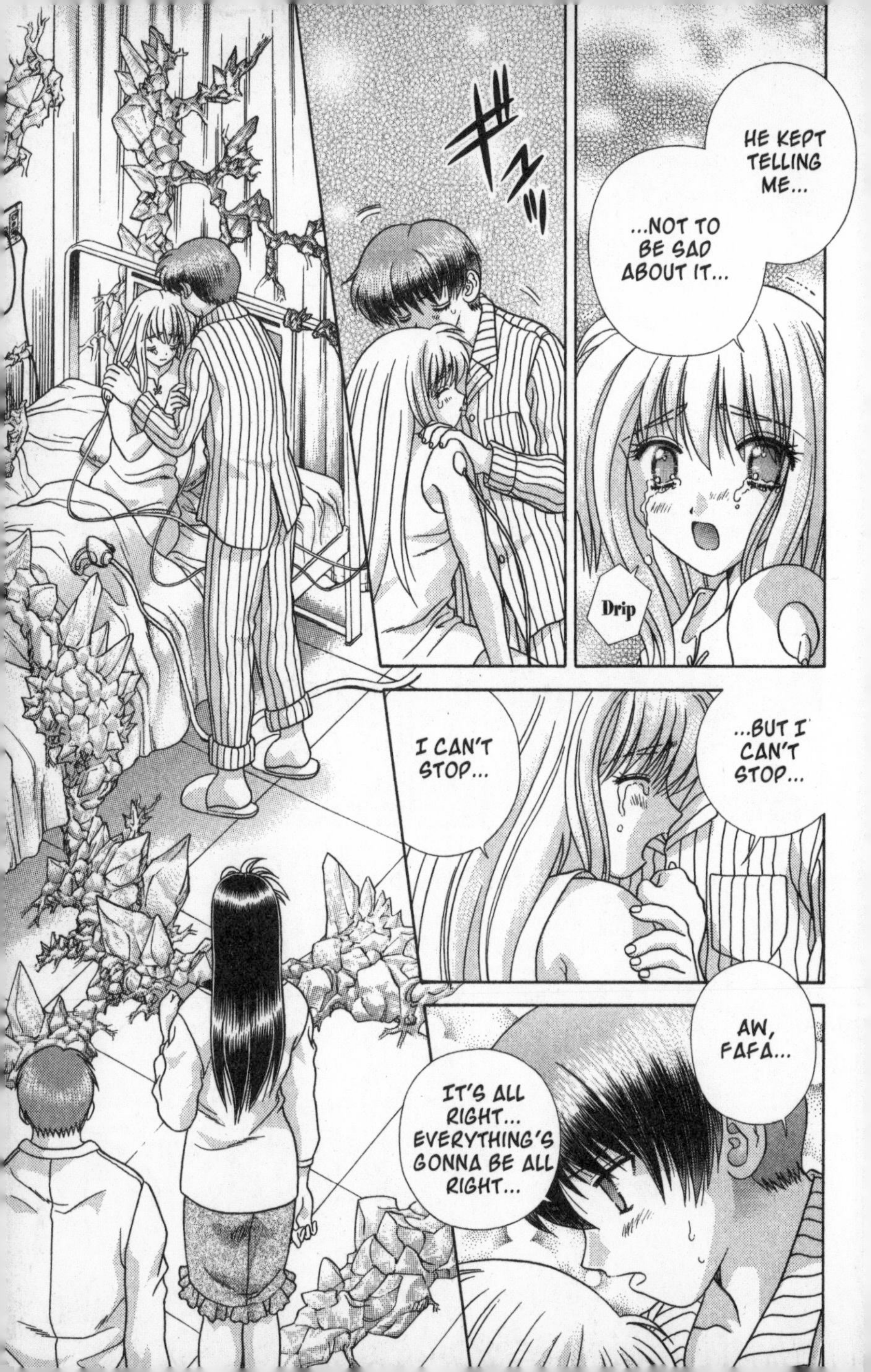
HE KEPT TELLING ME...
...NOT TO BE SAD ABOUT IT...
Drip
...BUT I CAN'T STOP...
I CAN'T STOP...
AW, FAFA...
IT'S ALL RIGHT... EVERYTHING'S GONNA BE ALL RIGHT...

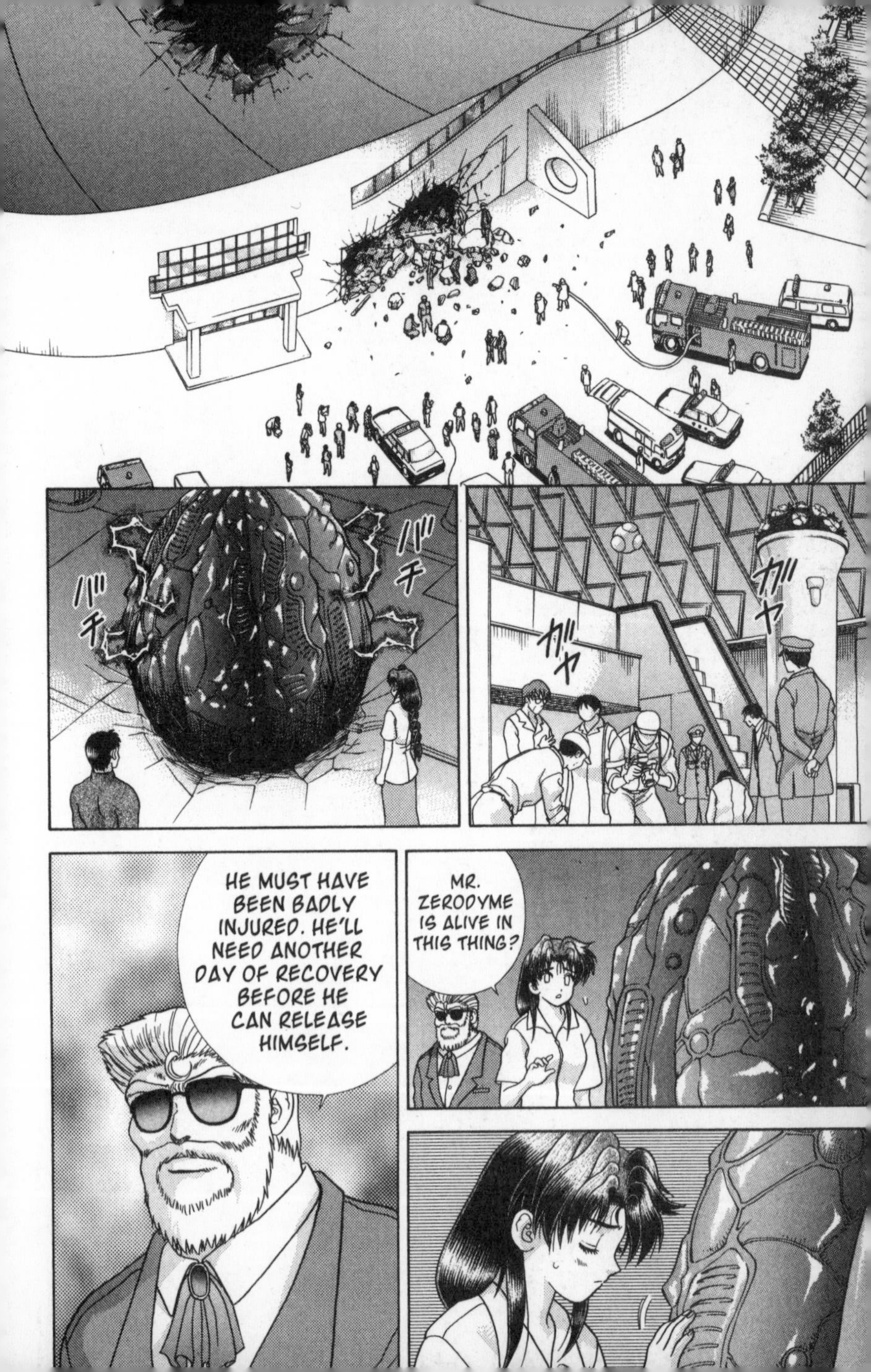
ガヤ
ガヤ
バチ
バチ
MR. ZERODYME IS ALIVE IN THIS THING?
HE MUST HAVE BEEN BADLY INJURED. HE'LL NEED ANOTHER DAY OF RECOVERY BEFORE HE CAN RELEASE HIMSELF.

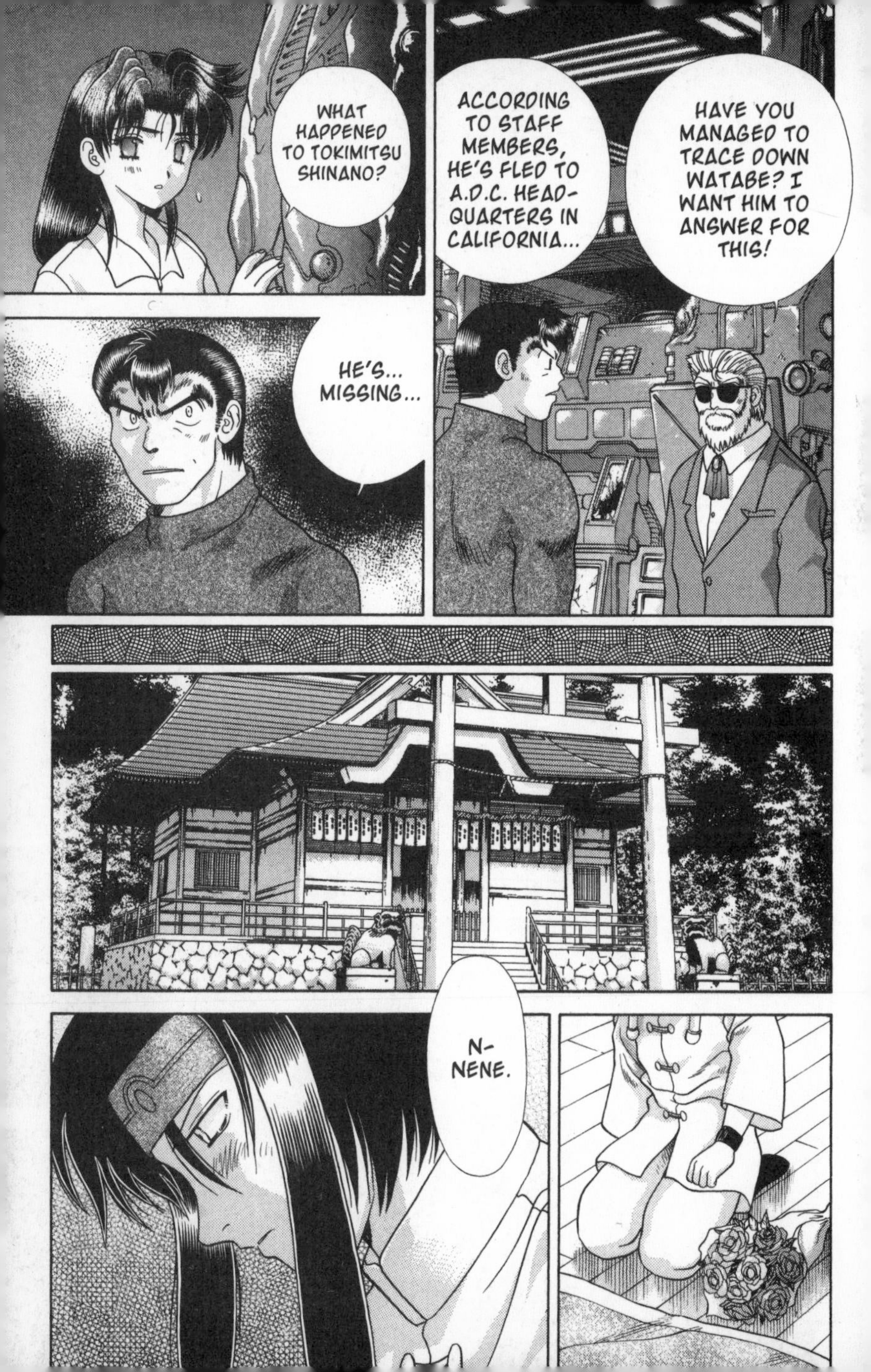
HAVE YOU MANAGED TO TRACE DOWN WATABE? I WANT HIM TO ANSWER FOR THIS!
ACCORDING TO STAFF MEMBERS, HE'S FLED TO A.D.C. HEAD-QUARTERS IN CALIFORNIA...
WHAT HAPPENED TO TOKIMITSU SHINANO?
HE'S... MISSING...
N- NENE.

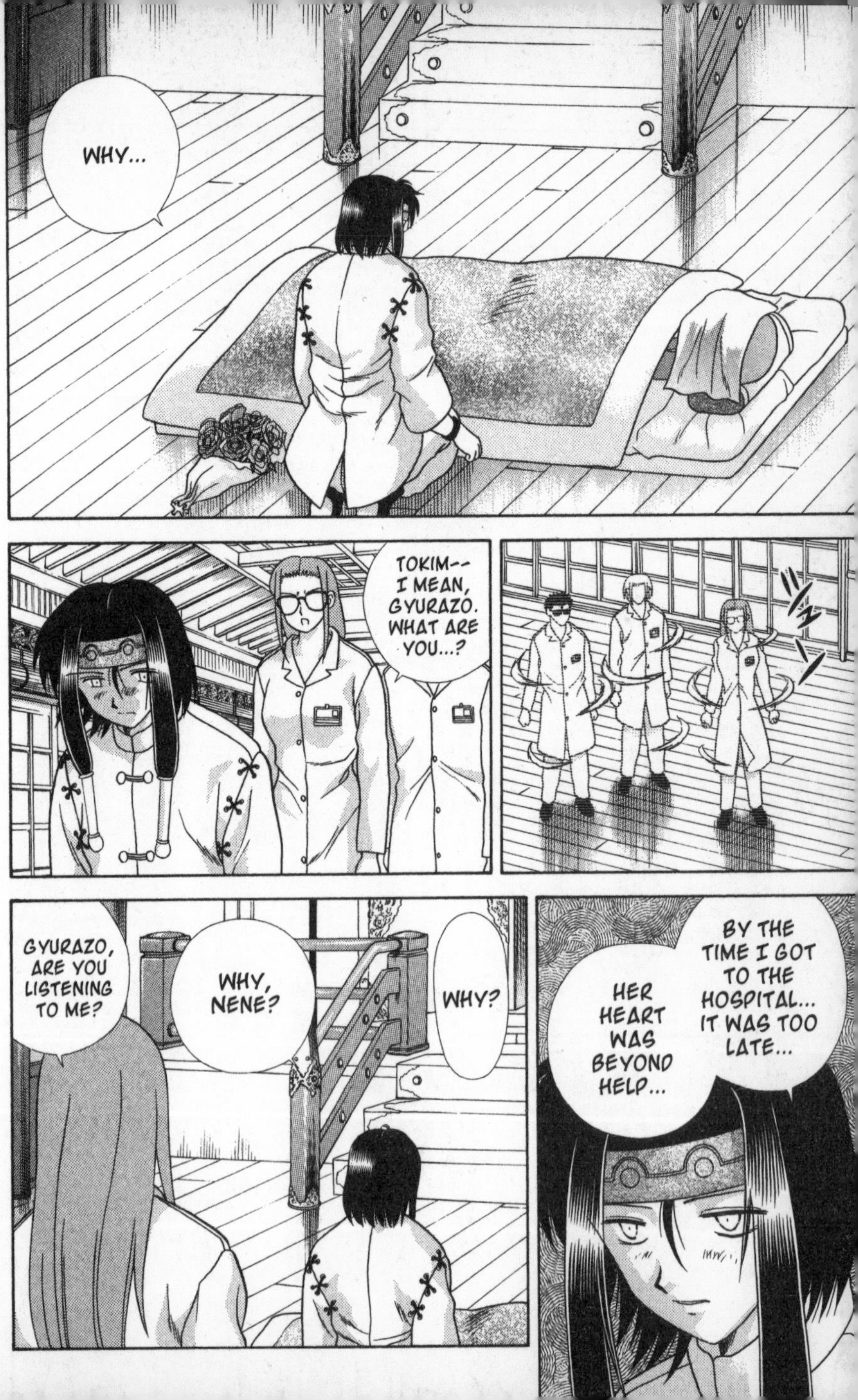
WHY...
TOKIM--
I MEAN,
GYURAZO.
WHAT ARE
YOU...?
BY THE
TIME I GOT
TO THE
HOSPITAL...
IT WAS TOO
LATE...
HER
HEART
WAS
BEYOND
HELP...
WHY?
WHY,
NENE?
GYURAZO,
ARE YOU
LISTENING
TO ME?

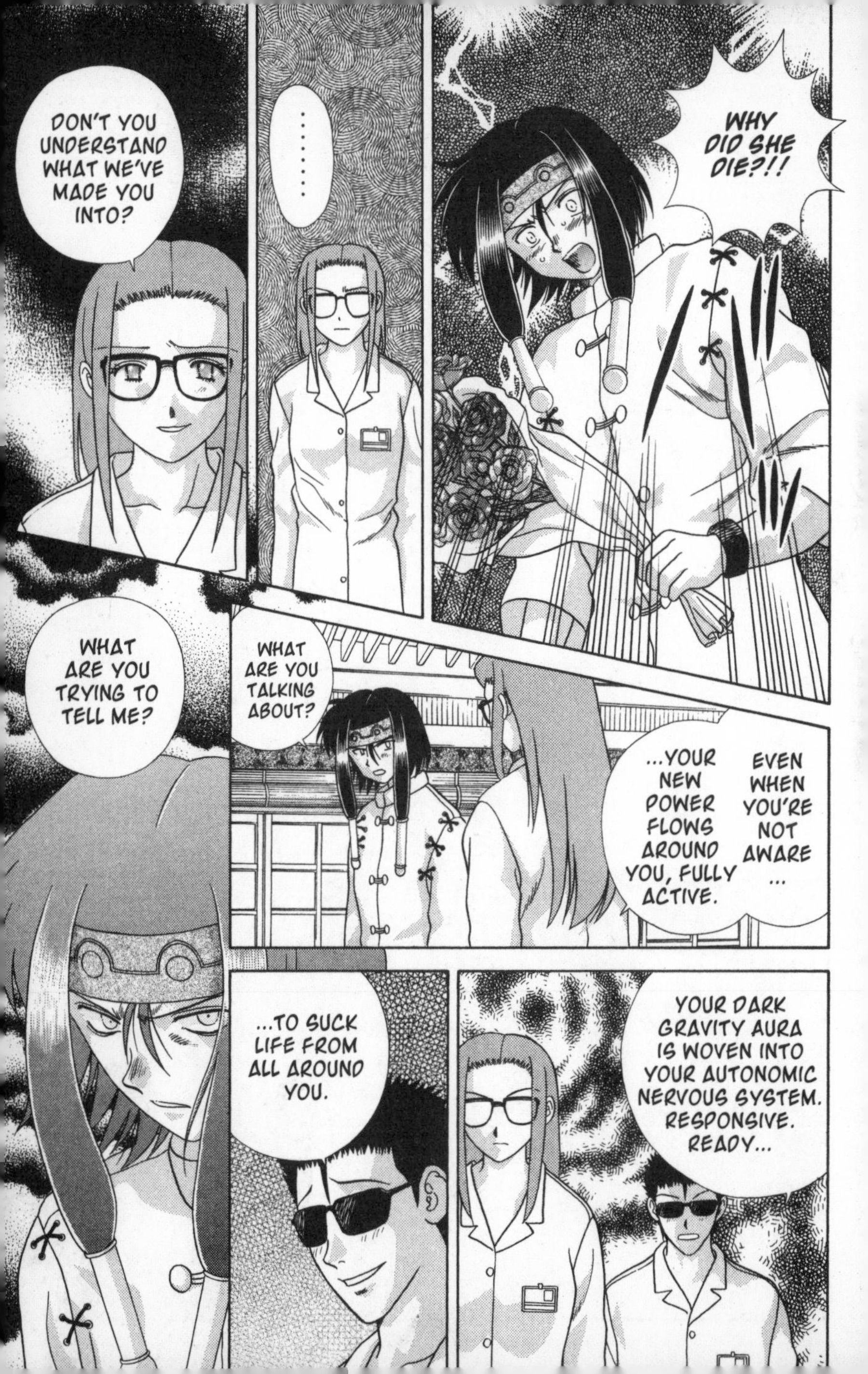
WHY DID SHE DIE?!!
......
DON'T YOU UNDERSTAND WHAT WE'VE MADE YOU INTO?
EVEN WHEN YOU'RE NOT AWARE ...
...YOUR NEW POWER FLOWS AROUND YOU, FULLY ACTIVE.
WHAT ARE YOU TALKING ABOUT?
YOUR DARK GRAVITY AURA IS WOVEN INTO YOUR AUTONOMIC NERVOUS SYSTEM. RESPONSIVE. READY...
...TO SUCK LIFE FROM ALL AROUND YOU.
WHAT ARE YOU TRYING TO TELL ME?

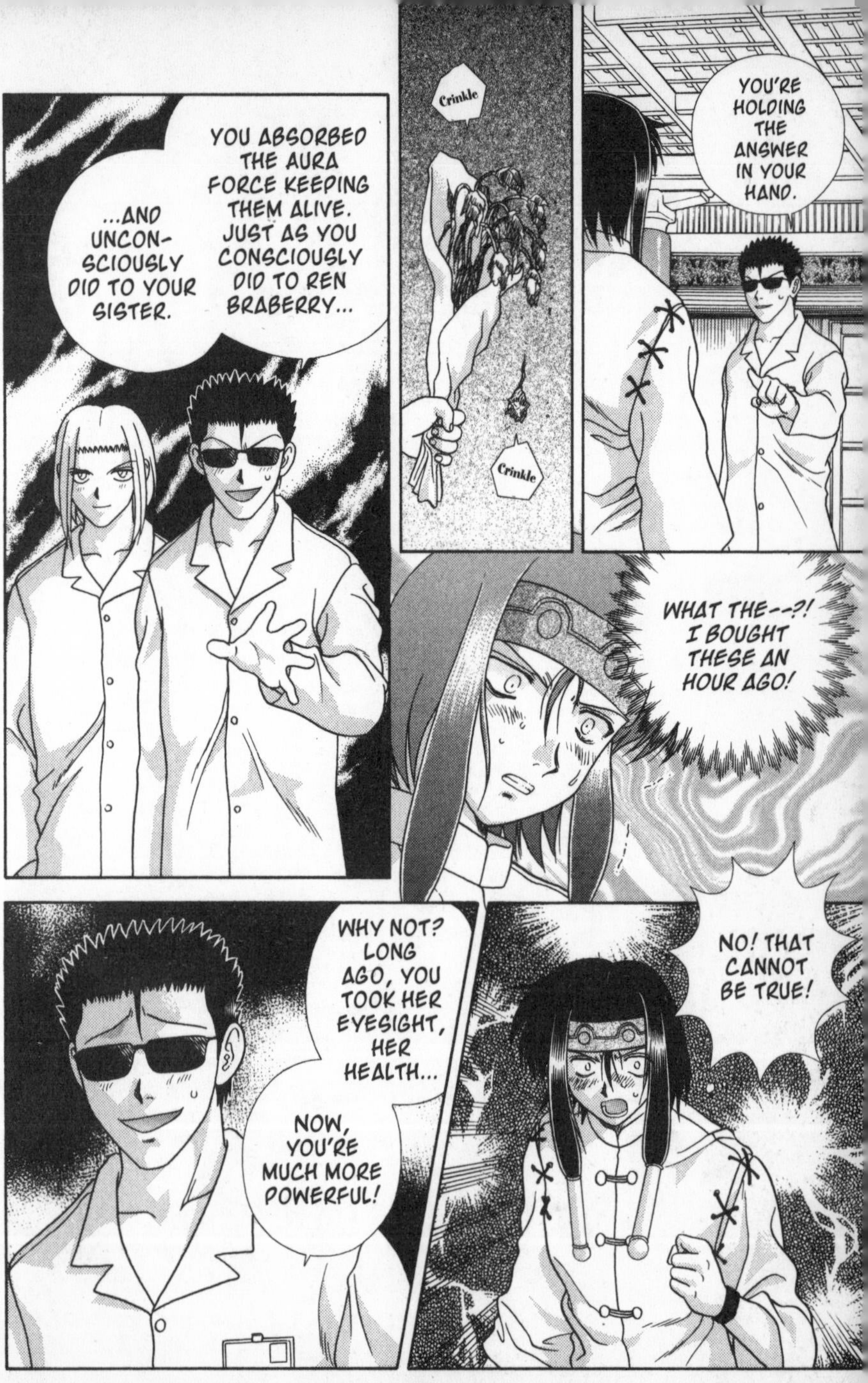

YOU'RE HOLDING THE ANSWER IN YOUR HAND.
Crinkle
Crinkle
WHAT THE--?! I BOUGHT THESE AN HOUR AGO!
YOU ABSORBED THE AURA FORCE KEEPING THEM ALIVE. JUST AS YOU CONSCIOUSLY DID TO REN BRABERRY...
...AND UNCON-SCIOUSLY DID TO YOUR SISTER.
NO! THAT CANNOT BE TRUE!
WHY NOT? LONG AGO, YOU TOOK HER EYESIGHT, HER HEALTH...
NOW, YOU'RE MUCH MORE POWERFUL!

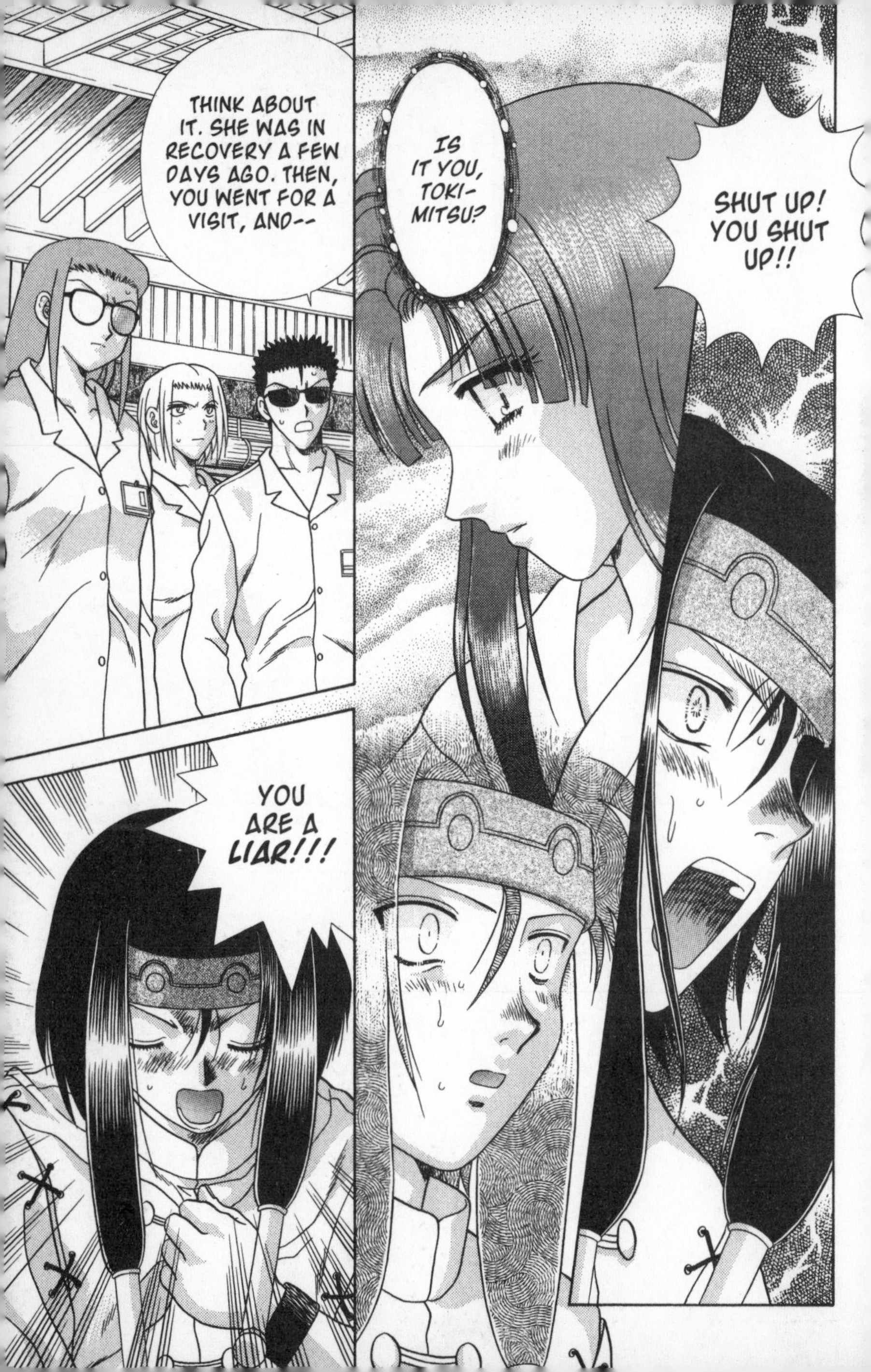
IS IT YOU, TOKI-MITSU?
SHUT UP! YOU SHUT UP!!
THINK ABOUT IT. SHE WAS IN RECOVERY A FEW DAYS AGO. THEN, YOU WENT FOR A VISIT, AND--
YOU ARE A LIAR!!!

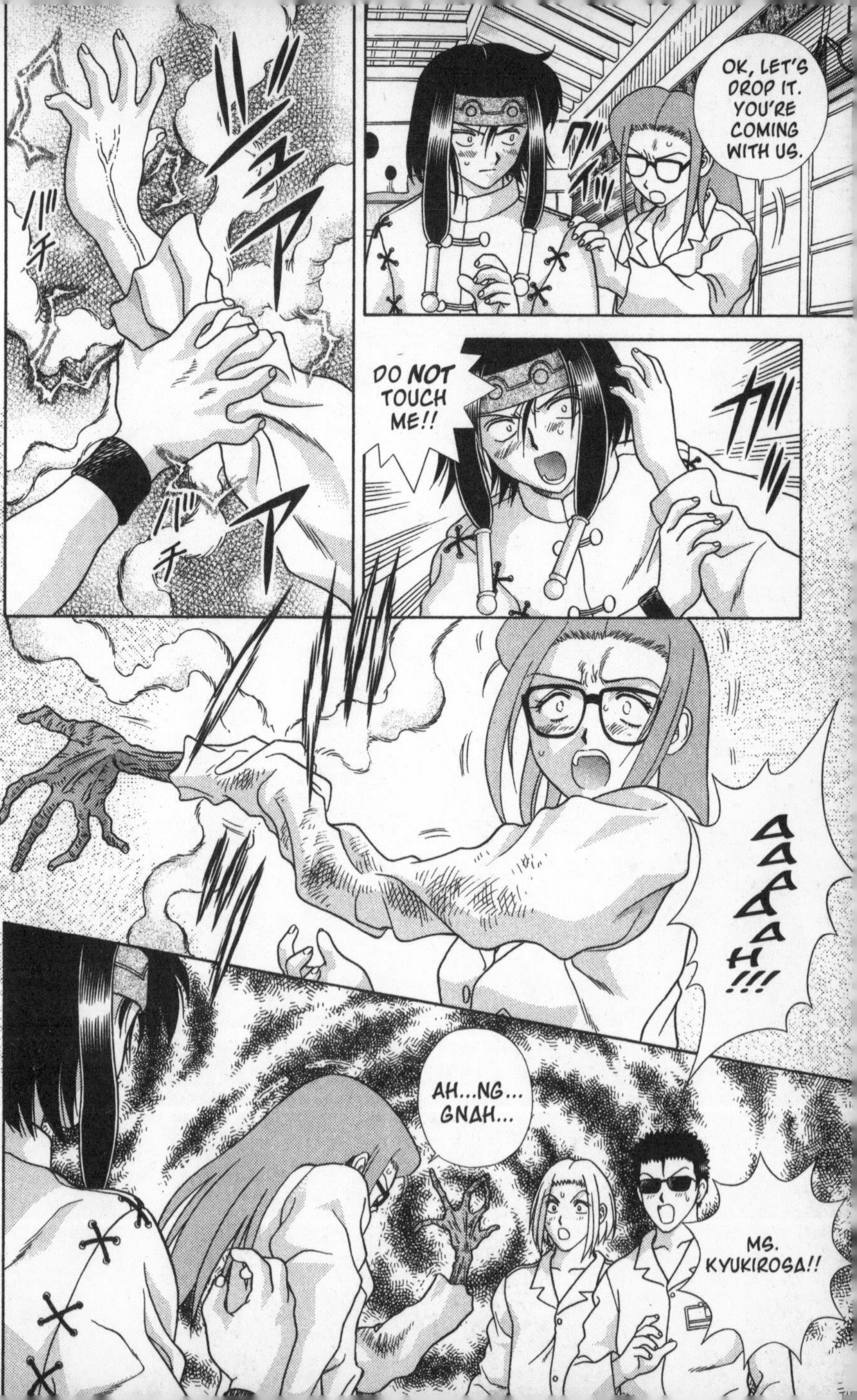
OK, LET'S DROP IT. YOU'RE COMING WITH US.
DO NOT TOUCH ME!!
AAAAAAH!!!
MS. KYUKIROSA!!
AH...NG... GNAH...

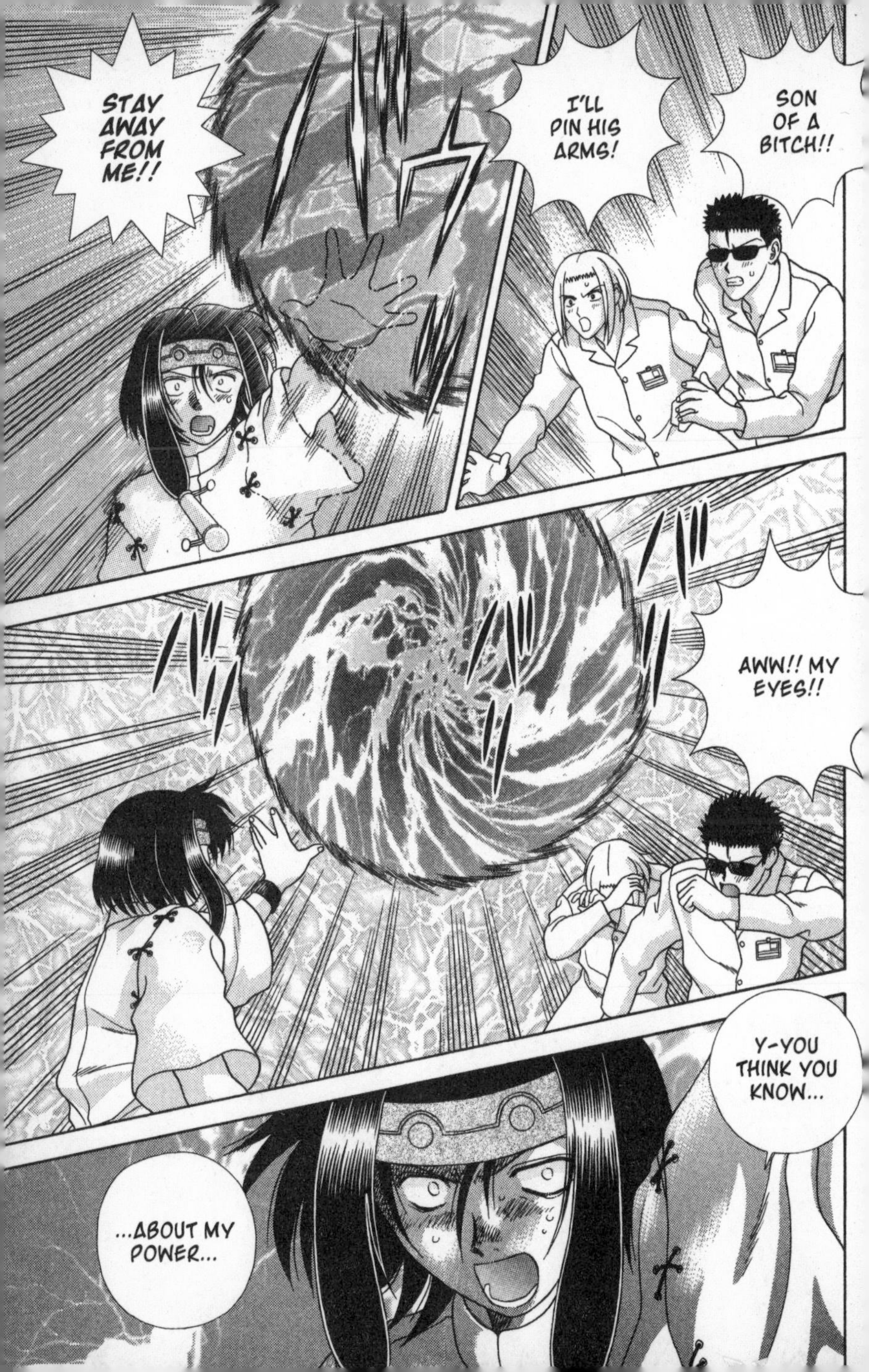
SON OF A BITCH!!
I'LL PIN HIS ARMS!
STAY AWAY FROM ME!!
AWW!! MY EYES!!
Y-YOU THINK YOU KNOW...
...ABOUT MY POWER...

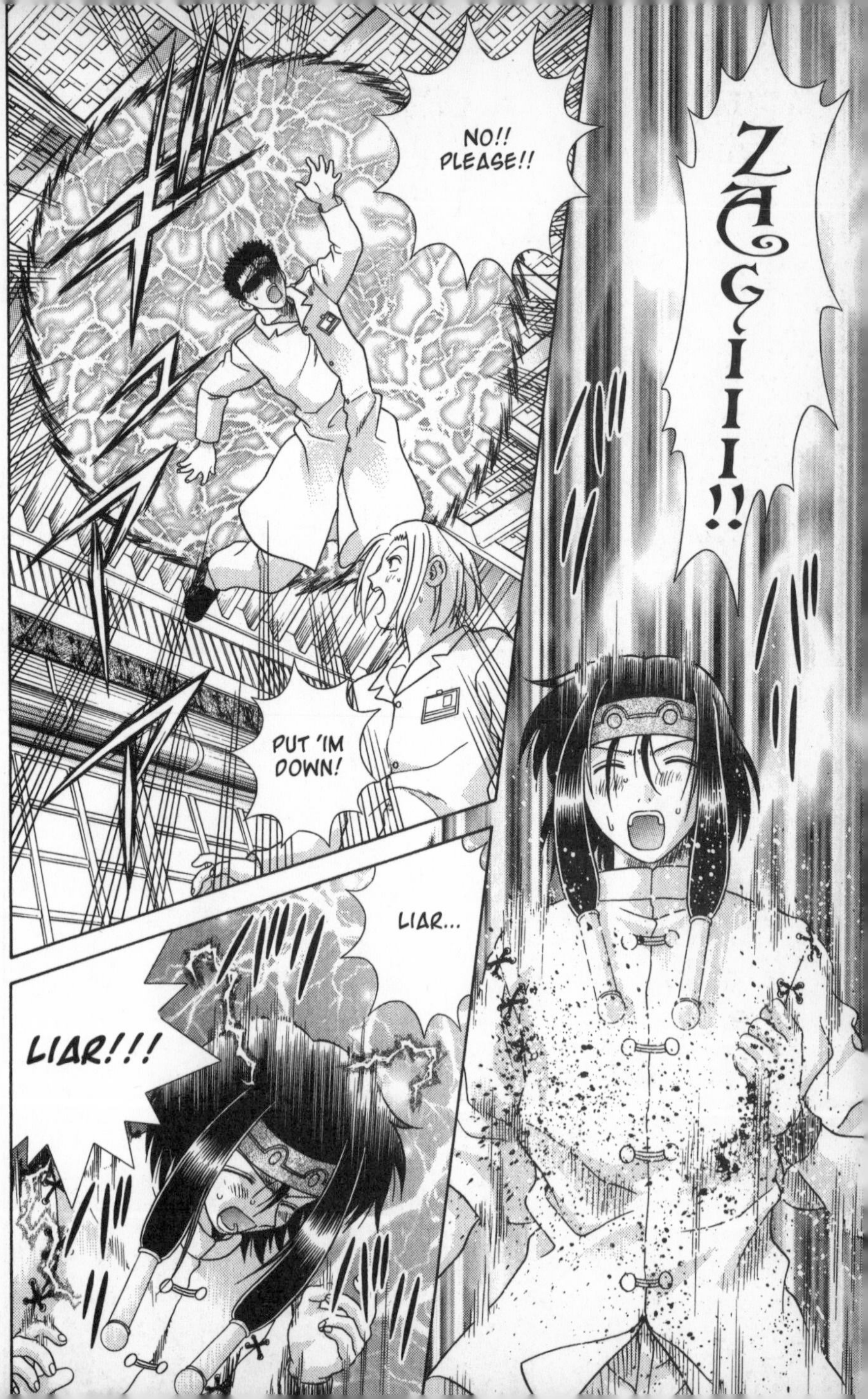
ZAGIII!!
NO!! PLEASE!!
PUT 'IM DOWN!
LIAR...
LIAR!!!

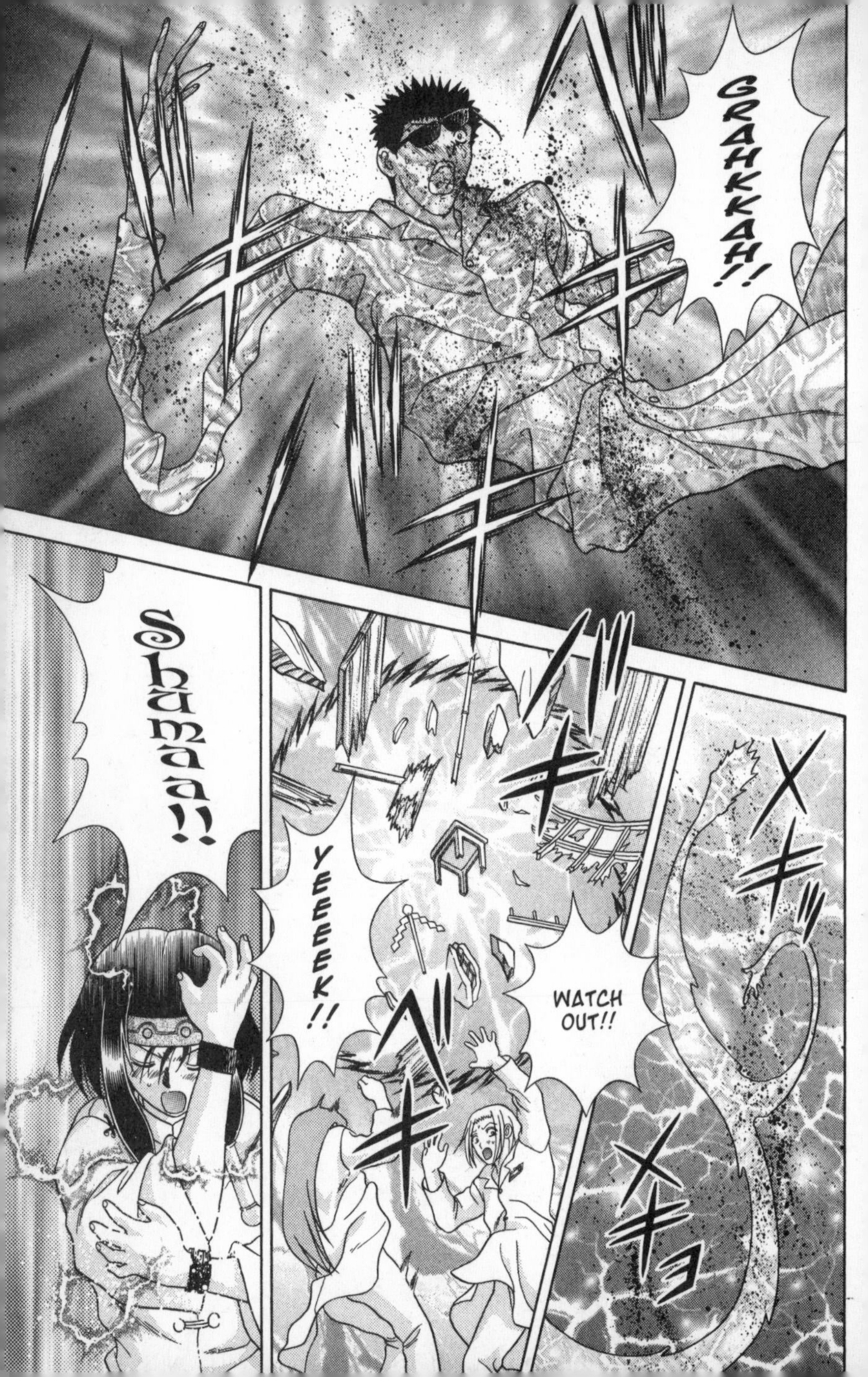
GRAHKKAH!!
YEEEEEK!!
WATCH OUT!!
Shumaa!!

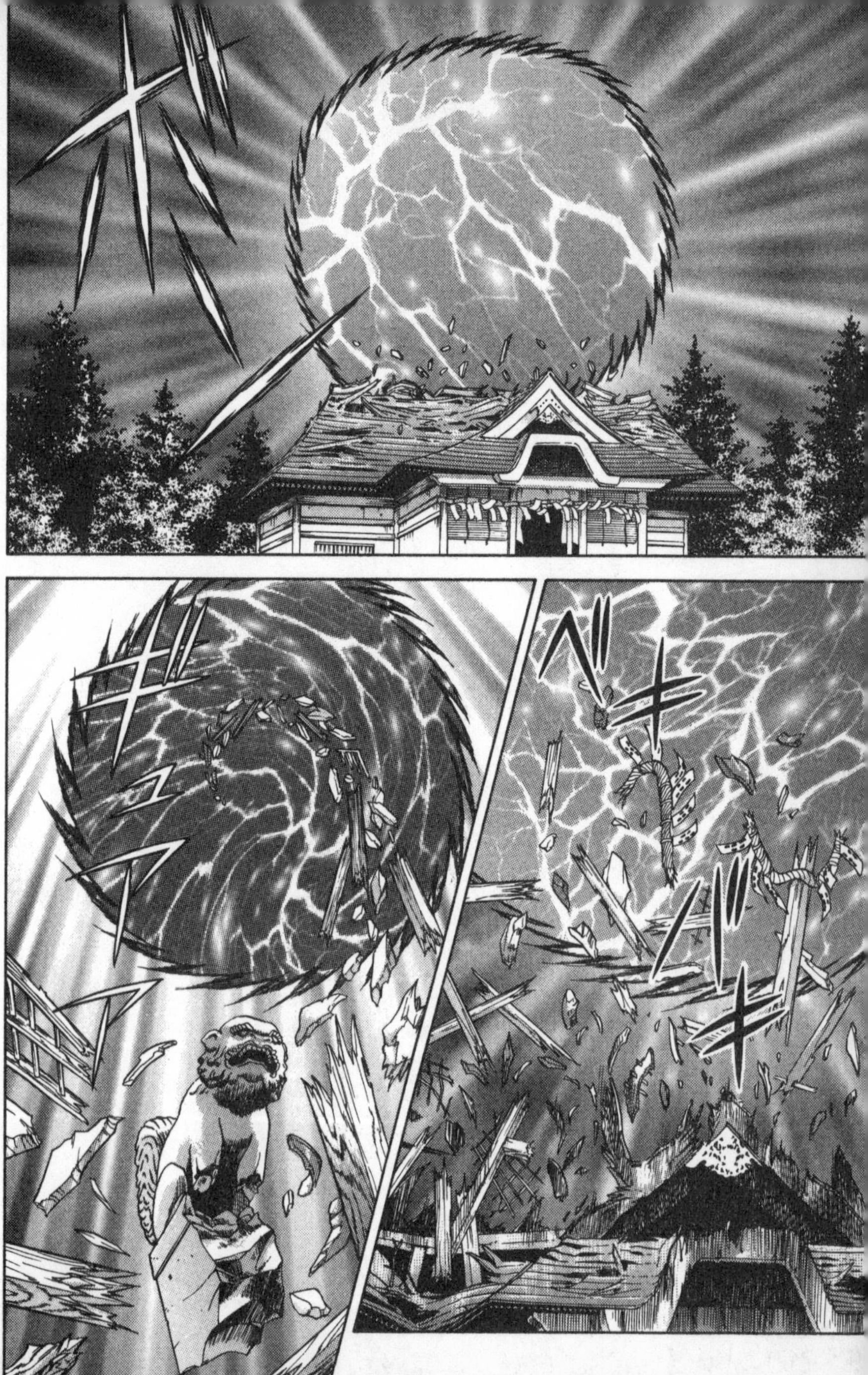

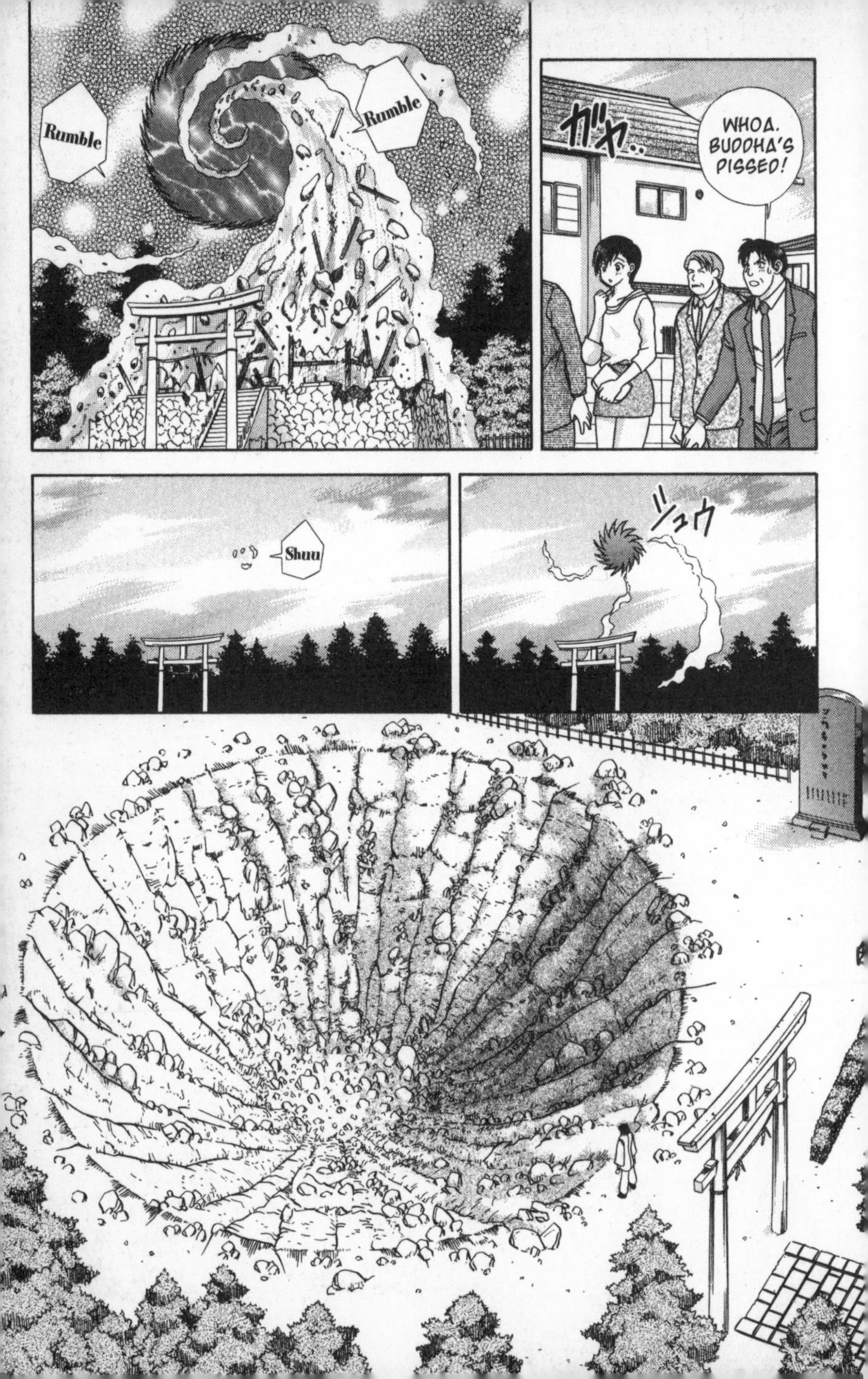
ガヤ..
WHOA. BUDDHA'S PISSED!
Rumble
Rumble
ジュウ
Shuu

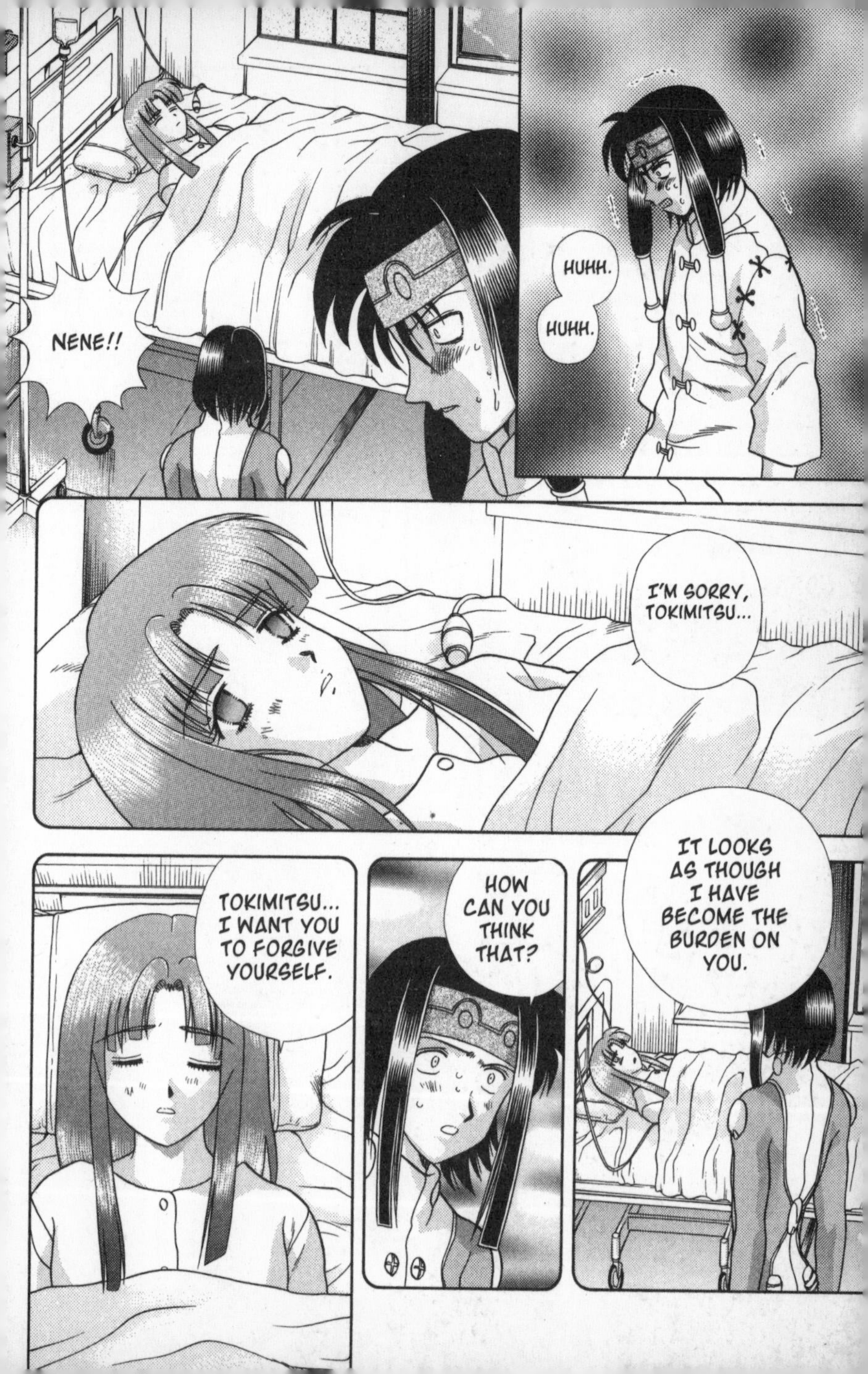
HUHH.
HUHH.
NENE!!
I'M SORRY, TOKIMITSU...
IT LOOKS AS THOUGH I HAVE BECOME THE BURDEN ON YOU.
HOW CAN YOU THINK THAT?
TOKIMITSU... I WANT YOU TO FORGIVE YOURSELF.

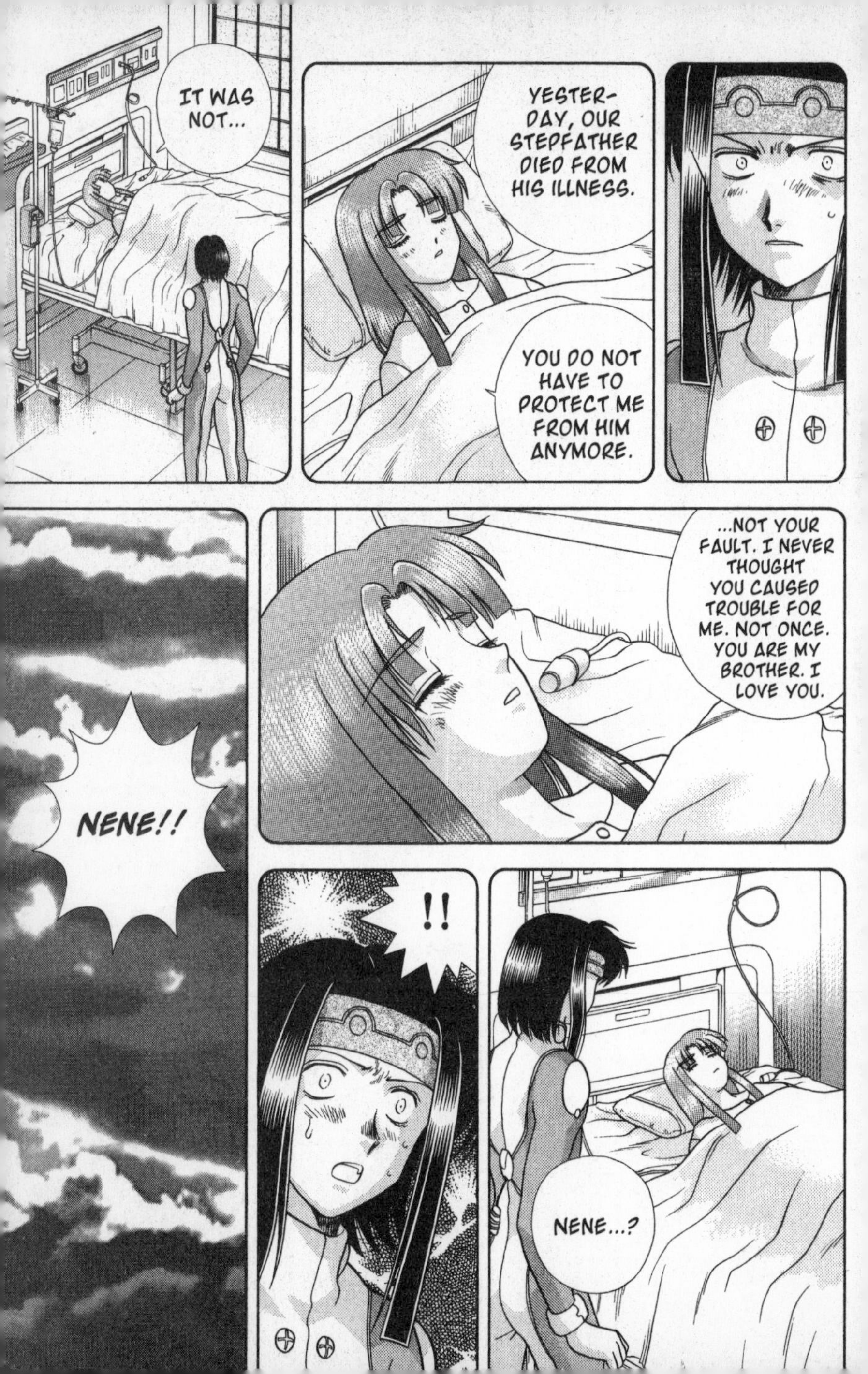
YESTER-DAY, OUR STEPFATHER DIED FROM HIS ILLNESS.
YOU DO NOT HAVE TO PROTECT ME FROM HIM ANYMORE.
IT WAS NOT...
...NOT YOUR FAULT. I NEVER THOUGHT YOU CAUSED TROUBLE FOR ME. NOT ONCE. YOU ARE MY BROTHER. I LOVE YOU.
NENE...?
!!
NENE!!

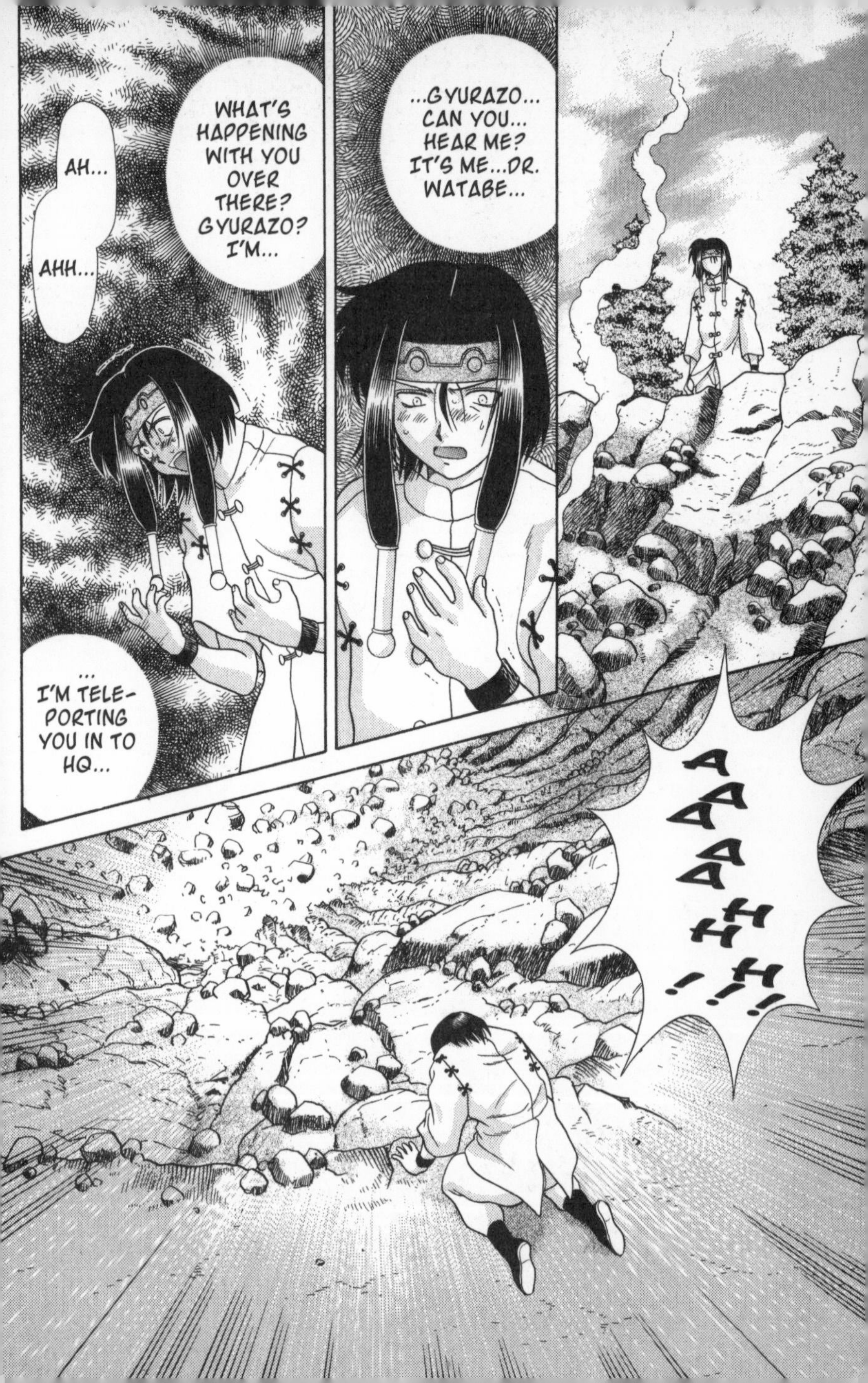
...GYURAZO... CAN YOU... HEAR ME? IT'S ME...DR. WATABE...
WHAT'S HAPPENING WITH YOU OVER THERE? GYURAZO? I'M...
AH...
AHH...
... I'M TELE-PORTING YOU IN TO HQ...
AAAAAHHH!!!

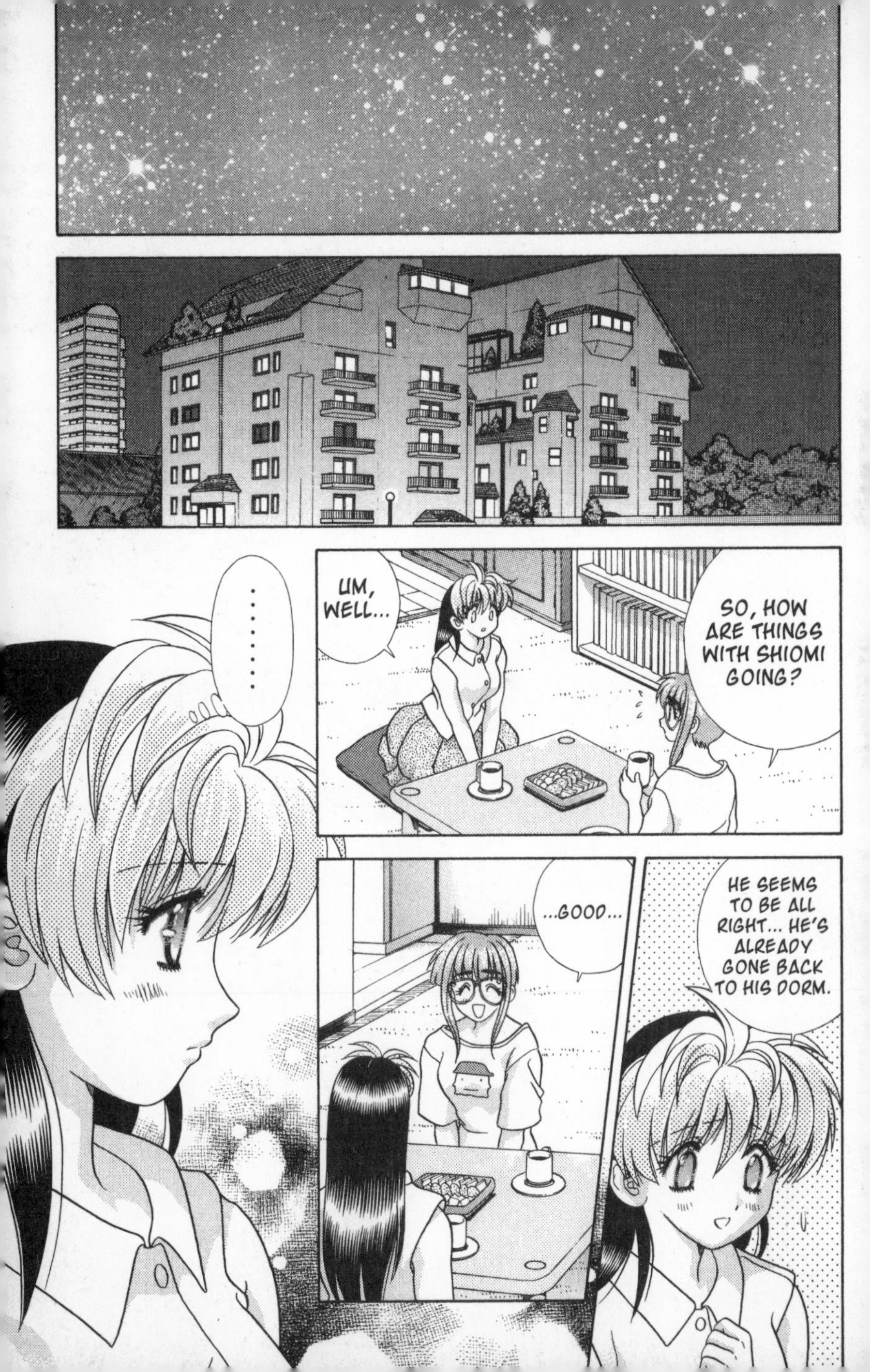
SO, HOW ARE THINGS WITH SHIOMI GOING?
UM, WELL...
HE SEEMS TO BE ALL RIGHT... HE'S ALREADY GONE BACK TO HIS DORM.
...GOOD...
....

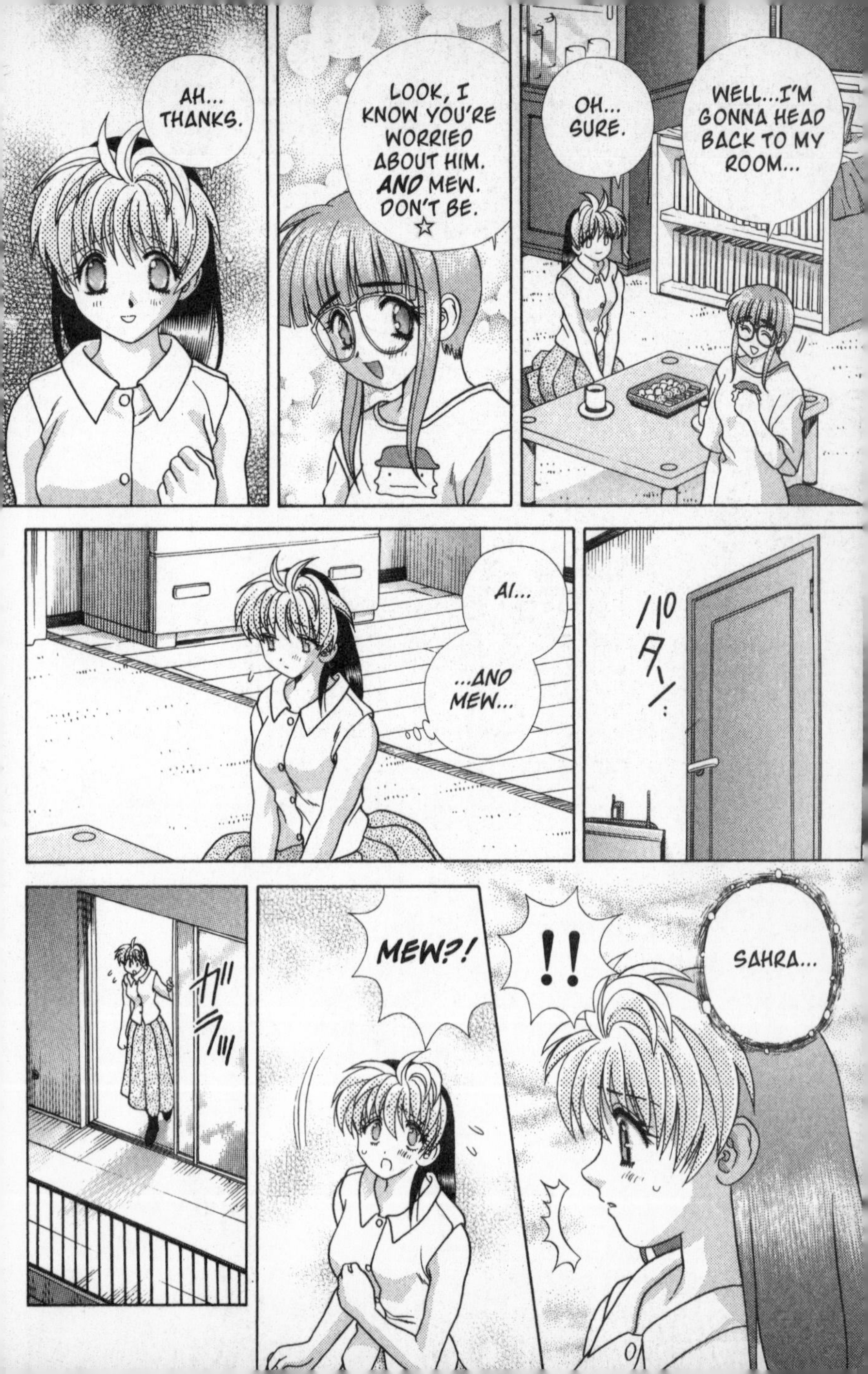
WELL...I'M GONNA HEAD BACK TO MY ROOM...
OH... SURE.
LOOK, I KNOW YOU'RE WORRIED ABOUT HIM. AND MEW. DON'T BE. ☆
AH... THANKS.
パタン
AI...
...AND MEW...
SAHRA...
!!
MEW?!
ガラッ

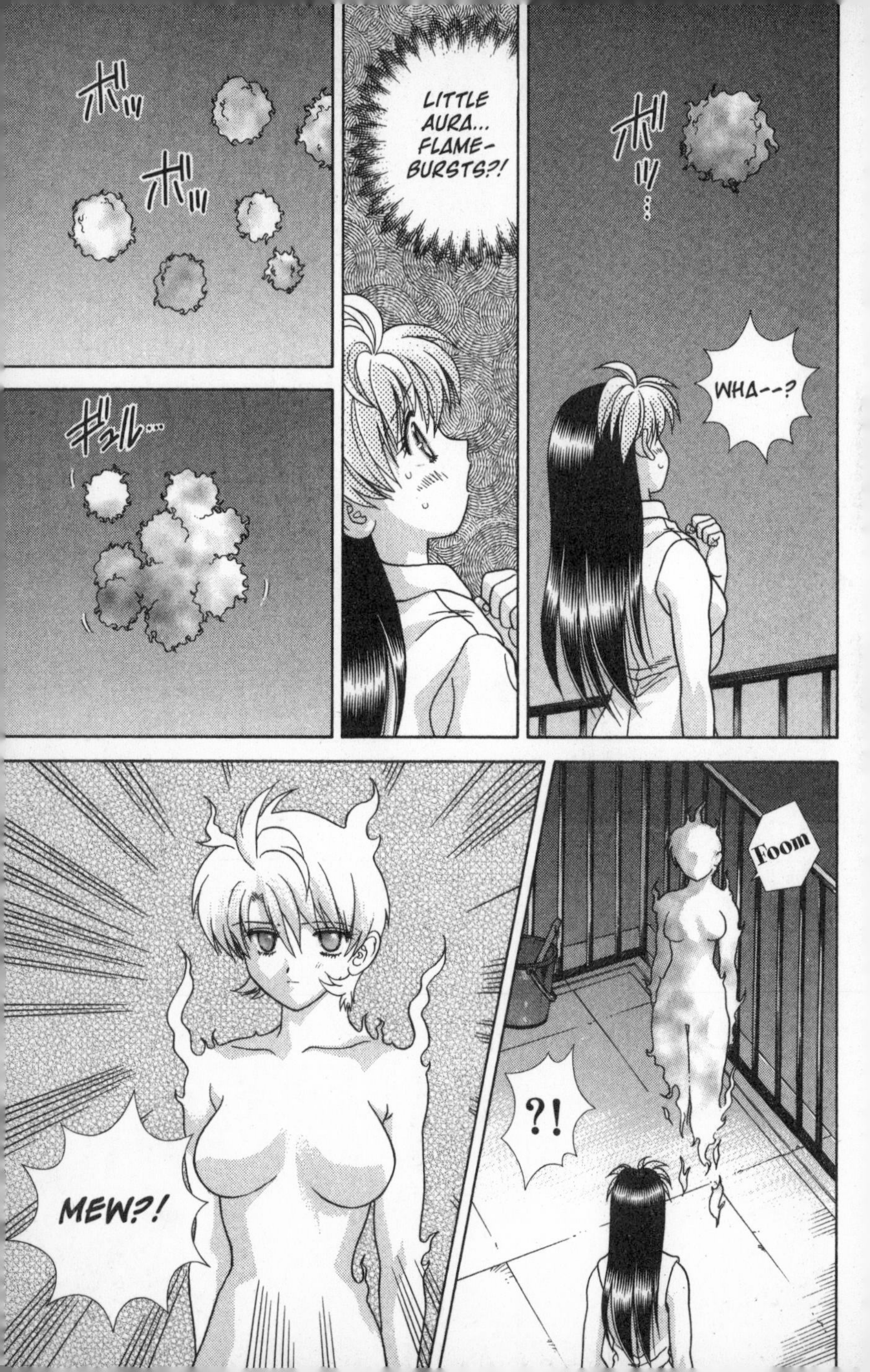

ボッ...
WHA--?
LITTLE AURA... FLAME-BURSTS?!
ボッ
ボッ
ギュル...
Foom
?!
MEW?!

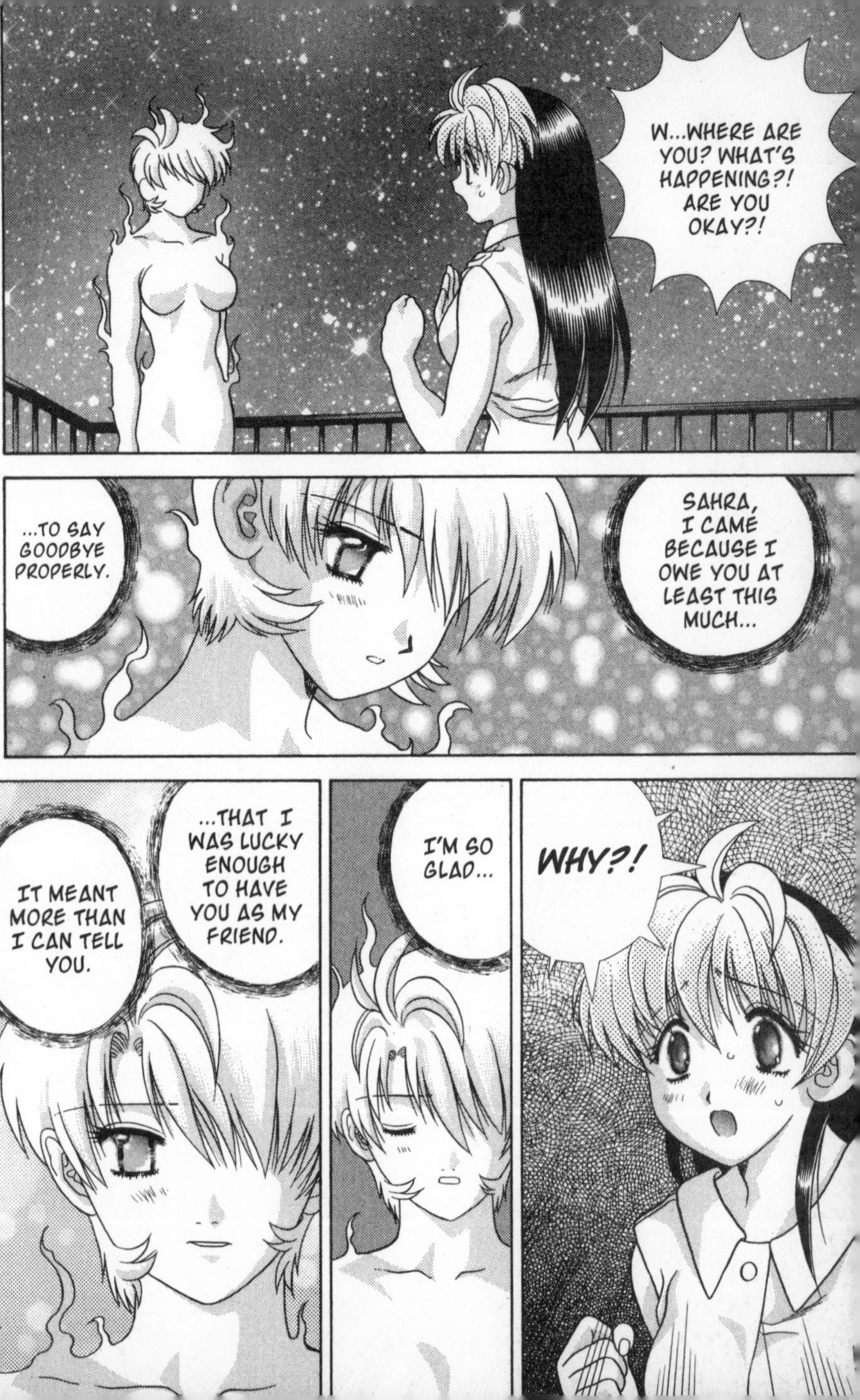
W...WHERE ARE YOU? WHAT'S HAPPENING?! ARE YOU OKAY?!
SAHRA, I CAME BECAUSE I OWE YOU AT LEAST THIS MUCH...
...TO SAY GOODBYE PROPERLY.
WHY?!
I'M SO GLAD...
...THAT I WAS LUCKY ENOUGH TO HAVE YOU AS MY FRIEND.
IT MEANT MORE THAN I CAN TELL YOU.

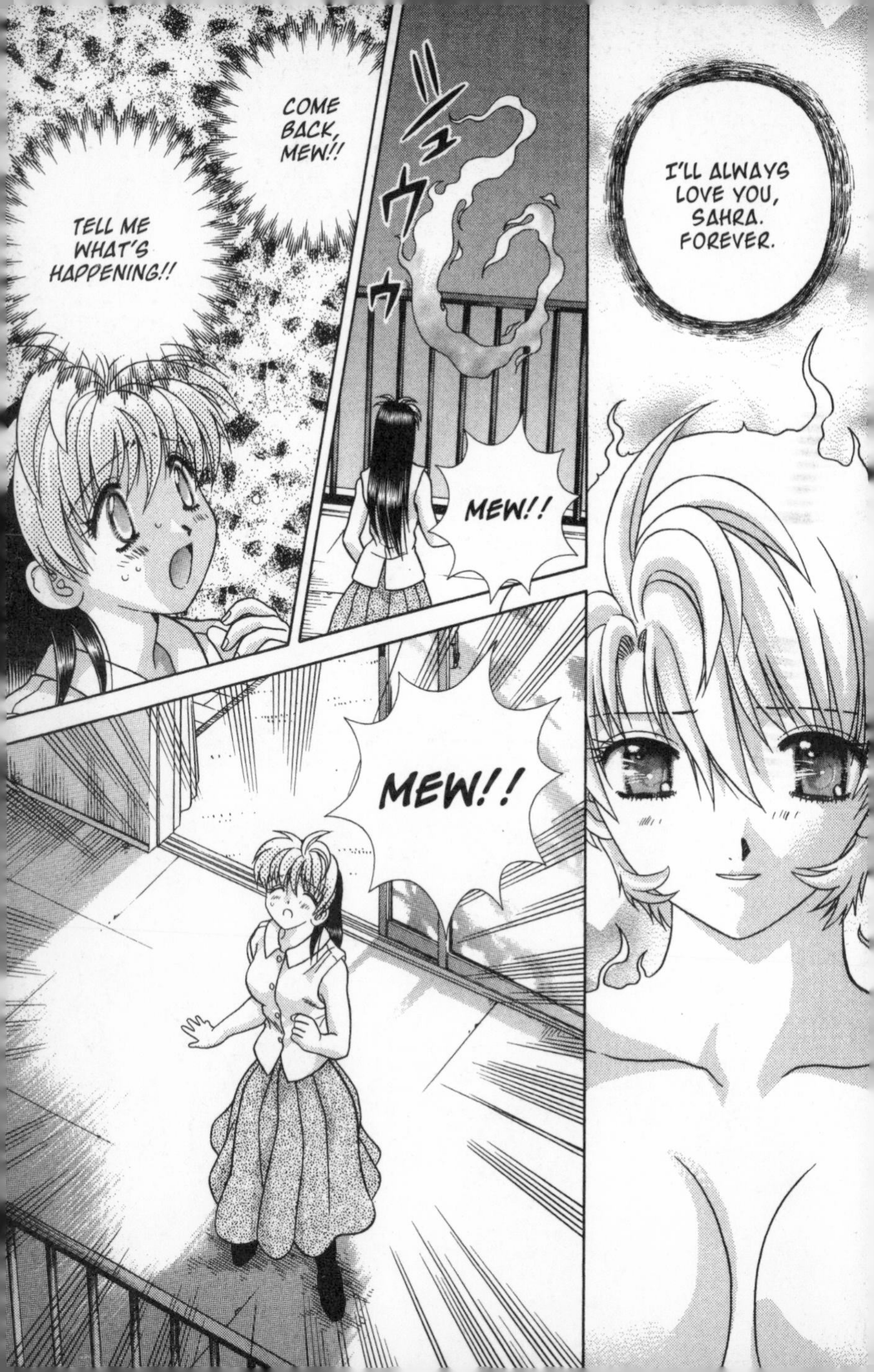
I'LL ALWAYS LOVE YOU, SAHRA. FOREVER.
ジュウゥ
MEW!!
COME BACK, MEW!!
TELL ME WHAT'S HAPPENING!!
MEW!!

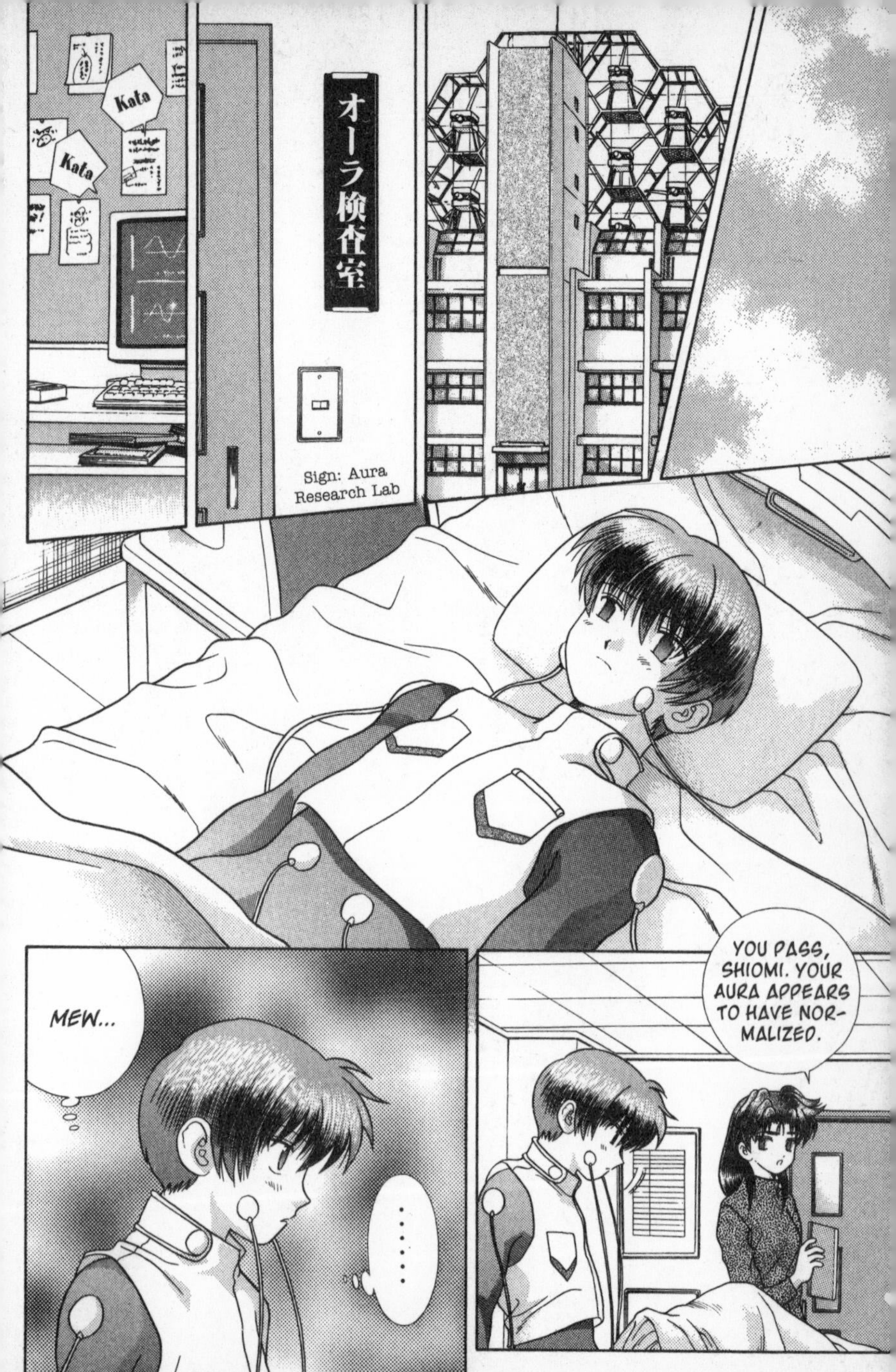

Kata
Kata
オーラ検査室
Sign: Aura Research Lab
YOU PASS, SHIOMI. YOUR AURA APPEARS TO HAVE NOR-MALIZED.
MEW...
......

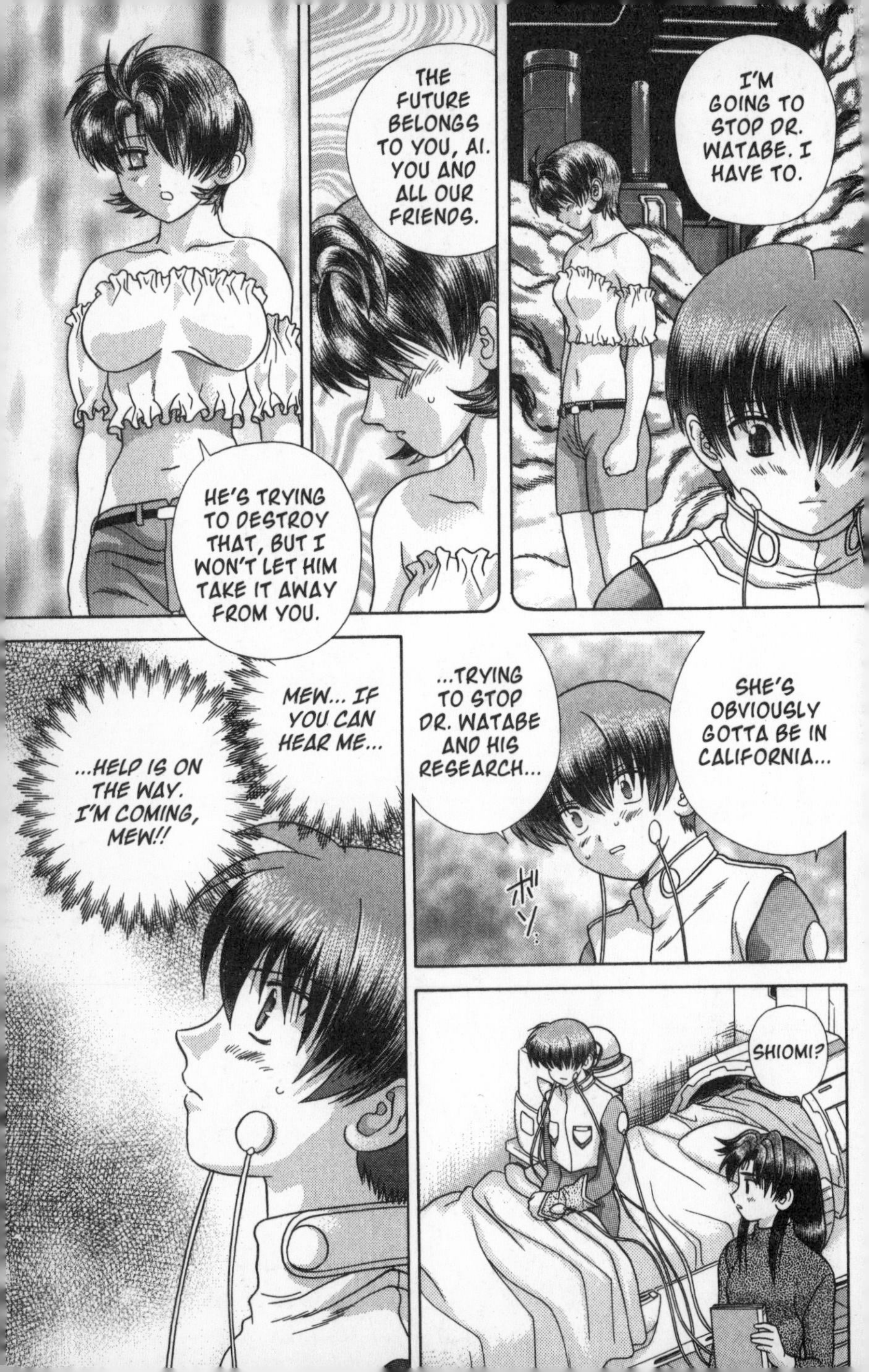
I'M GOING TO STOP DR. WATABE. I HAVE TO.
THE FUTURE BELONGS TO YOU, AI. YOU AND ALL OUR FRIENDS.
HE'S TRYING TO DESTROY THAT, BUT I WON'T LET HIM TAKE IT AWAY FROM YOU.
SHE'S OBVIOUSLY GOTTA BE IN CALIFORNIA...
...TRYING TO STOP DR. WATABE AND HIS RESEARCH...
ボソ
SHIOMI?
MEW... IF YOU CAN HEAR ME...
...HELP IS ON THE WAY. I'M COMING, MEW!!

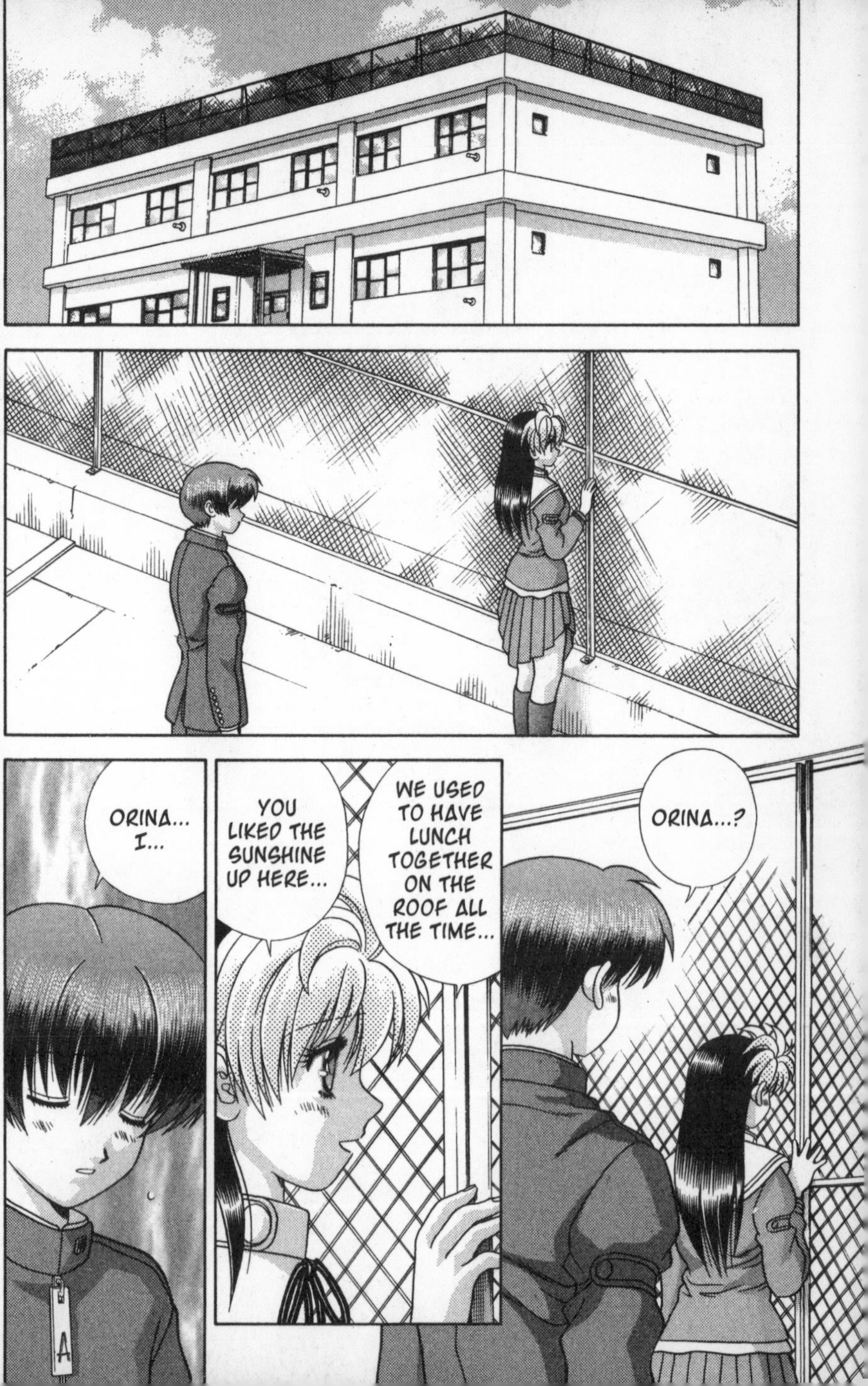
ORINA...?
WE USED TO HAVE LUNCH TOGETHER ON THE ROOF ALL THE TIME...
YOU LIKED THE SUNSHINE UP HERE...
ORINA... I...

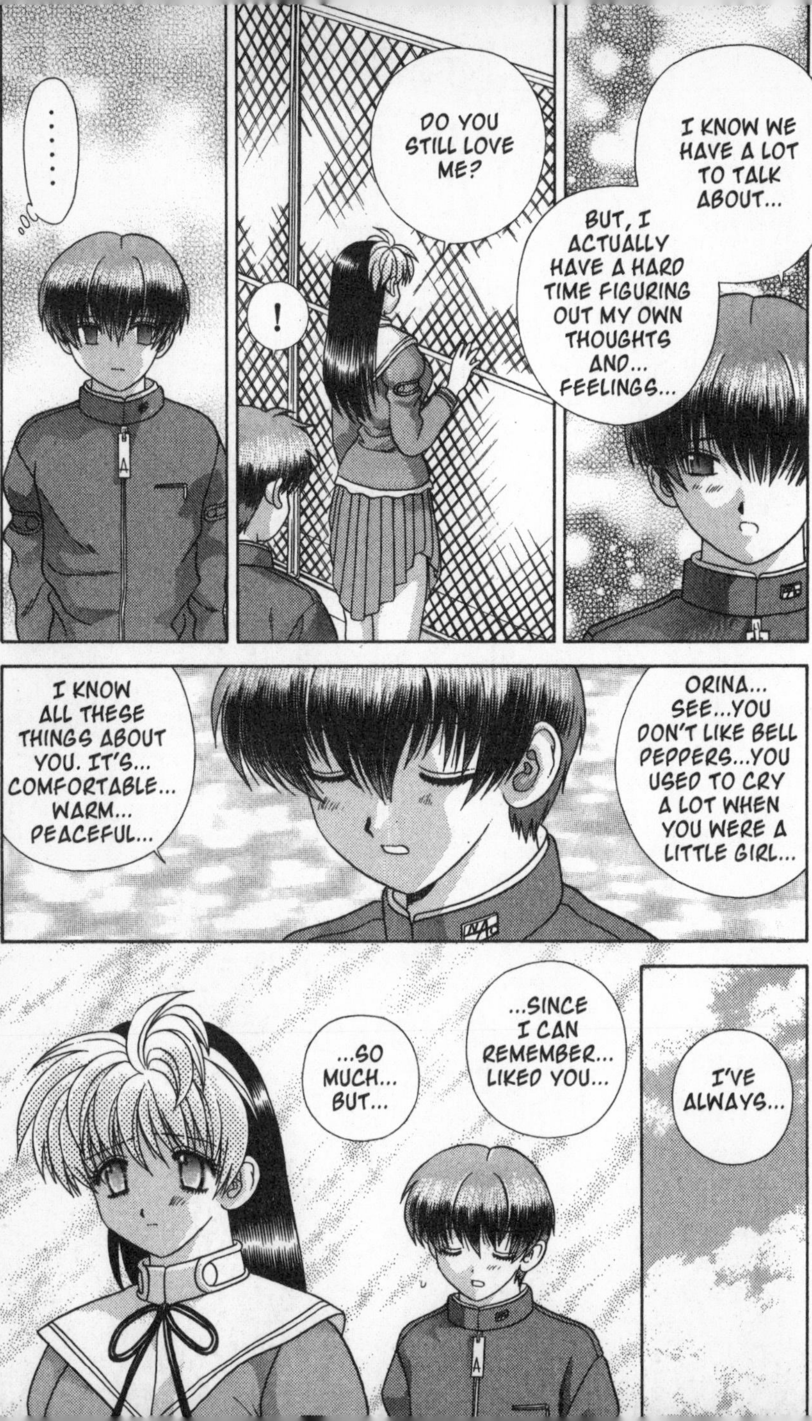
I KNOW WE HAVE A LOT TO TALK ABOUT...
BUT, I ACTUALLY HAVE A HARD TIME FIGURING OUT MY OWN THOUGHTS AND... FEELINGS...
DO YOU STILL LOVE ME?
!
......
ORINA... SEE...YOU DON'T LIKE BELL PEPPERS...YOU USED TO CRY A LOT WHEN YOU WERE A LITTLE GIRL...
I KNOW ALL THESE THINGS ABOUT YOU. IT'S... COMFORTABLE... WARM... PEACEFUL...
I'VE ALWAYS...
...SINCE I CAN REMEMBER... LIKED YOU...
...SO MUCH... BUT...

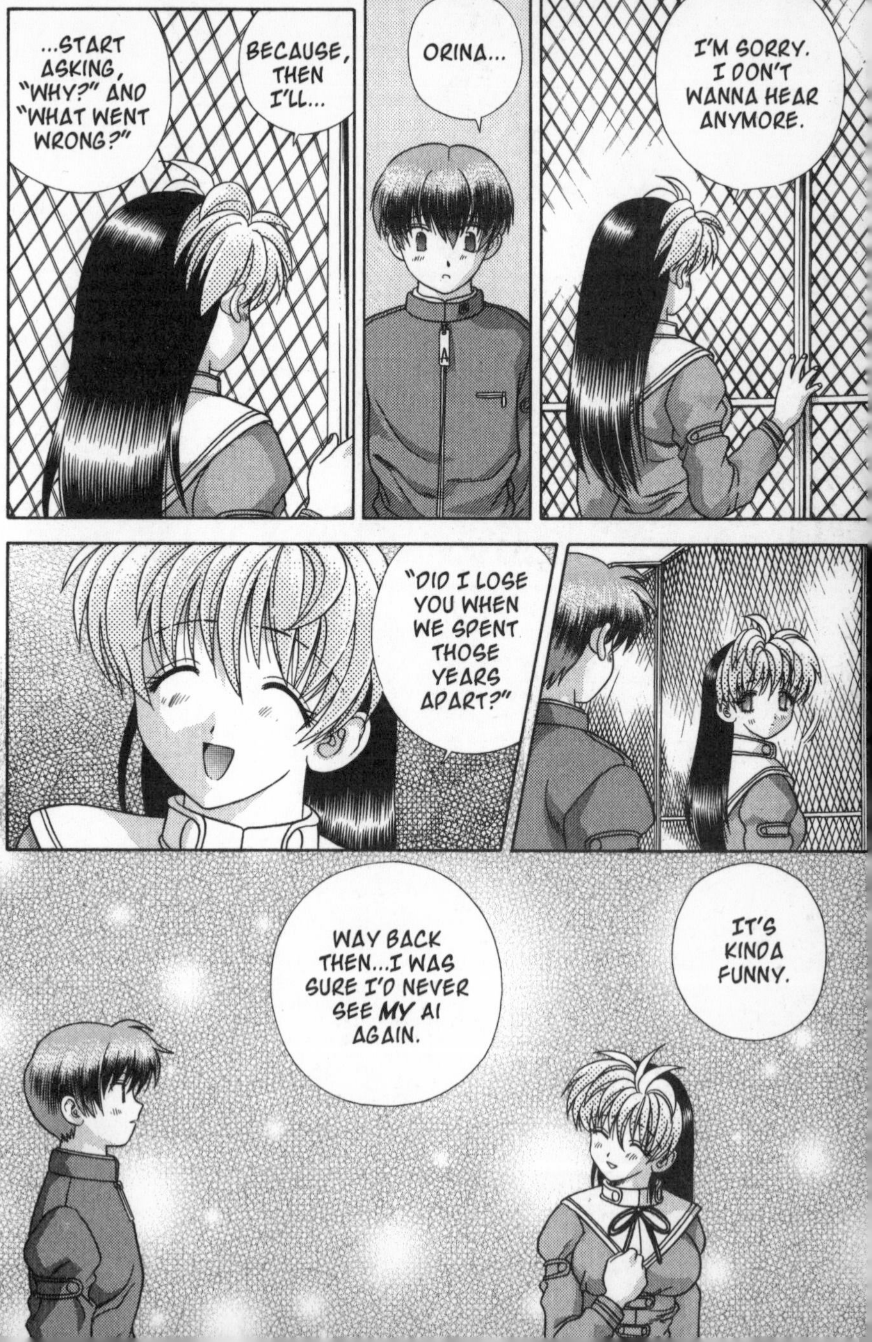
I'M SORRY. I DON'T WANNA HEAR ANYMORE.
ORINA...
BECAUSE, THEN I'LL...
...START ASKING, "WHY?" AND "WHAT WENT WRONG?"
"DID I LOSE YOU WHEN WE SPENT THOSE YEARS APART?"
IT'S KINDA FUNNY.
WAY BACK THEN...I WAS SURE I'D NEVER SEE *MY* AI AGAIN.

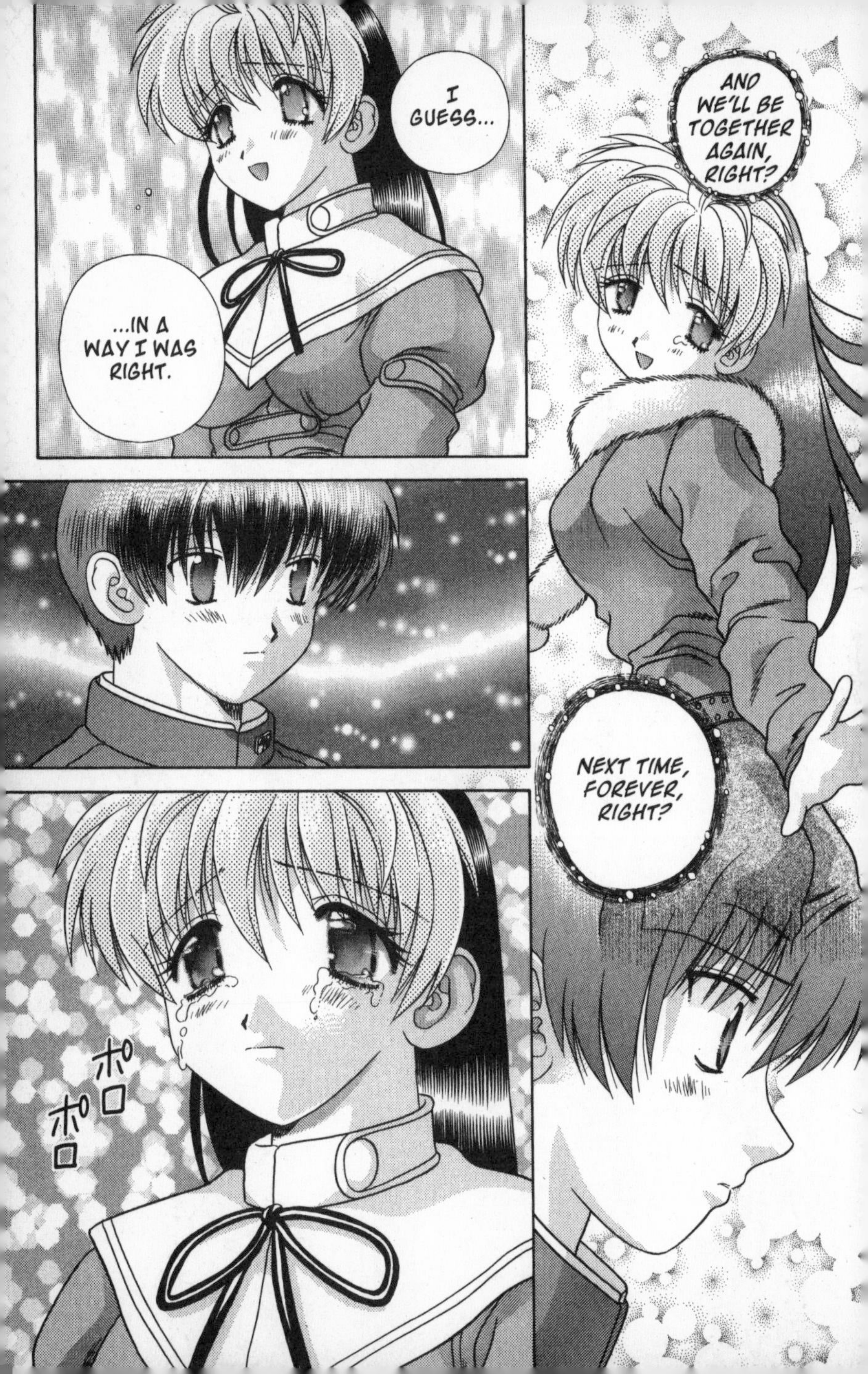
AND WE'LL BE TOGETHER AGAIN, RIGHT?
NEXT TIME, FOREVER, RIGHT?
I GUESS...
...IN A WAY I WAS RIGHT.
ポロポロ

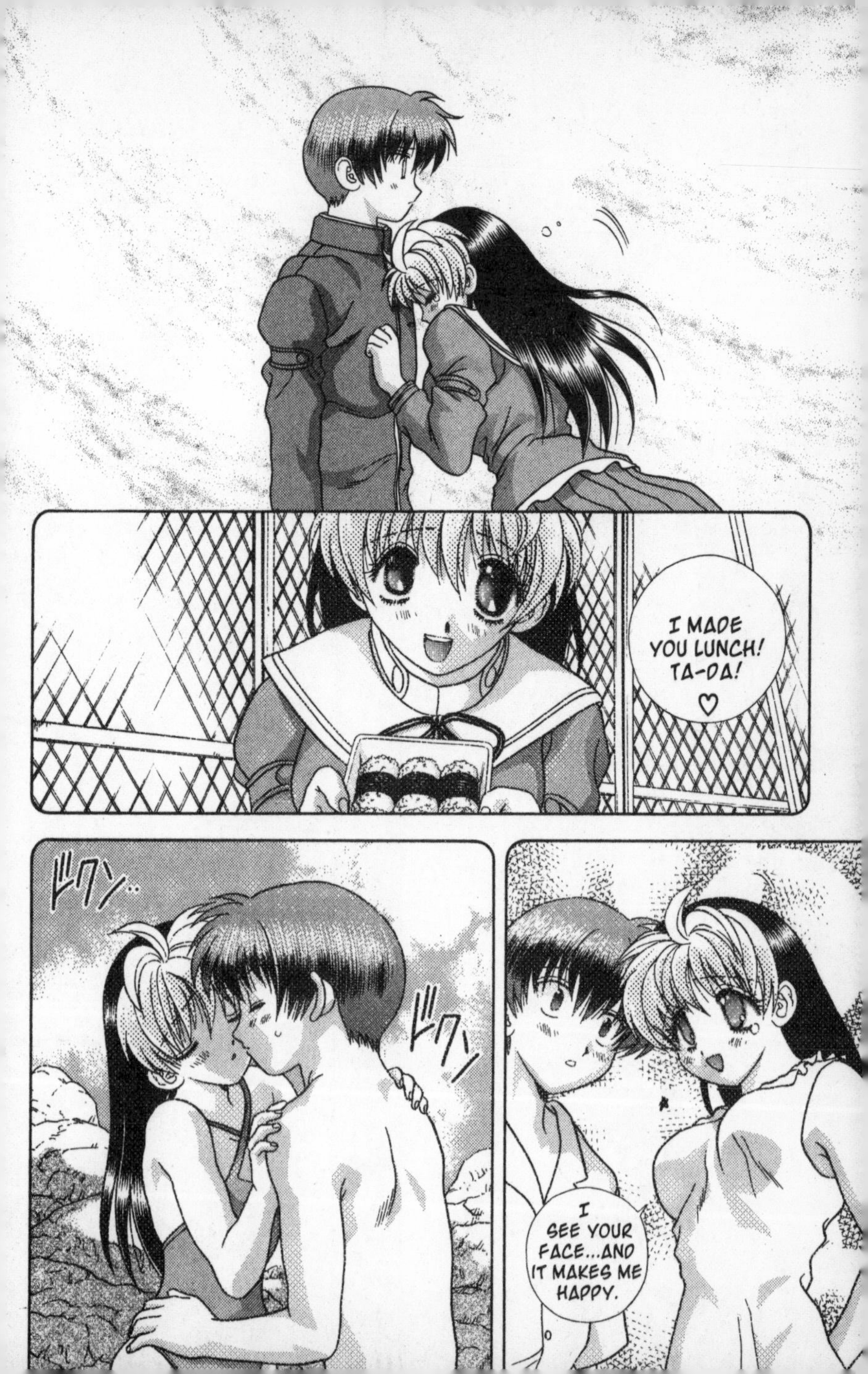
I MADE YOU LUNCH! TA-DA! ♥
I SEE YOUR FACE...AND IT MAKES ME HAPPY.
ドクン..
ドクン

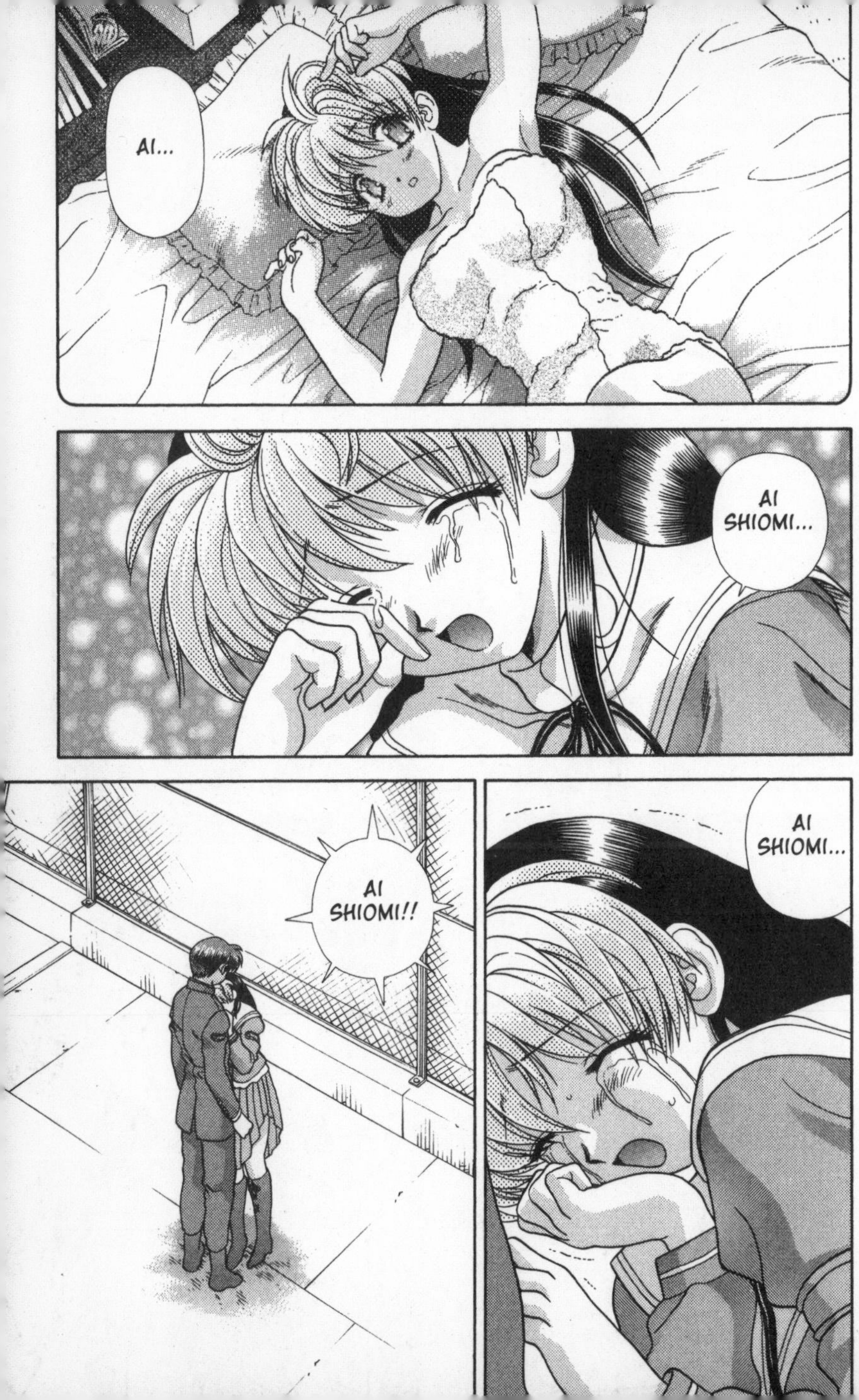
AI...
AI SHIOMI...
AI SHIOMI...
AI SHIOMI!!

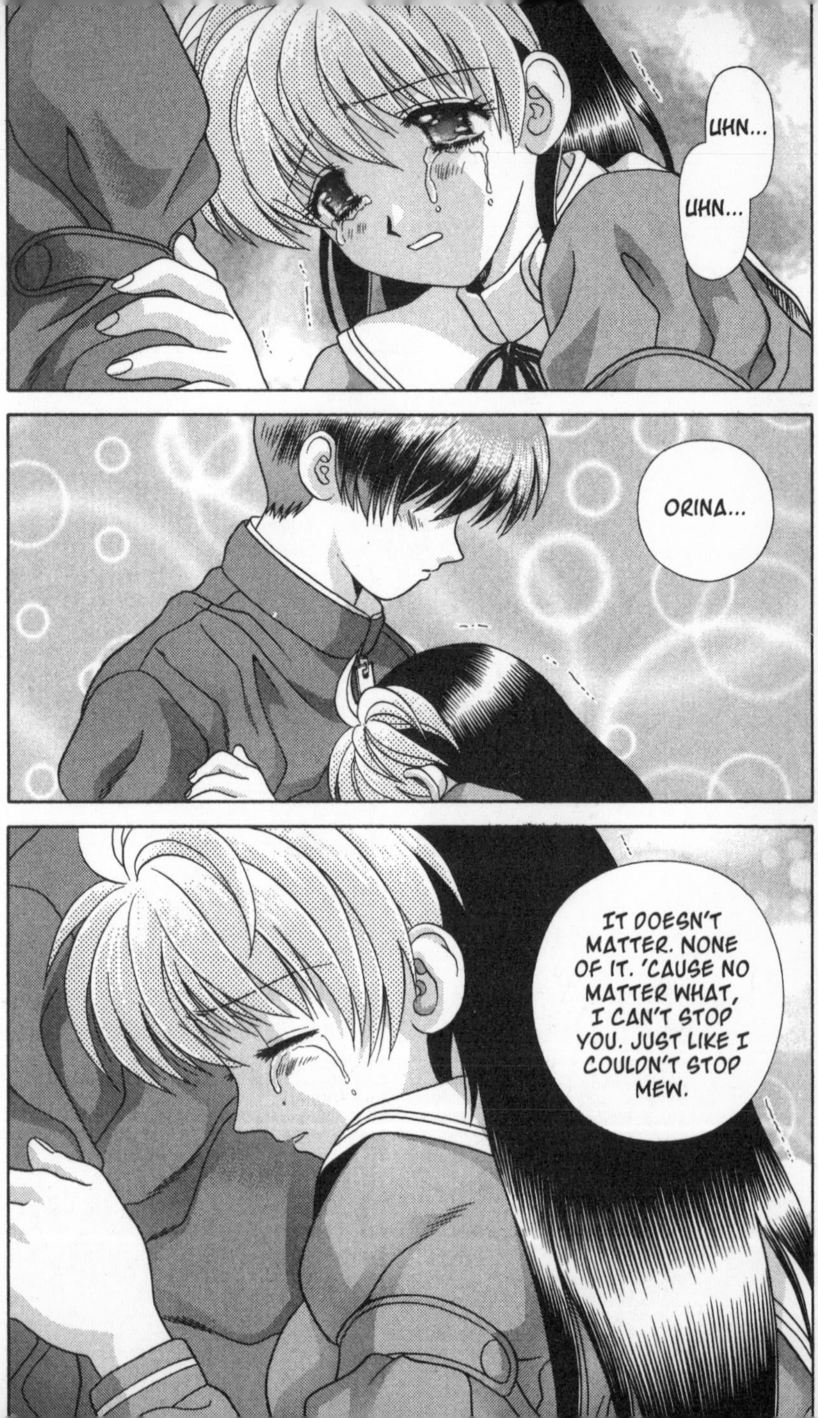
UHN...
UHN...
ORINA...
IT DOESN'T MATTER. NONE OF IT. 'CAUSE NO MATTER WHAT, I CAN'T STOP YOU. JUST LIKE I COULDN'T STOP MEW.

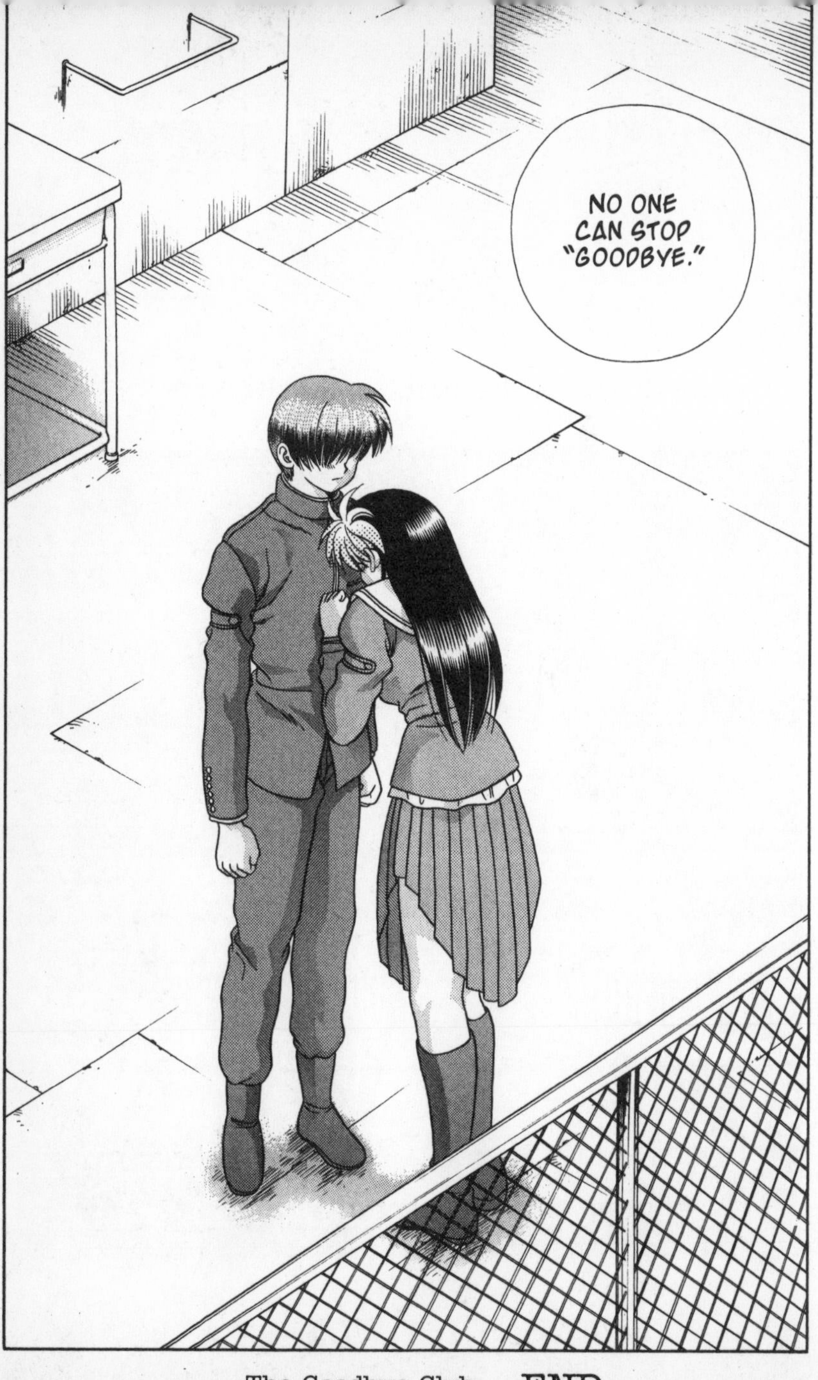
NO ONE CAN STOP "GOODBYE."

The Goodbye Club END

Chapter 37: Past the Point of No Return

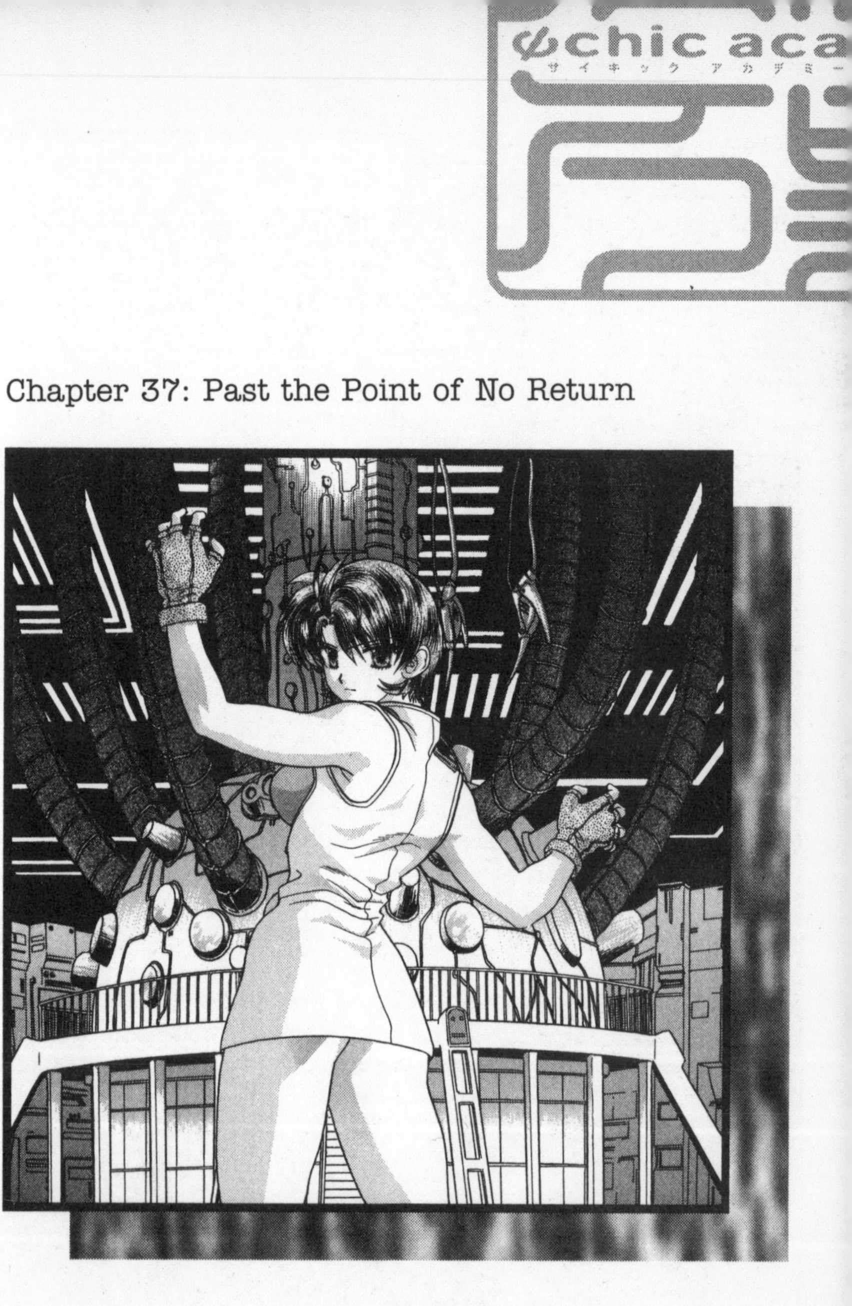

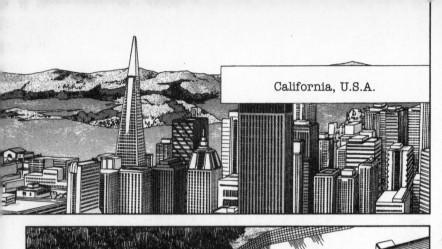

California, U.S.A.

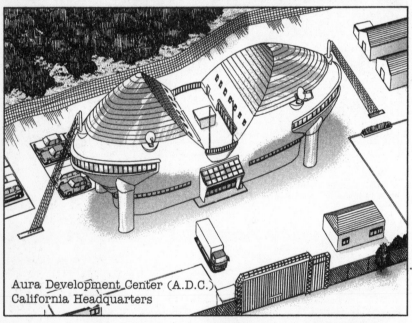

Aura Development Center (A.D.C.)
California Headquarters

I'M MEW BARAUE.

IDENTIFY YOUR- SELF!

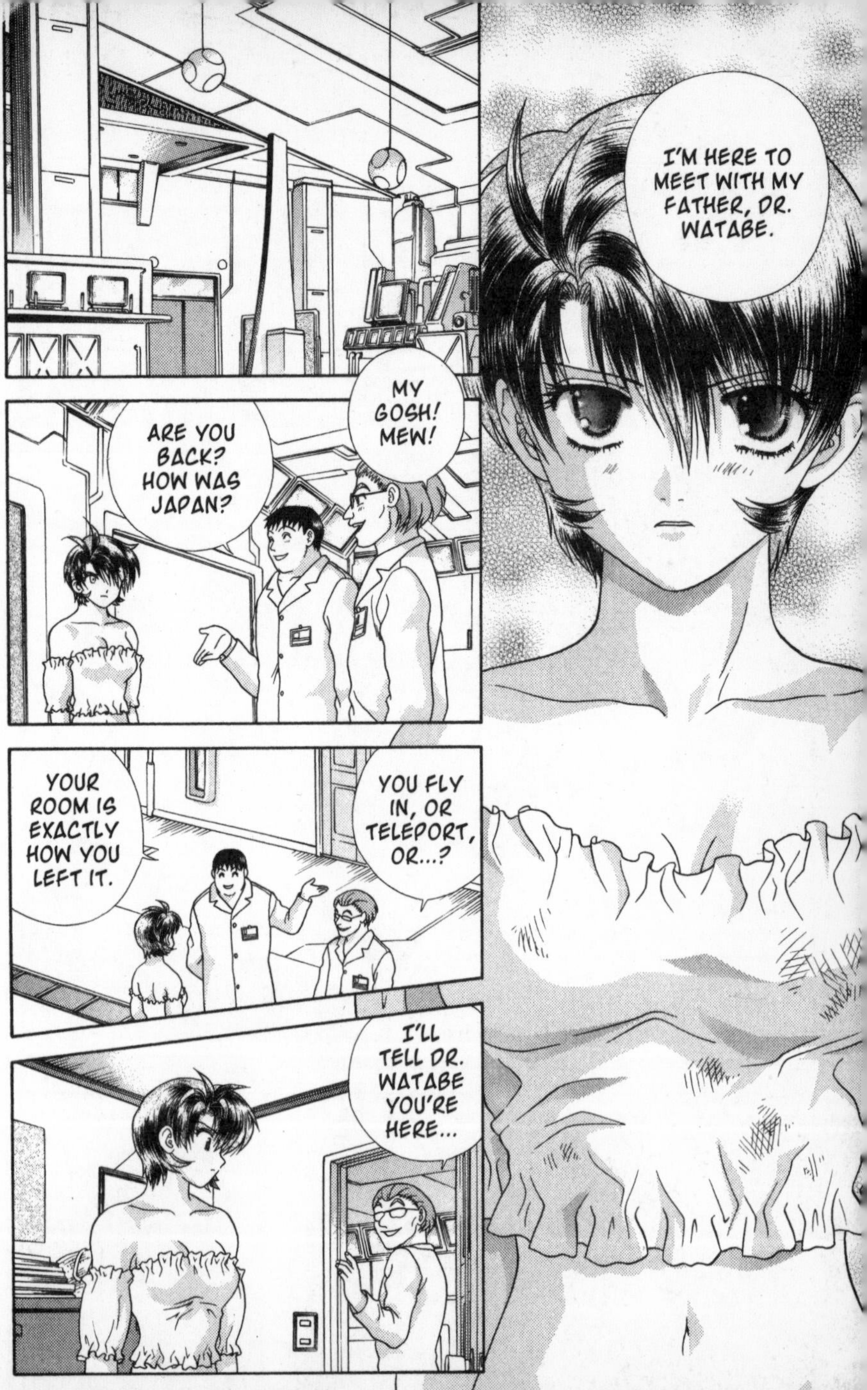
I'M HERE TO MEET WITH MY FATHER, DR. WATABE.
MY GOSH! MEW!
ARE YOU BACK? HOW WAS JAPAN?
YOU FLY IN, OR TELEPORT, OR...?
YOUR ROOM IS EXACTLY HOW YOU LEFT IT.
I'LL TELL DR. WATABE YOU'RE HERE...

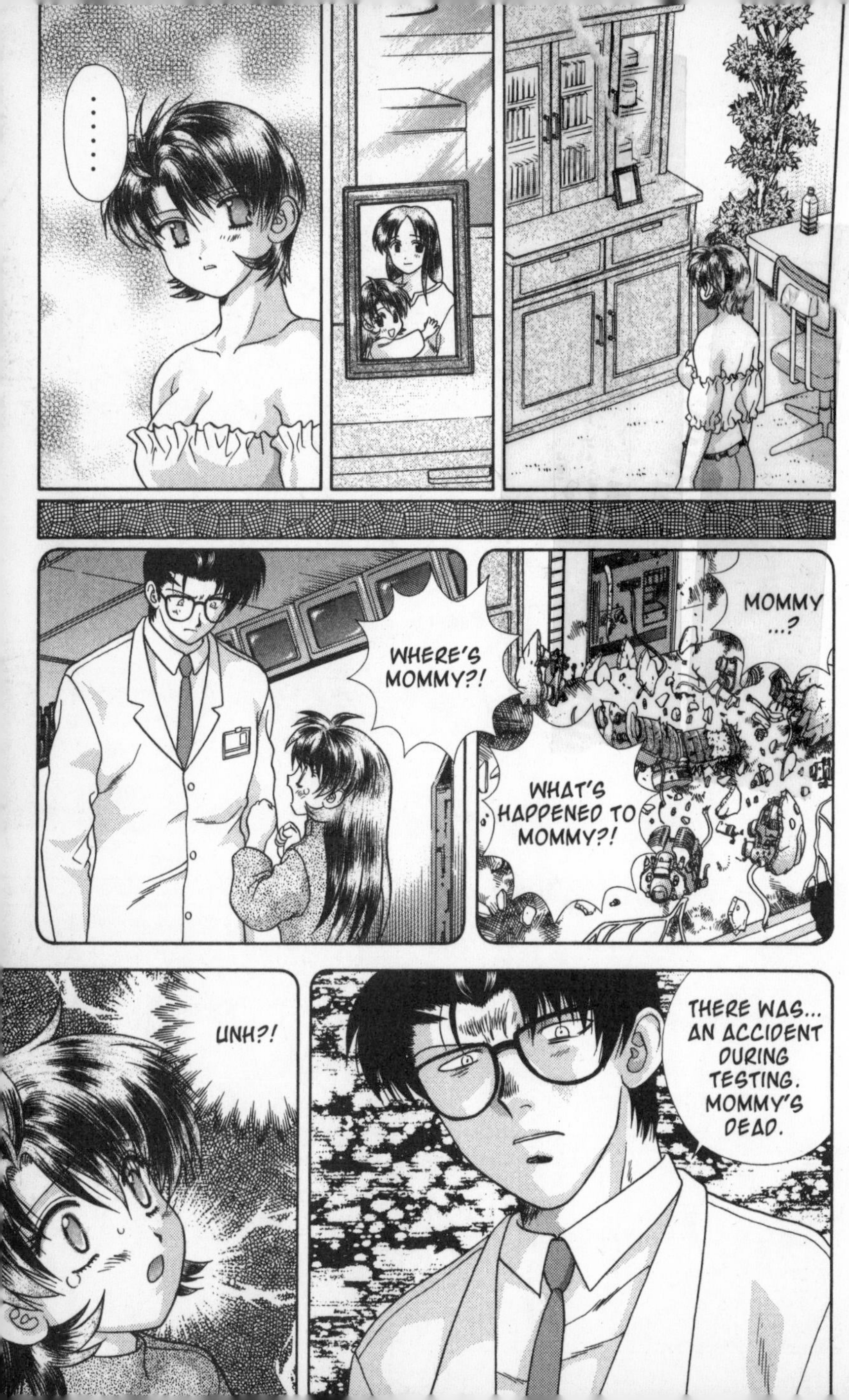
......
MOMMY ...?
WHAT'S HAPPENED TO MOMMY?!
WHERE'S MOMMY?!
THERE WAS... AN ACCIDENT DURING TESTING. MOMMY'S DEAD.
UNH?!

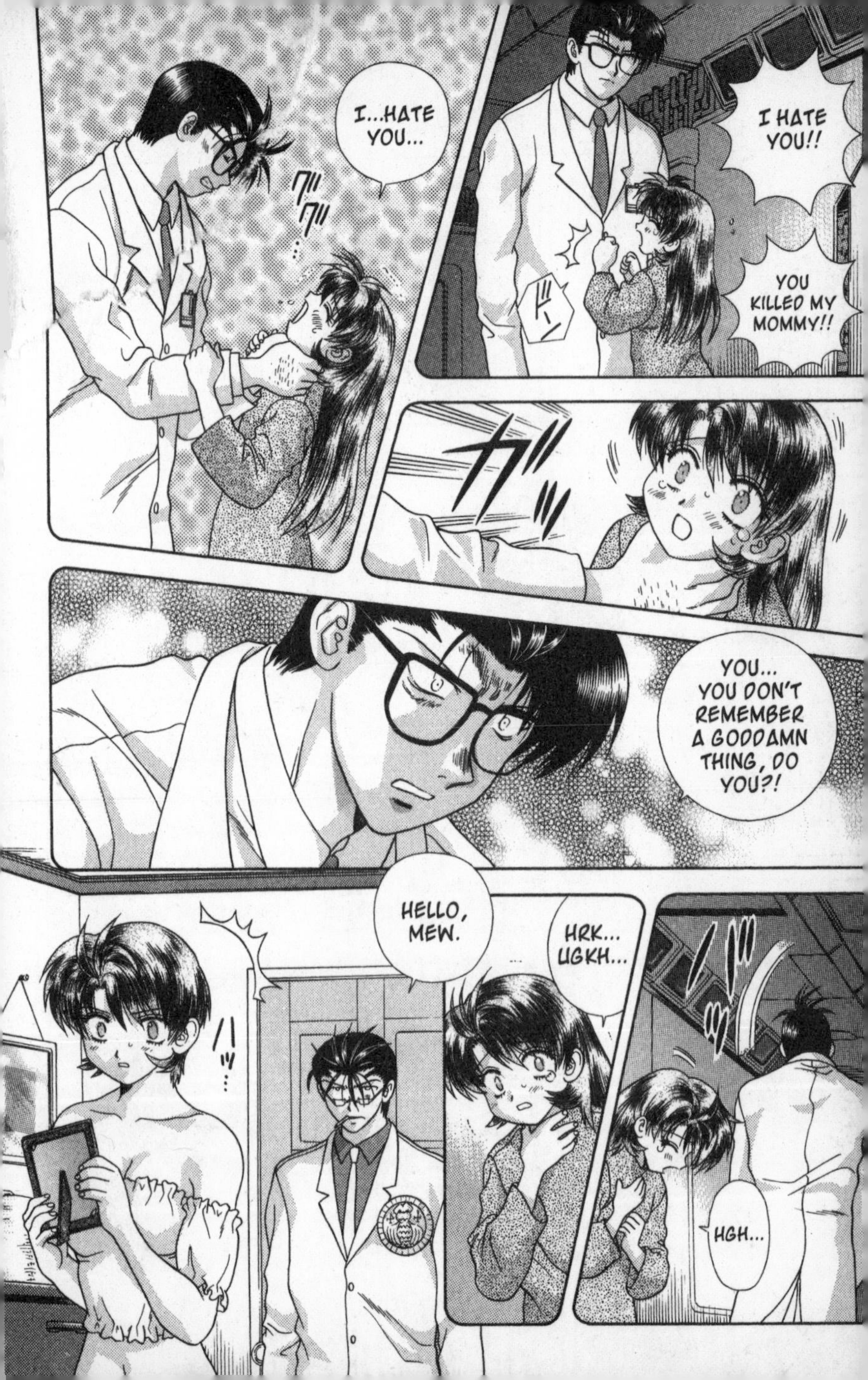
I HATE YOU!!
YOU KILLED MY MOMMY!!
I...HATE YOU...
YOU... YOU DON'T REMEMBER A GODDAMN THING, DO YOU?!
HGH...
HRK... UGKH...
HELLO, MEW.

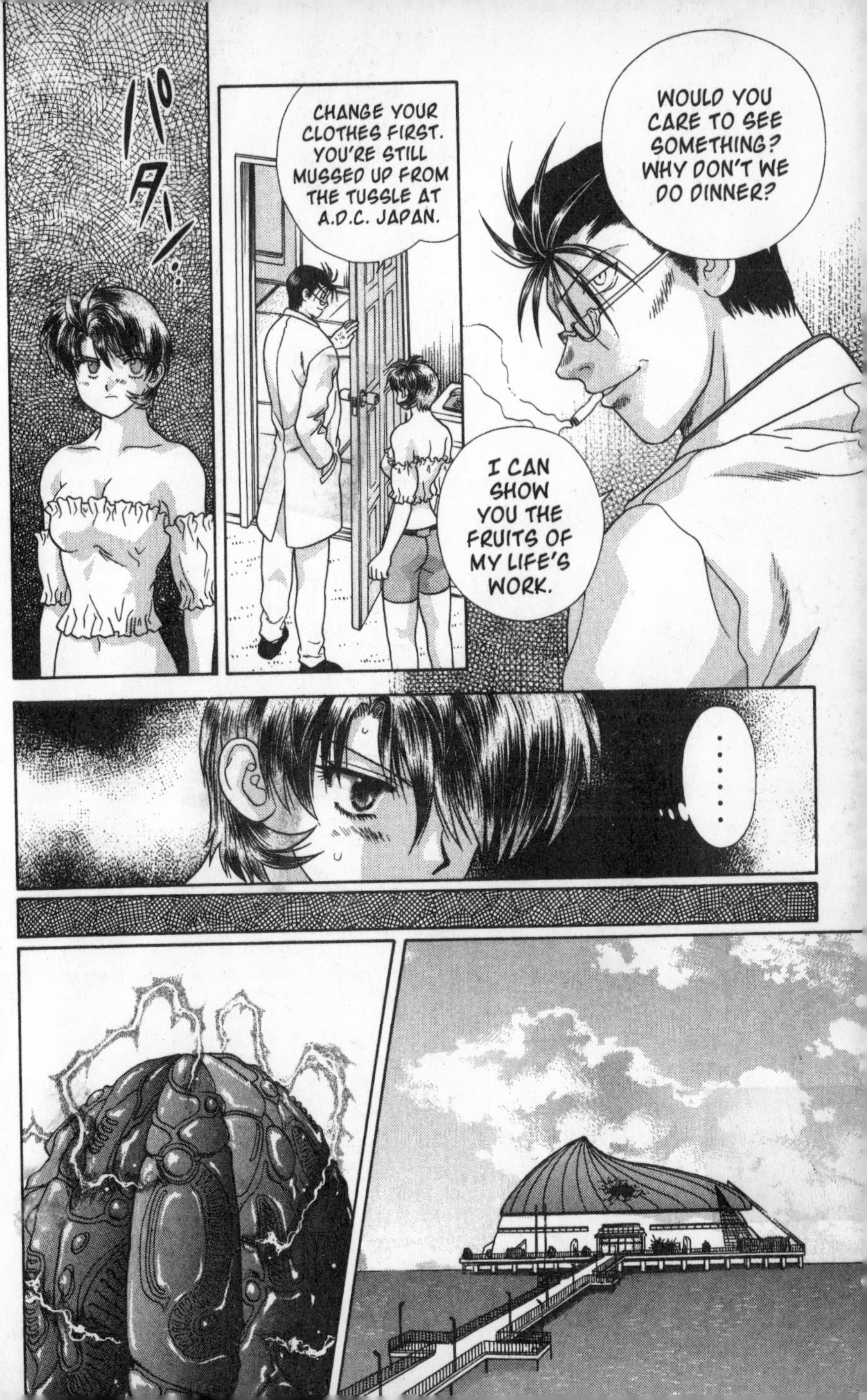
WOULD YOU CARE TO SEE SOMETHING? WHY DON'T WE DO DINNER?
I CAN SHOW YOU THE FRUITS OF MY LIFE'S WORK.
CHANGE YOUR CLOTHES FIRST. YOU'RE STILL MUSSED UP FROM THE TUSSLE AT A.D.C. JAPAN.
パタン…
……
…

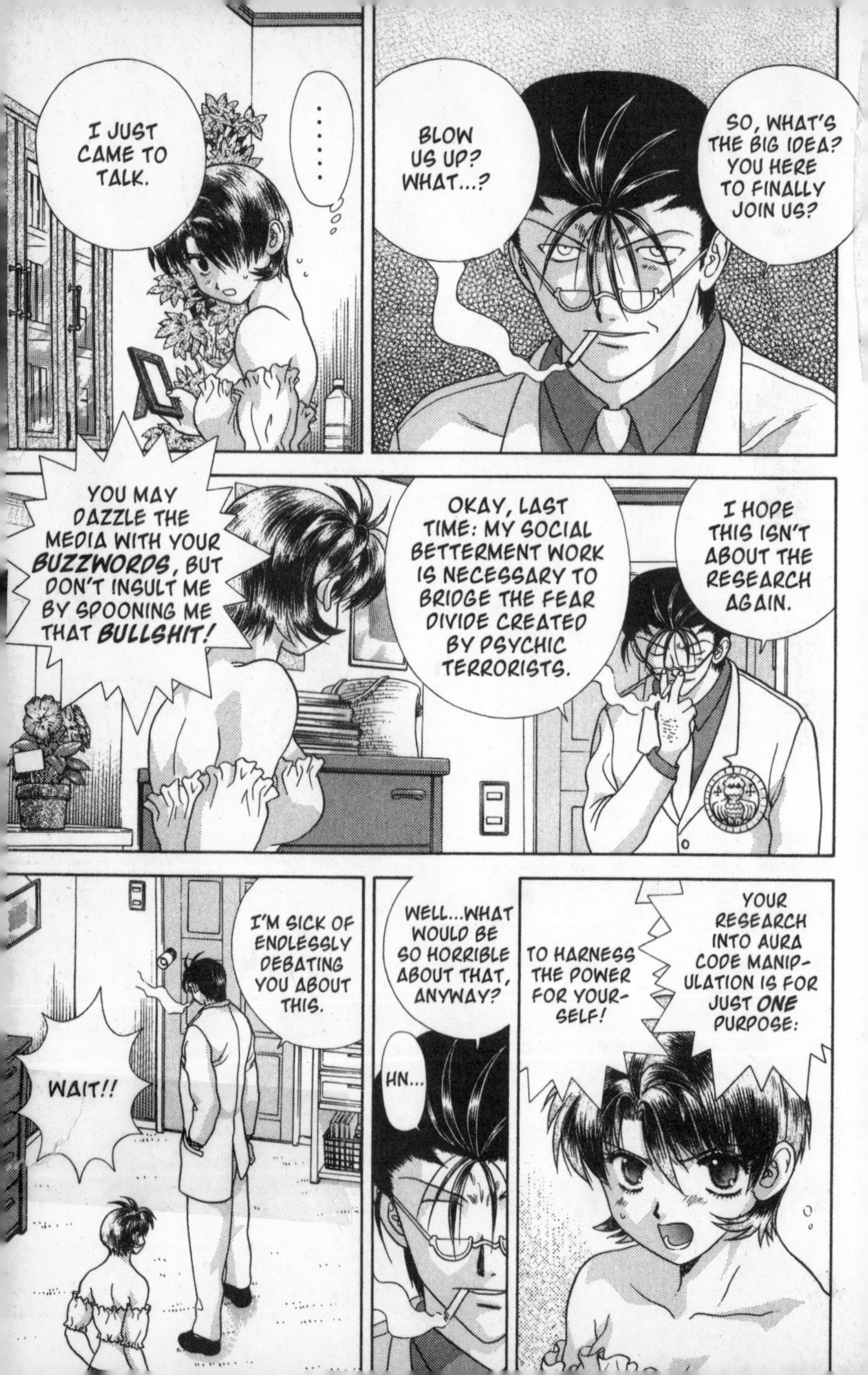
SO, WHAT'S THE BIG IDEA? YOU HERE TO FINALLY JOIN US?
BLOW US UP? WHAT...?
......
I JUST CAME TO TALK.
I HOPE THIS ISN'T ABOUT THE RESEARCH AGAIN.
OKAY, LAST TIME: MY SOCIAL BETTERMENT WORK IS NECESSARY TO BRIDGE THE FEAR DIVIDE CREATED BY PSYCHIC TERRORISTS.
YOU MAY DAZZLE THE MEDIA WITH YOUR BUZZWORDS, BUT DON'T INSULT ME BY SPOONING ME THAT BULLSHIT!
YOUR RESEARCH INTO AURA CODE MANIPULATION IS FOR JUST ONE PURPOSE:
TO HARNESS THE POWER FOR YOURSELF!
WELL...WHAT WOULD BE SO HORRIBLE ABOUT THAT, ANYWAY?
HN...
I'M SICK OF ENDLESSLY DEBATING YOU ABOUT THIS.
WAIT!!

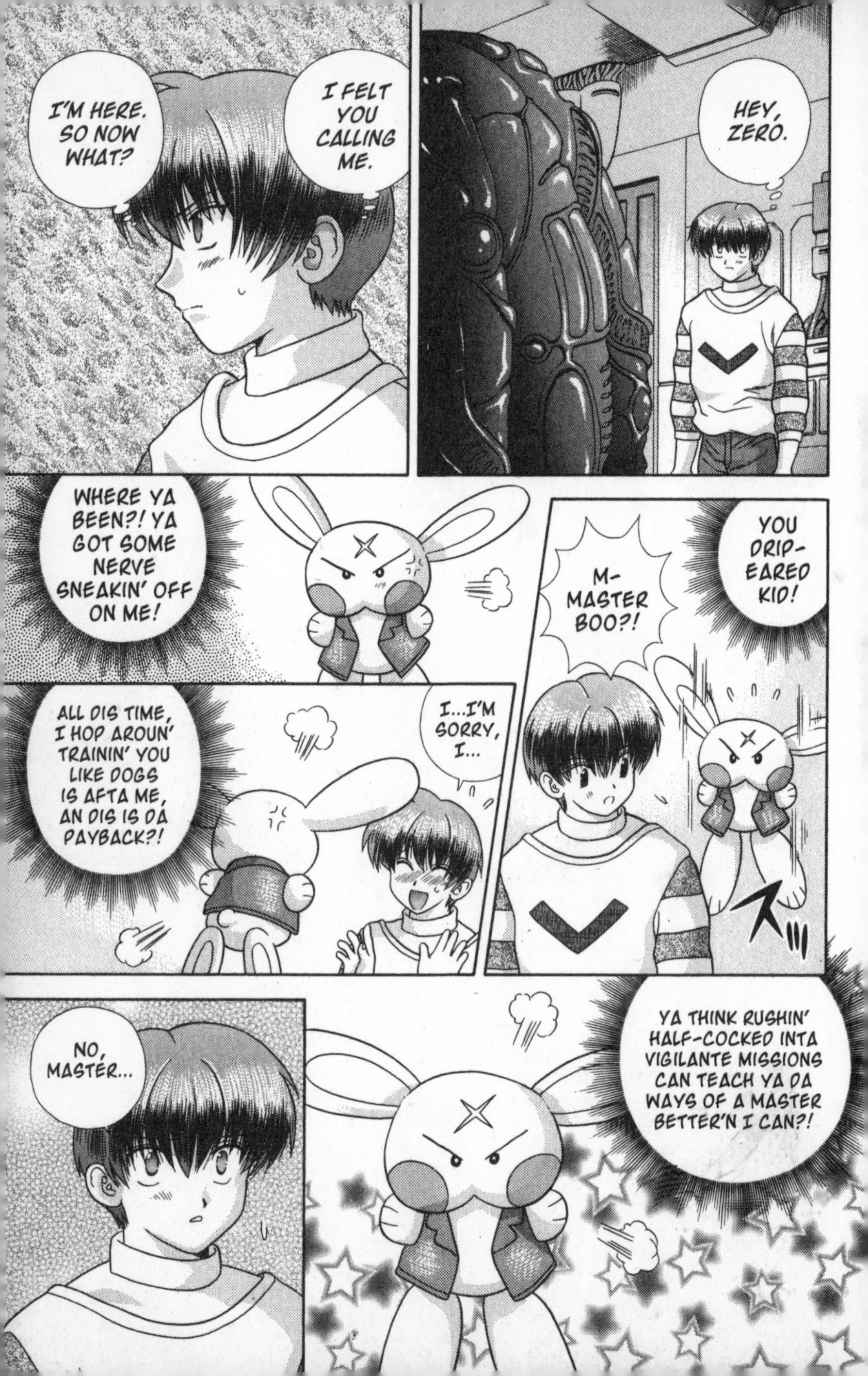
HEY, ZERO.
I FELT YOU CALLING ME.
I'M HERE. SO NOW WHAT?
YOU DRIP-EARED KID!
M-MASTER BOO?!
WHERE YA BEEN?! YA GOT SOME NERVE SNEAKIN' OFF ON ME!
I...I'M SORRY, I...
ALL DIS TIME, I HOP AROUN' TRAININ' YOU LIKE DOGS IS AFTA ME, AN DIS IS DA PAYBACK?!
YA THINK RUSHIN' HALF-COCKED INTA VIGILANTE MISSIONS CAN TEACH YA DA WAYS OF A MASTER BETTER'N I CAN?!
NO, MASTER...

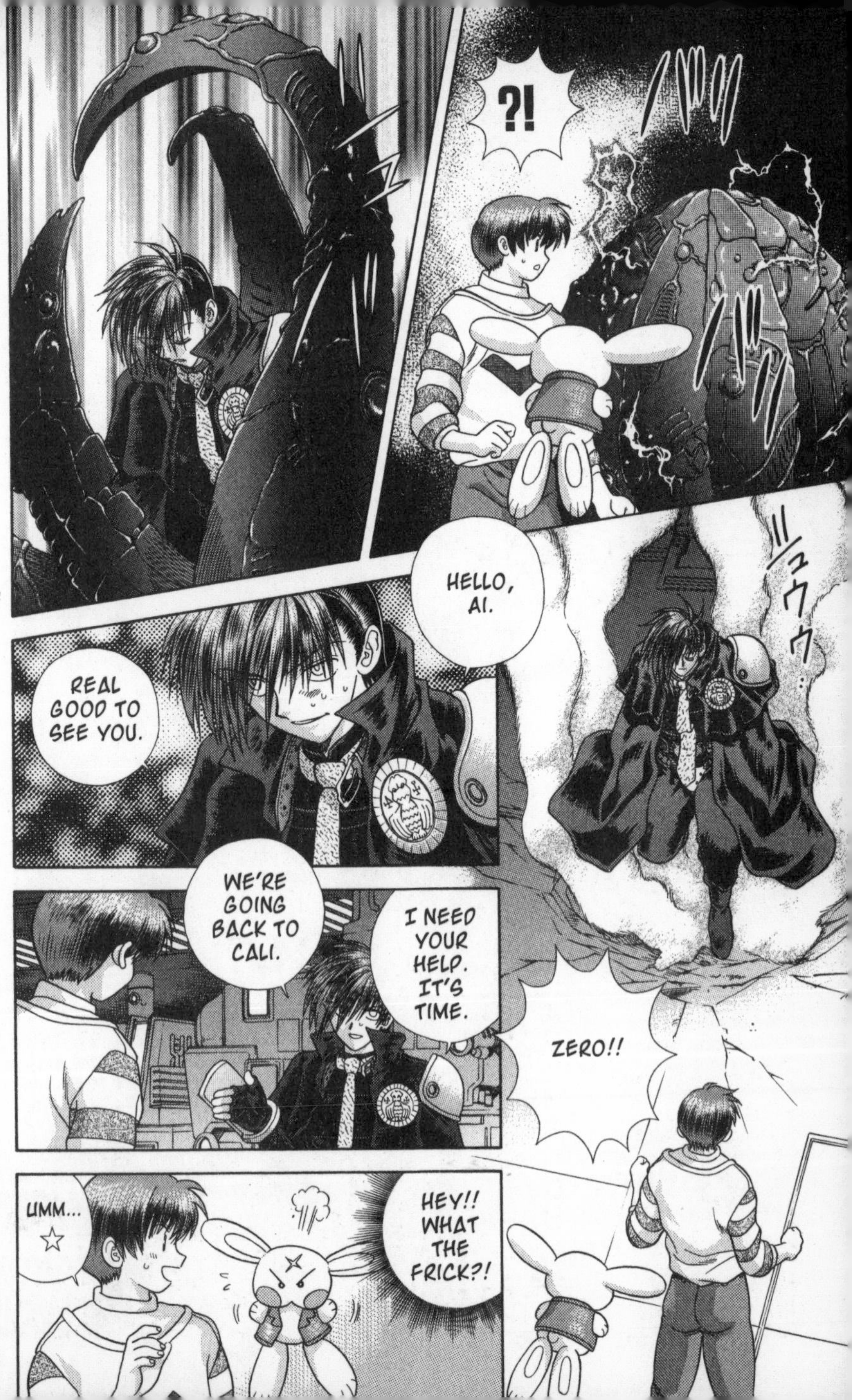
?!
HELLO, AI.
ZERO!!
REAL GOOD TO SEE YOU.
WE'RE GOING BACK TO CALI.
I NEED YOUR HELP. IT'S TIME.
HEY!! WHAT THE FRICK?!
UMM... ☆

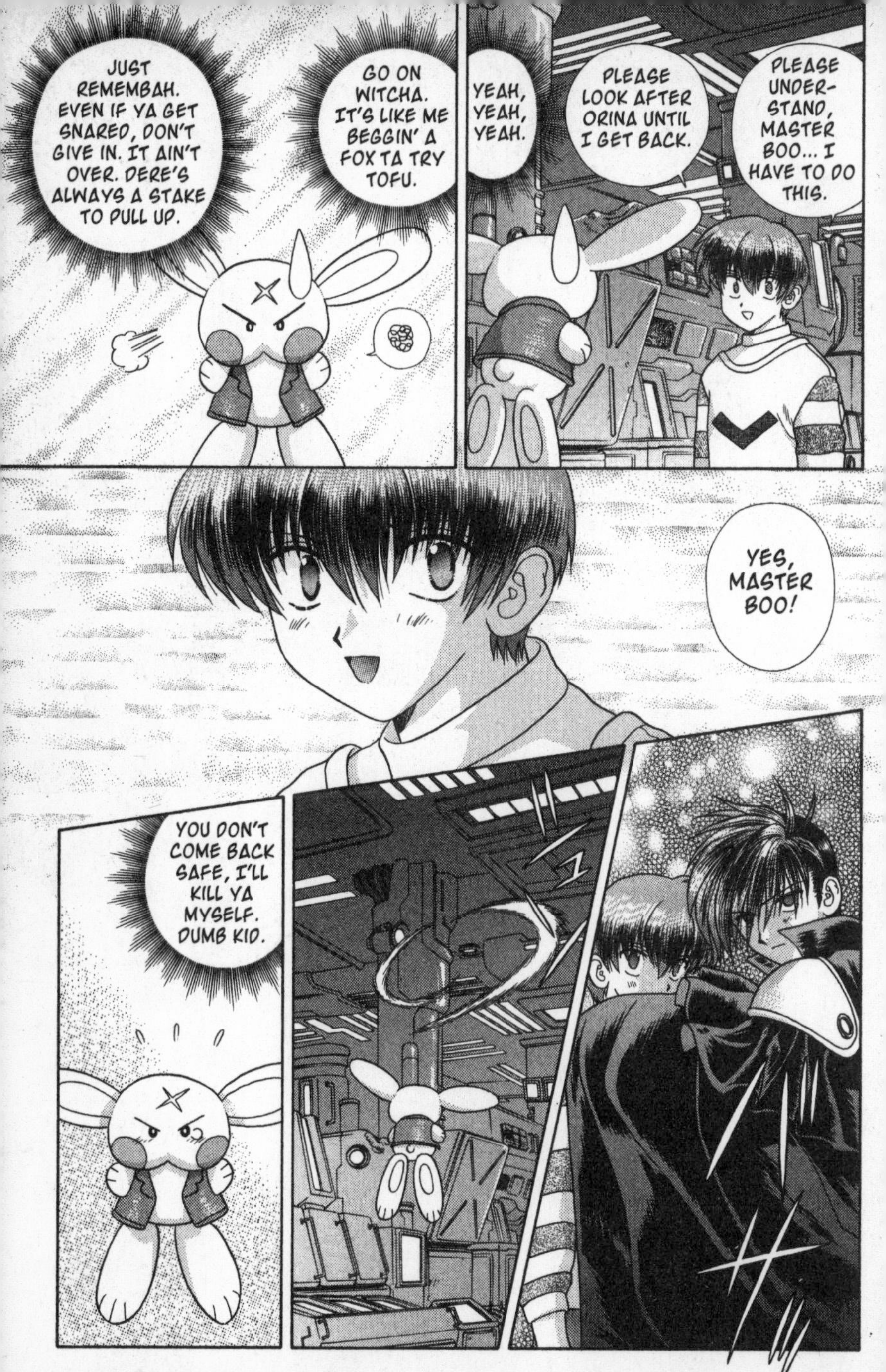
PLEASE UNDER-STAND, MASTER BOO... I HAVE TO DO THIS.
PLEASE LOOK AFTER ORINA UNTIL I GET BACK.
YEAH, YEAH, YEAH.
GO ON WITCHA. IT'S LIKE ME BEGGIN' A FOX TA TRY TOFU.
JUST REMEMBAH. EVEN IF YA GET SNARED, DON'T GIVE IN. IT AIN'T OVER. DERE'S ALWAYS A STAKE TO PULL UP.
YES, MASTER BOO!
YOU DON'T COME BACK SAFE, I'LL KILL YA MYSELF. DUMB KID.

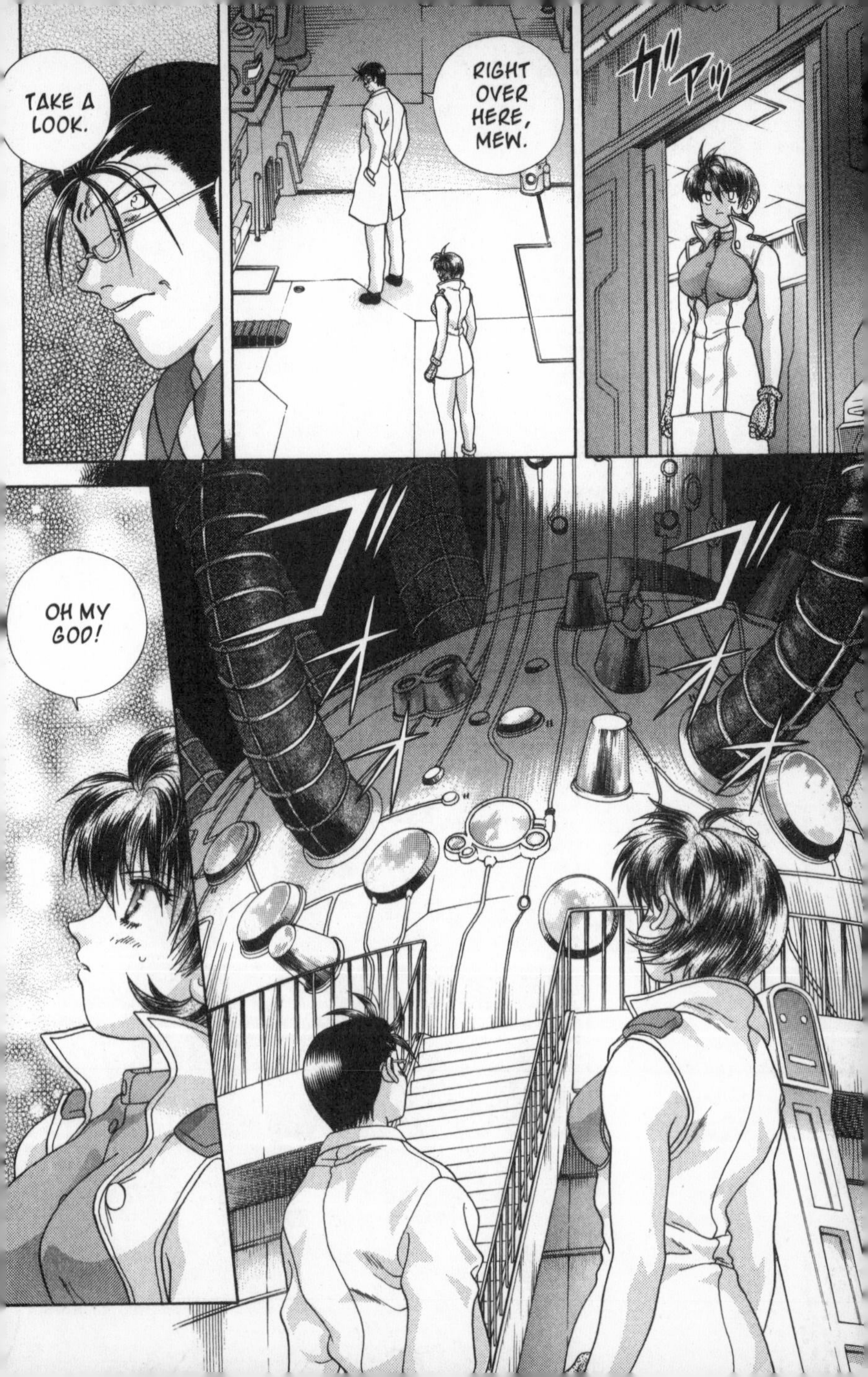
ガァッ
RIGHT OVER HERE, MEW.
TAKE A LOOK.
OH MY GOD!

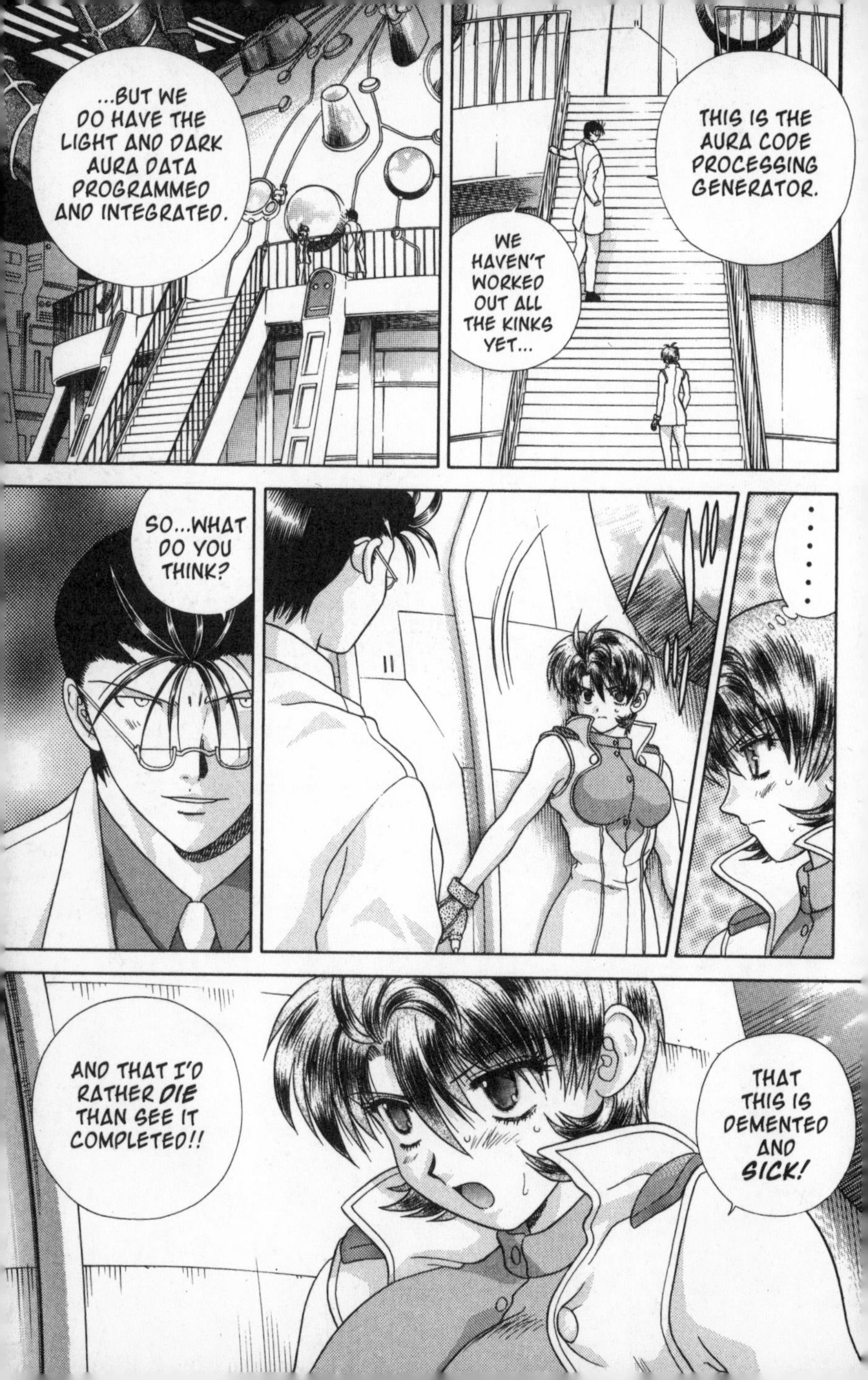
THIS IS THE AURA CODE PROCESSING GENERATOR.
WE HAVEN'T WORKED OUT ALL THE KINKS YET...
...BUT WE DO HAVE THE LIGHT AND DARK AURA DATA PROGRAMMED AND INTEGRATED.
......
SO...WHAT DO YOU THINK?
THAT THIS IS DEMENTED AND SICK!
AND THAT I'D RATHER DIE THAN SEE IT COMPLETED!!

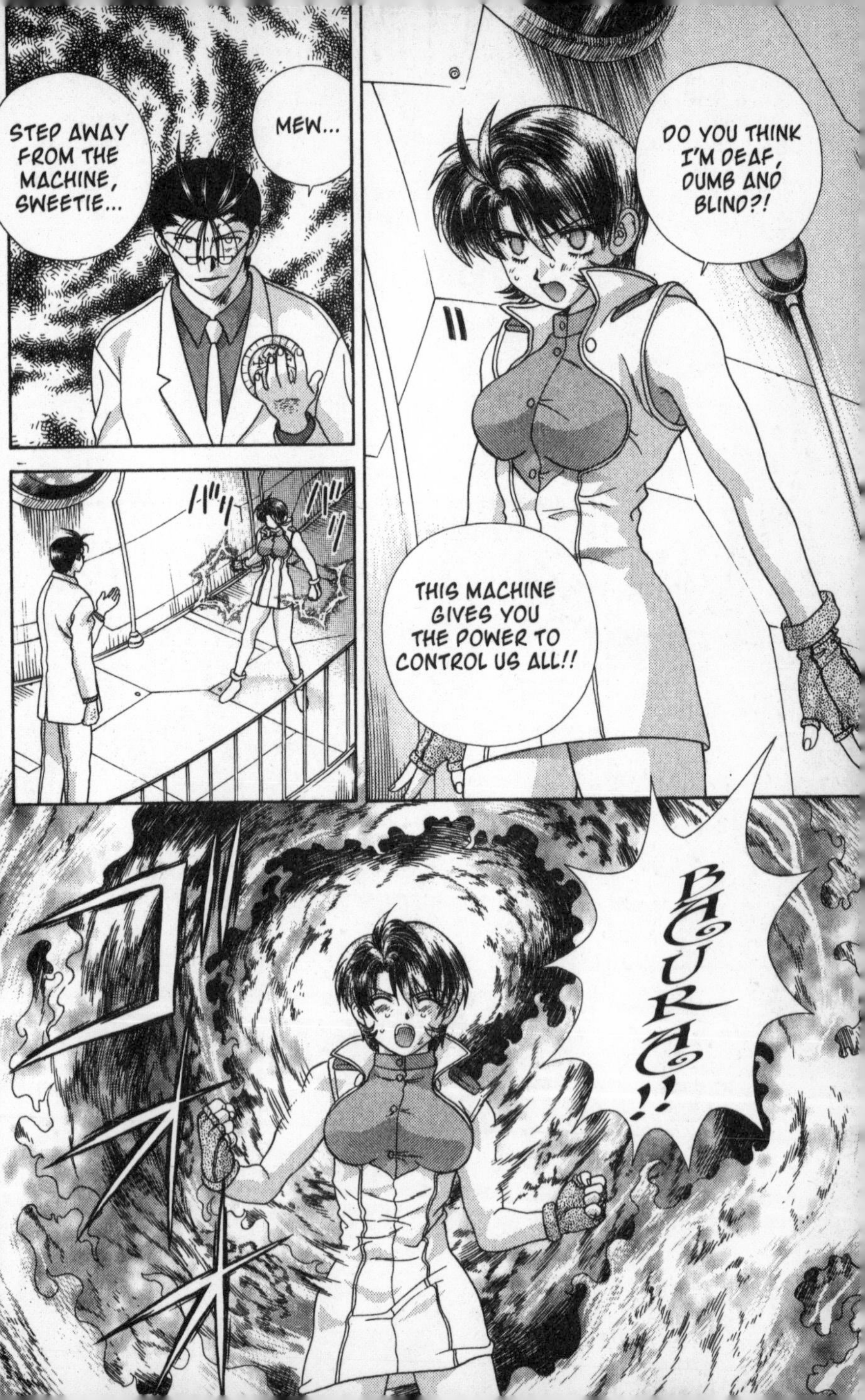

DO YOU THINK I'M DEAF, DUMB AND BLIND?!
THIS MACHINE GIVES YOU THE POWER TO CONTROL US ALL!!
MEW...
STEP AWAY FROM THE MACHINE, SWEETIE...
BAGURAG!!

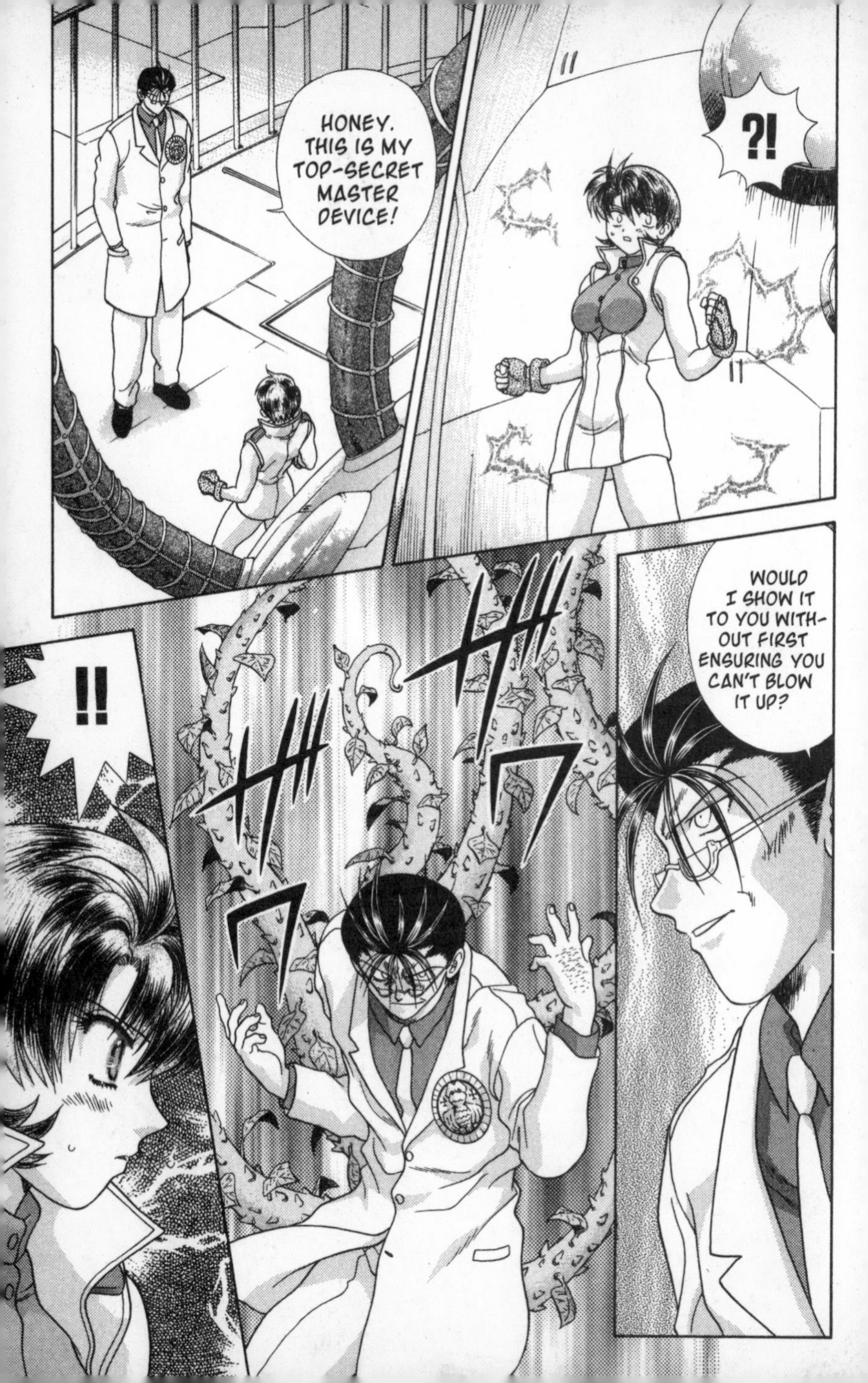
?!
HONEY. THIS IS MY TOP-SECRET MASTER DEVICE!
WOULD I SHOW IT TO YOU WITH-OUT FIRST ENSURING YOU CAN'T BLOW IT UP?
!!

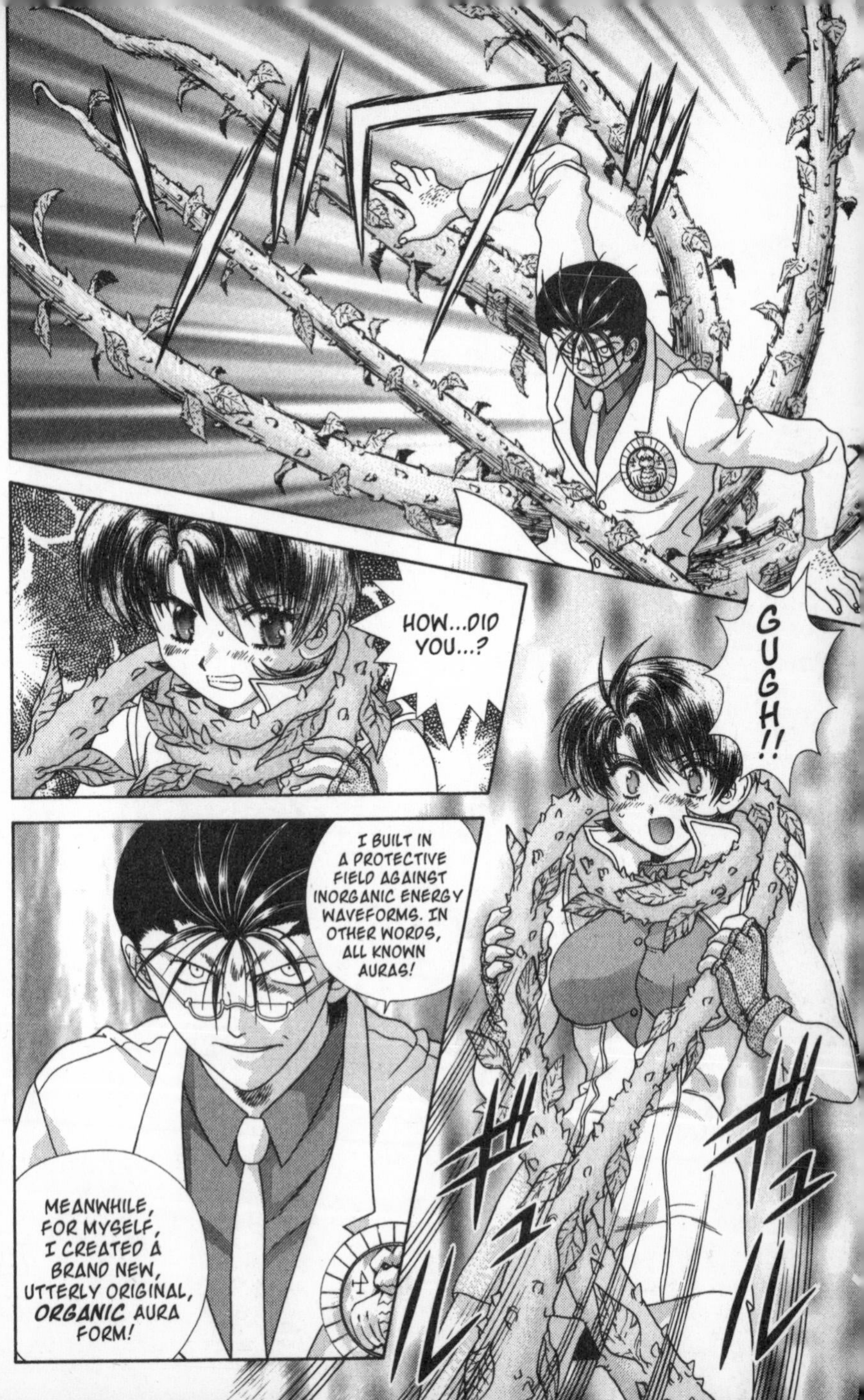
GUGH!!
HOW...DID YOU...?
I BUILT IN A PROTECTIVE FIELD AGAINST INORGANIC ENERGY WAVEFORMS. IN OTHER WORDS, ALL KNOWN AURAS!
MEANWHILE, FOR MYSELF, I CREATED A BRAND NEW, UTTERLY ORIGINAL, **ORGANIC** AURA FORM!

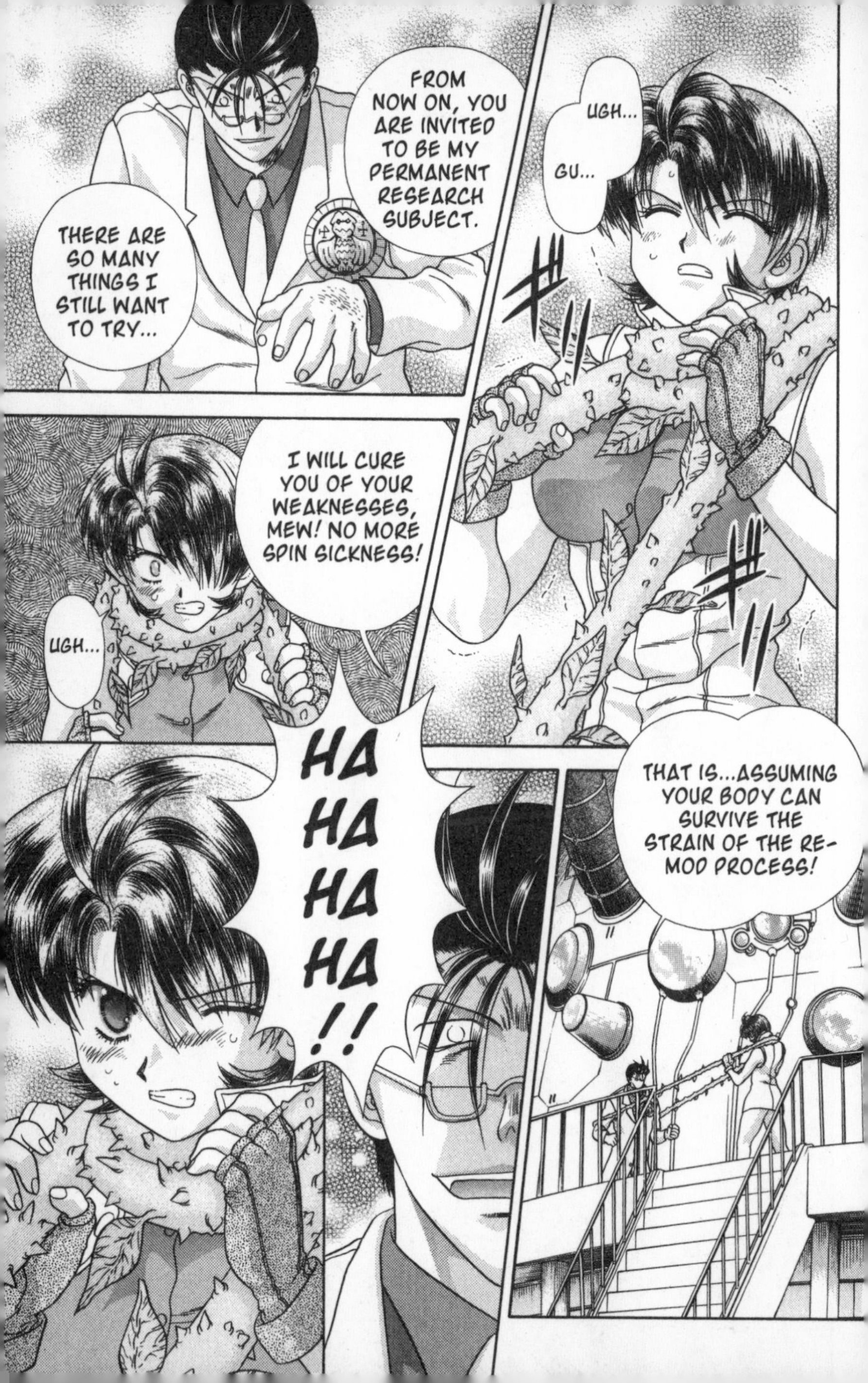
UGH...
GU...
FROM NOW ON, YOU ARE INVITED TO BE MY PERMANENT RESEARCH SUBJECT.
THERE ARE SO MANY THINGS I STILL WANT TO TRY...
I WILL CURE YOU OF YOUR WEAKNESSES, MEW! NO MORE SPIN SICKNESS!
UGH...
THAT IS...ASSUMING YOUR BODY CAN SURVIVE THE STRAIN OF THE RE-MOD PROCESS!
HA HA HA HA HA!!

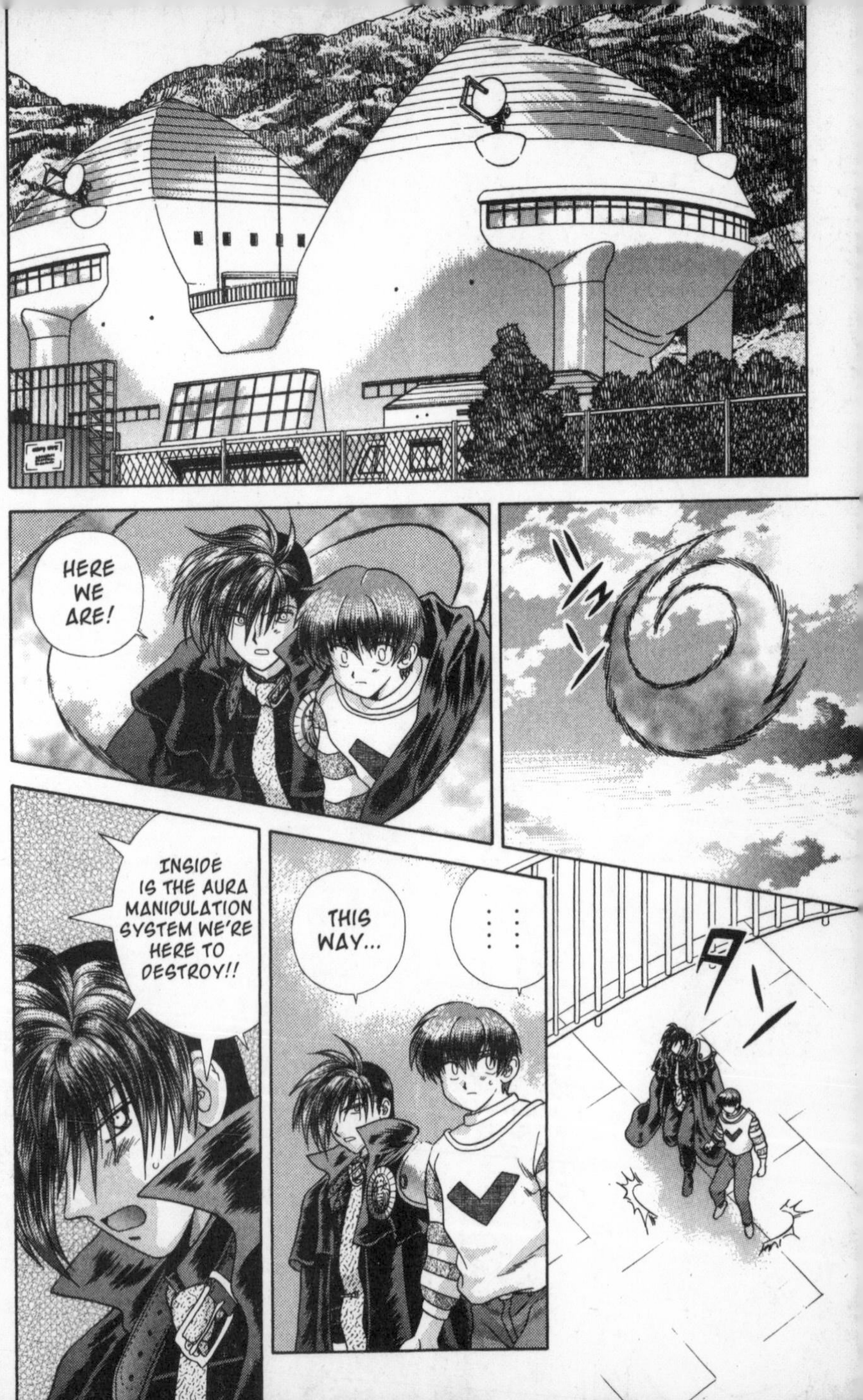
HERE WE ARE!
......
THIS WAY...
INSIDE IS THE AURA MANIPULATION SYSTEM WE'RE HERE TO DESTROY!!

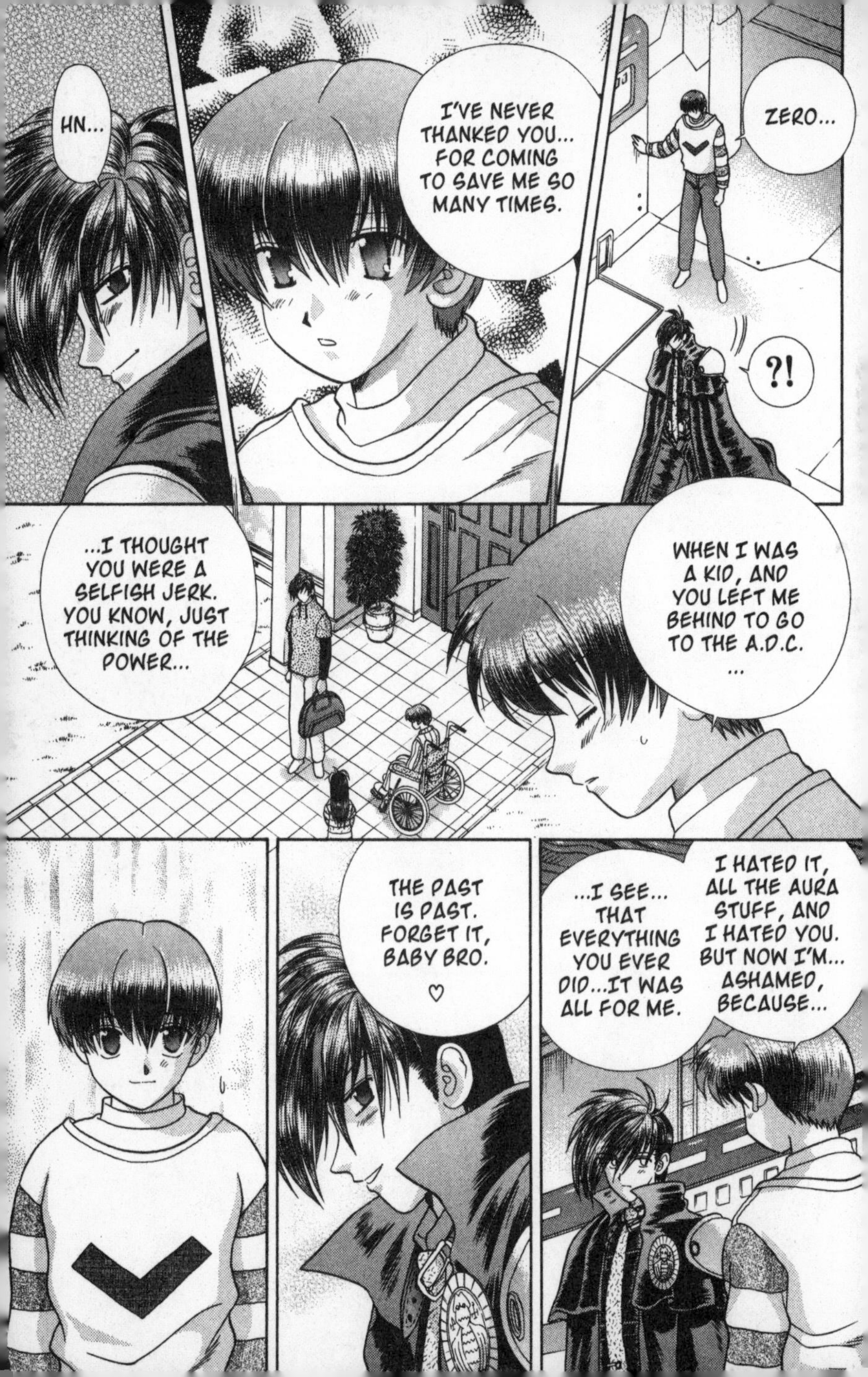
ZERO...
?!
I'VE NEVER THANKED YOU... FOR COMING TO SAVE ME SO MANY TIMES.
HN...
WHEN I WAS A KID, AND YOU LEFT ME BEHIND TO GO TO THE A.D.C. ...
...I THOUGHT YOU WERE A SELFISH JERK. YOU KNOW, JUST THINKING OF THE POWER...
I HATED IT, ALL THE AURA STUFF, AND I HATED YOU. BUT NOW I'M... ASHAMED, BECAUSE...
...I SEE... THAT EVERYTHING YOU EVER DID...IT WAS ALL FOR ME.
THE PAST IS PAST. FORGET IT, BABY BRO. ♡

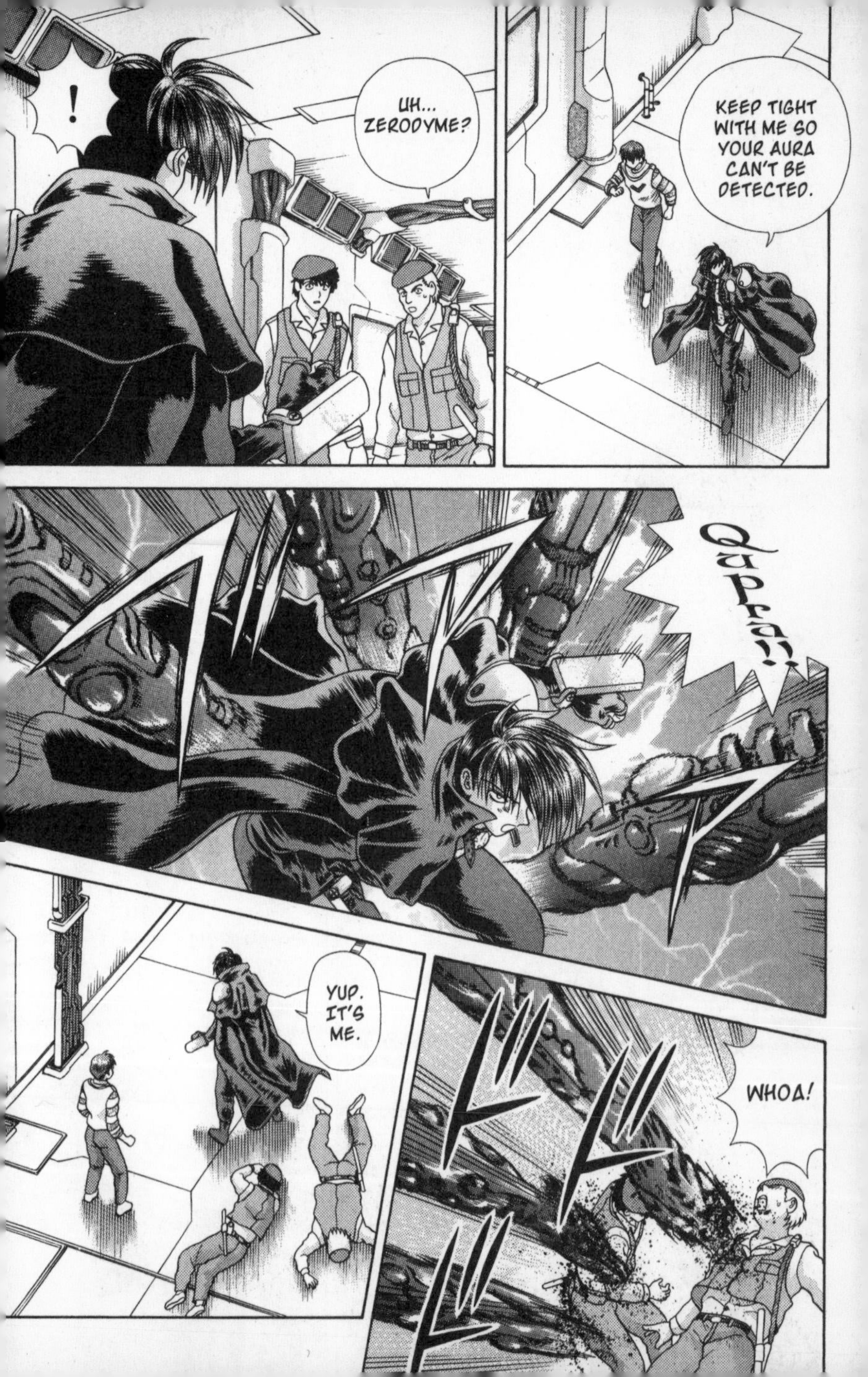
KEEP TIGHT WITH ME SO YOUR AURA CAN'T BE DETECTED.
!
UH... ZERODYME?
Qupra!!
WHOA!
YUP. IT'S ME.

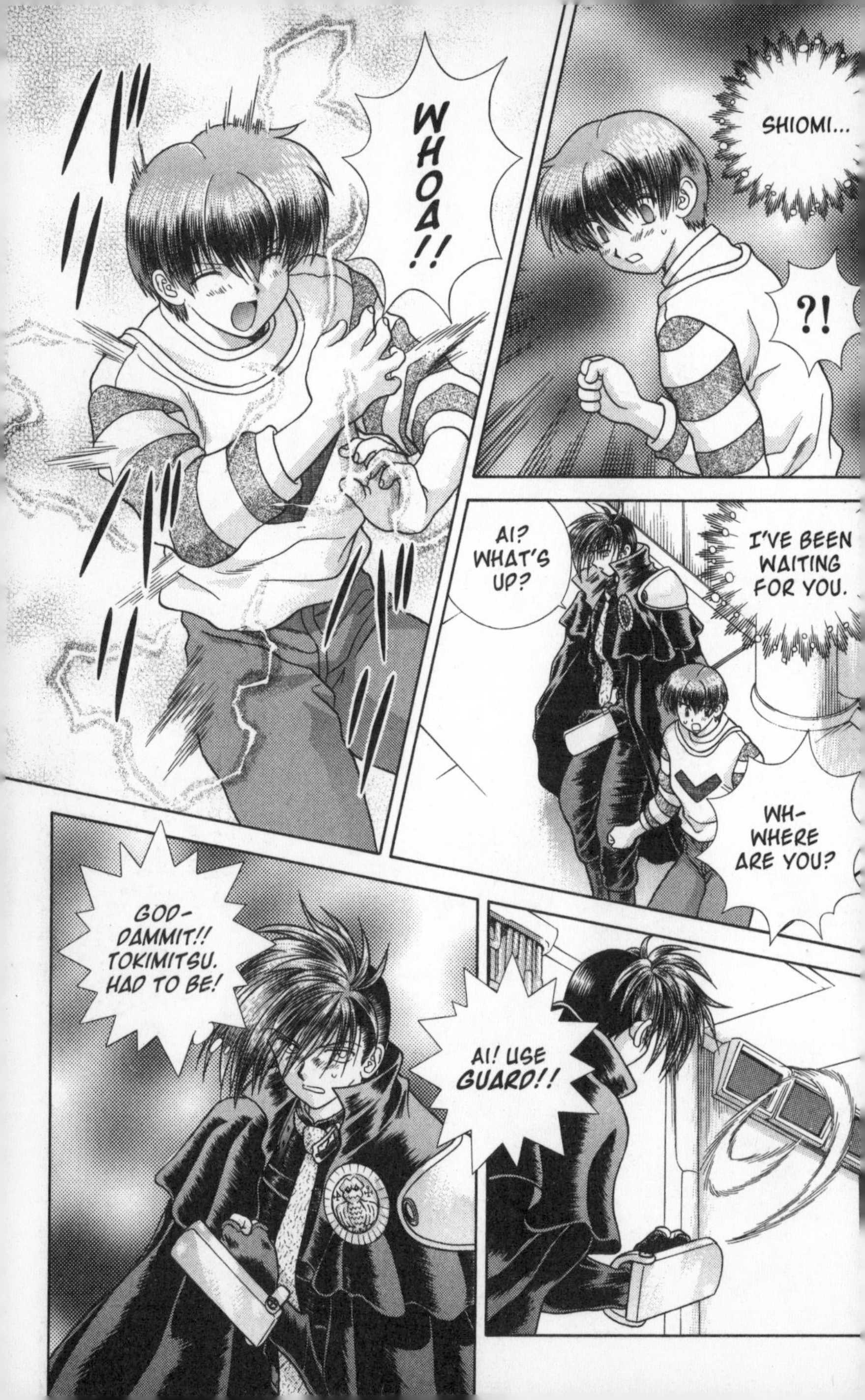
SHIOMI...
?!
I'VE BEEN WAITING FOR YOU.
AI? WHAT'S UP?
WH-WHERE ARE YOU?
WHOA!!
AI! USE GUARD!!
GOD-DAMMIT!! TOKIMITSU. HAD TO BE!

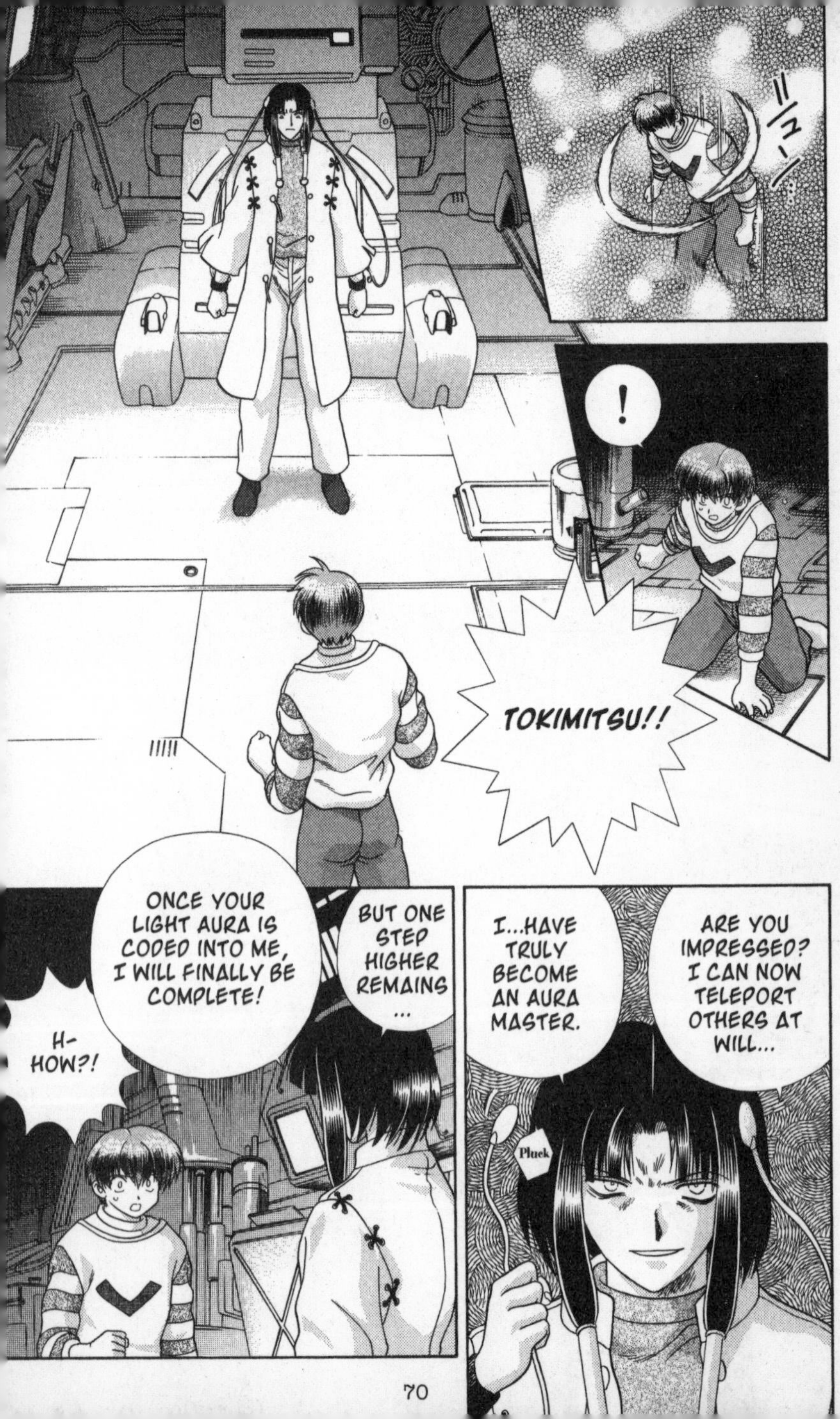
!
TOKIMITSU!!
ARE YOU IMPRESSED? I CAN NOW TELEPORT OTHERS AT WILL...
I...HAVE TRULY BECOME AN AURA MASTER.
Pluck
BUT ONE STEP HIGHER REMAINS ...
ONCE YOUR LIGHT AURA IS CODED INTO ME, I WILL FINALLY BE COMPLETE!
H- HOW?!

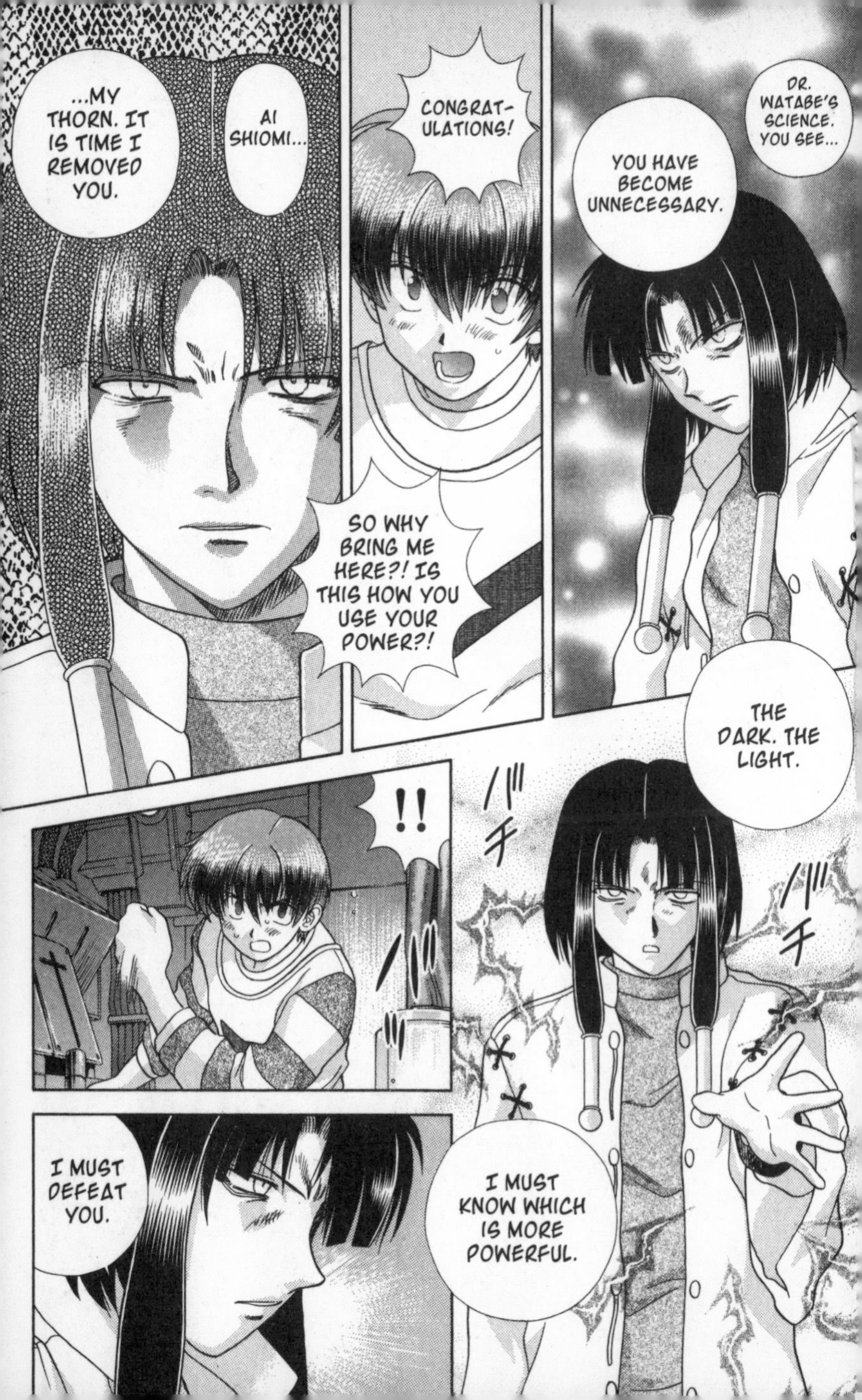
DR. WATABE'S SCIENCE. YOU SEE...
YOU HAVE BECOME UNNECESSARY.
CONGRAT-ULATIONS!
SO WHY BRING ME HERE?! IS THIS HOW YOU USE YOUR POWER?!
AI SHIOMI...
...MY THORN. IT IS TIME I REMOVED YOU.
THE DARK. THE LIGHT.
バチ
バチ
I MUST KNOW WHICH IS MORE POWERFUL.
!!
I MUST DEFEAT YOU.

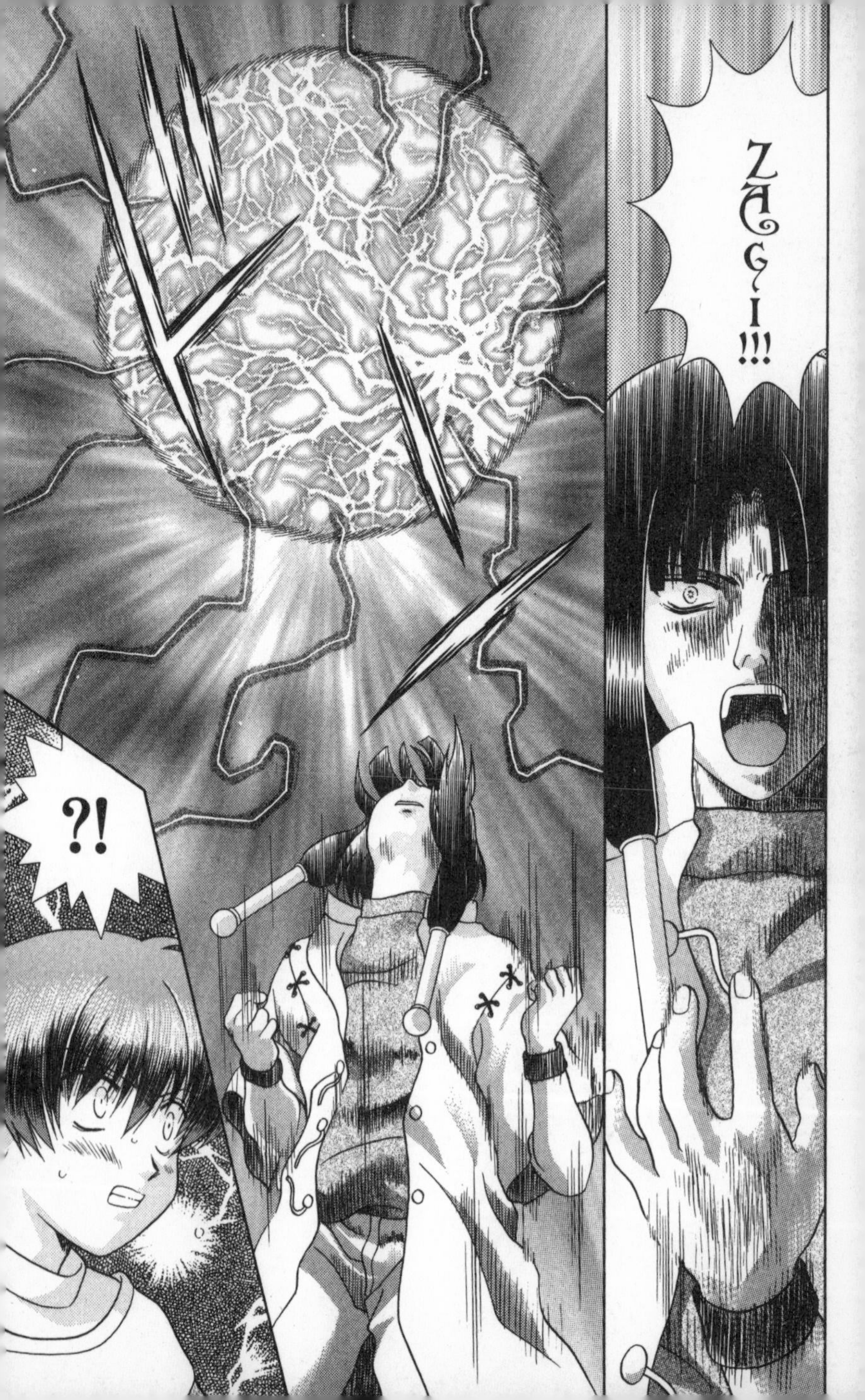
ZAGI!!!
?!

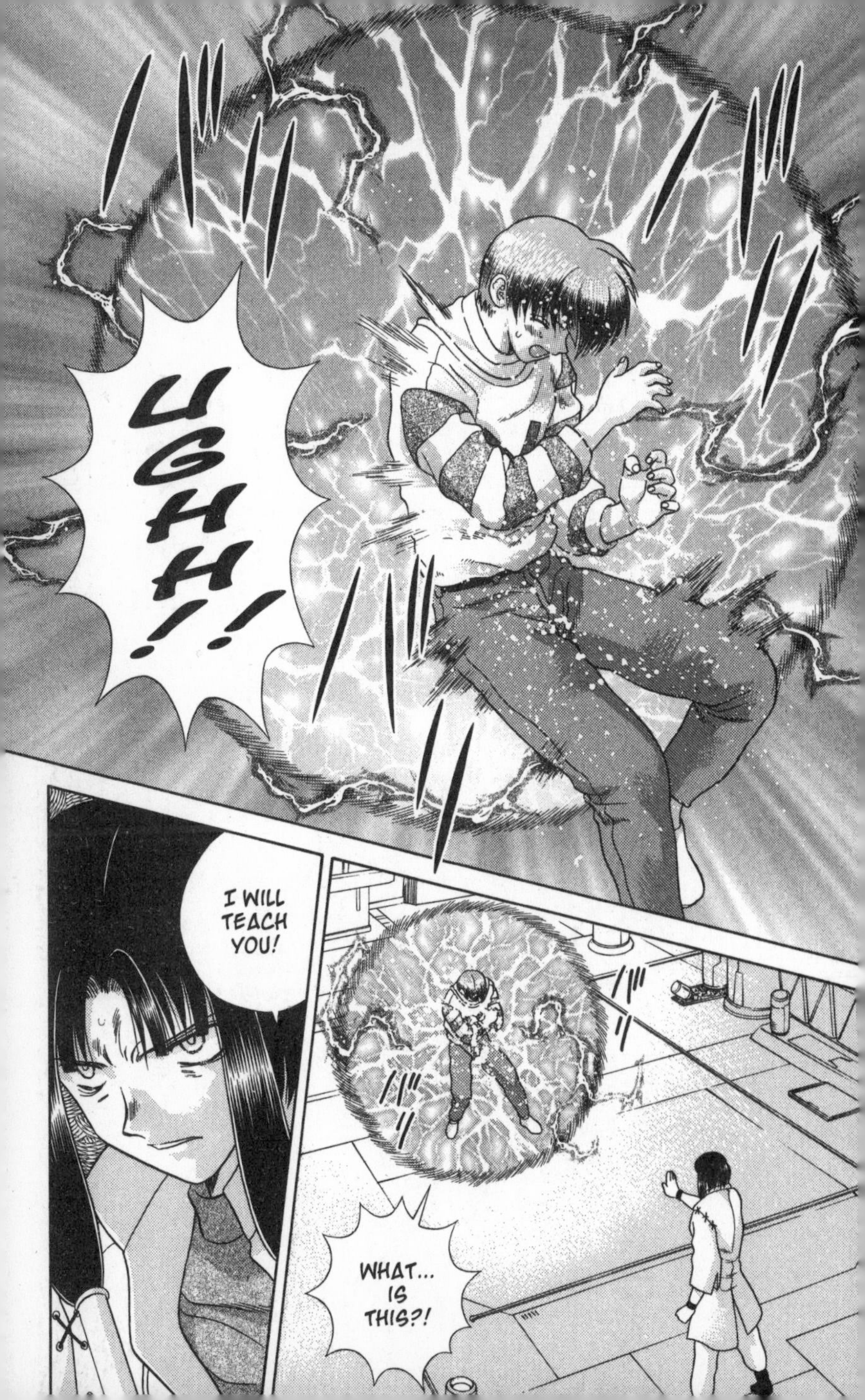
UGHH!!
I WILL TEACH YOU!
WHAT... IS THIS?!

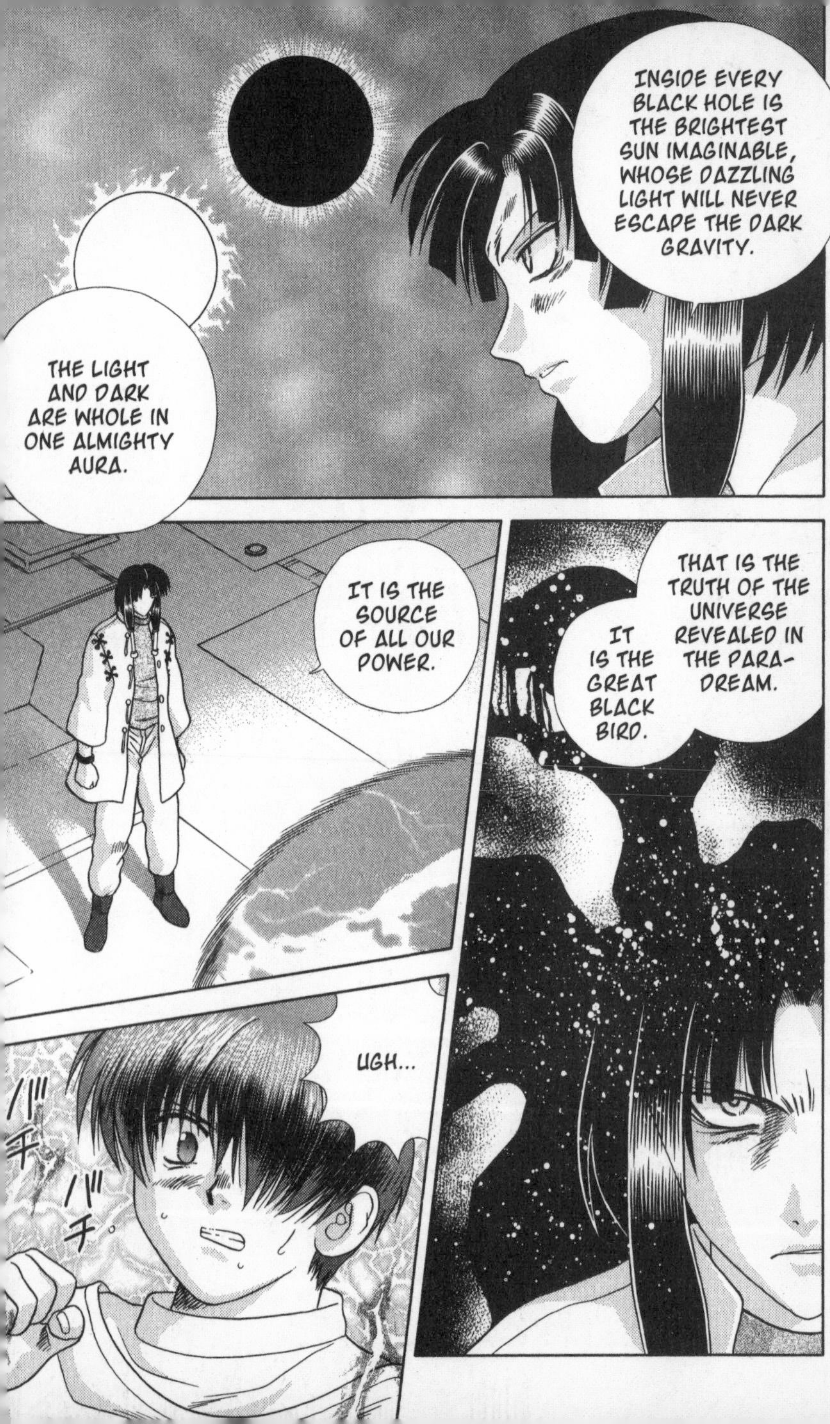
INSIDE EVERY BLACK HOLE IS THE BRIGHTEST SUN IMAGINABLE, WHOSE DAZZLING LIGHT WILL NEVER ESCAPE THE DARK GRAVITY.
THE LIGHT AND DARK ARE WHOLE IN ONE ALMIGHTY AURA.
THAT IS THE TRUTH OF THE UNIVERSE REVEALED IN THE PARA-DREAM.
IT IS THE GREAT BLACK BIRD.
IT IS THE SOURCE OF ALL OUR POWER.
UGH...
バチ
バチ

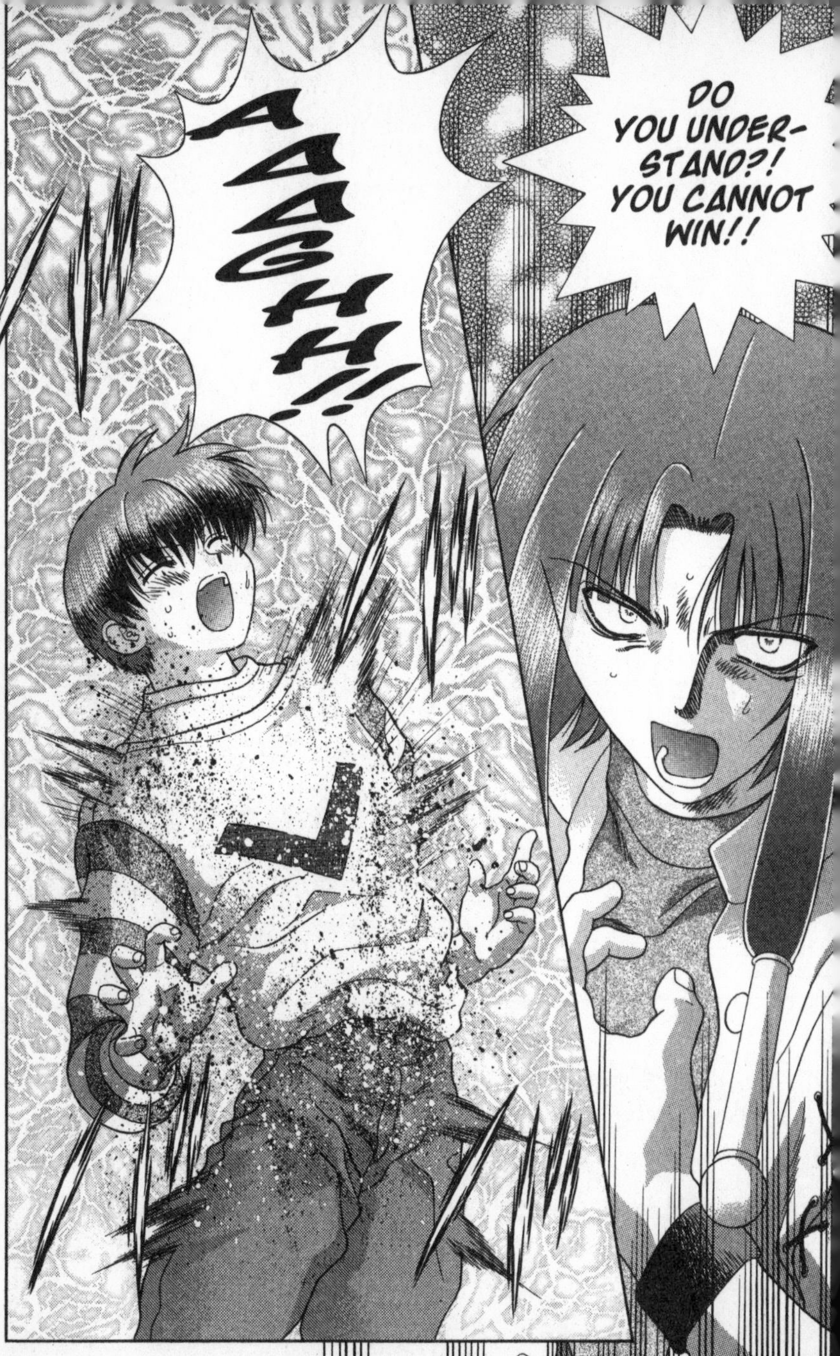
DO YOU UNDER-STAND?! YOU CANNOT WIN!!
AAAGHH!!...

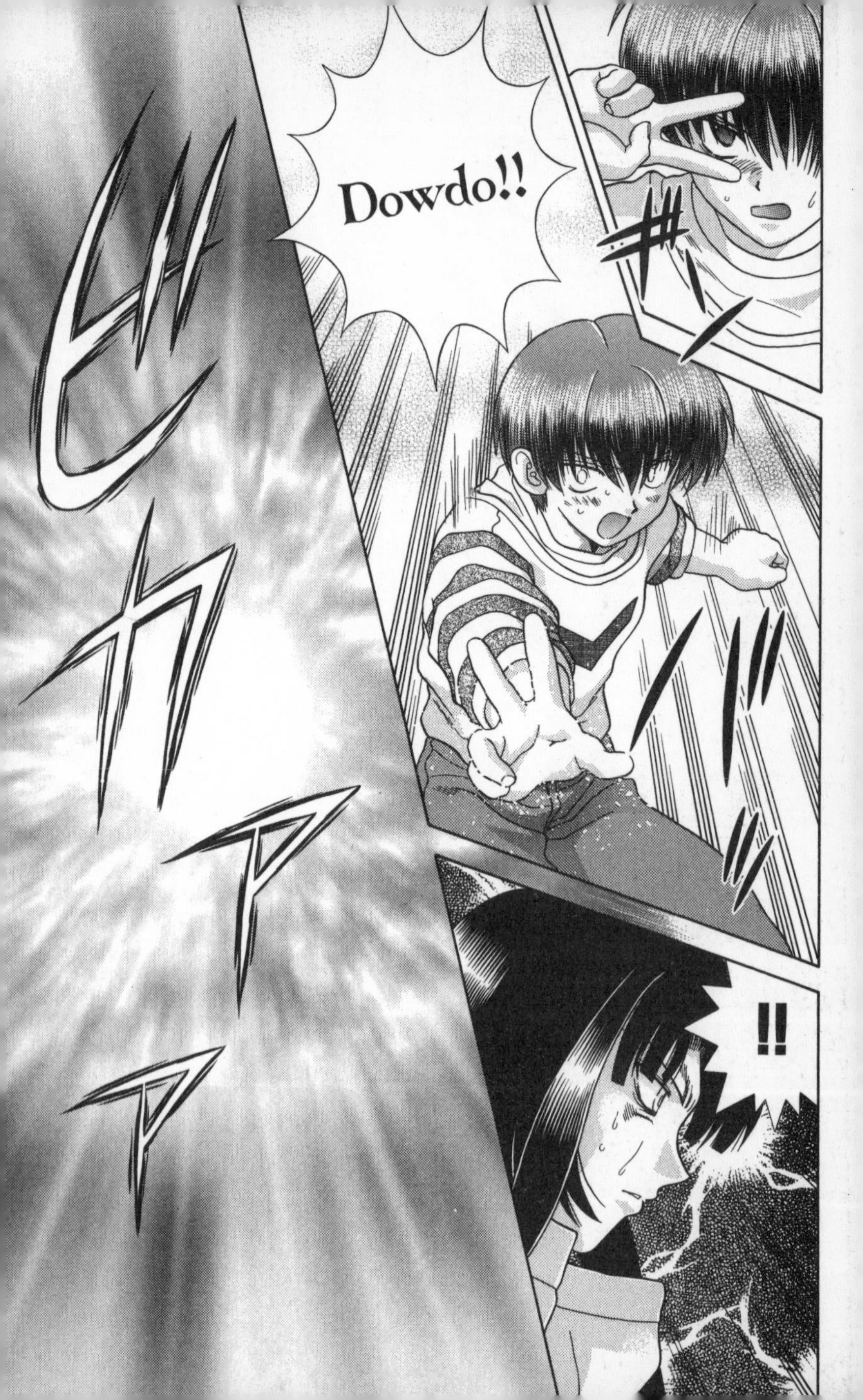

Dowdo!!
!!

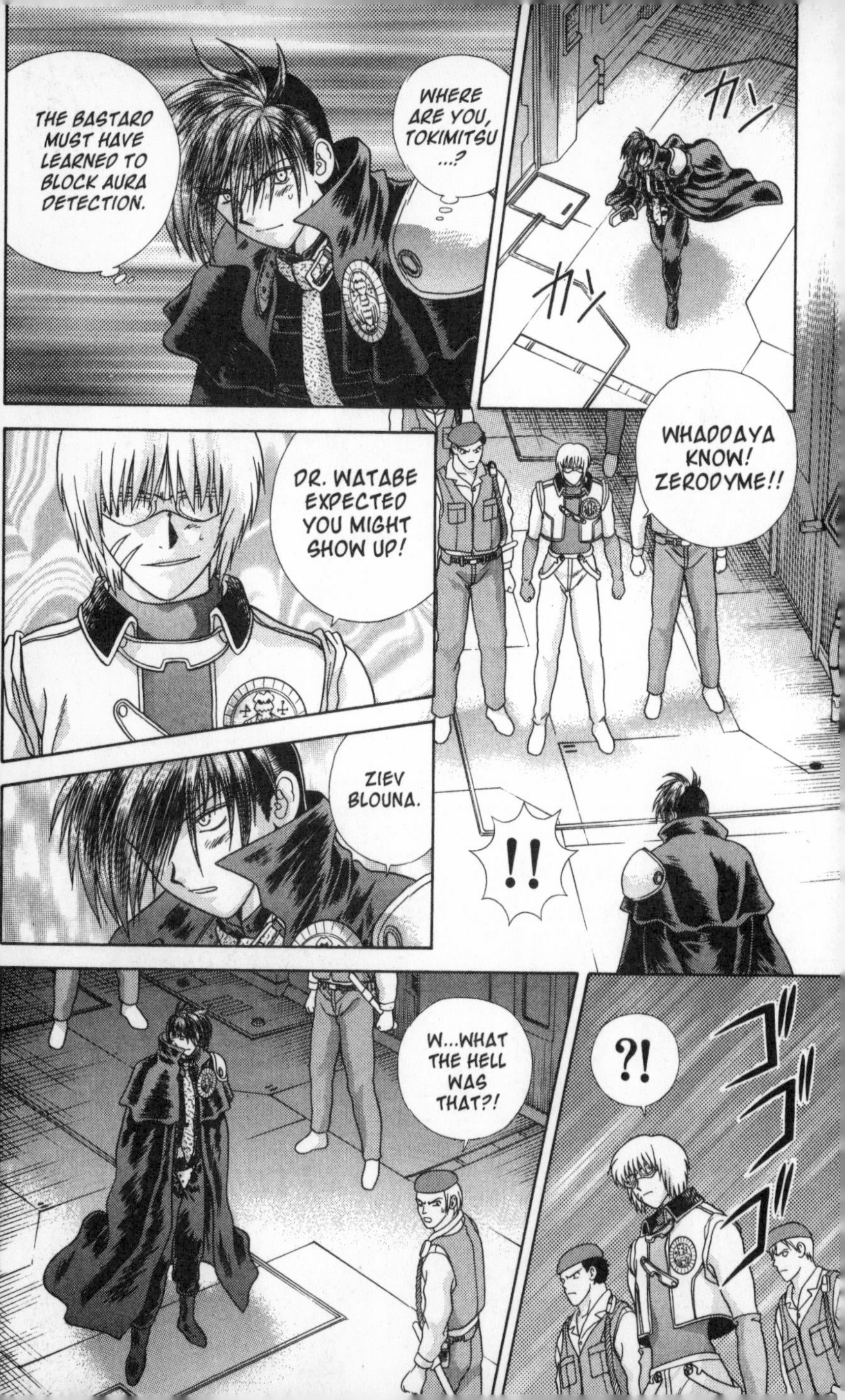
カン
カン
WHERE ARE YOU, TOKIMITSU...?
THE BASTARD MUST HAVE LEARNED TO BLOCK AURA DETECTION.
WHADDAYA KNOW! ZERODYME!!
!!
DR. WATABE EXPECTED YOU MIGHT SHOW UP!
ZIEV BLOUNA.
?!
ゴゴゴゴ
W...WHAT THE HELL WAS THAT?!

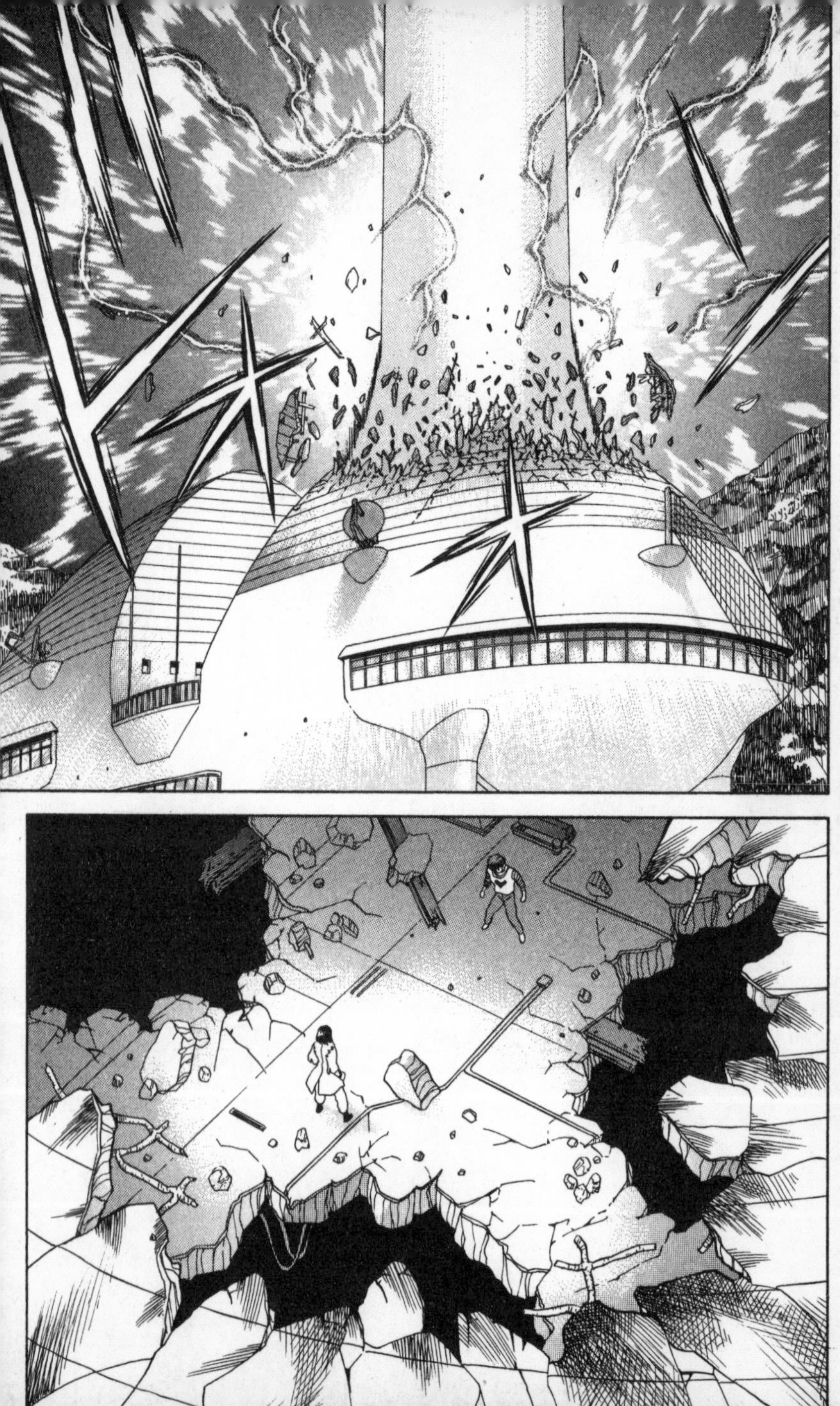

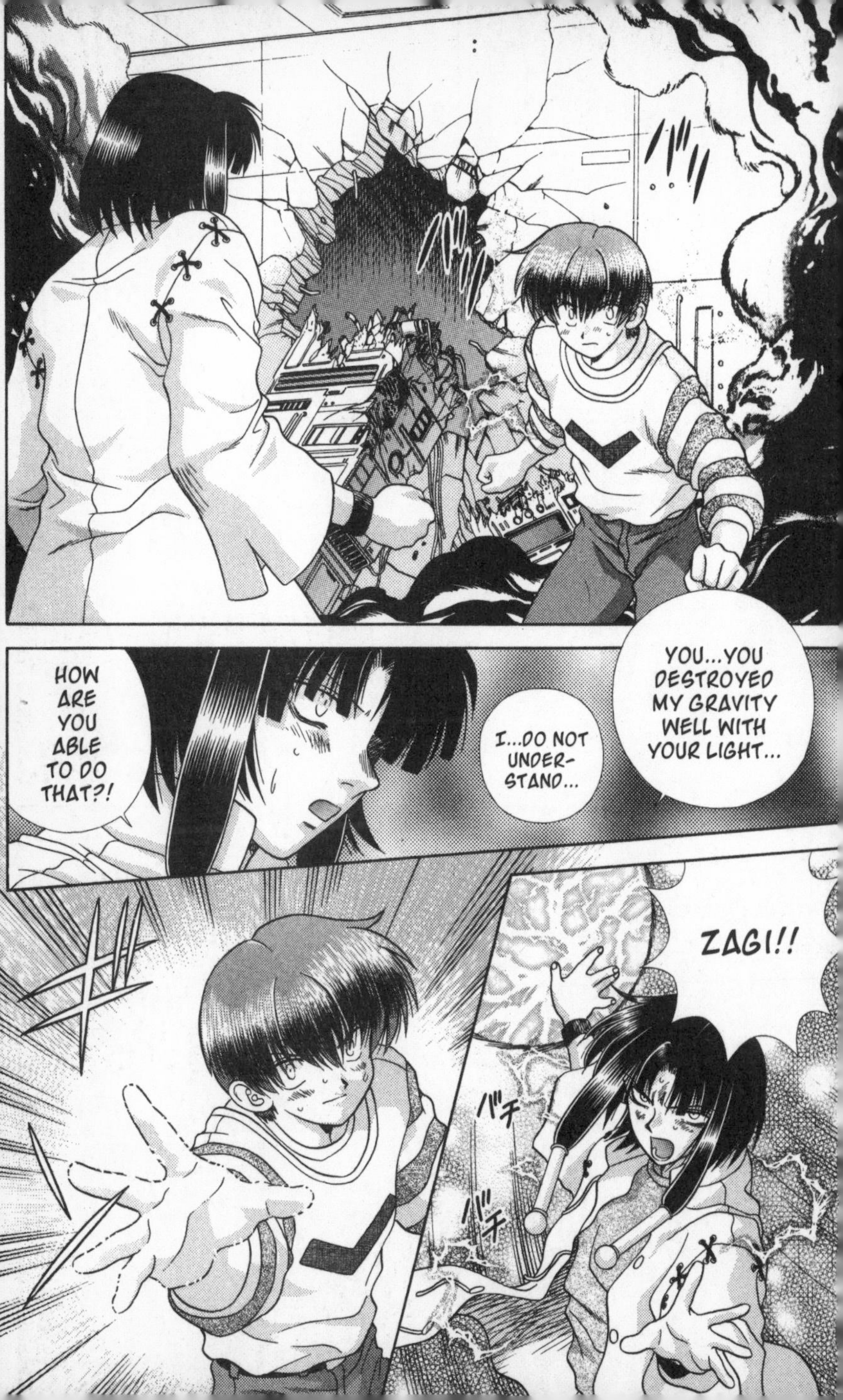
YOU...YOU DESTROYED MY GRAVITY WELL WITH YOUR LIGHT...
I...DO NOT UNDER-STAND...
HOW ARE YOU ABLE TO DO THAT?!
ZAGI!!
バチ
バチ

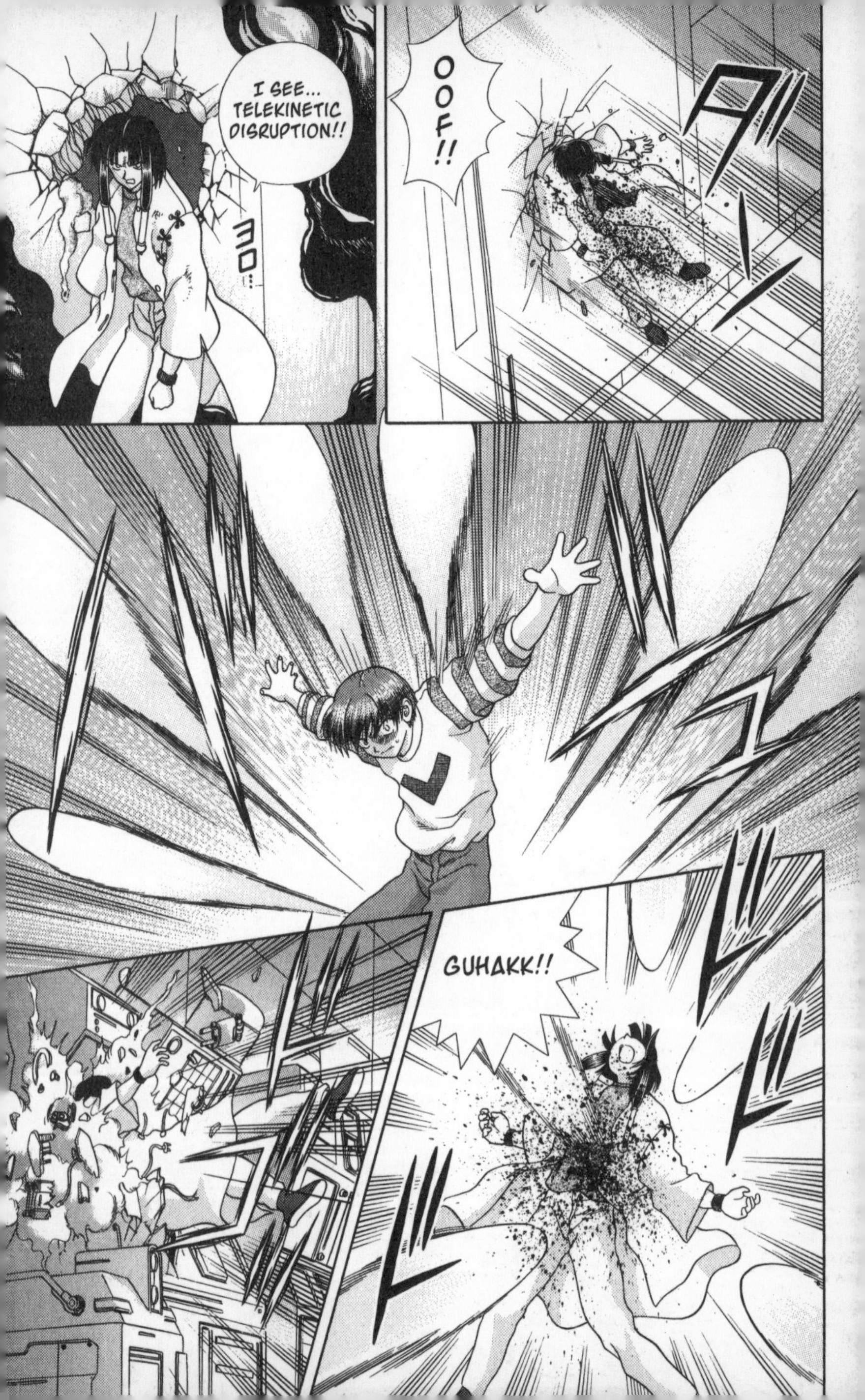
OOF!!
I SEE... TELEKINETIC DISRUPTION!!
GUHAKK!!

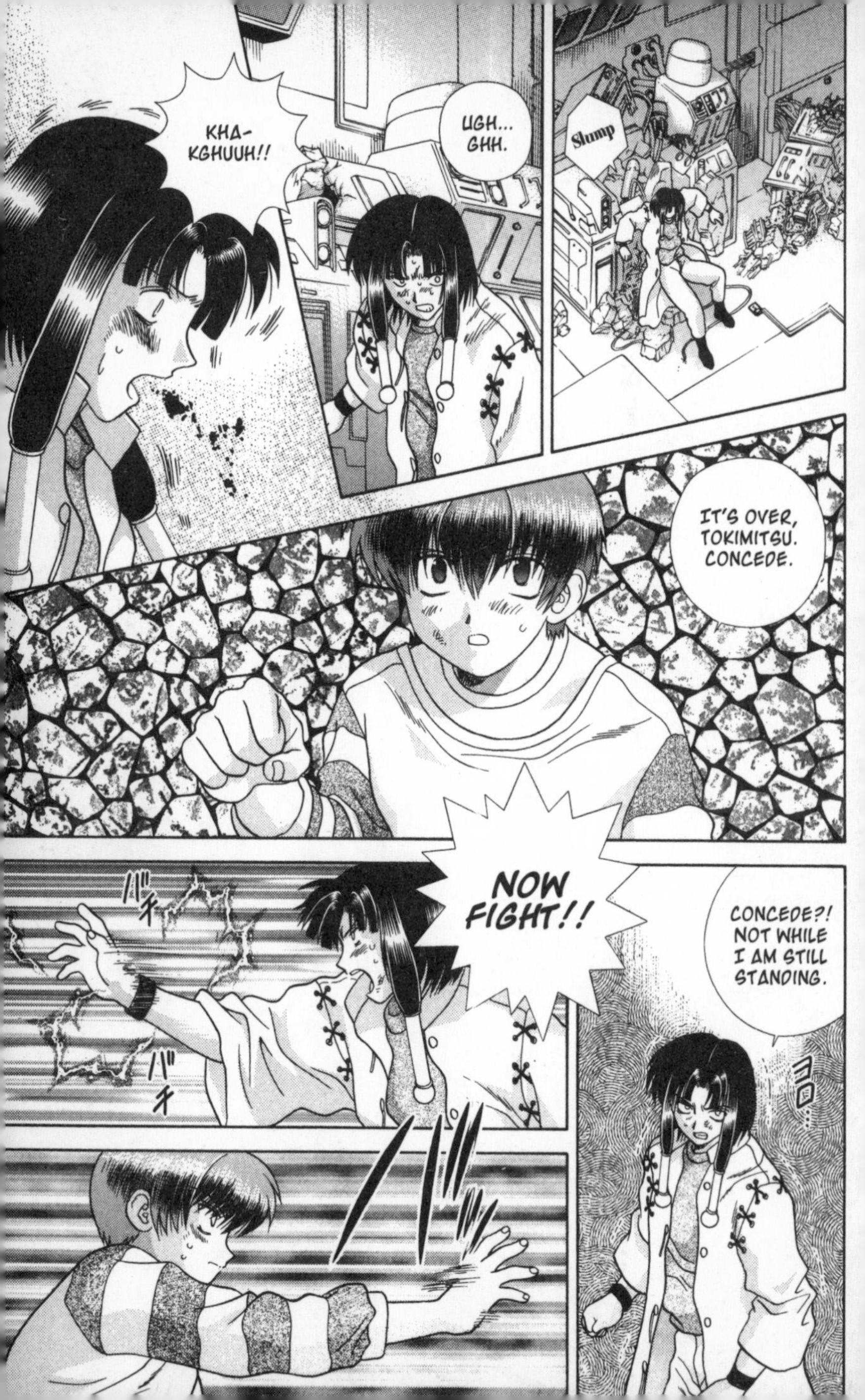
Slump
UGH... GHH.
KHA-KGHUUH!!
IT'S OVER, TOKIMITSU. CONCEDE.
CONCEDE?! NOT WHILE I AM STILL STANDING.
ヨロ...
NOW FIGHT!!
バチ
バチ

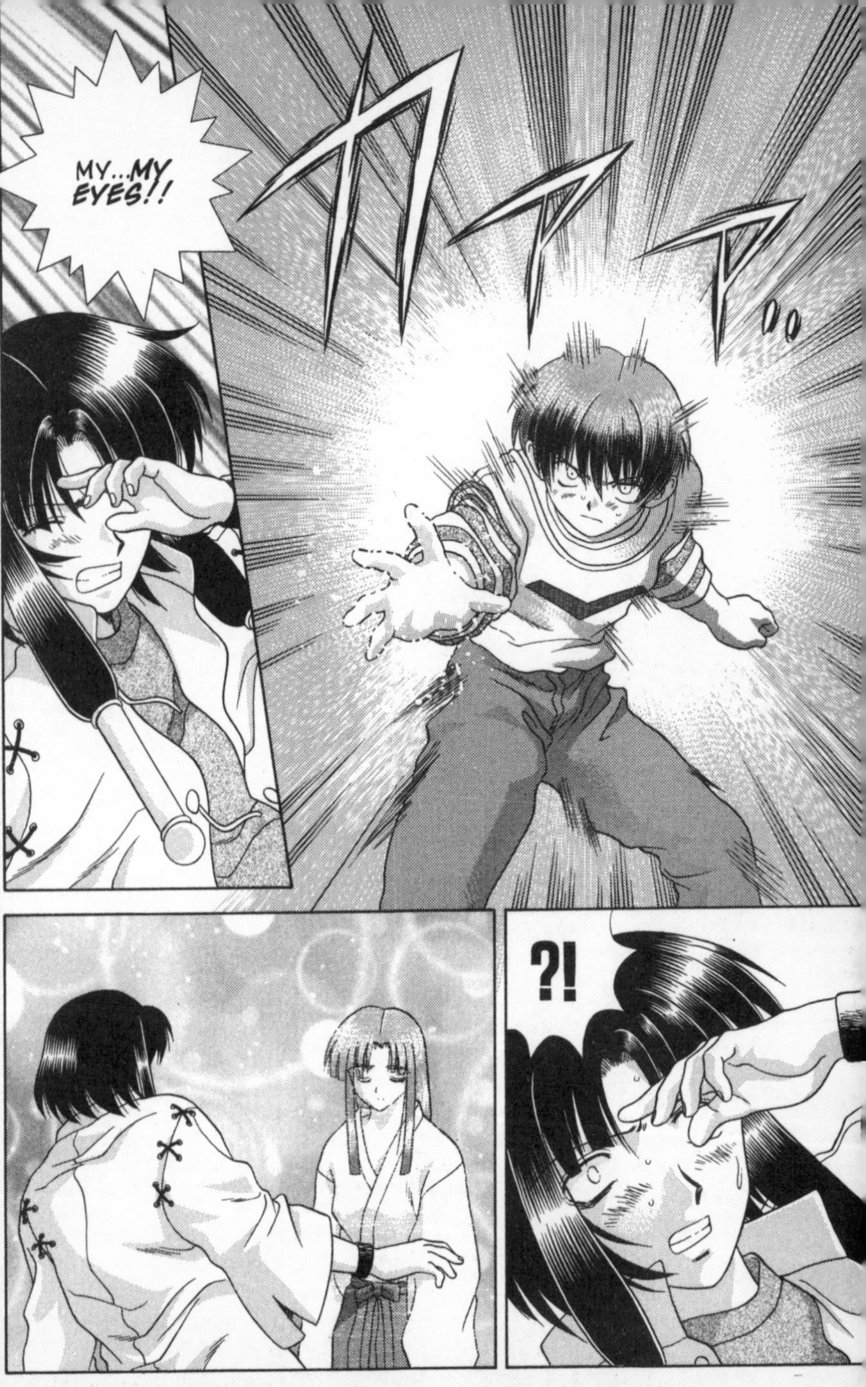
MY...MY EYES!!
カアア..
?!

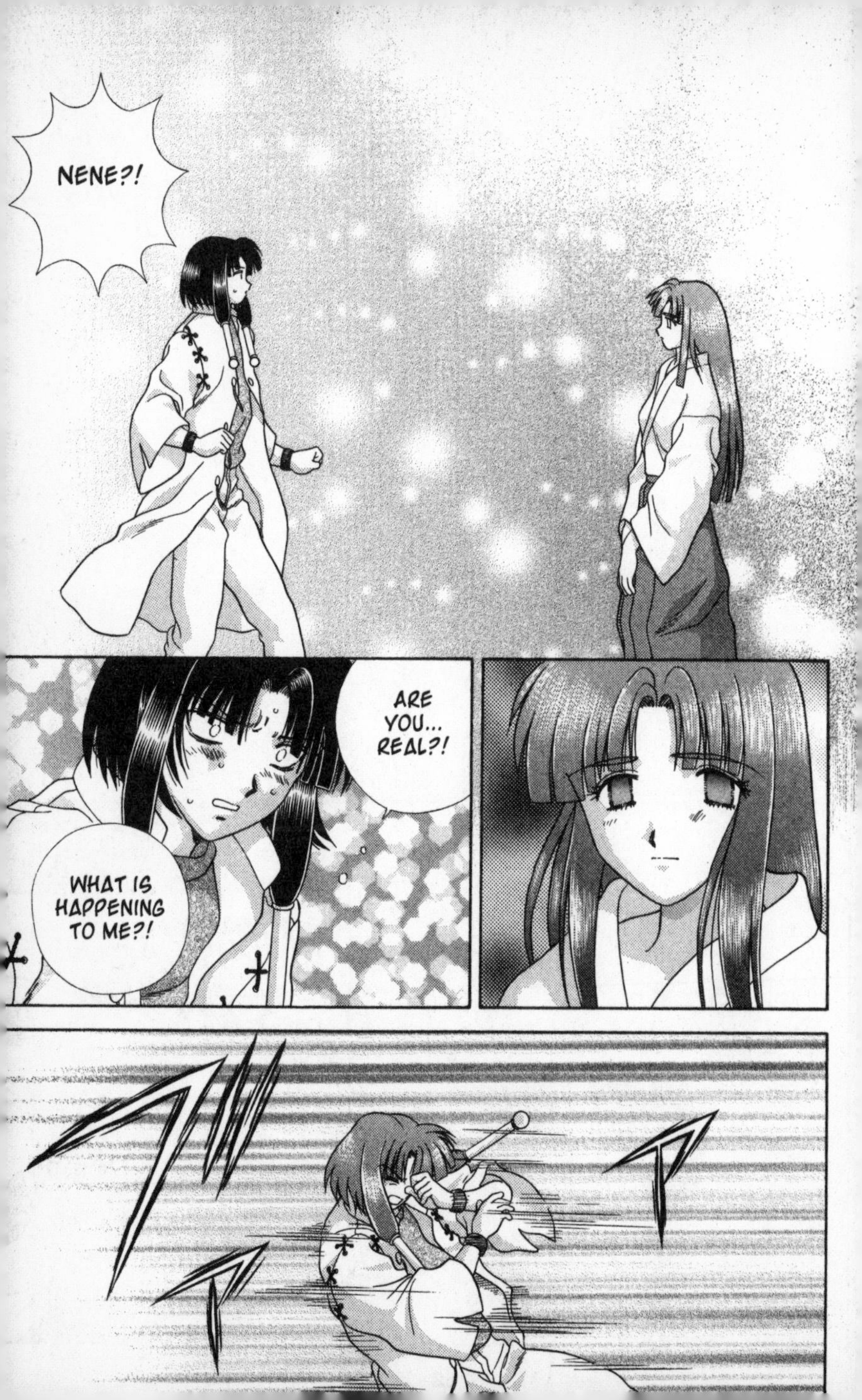
NENE?!
ARE YOU... REAL?!
WHAT IS HAPPENING TO ME?!

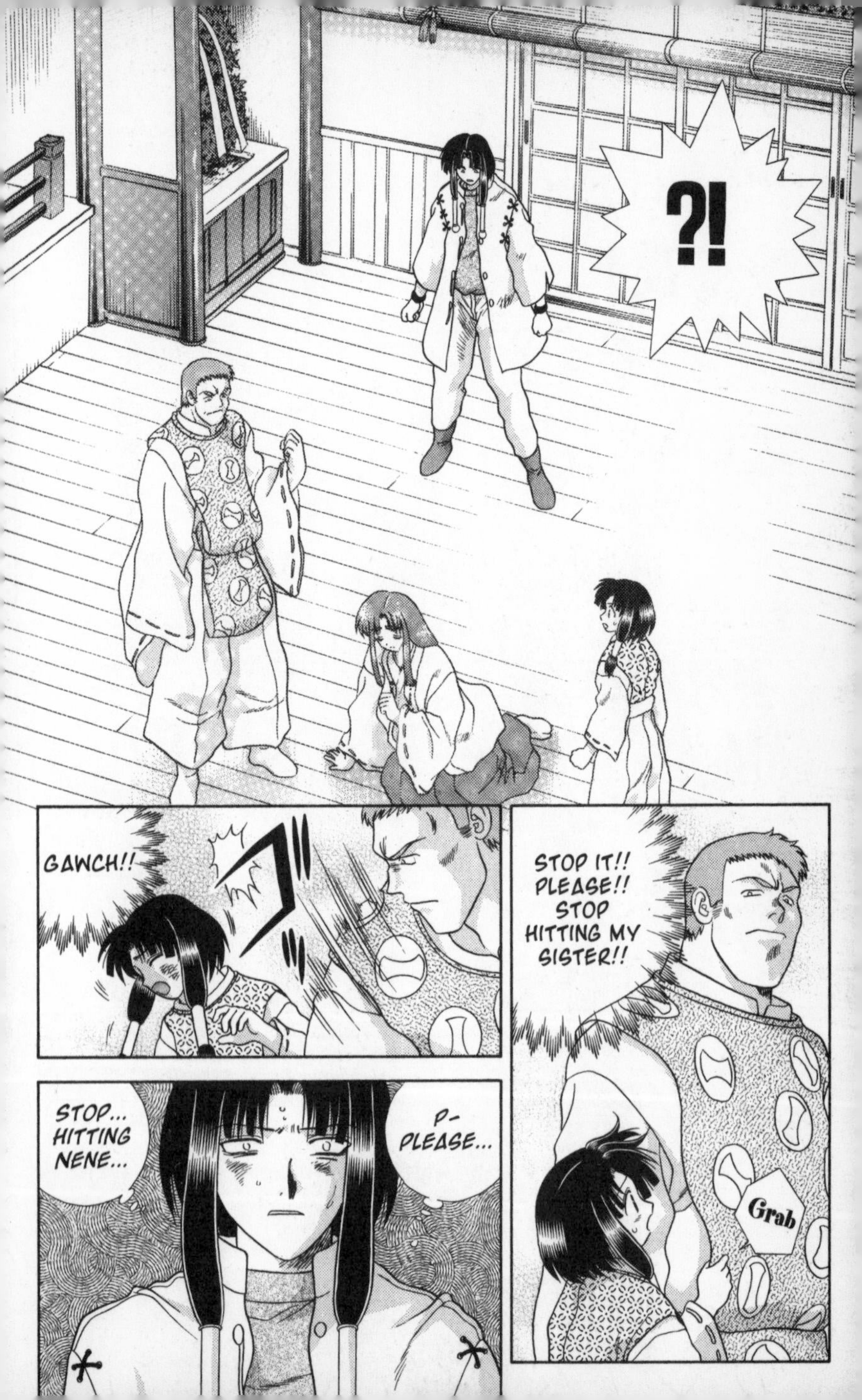
?!
STOP IT!! PLEASE!! STOP HITTING MY SISTER!!
Grab
GAWCH!!
P-PLEASE...
STOP... HITTING NENE...

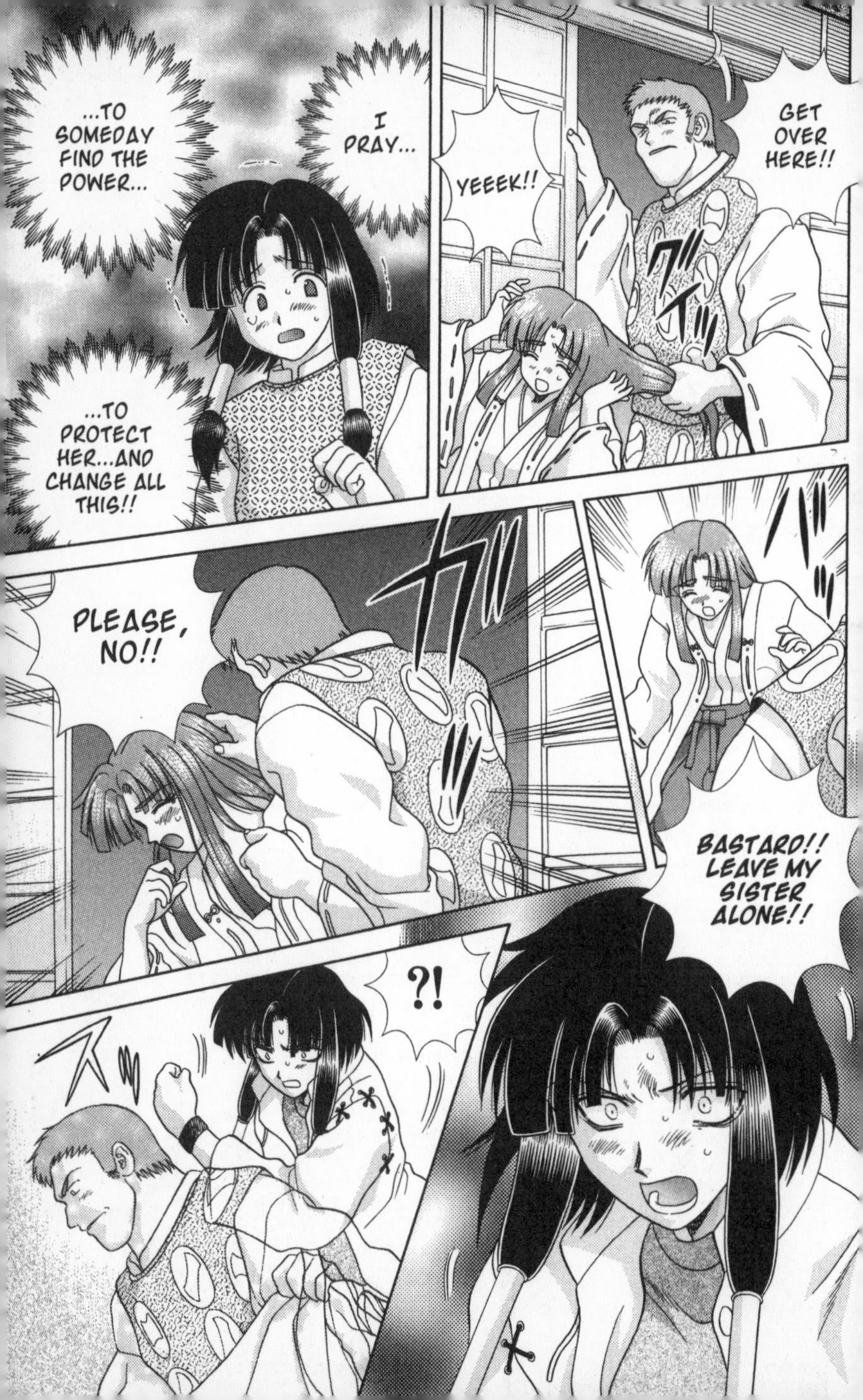
GET OVER HERE!!
YEEEK!!
I PRAY...
...TO SOMEDAY FIND THE POWER...
...TO PROTECT HER...AND CHANGE ALL THIS!!
PLEASE, NO!!
BASTARD!! LEAVE MY SISTER ALONE!!
?!

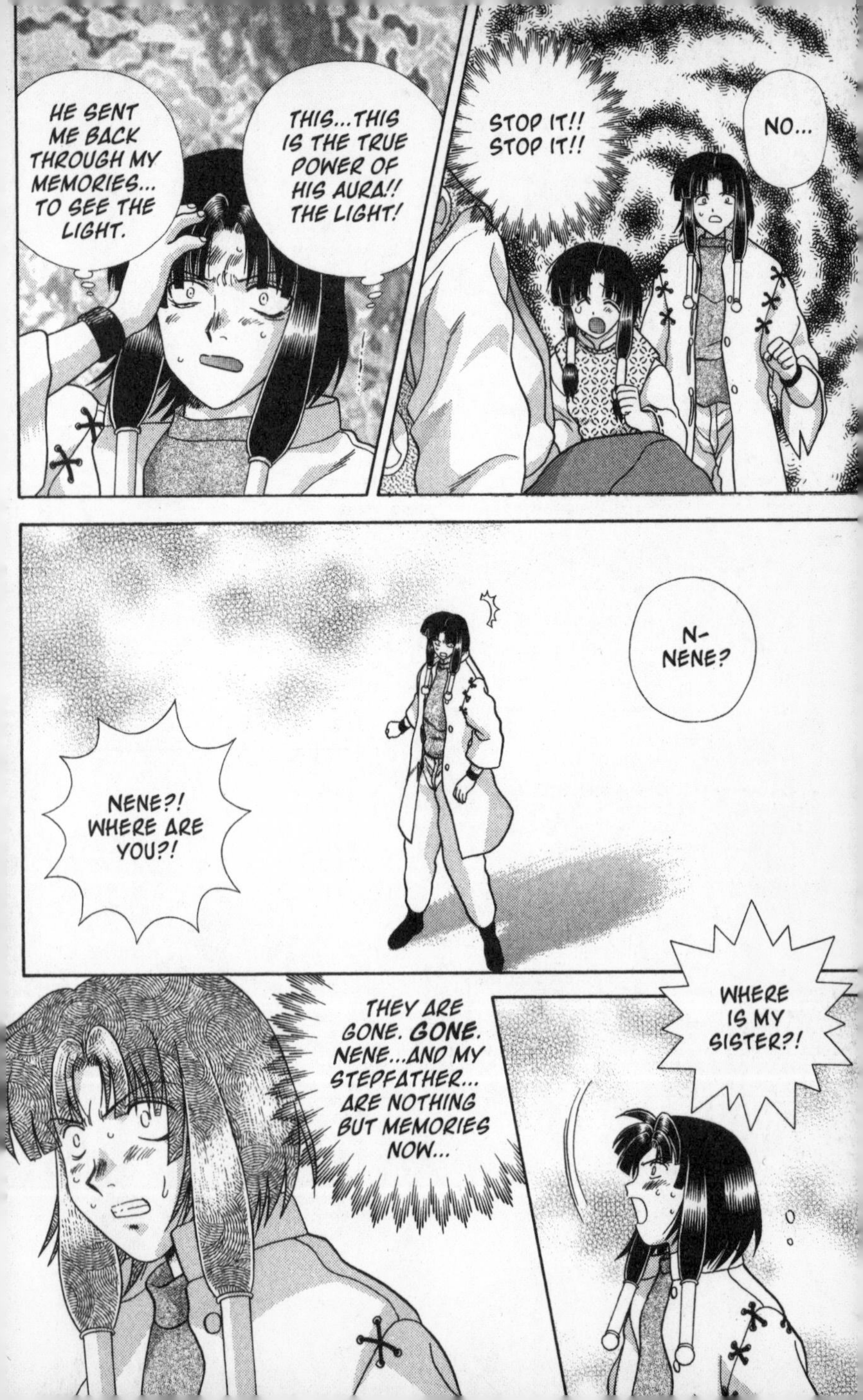
NO...
STOP IT!! STOP IT!!
THIS...THIS IS THE TRUE POWER OF HIS AURA!! THE LIGHT!
HE SENT ME BACK THROUGH MY MEMORIES... TO SEE THE LIGHT.
N- NENE?
NENE?! WHERE ARE YOU?!
WHERE IS MY SISTER?!
THEY ARE GONE. GONE. NENE...AND MY STEPFATHER... ARE NOTHING BUT MEMORIES NOW...

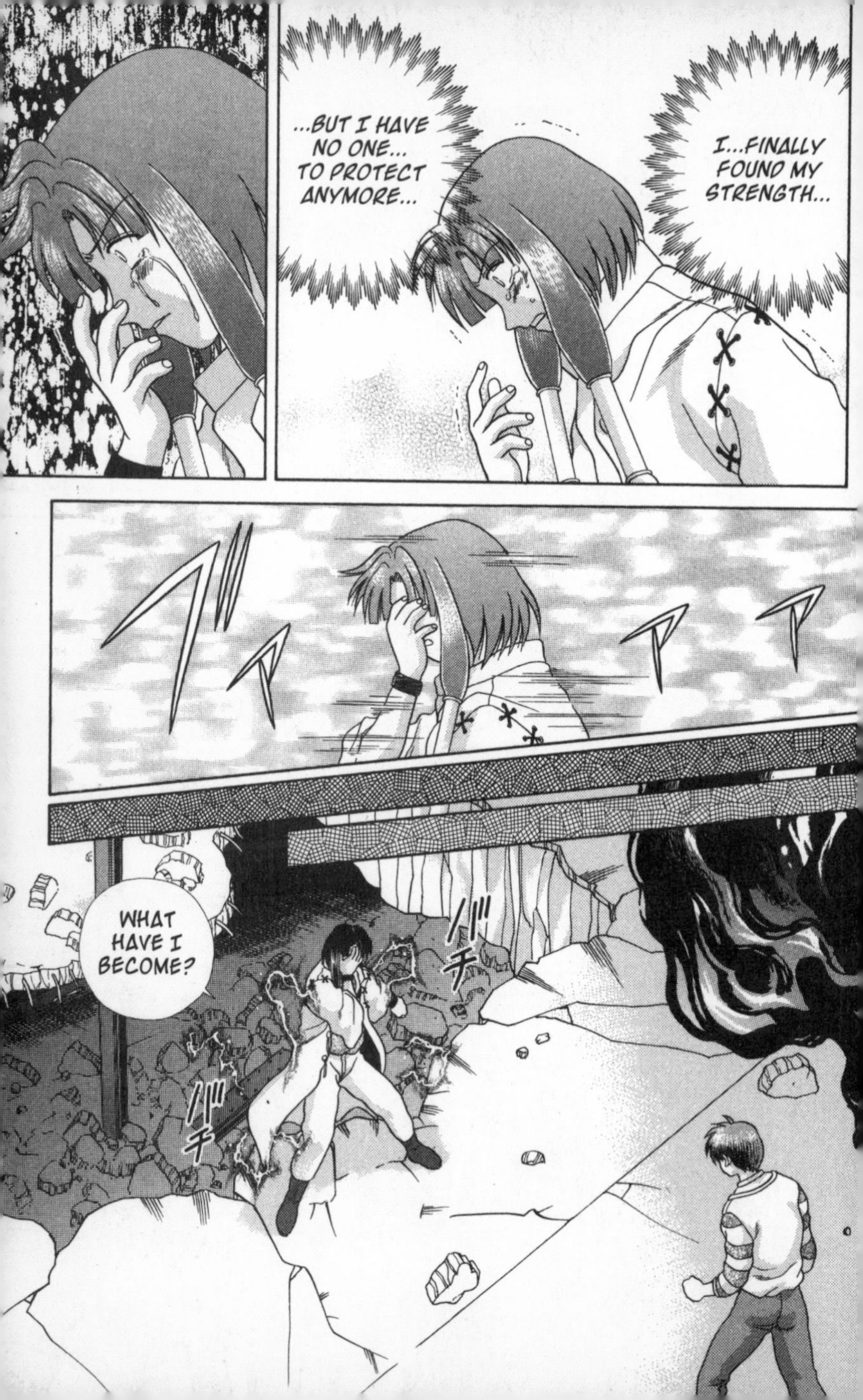
I...FINALLY FOUND MY STRENGTH...
...BUT I HAVE NO ONE... TO PROTECT ANYMORE...
バチ
WHAT HAVE I BECOME?
バチ

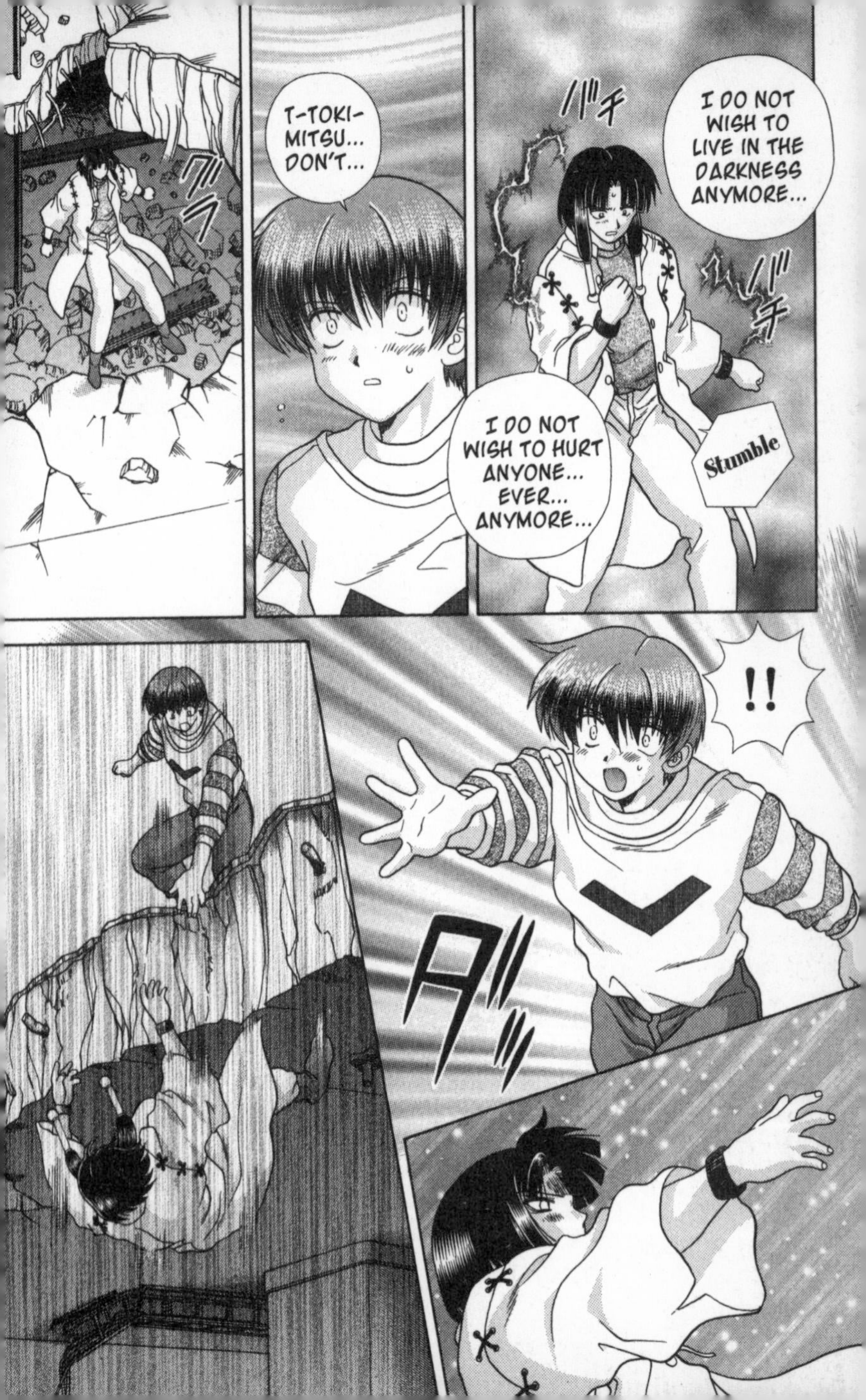
I DO NOT WISH TO LIVE IN THE DARKNESS ANYMORE...
I DO NOT WISH TO HURT ANYONE... EVER... ANYMORE...
Stumble
T-TOKI-MITSU... DON'T...
!!

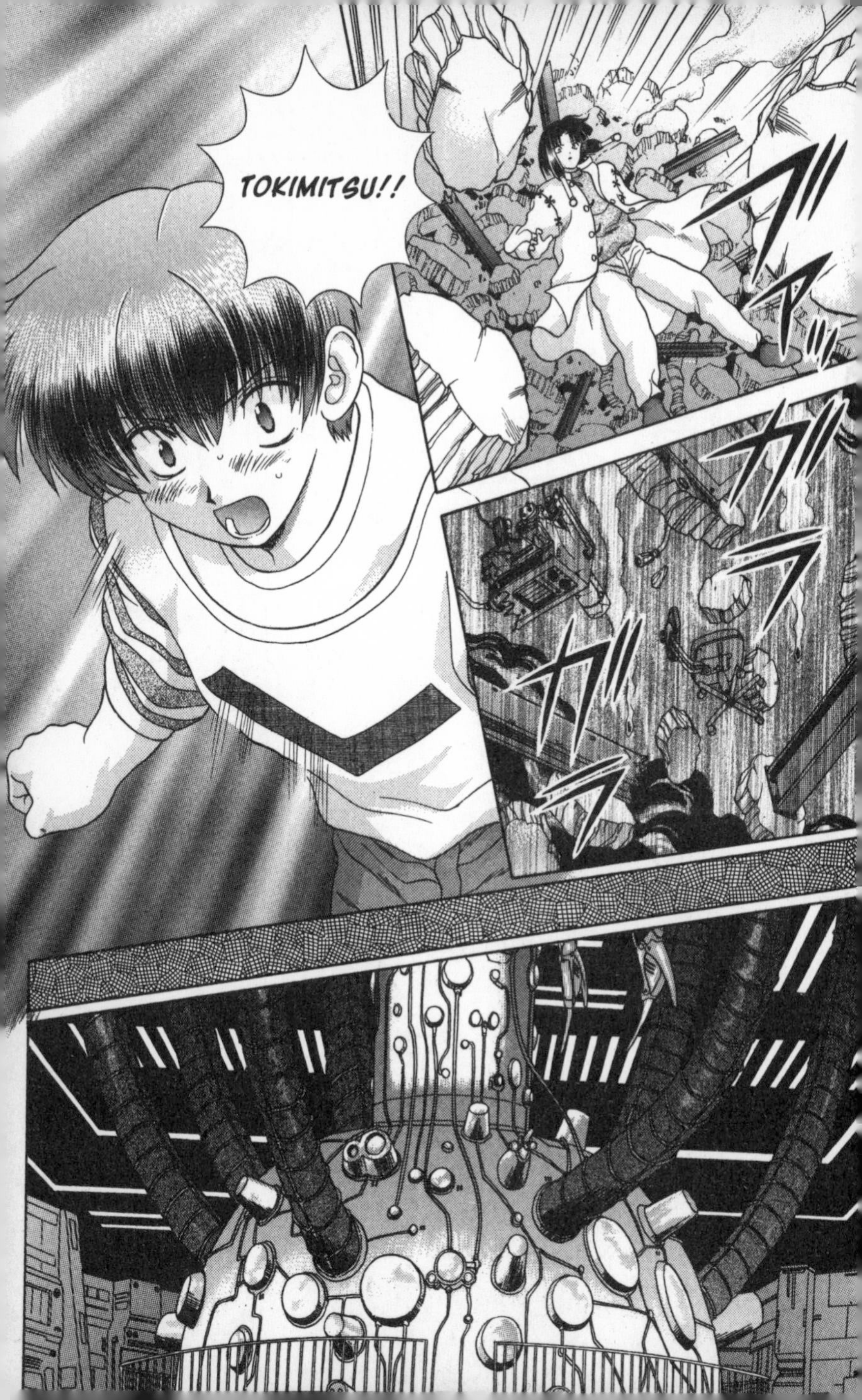
TOKIMITSU!!

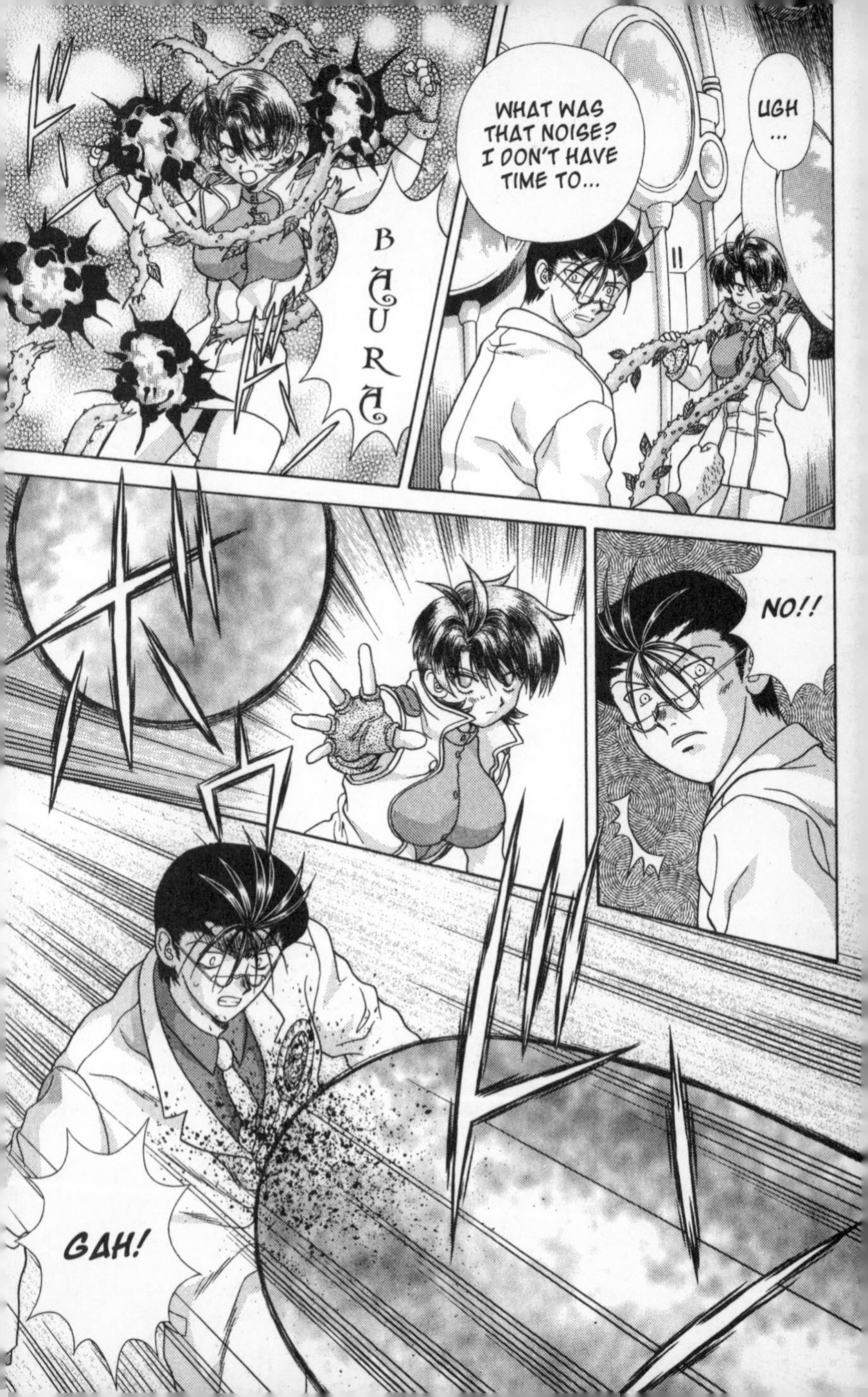
UGH ...
WHAT WAS THAT NOISE? I DON'T HAVE TIME TO...
BAURA
NO!!
GAH!

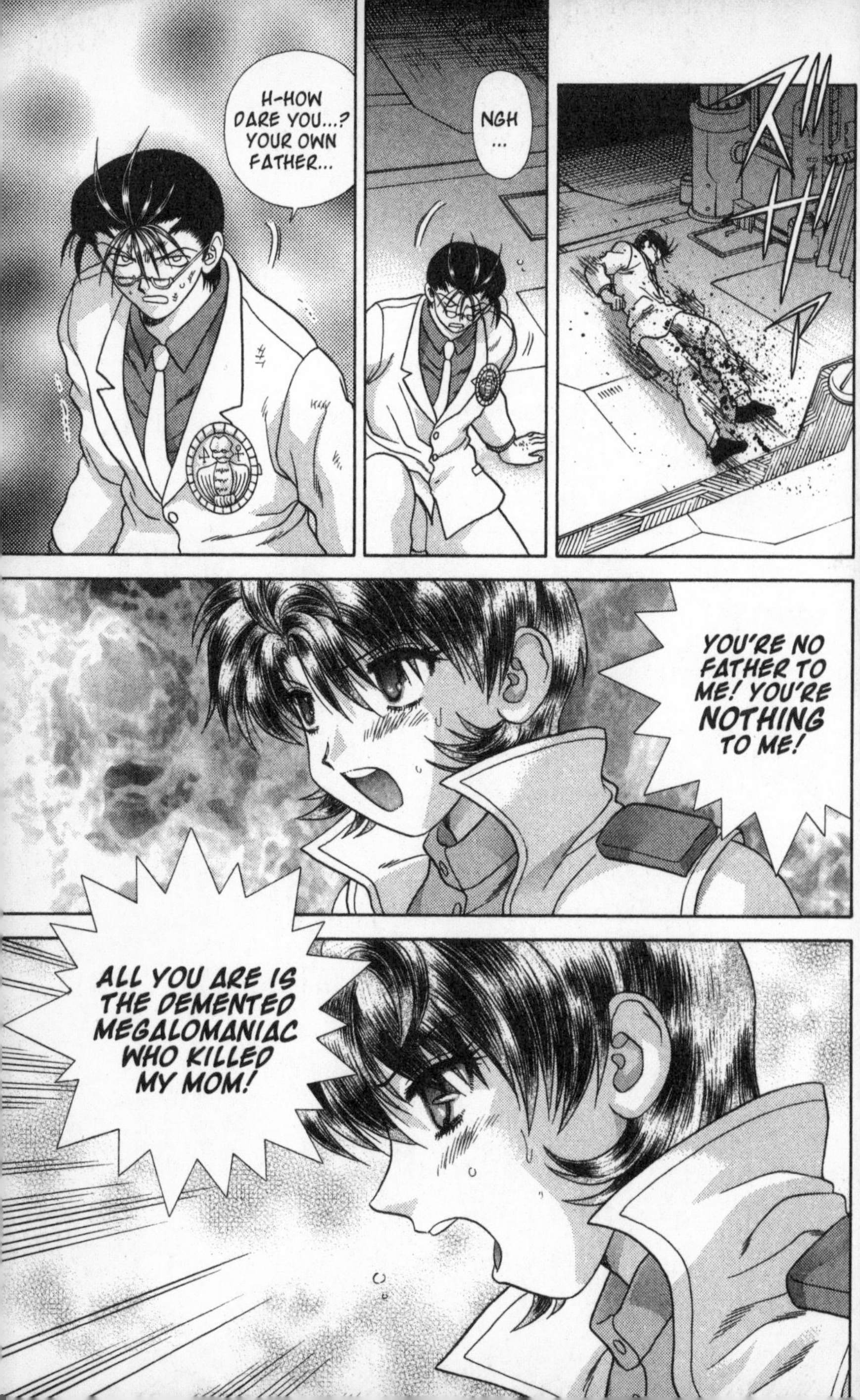
NGH ...
H-HOW DARE YOU...? YOUR OWN FATHER...
YOU'RE NO FATHER TO ME! YOU'RE NOTHING TO ME!
ALL YOU ARE IS THE DEMENTED MEGALOMANIAC WHO KILLED MY MOM!

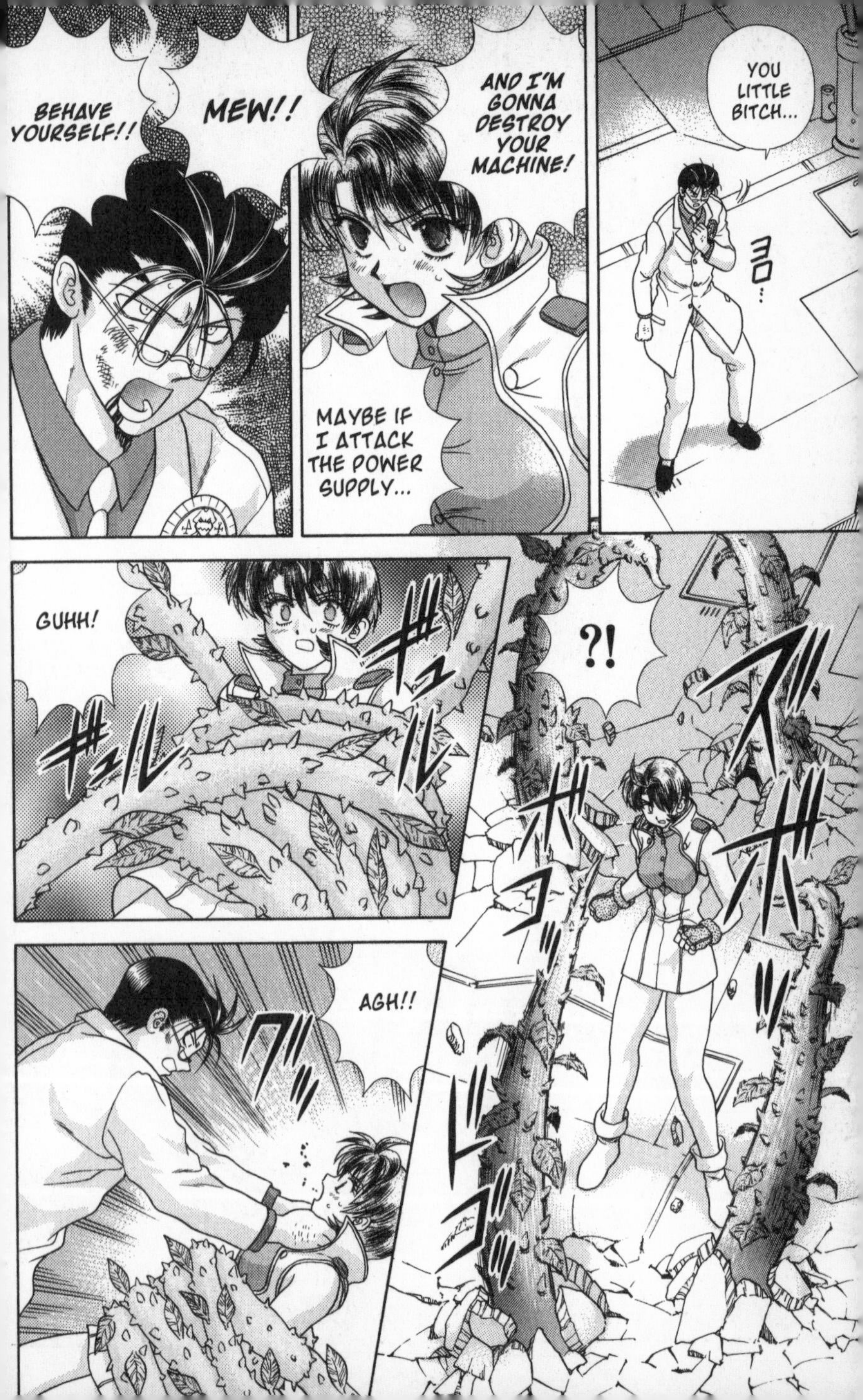
YOU LITTLE BITCH...
AND I'M GONNA DESTROY YOUR MACHINE!
MEW!!
MAYBE IF I ATTACK THE POWER SUPPLY...
BEHAVE YOURSELF!!
?!
GUHH!
AGH!!

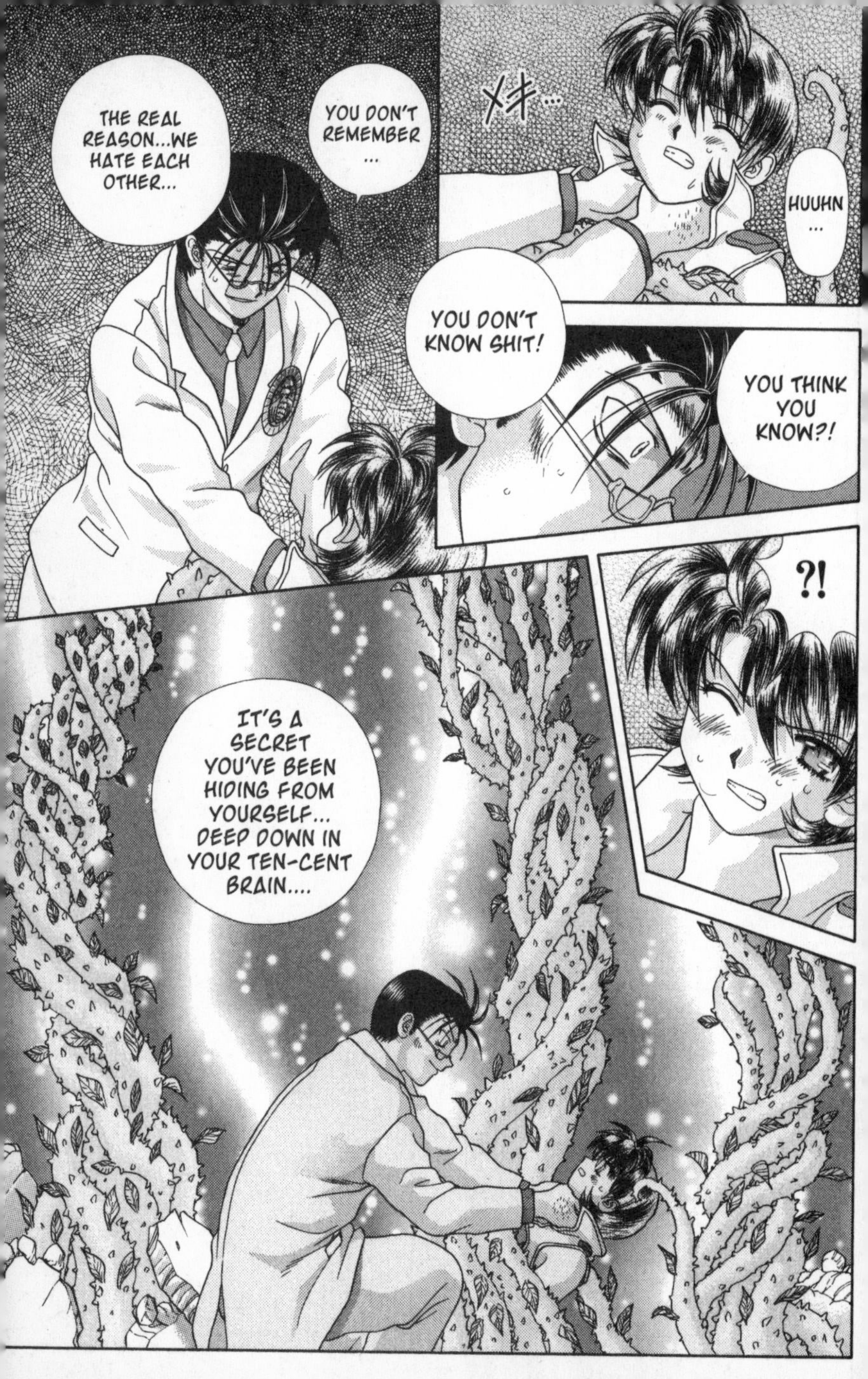

メキ…
HUUHN ...
YOU THINK YOU KNOW?!
YOU DON'T KNOW SHIT!
YOU DON'T REMEMBER ...
THE REAL REASON...WE HATE EACH OTHER...
?!
IT'S A SECRET YOU'VE BEEN HIDING FROM YOURSELF... DEEP DOWN IN YOUR TEN-CENT BRAIN....

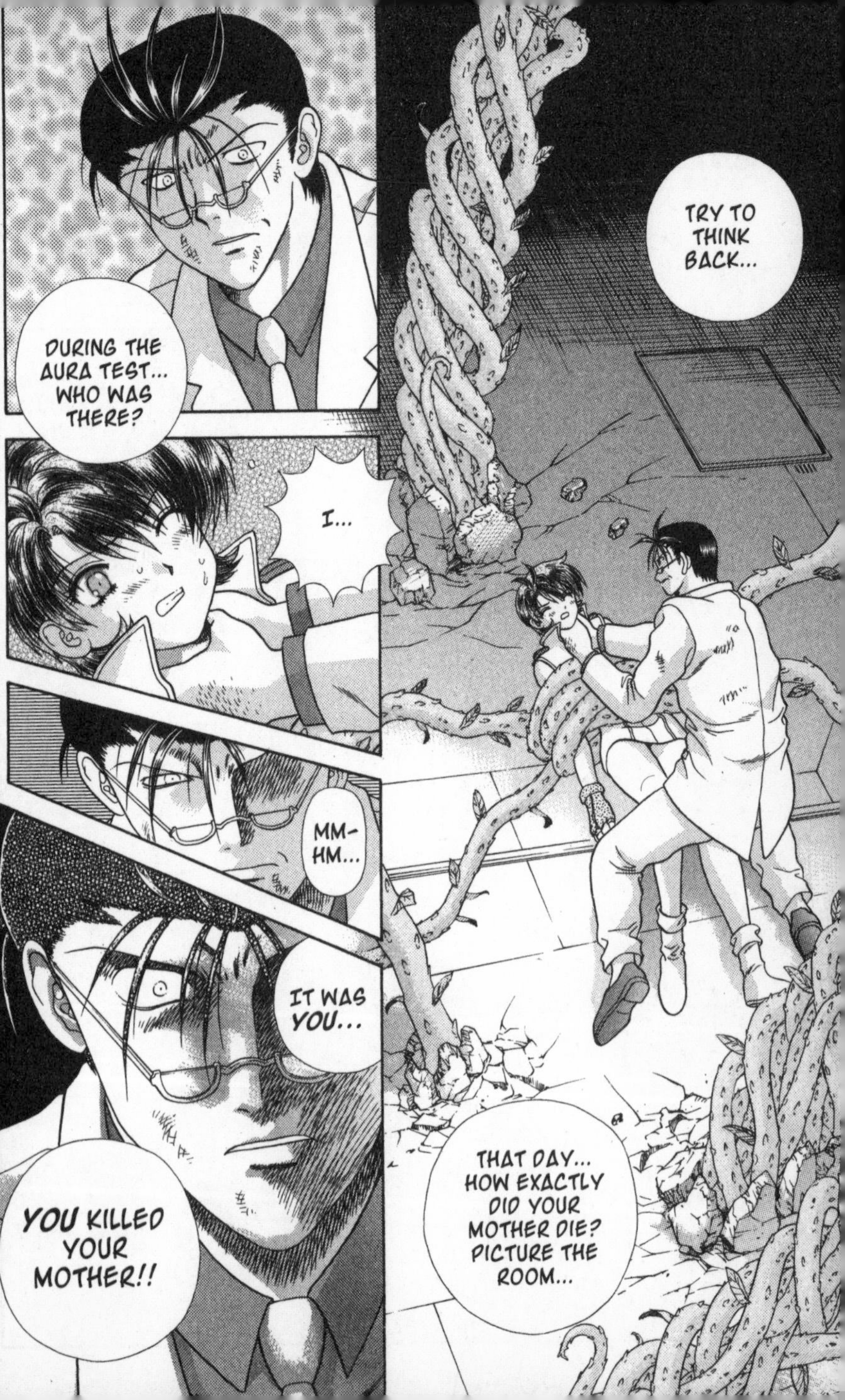
TRY TO THINK BACK...
THAT DAY... HOW EXACTLY DID YOUR MOTHER DIE? PICTURE THE ROOM...
DURING THE AURA TEST... WHO WAS THERE?
I...
MM-HM...
IT WAS *YOU*...
YOU KILLED YOUR MOTHER!!

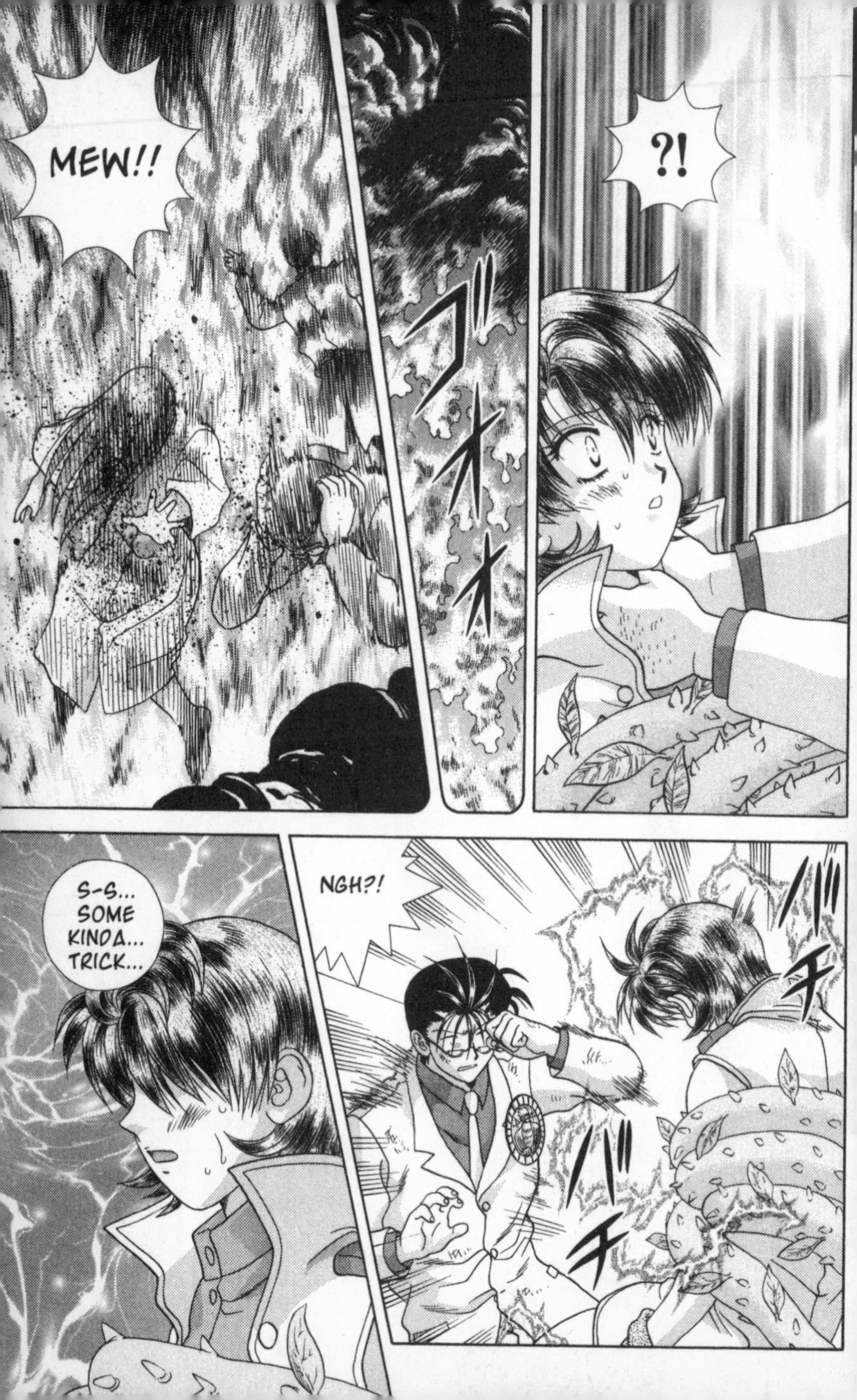
?!
ゴオオオ
MEW!!
NGH?!
バチ
バチ
S-S... SOME KINDA... TRICK...

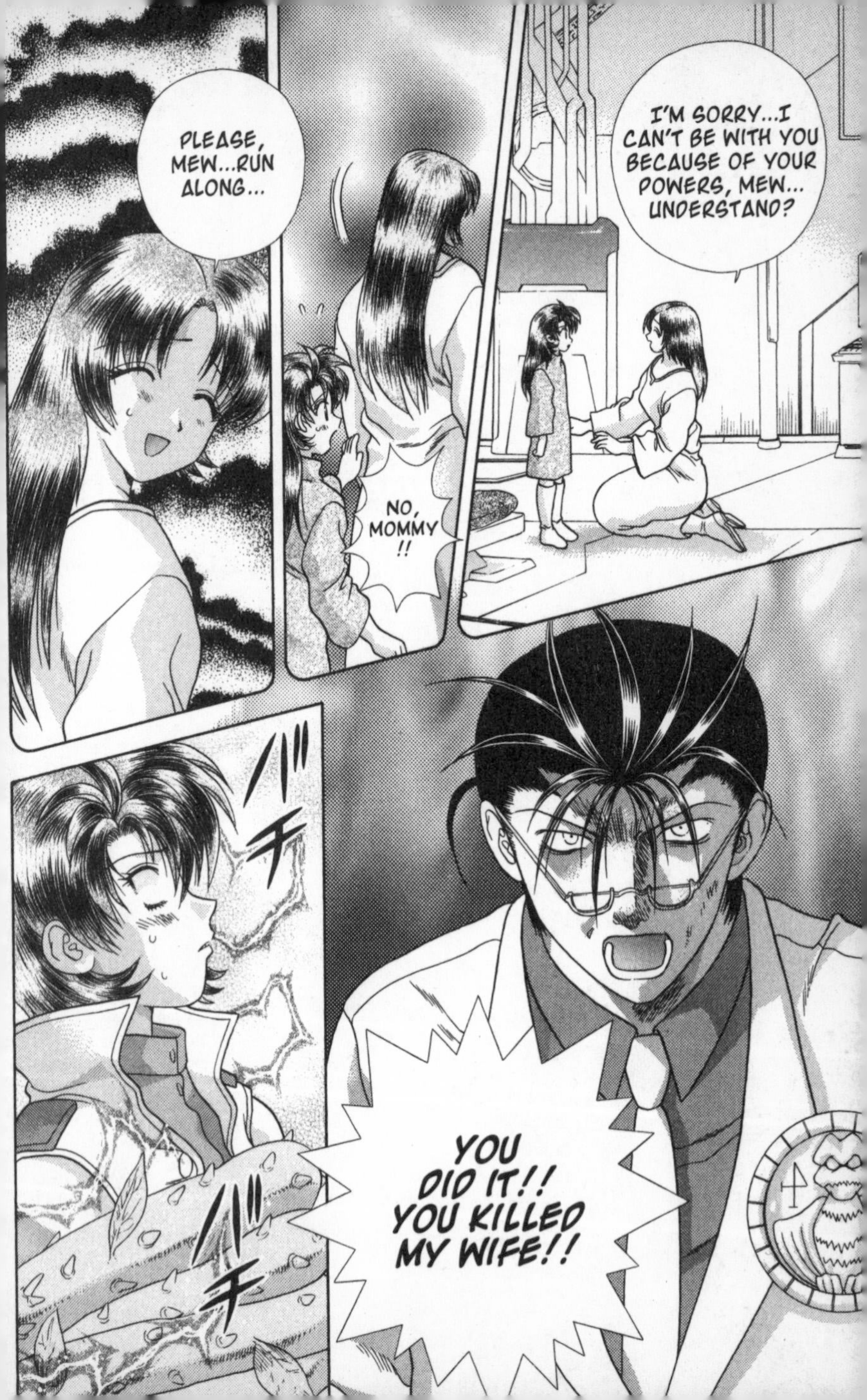
I'M SORRY...I CAN'T BE WITH YOU BECAUSE OF YOUR POWERS, MEW... UNDERSTAND?
NO, MOMMY!!
PLEASE, MEW...RUN ALONG...
YOU DID IT!! YOU KILLED MY WIFE!!
バチ
バチ

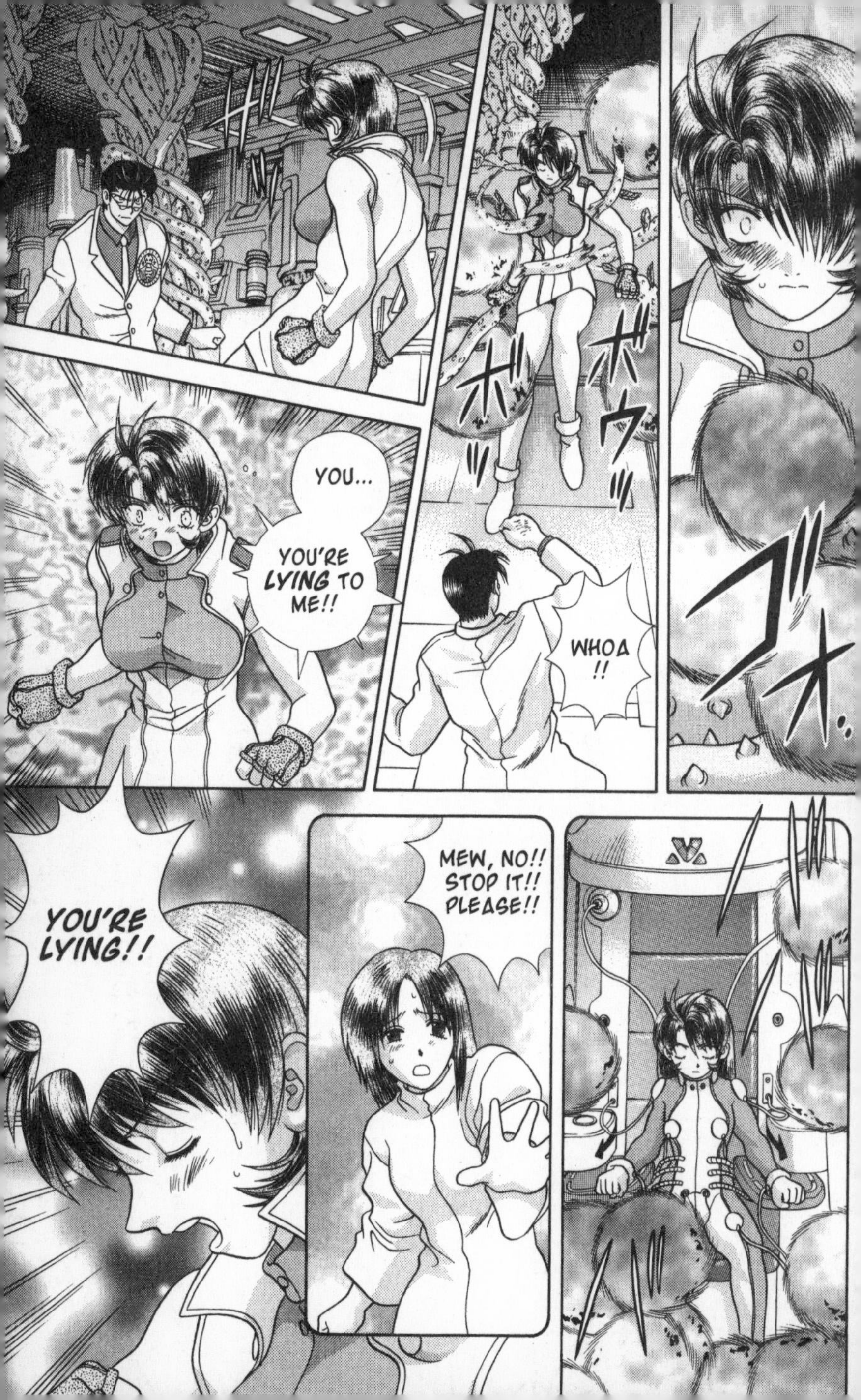
ゴオ…
ボウ
WHOA!!
YOU...
YOU'RE *LYING* TO ME!!
MEW, NO!! STOP IT!! PLEASE!!
YOU'RE LYING!!

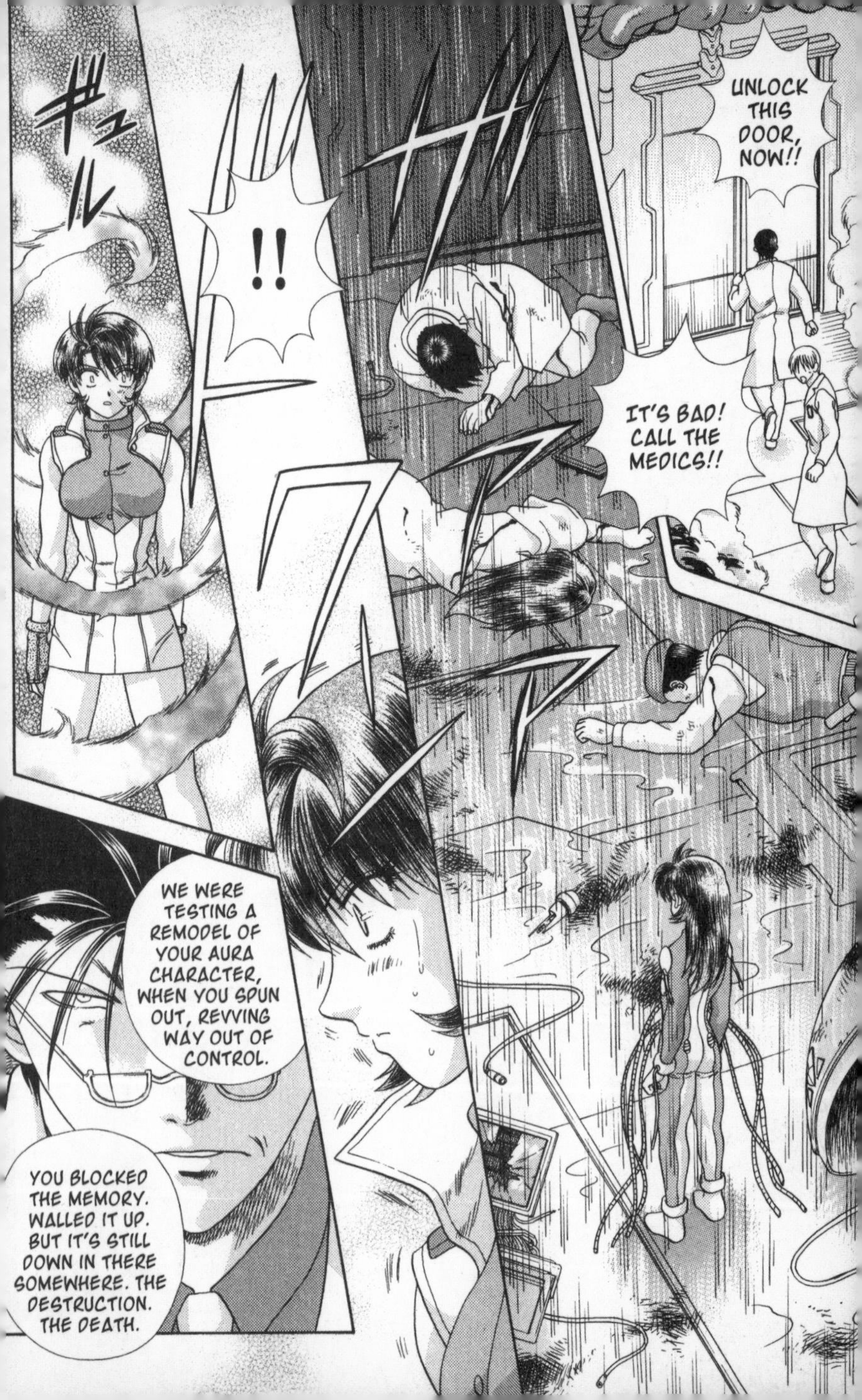
UNLOCK THIS DOOR, NOW!!
IT'S BAD! CALL THE MEDICS!!
!!
ギュル
WE WERE TESTING A REMODEL OF YOUR AURA CHARACTER, WHEN YOU SPUN OUT, REVVING WAY OUT OF CONTROL.
YOU BLOCKED THE MEMORY. WALLED IT UP. BUT IT'S STILL DOWN IN THERE SOMEWHERE. THE DESTRUCTION. THE DEATH.

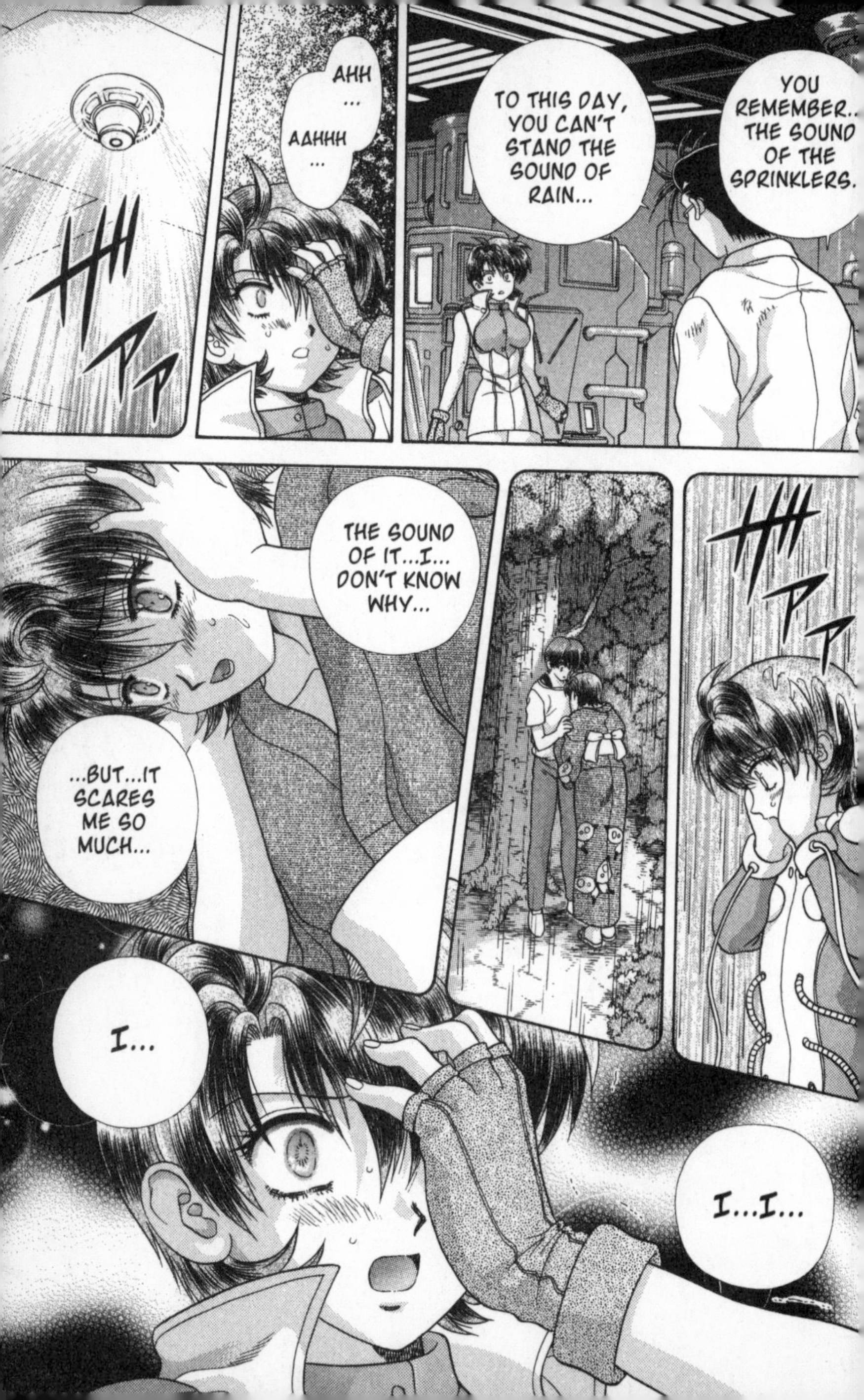
YOU REMEMBER... THE SOUND OF THE SPRINKLERS.
TO THIS DAY, YOU CAN'T STAND THE SOUND OF RAIN...
AHH ... AAHHH ...
THE SOUND OF IT...I... DON'T KNOW WHY...
...BUT...IT SCARES ME SO MUCH...
I...
I...I...

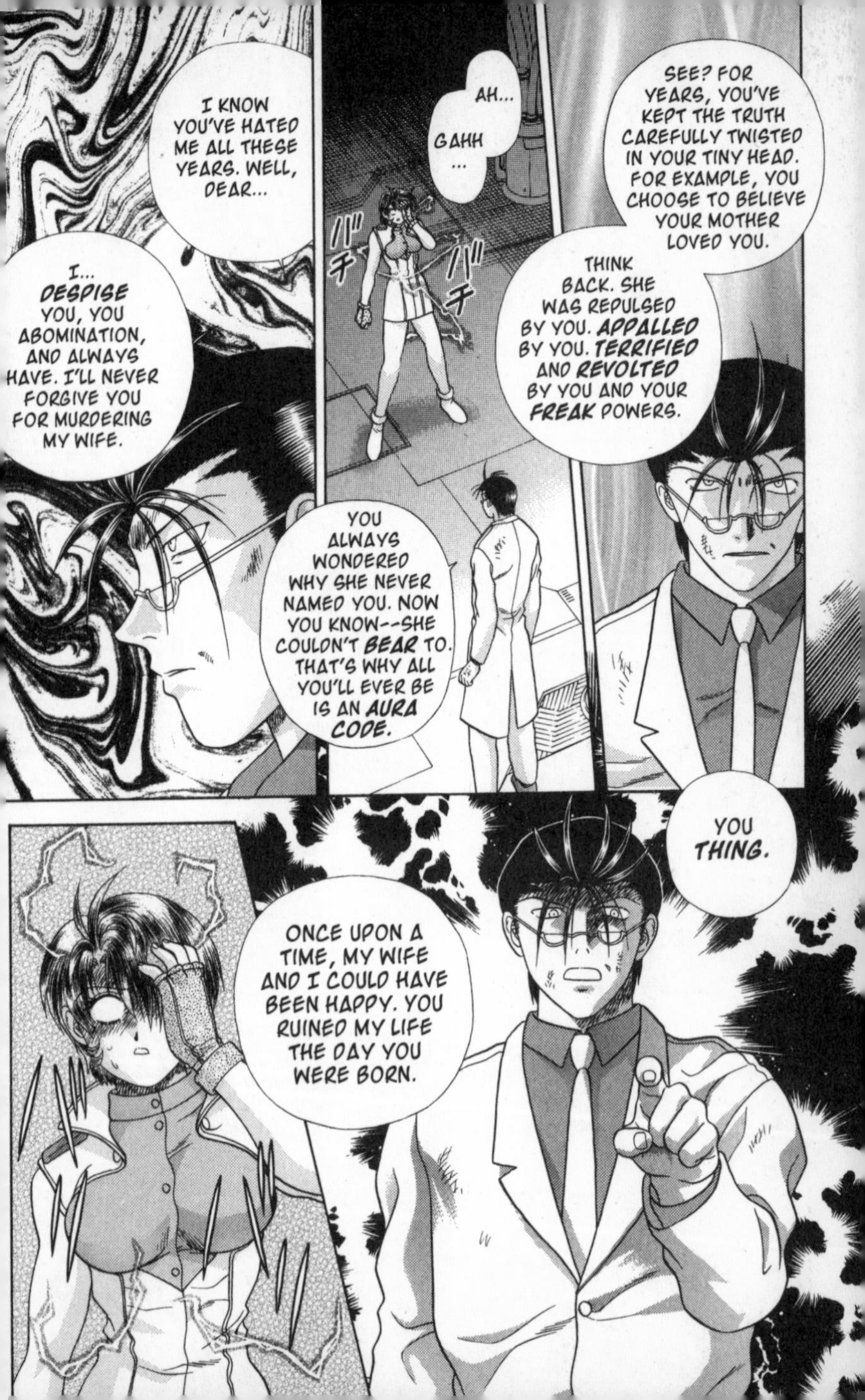

SEE? FOR YEARS, YOU'VE KEPT THE TRUTH CAREFULLY TWISTED IN YOUR TINY HEAD. FOR EXAMPLE, YOU CHOOSE TO BELIEVE YOUR MOTHER LOVED YOU.
THINK BACK. SHE WAS REPULSED BY YOU. APPALLED BY YOU. TERRIFIED AND REVOLTED BY YOU AND YOUR FREAK POWERS.
AH...
GAHH ...
バチ
バチ
YOU ALWAYS WONDERED WHY SHE NEVER NAMED YOU. NOW YOU KNOW--SHE COULDN'T BEAR TO. THAT'S WHY ALL YOU'LL EVER BE IS AN AURA CODE.
I KNOW YOU'VE HATED ME ALL THESE YEARS. WELL, DEAR...
I... DESPISE YOU, YOU ABOMINATION, AND ALWAYS HAVE. I'LL NEVER FORGIVE YOU FOR MURDERING MY WIFE.
YOU THING.
ONCE UPON A TIME, MY WIFE AND I COULD HAVE BEEN HAPPY. YOU RUINED MY LIFE THE DAY YOU WERE BORN.

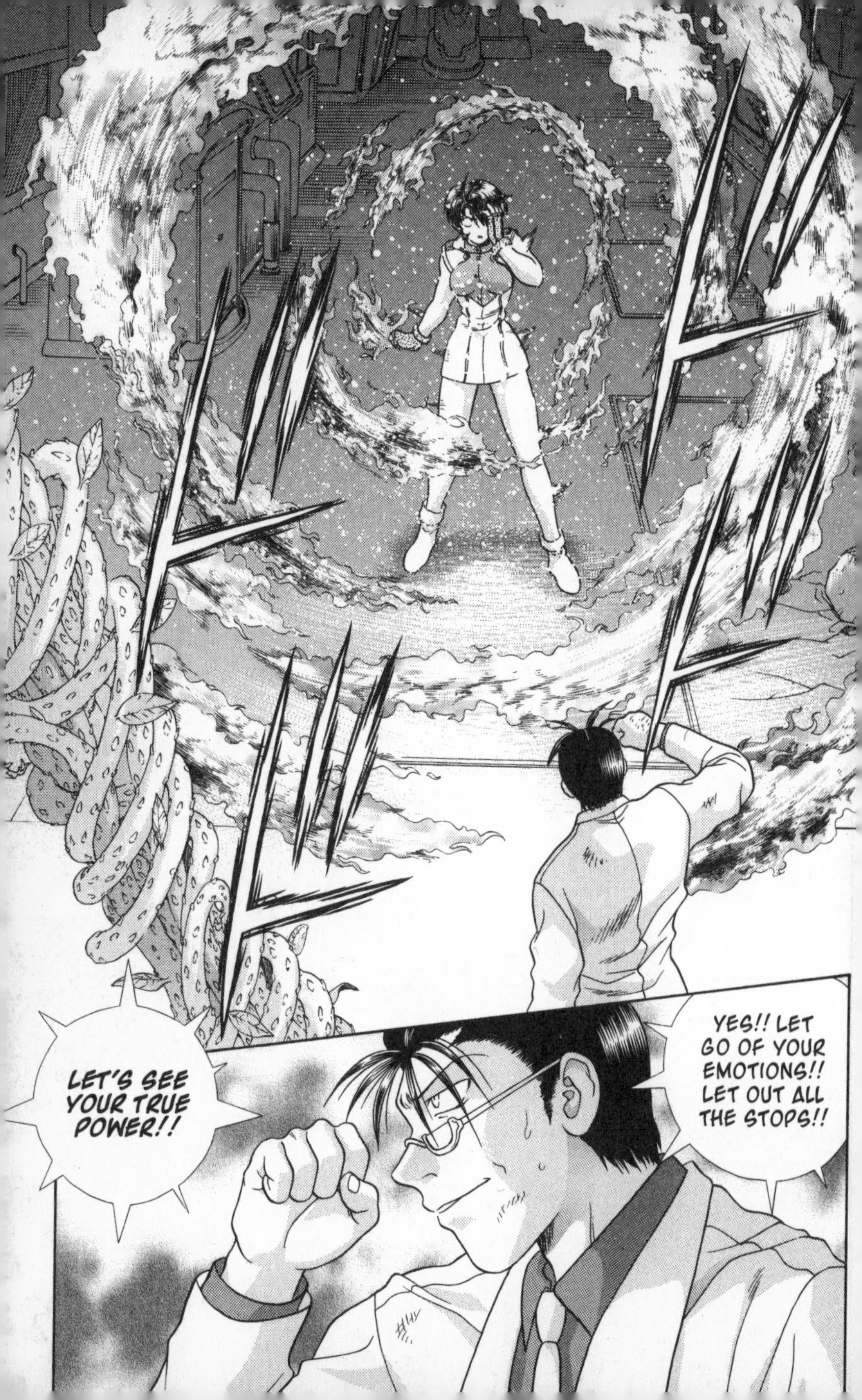
YES!! LET GO OF YOUR EMOTIONS!! LET OUT ALL THE STOPS!!
LET'S SEE YOUR TRUE POWER!!

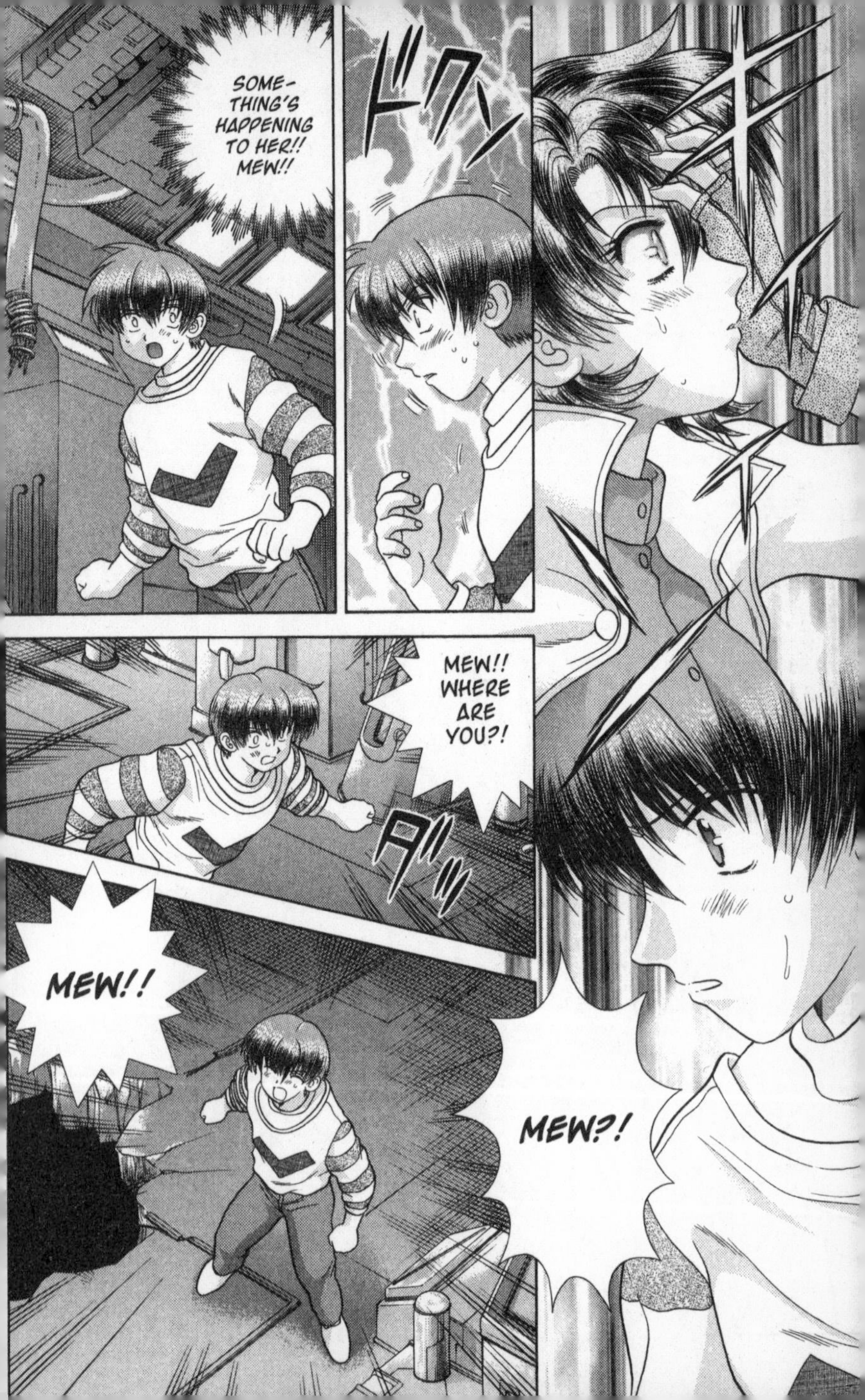
MEW?!
ドクン
SOME-THING'S HAPPENING TO HER!! MEW!!
MEW!! WHERE ARE YOU?!
ダッ
MEW!!

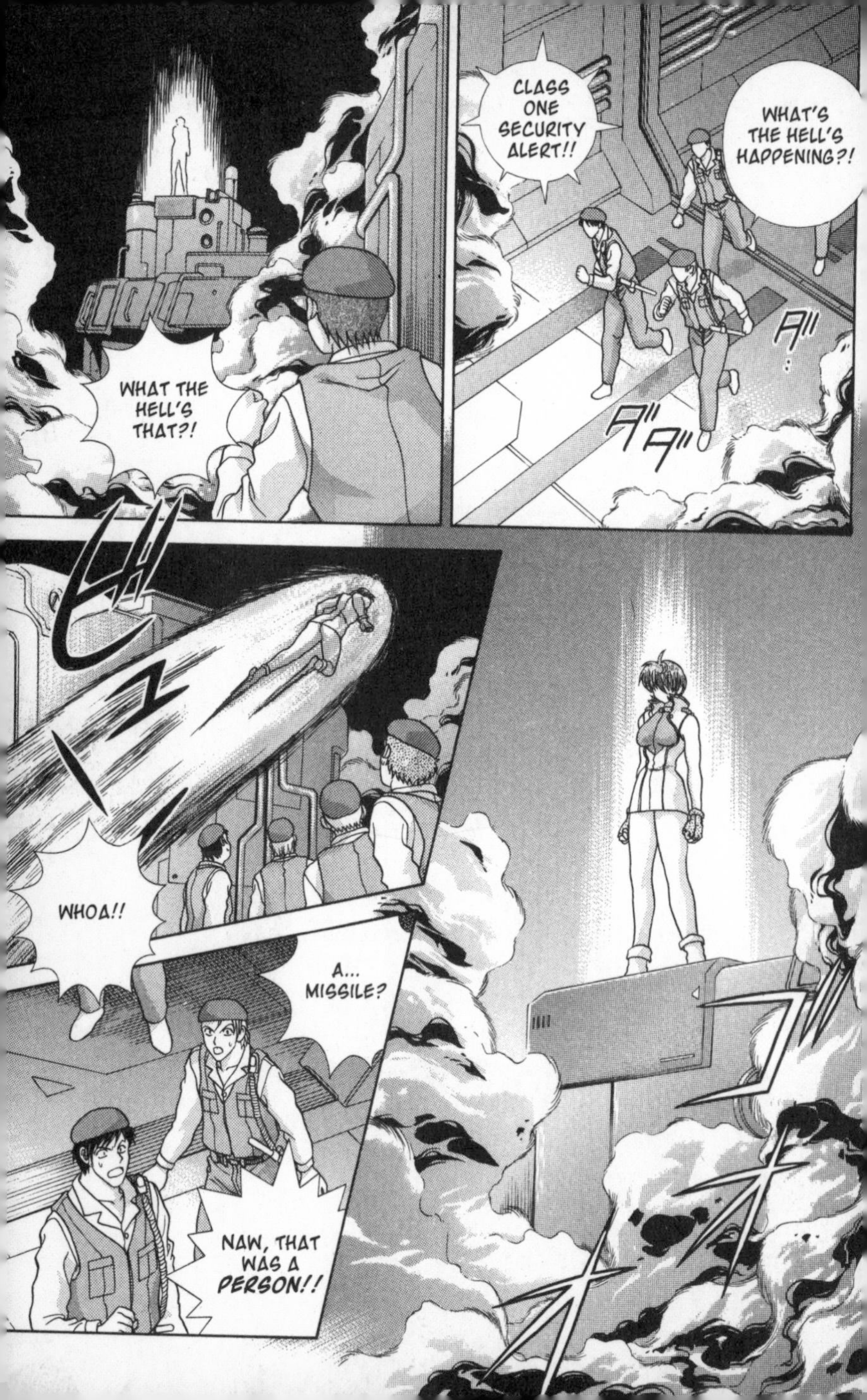
CLASS ONE SECURITY ALERT!!
WHAT'S THE HELL'S HAPPENING?!
WHAT THE HELL'S THAT?!
WHOA!!
A... MISSILE?
NAW, THAT WAS A PERSON!!

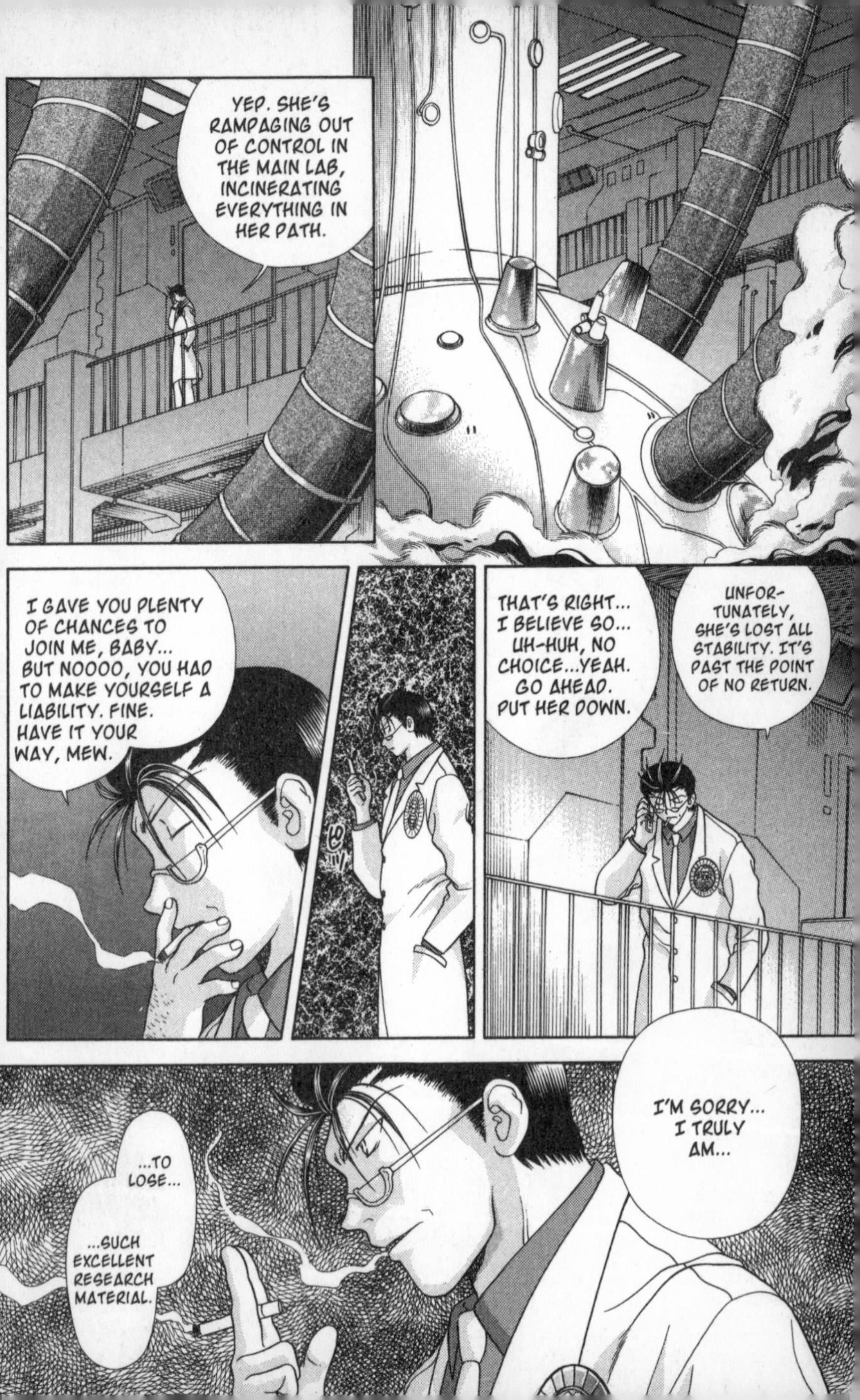
YEP. SHE'S RAMPAGING OUT OF CONTROL IN THE MAIN LAB, INCINERATING EVERYTHING IN HER PATH.
UNFOR-TUNATELY, SHE'S LOST ALL STABILITY. IT'S PAST THE POINT OF NO RETURN.
THAT'S RIGHT... I BELIEVE SO... UH-HUH, NO CHOICE...YEAH. GO AHEAD. PUT HER DOWN.
I GAVE YOU PLENTY OF CHANCES TO JOIN ME, BABY... BUT NOOOO, YOU HAD TO MAKE YOURSELF A LIABILITY. FINE. HAVE IT YOUR WAY, MEW.
I'M SORRY... I TRULY AM...
...TO LOSE...
...SUCH EXCELLENT RESEARCH MATERIAL.

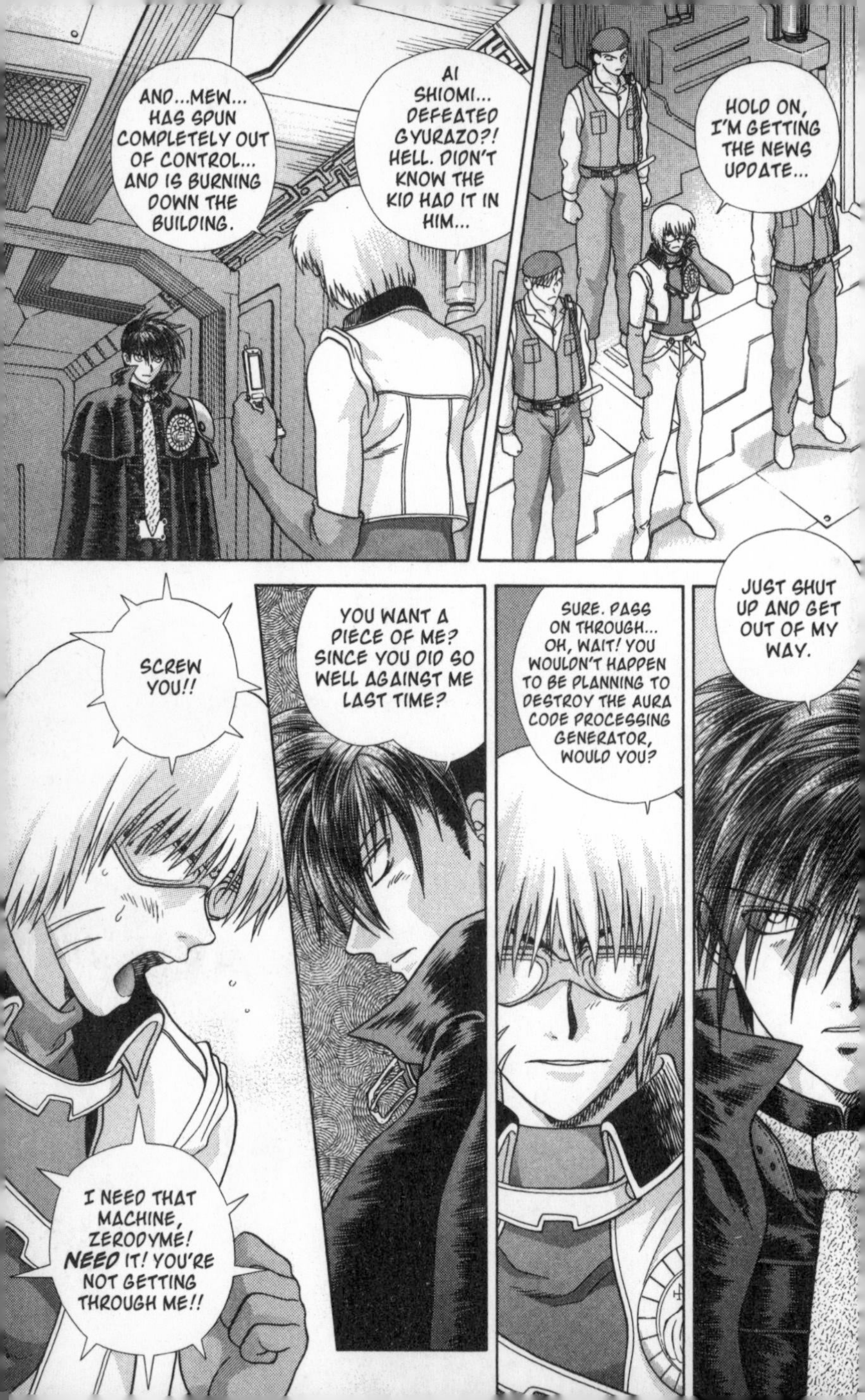
HOLD ON, I'M GETTING THE NEWS UPDATE...
AI SHIOMI... DEFEATED GYURAZO?! HELL. DIDN'T KNOW THE KID HAD IT IN HIM...
AND...MEW... HAS SPUN COMPLETELY OUT OF CONTROL... AND IS BURNING DOWN THE BUILDING.
JUST SHUT UP AND GET OUT OF MY WAY.
SURE. PASS ON THROUGH... OH, WAIT! YOU WOULDN'T HAPPEN TO BE PLANNING TO DESTROY THE AURA CODE PROCESSING GENERATOR, WOULD YOU?
YOU WANT A PIECE OF ME? SINCE YOU DID SO WELL AGAINST ME LAST TIME?
SCREW YOU!!
I NEED THAT MACHINE, ZERODYME! **NEED** IT! YOU'RE NOT GETTING THROUGH ME!!

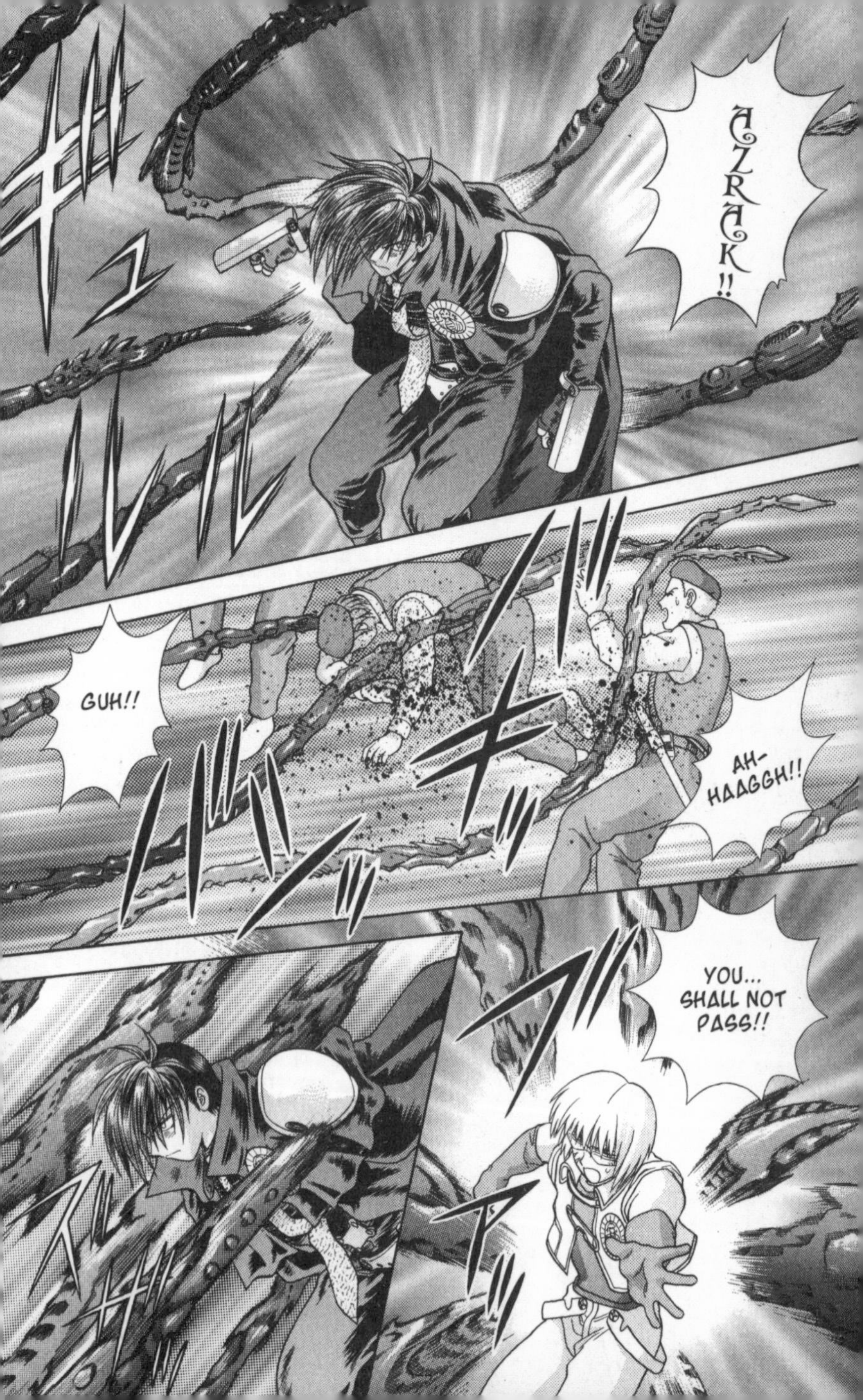
AZRAK!!
AH-HAAGGH!!
GUH!!
YOU... SHALL NOT PASS!!

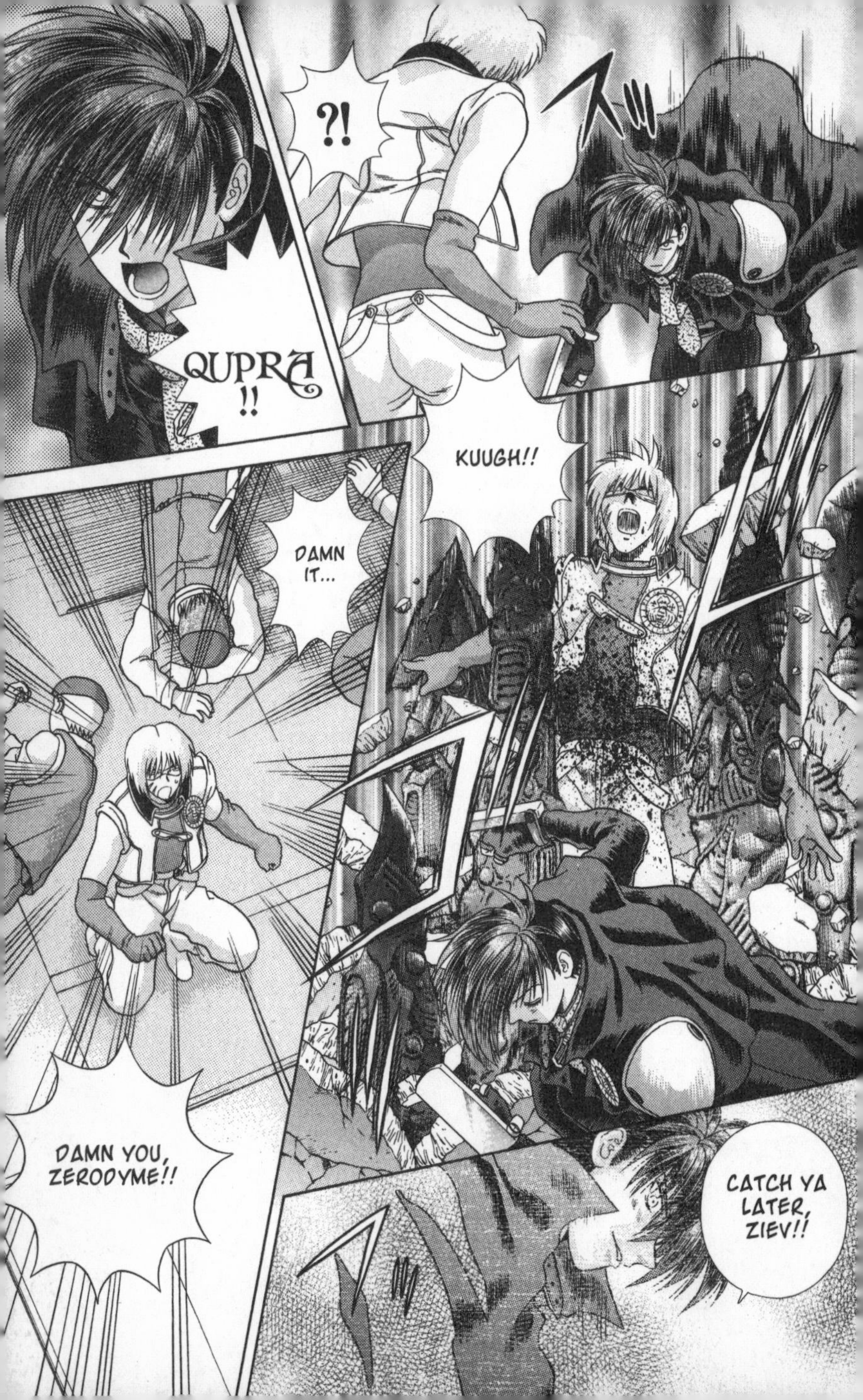
?!
QUPRA !!
KUUGH!!
CATCH YA LATER, ZIEV!!
DAMN IT...
DAMN YOU, ZERODYME!!

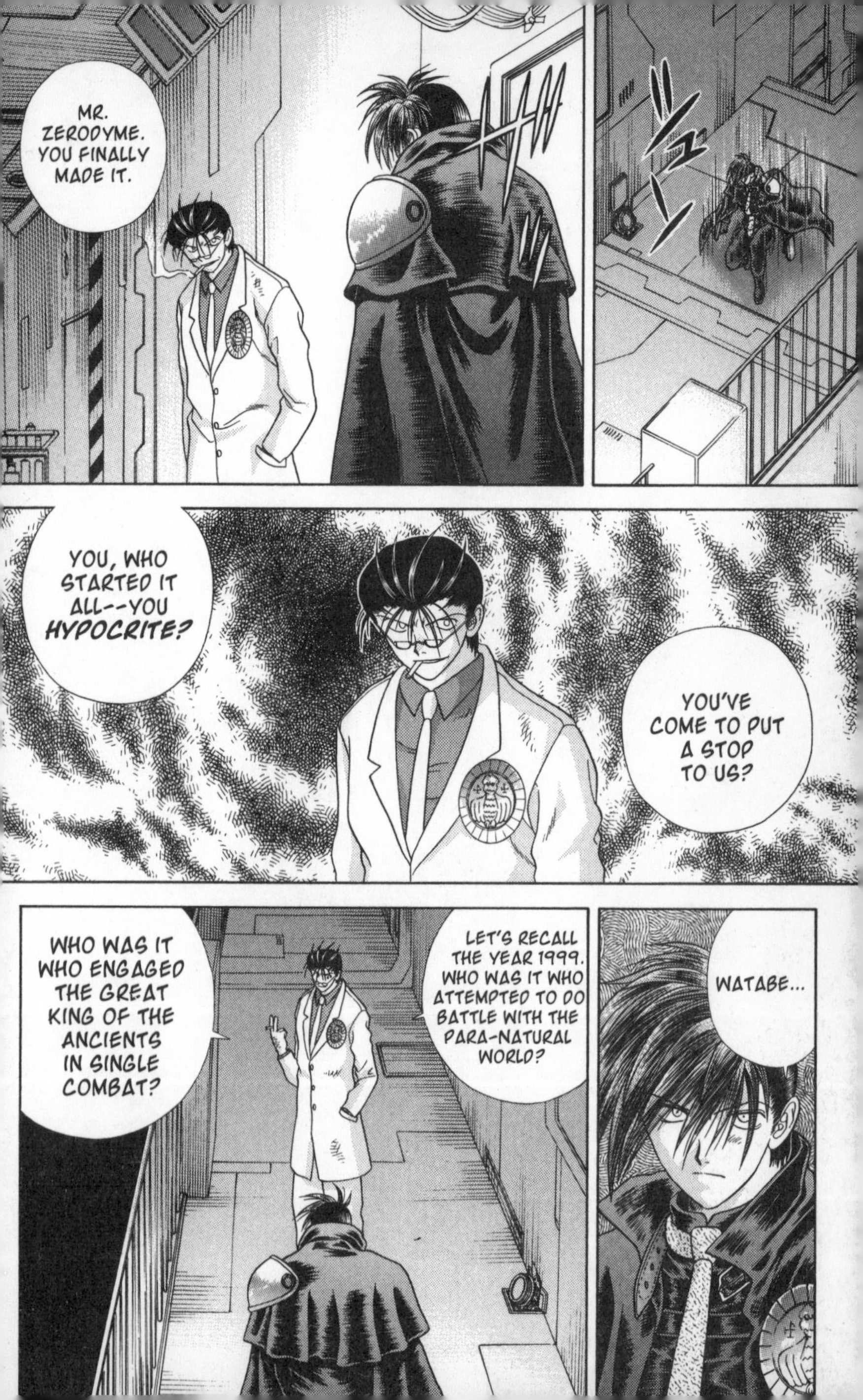
MR. ZERODYME. YOU FINALLY MADE IT.
YOU'VE COME TO PUT A STOP TO US?
YOU, WHO STARTED IT ALL--YOU *HYPOCRITE?*
WATABE...
LET'S RECALL THE YEAR 1999. WHO WAS IT WHO ATTEMPTED TO DO BATTLE WITH THE PARA-NATURAL WORLD?
WHO WAS IT WHO ENGAGED THE GREAT KING OF THE ANCIENTS IN SINGLE COMBAT?

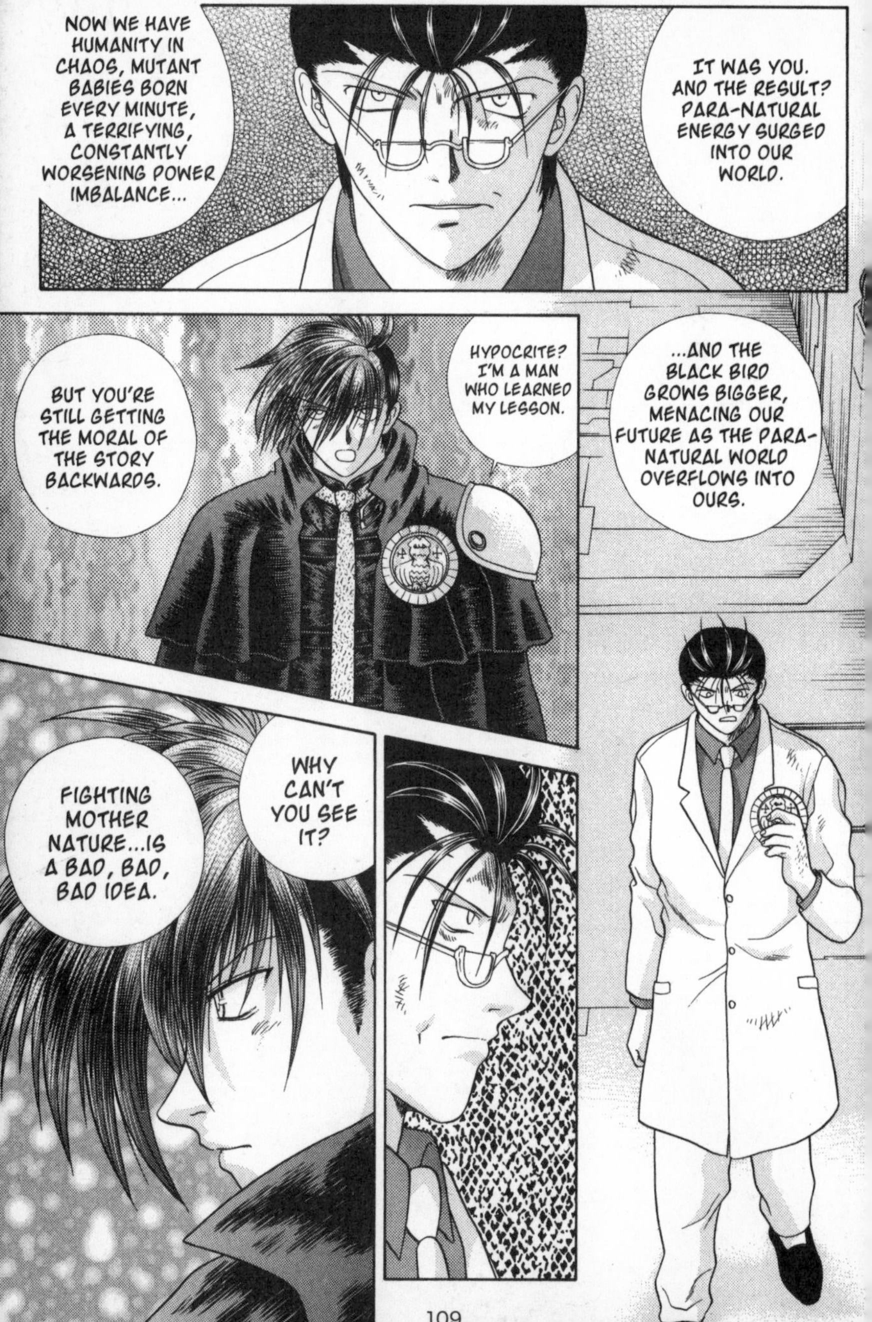
IT WAS YOU. AND THE RESULT? PARA-NATURAL ENERGY SURGED INTO OUR WORLD.
NOW WE HAVE HUMANITY IN CHAOS, MUTANT BABIES BORN EVERY MINUTE, A TERRIFYING, CONSTANTLY WORSENING POWER IMBALANCE...
...AND THE BLACK BIRD GROWS BIGGER, MENACING OUR FUTURE AS THE PARA-NATURAL WORLD OVERFLOWS INTO OURS.
HYPOCRITE? I'M A MAN WHO LEARNED MY LESSON.
BUT YOU'RE STILL GETTING THE MORAL OF THE STORY BACKWARDS.
WHY CAN'T YOU SEE IT?
FIGHTING MOTHER NATURE...IS A BAD, BAD, BAD IDEA.

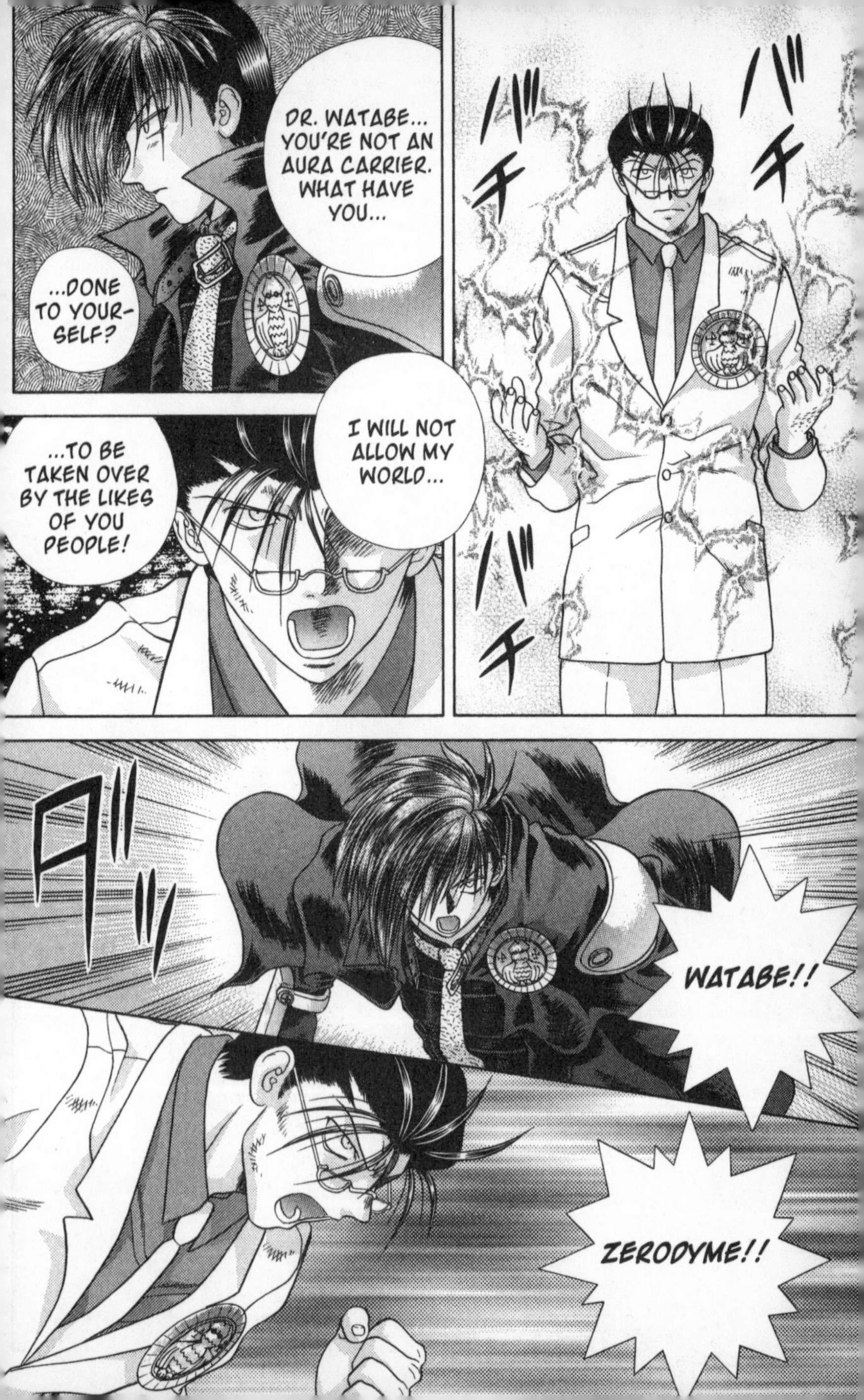

バチ
バチ
DR. WATABE... YOU'RE NOT AN AURA CARRIER. WHAT HAVE YOU...
...DONE TO YOURSELF?
I WILL NOT ALLOW MY WORLD...
...TO BE TAKEN OVER BY THE LIKES OF YOU PEOPLE!
WATABE!!
ダッ
ZERODYME!!

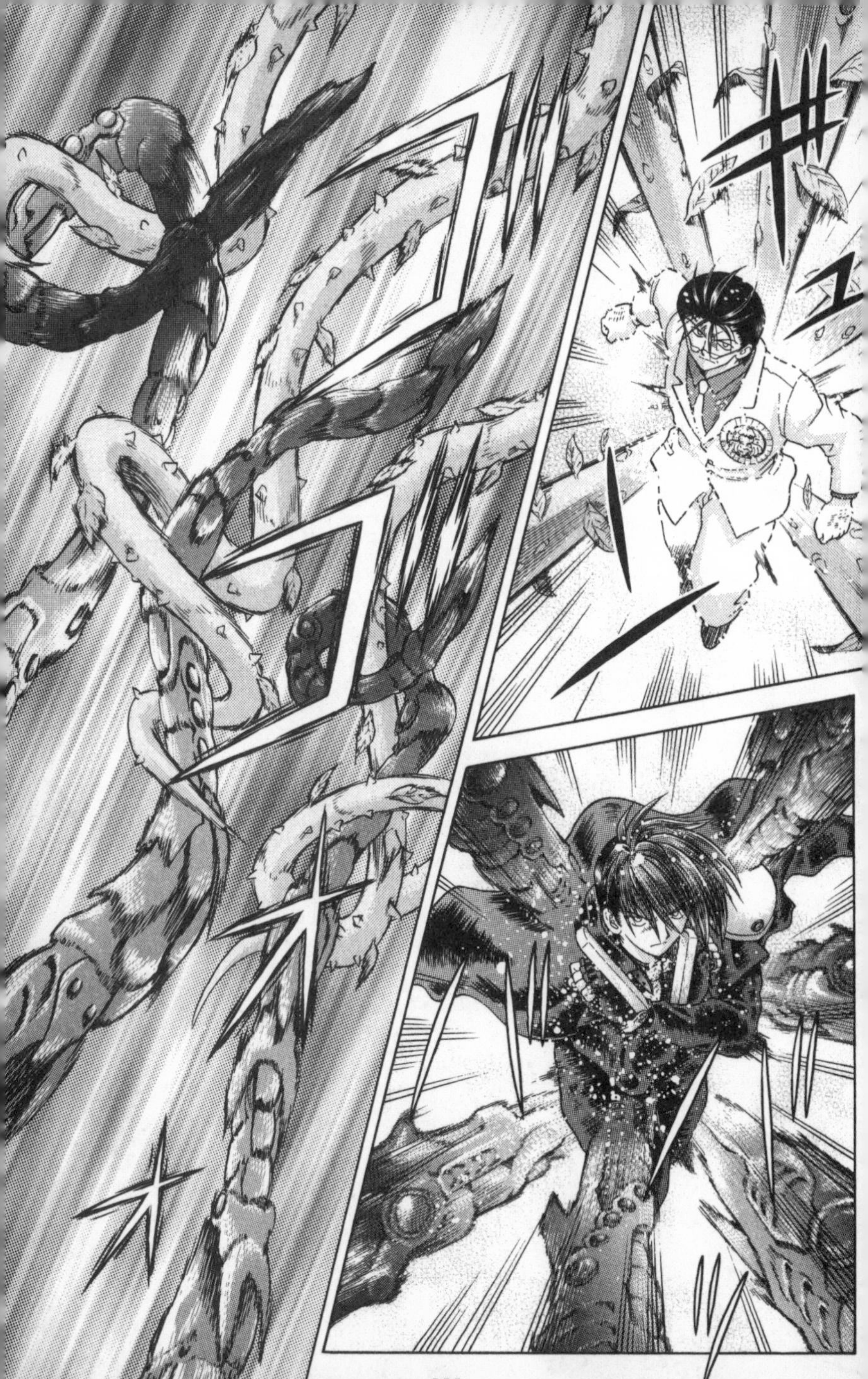

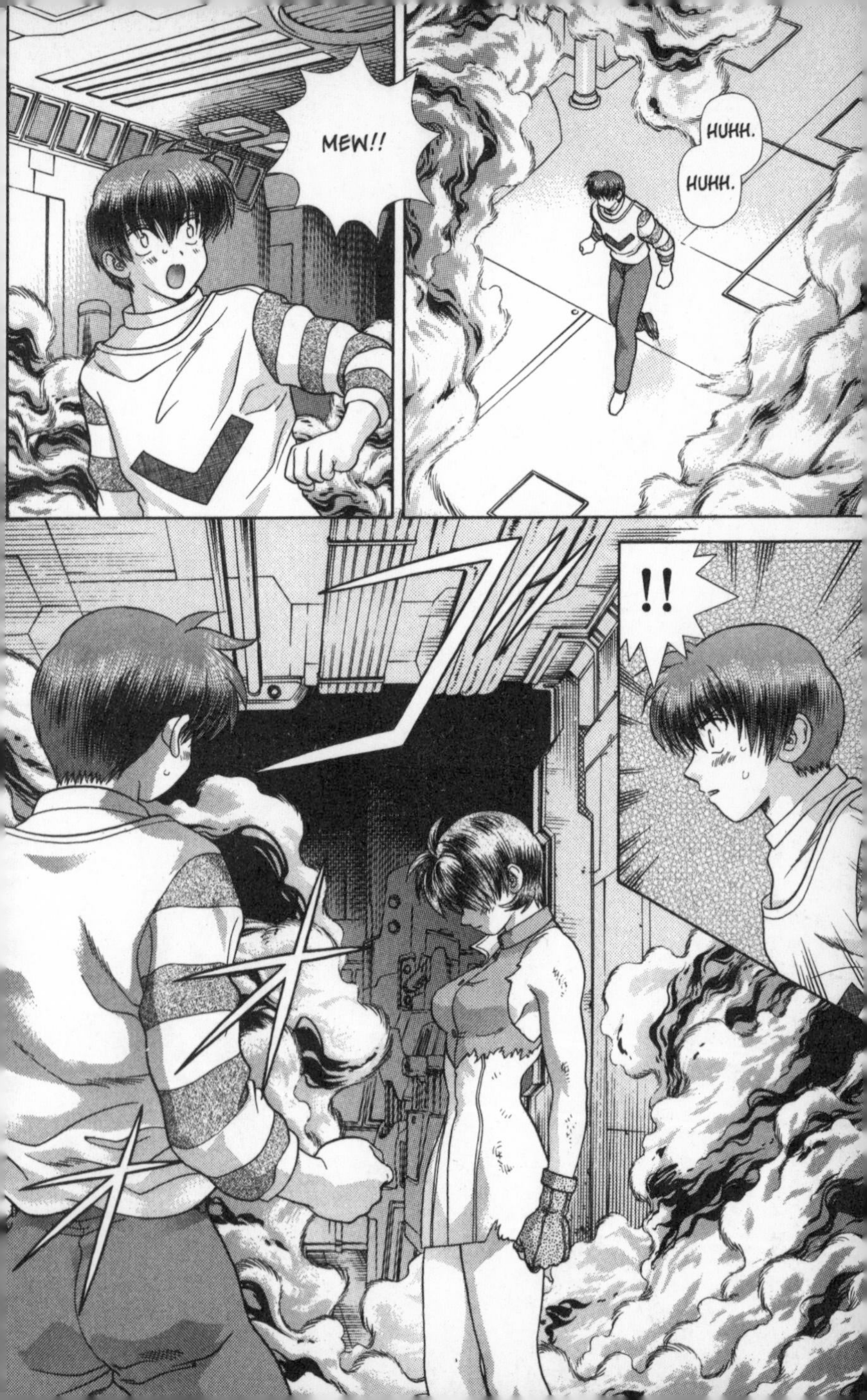
HUHH.
HUHH.
MEW!!
!!

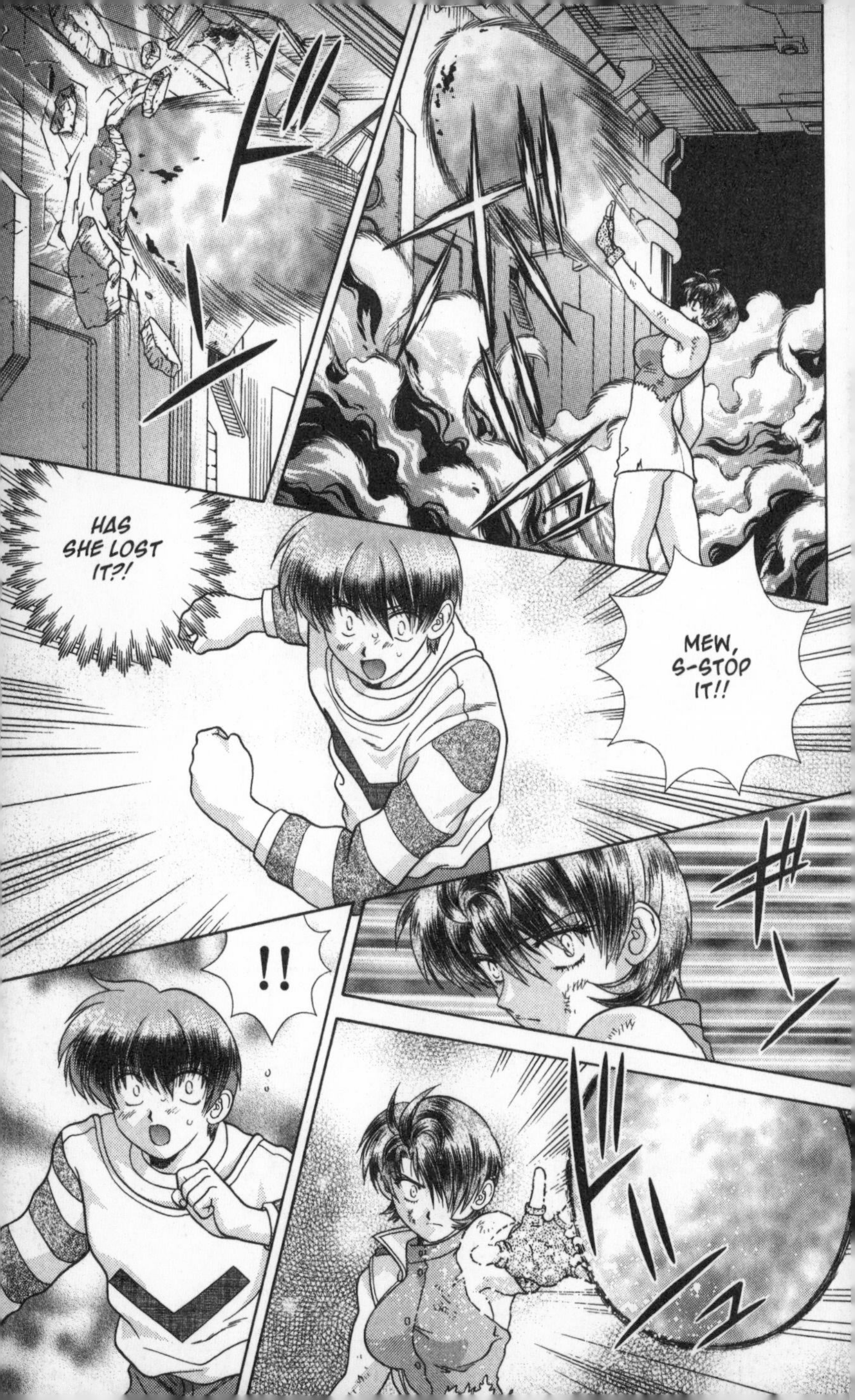
MEW, S-STOP IT!!
HAS SHE LOST IT?!
!!

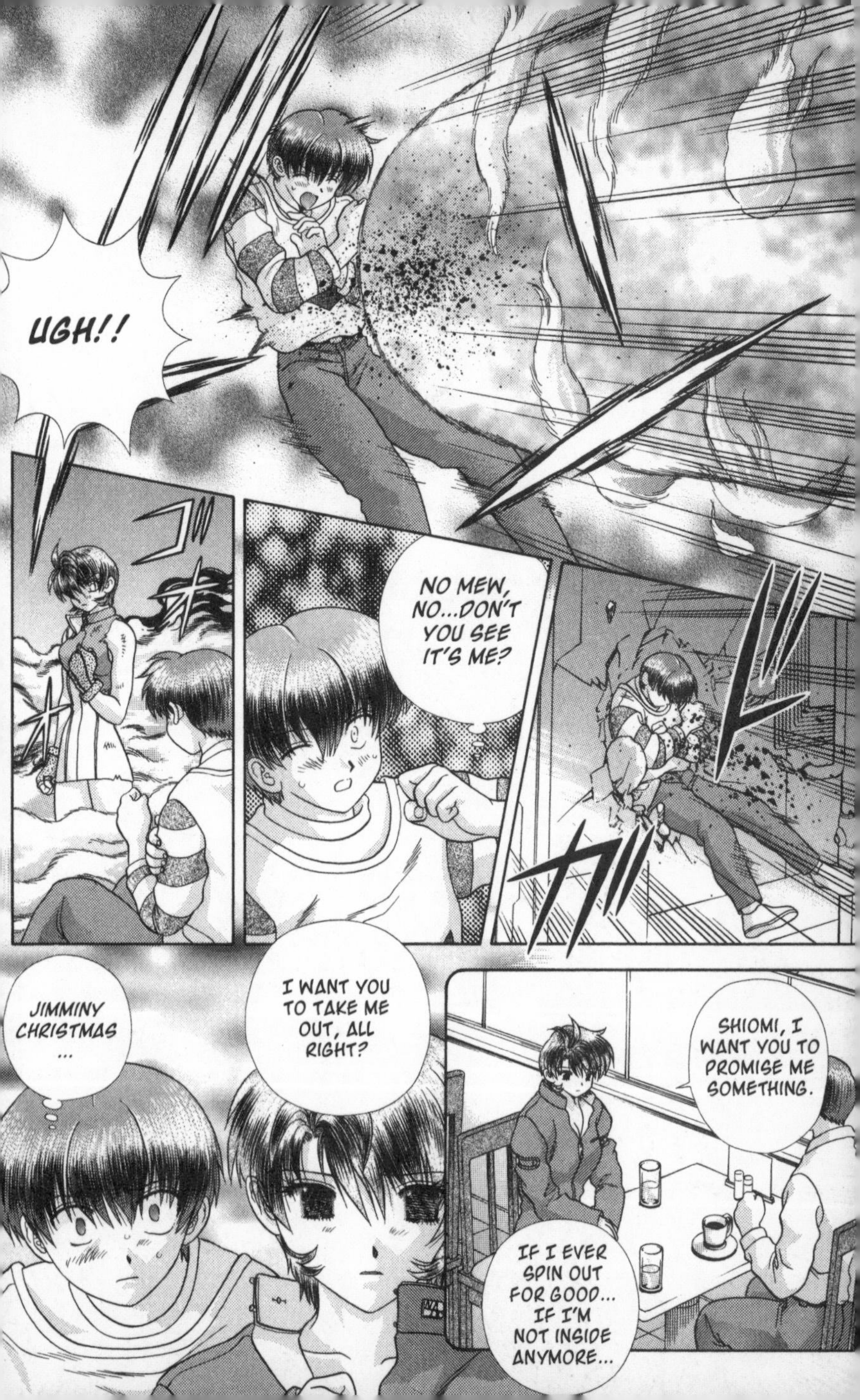
UGH!!
NO MEW, NO...DON'T YOU SEE IT'S ME?
SHIOMI, I WANT YOU TO PROMISE ME SOMETHING.
IF I EVER SPIN OUT FOR GOOD... IF I'M NOT INSIDE ANYMORE...
I WANT YOU TO TAKE ME OUT, ALL RIGHT?
JIMMINY CHRISTMAS ...

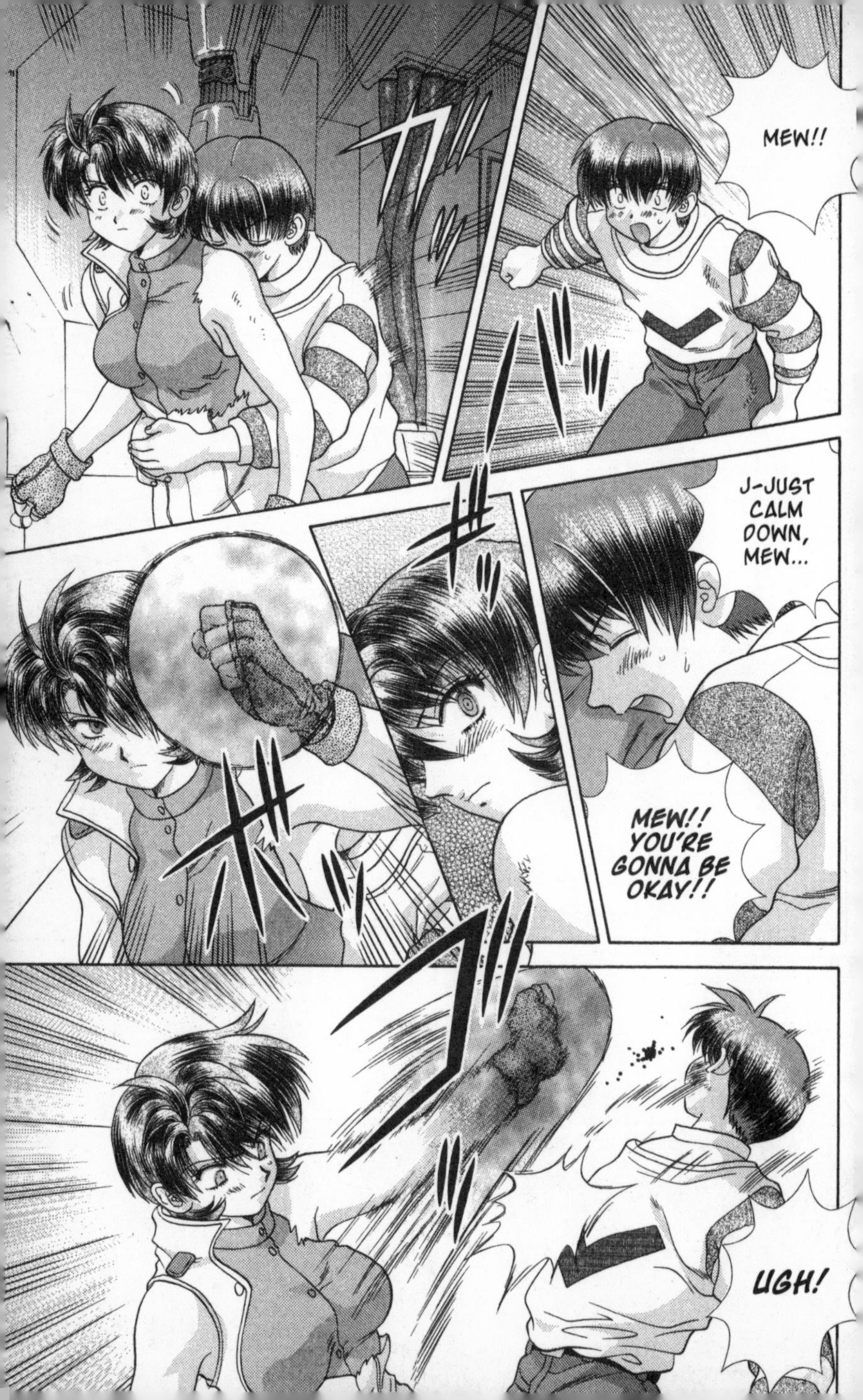
MEW!!
J-JUST CALM DOWN, MEW...
MEW!! YOU'RE GONNA BE OKAY!!
UGH!

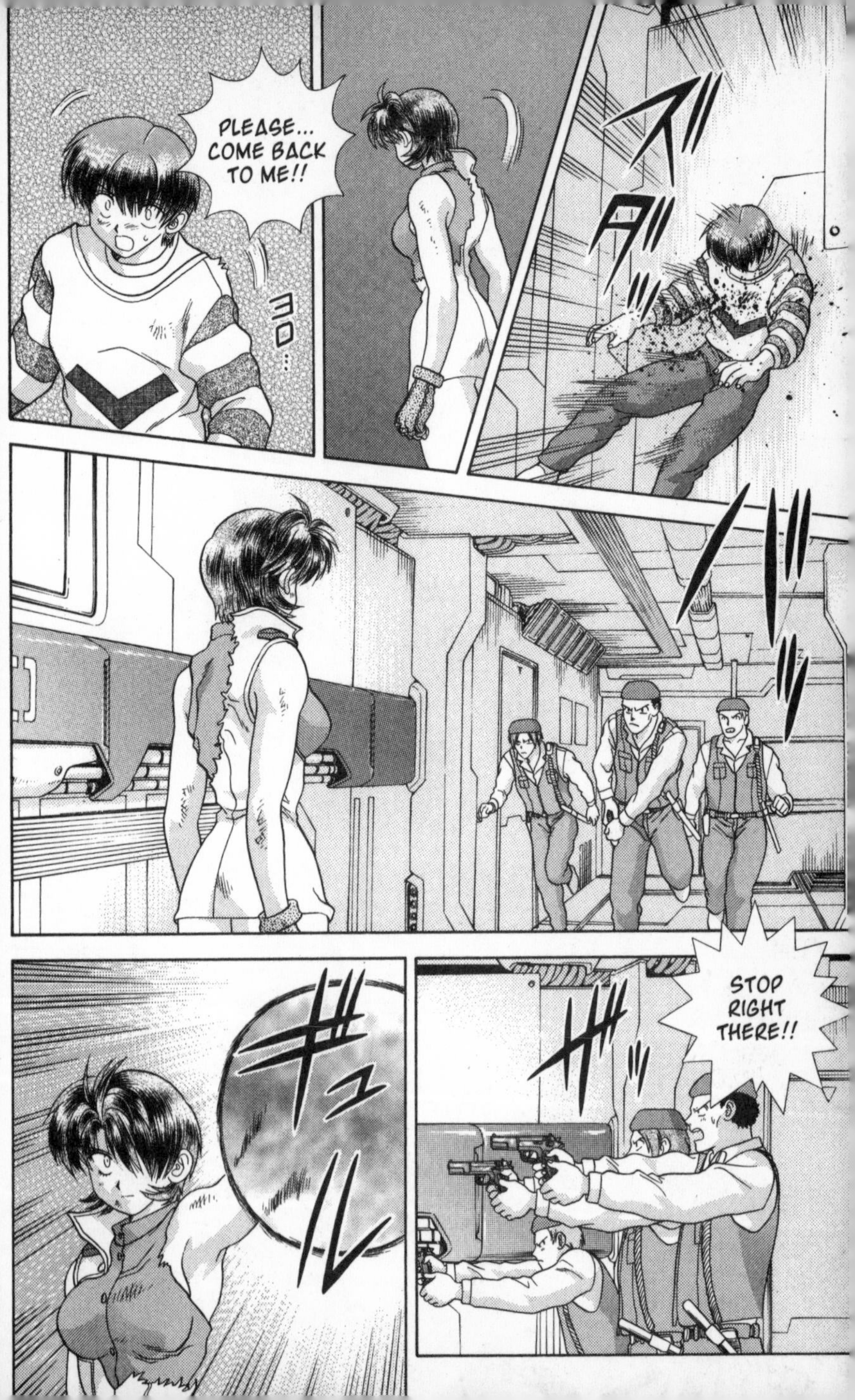
ズダ
PLEASE... COME BACK TO ME!!
ヨロ…
STOP RIGHT THERE!!
ザ
ギュル

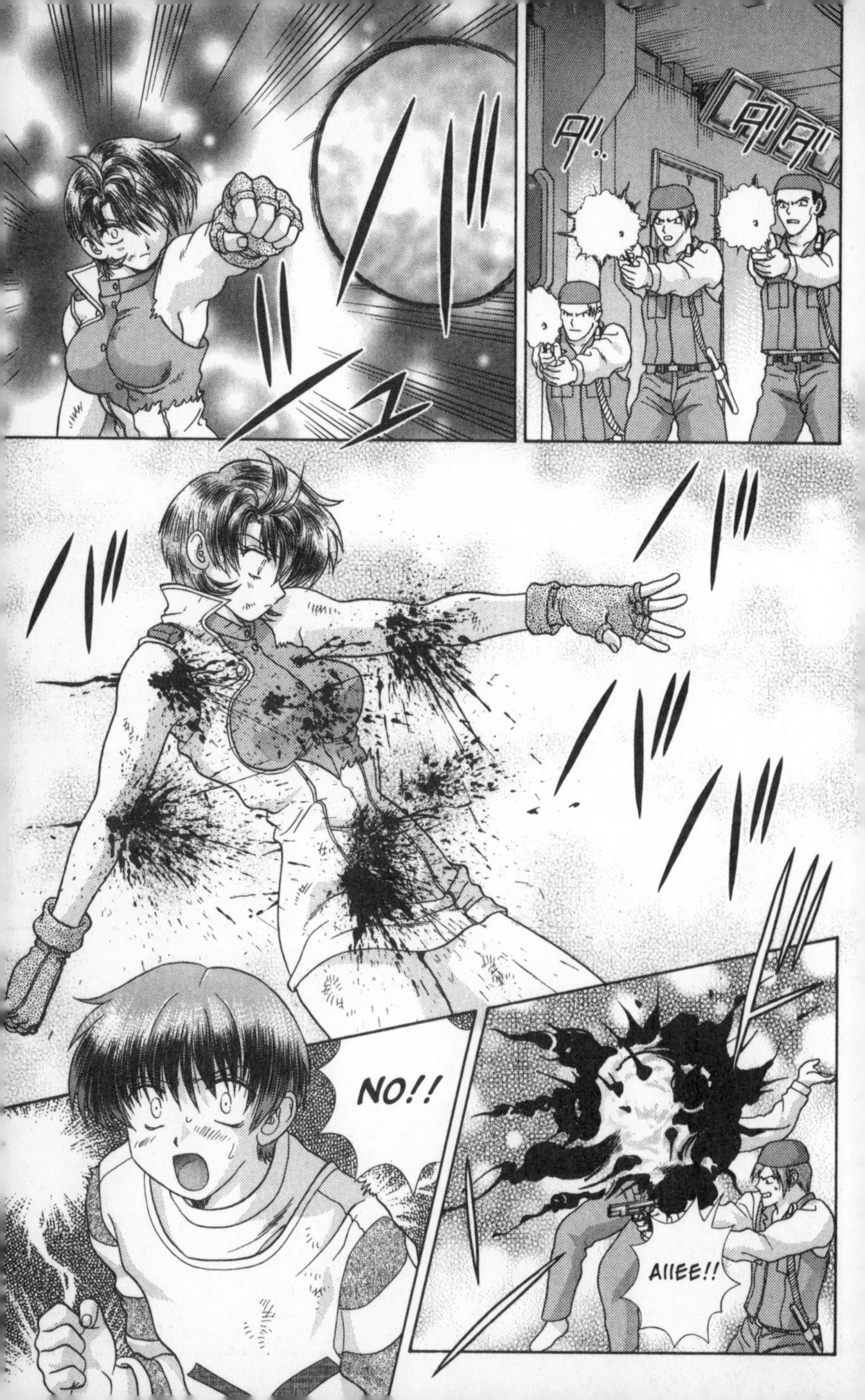
AIIEE!!
NO!!

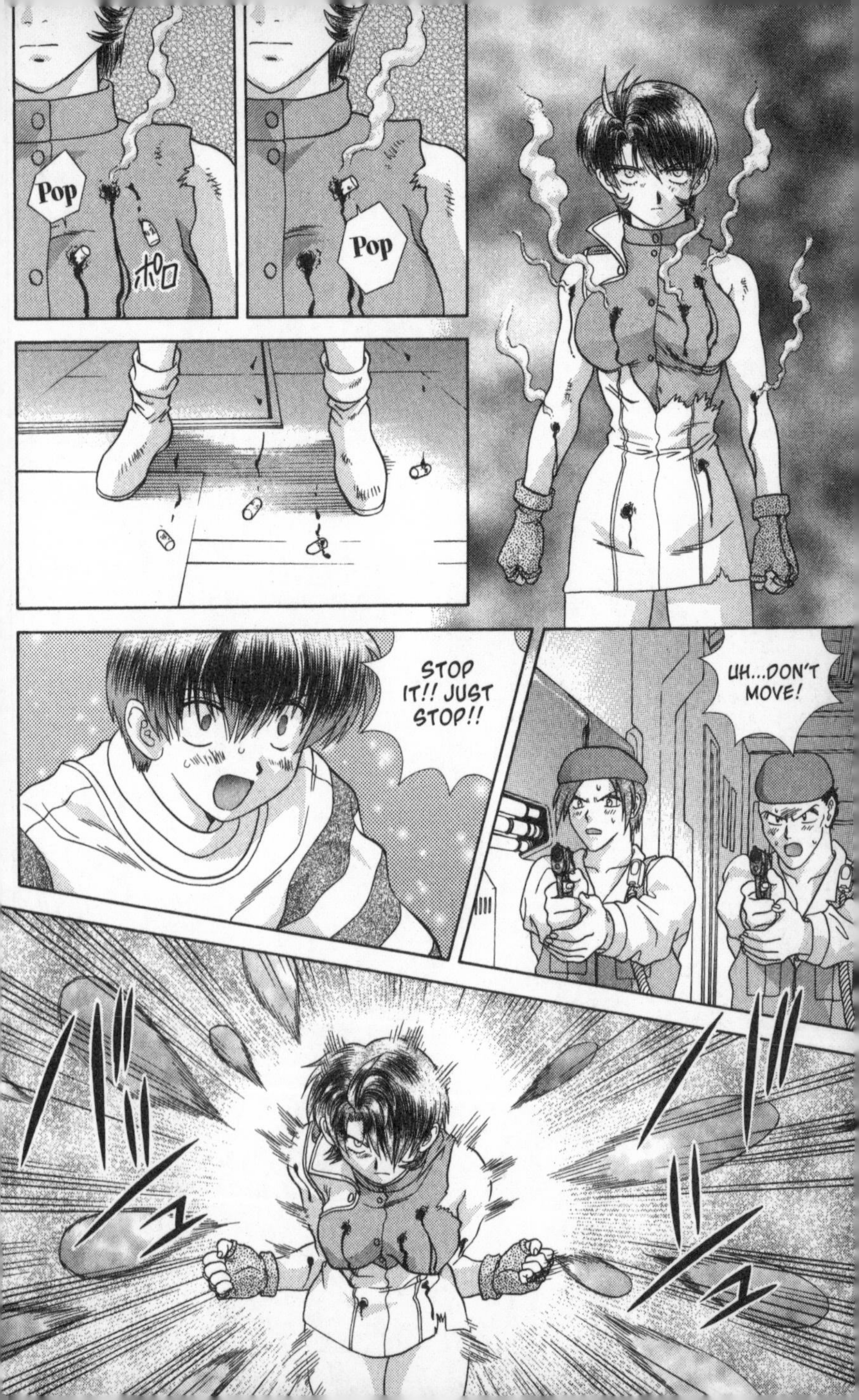

Pop
Pop
ポロ
UH...DON'T MOVE!
STOP IT!! JUST STOP!!

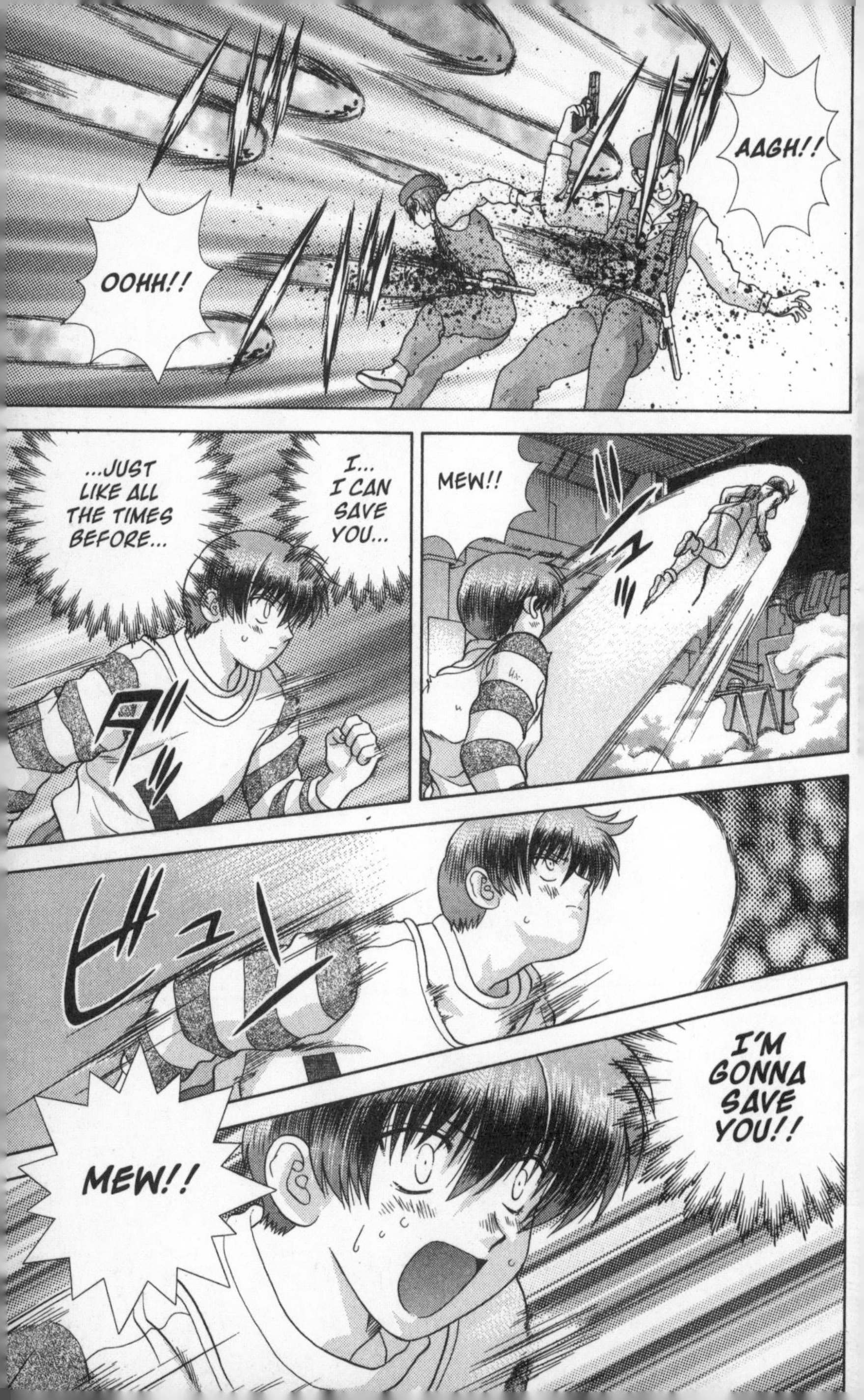
AAGH!!
OOHH!!
MEW!!
I... I CAN SAVE YOU...
...JUST LIKE ALL THE TIMES BEFORE...
I'M GONNA SAVE YOU!!
MEW!!

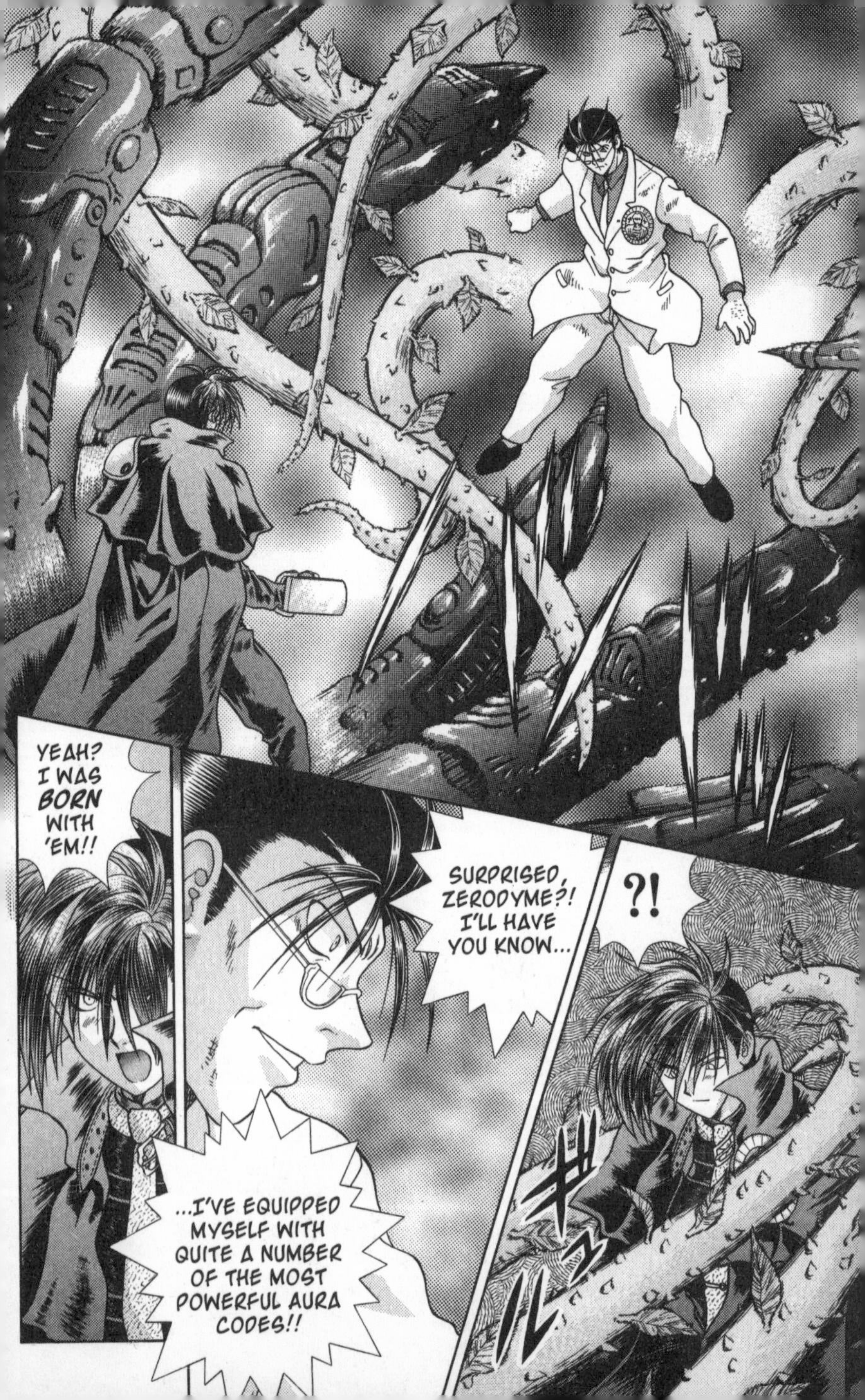
?!
SURPRISED, ZERODYME?! I'LL HAVE YOU KNOW...
...I'VE EQUIPPED MYSELF WITH QUITE A NUMBER OF THE MOST POWERFUL AURA CODES!!
YEAH? I WAS BORN WITH 'EM!!

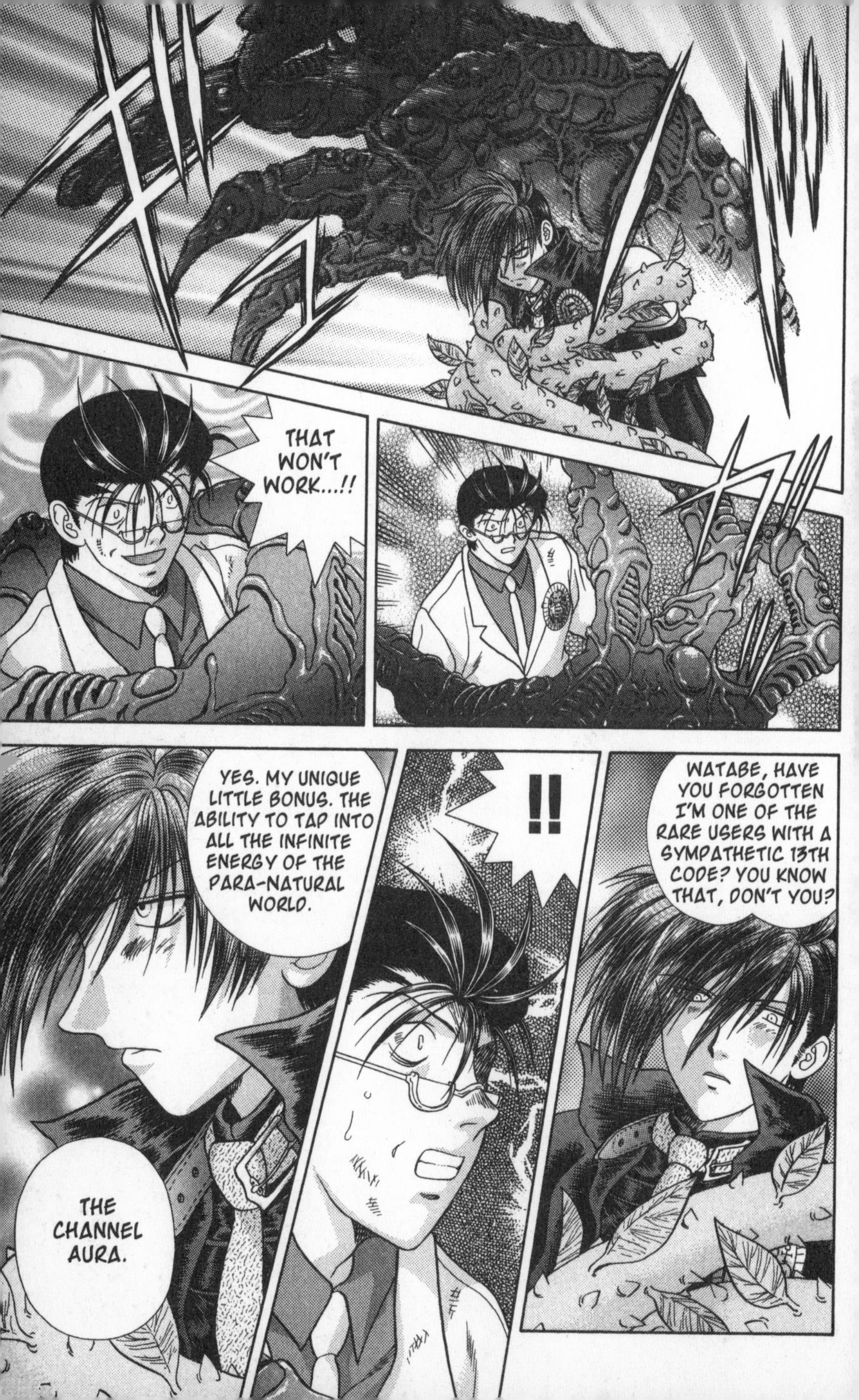
THAT WON'T WORK...!!
WATABE, HAVE YOU FORGOTTEN I'M ONE OF THE RARE USERS WITH A SYMPATHETIC 13TH CODE? YOU KNOW THAT, DON'T YOU?
!!
YES. MY UNIQUE LITTLE BONUS. THE ABILITY TO TAP INTO ALL THE INFINITE ENERGY OF THE PARA-NATURAL WORLD.
THE CHANNEL AURA.

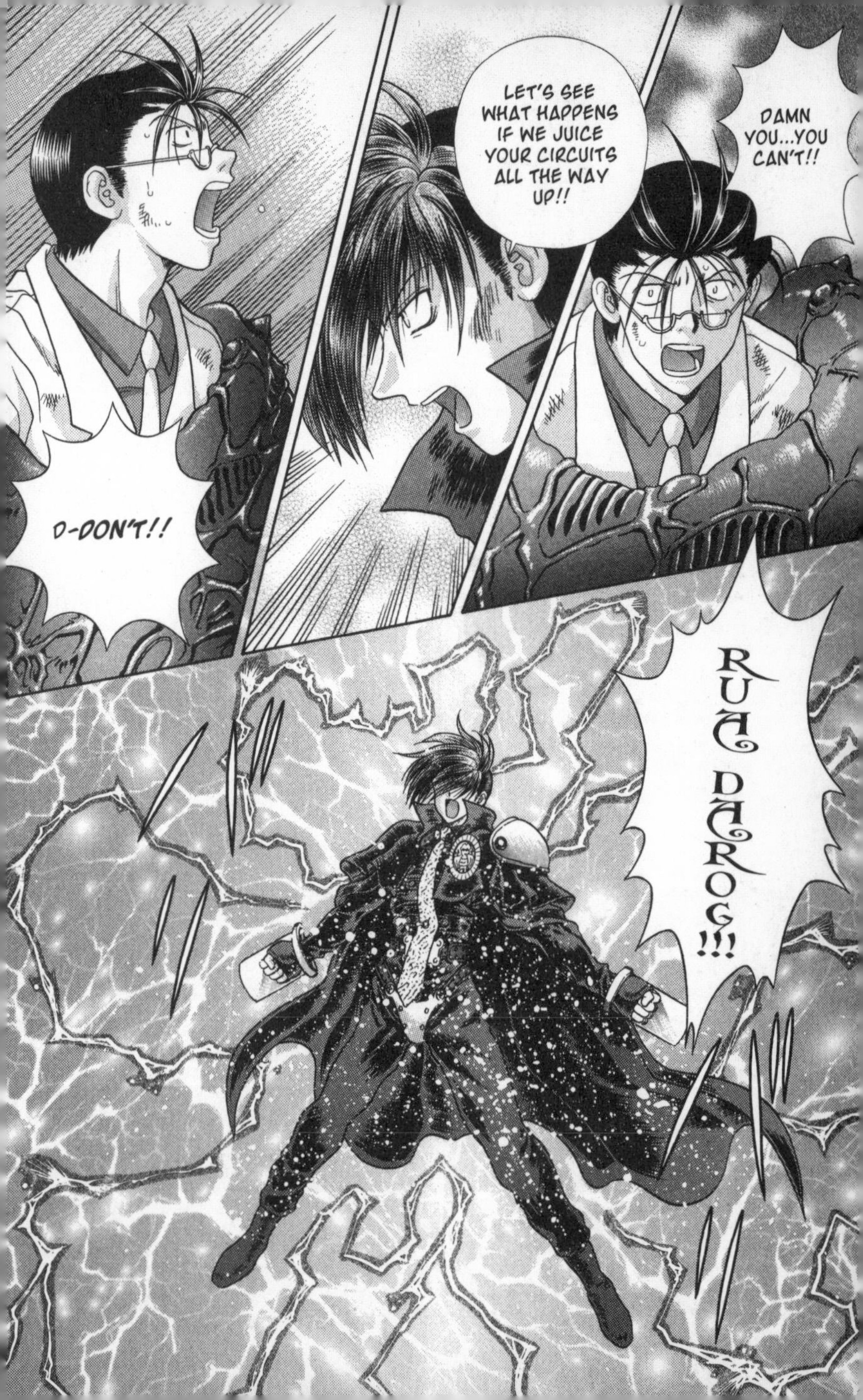
DAMN YOU...YOU CAN'T!!
LET'S SEE WHAT HAPPENS IF WE JUICE YOUR CIRCUITS ALL THE WAY UP!!
D-DON'T!!
RUA DAROG!!!

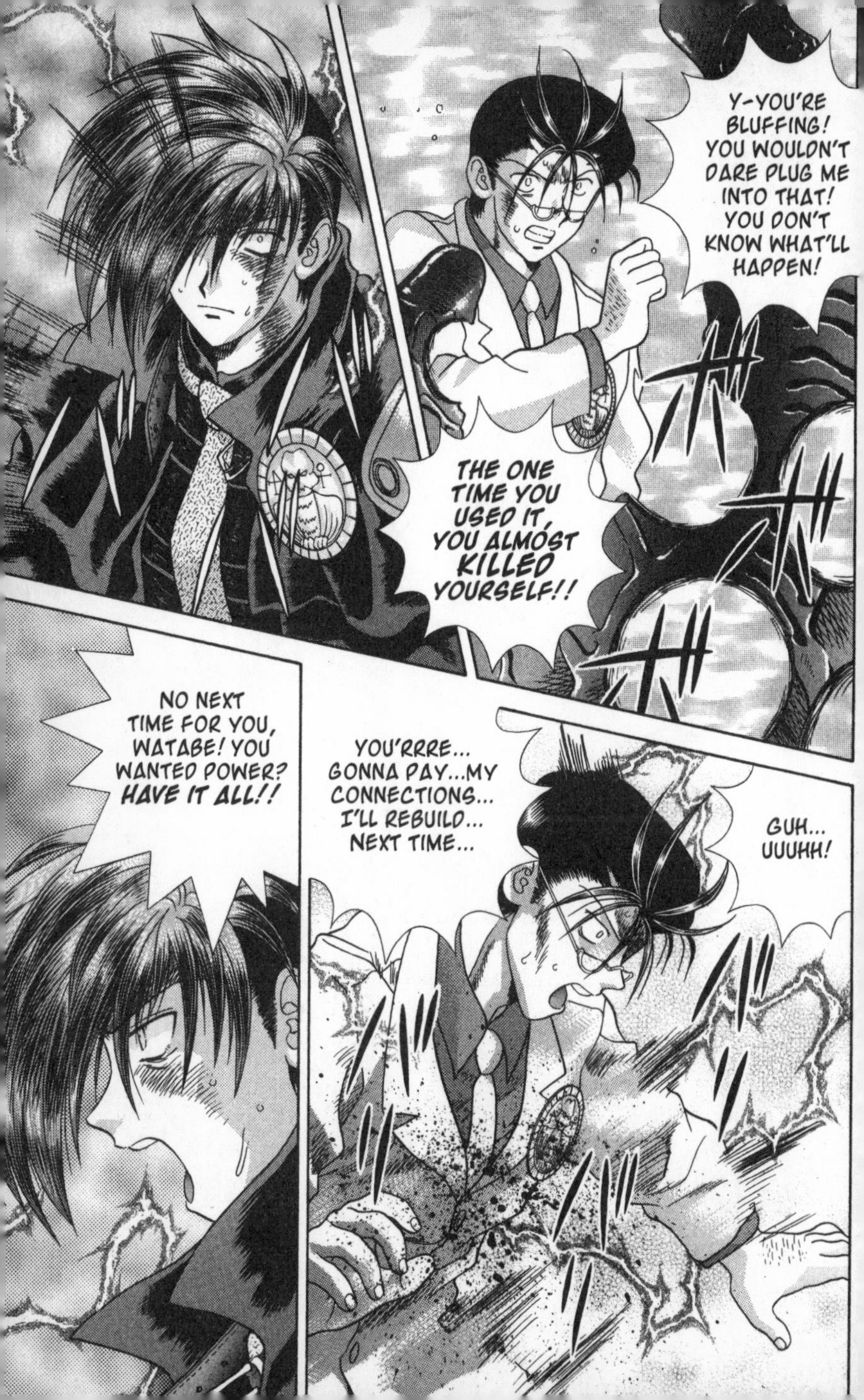
Y-YOU'RE BLUFFING! YOU WOULDN'T DARE PLUG ME INTO THAT! YOU DON'T KNOW WHAT'LL HAPPEN!
THE ONE TIME YOU USED IT, YOU ALMOST KILLED YOURSELF!!
GUH... UUUHH!
YOU'RRRE... GONNA PAY...MY CONNECTIONS... I'LL REBUILD... NEXT TIME...
NO NEXT TIME FOR YOU, WATABE! YOU WANTED POWER? HAVE IT ALL!!

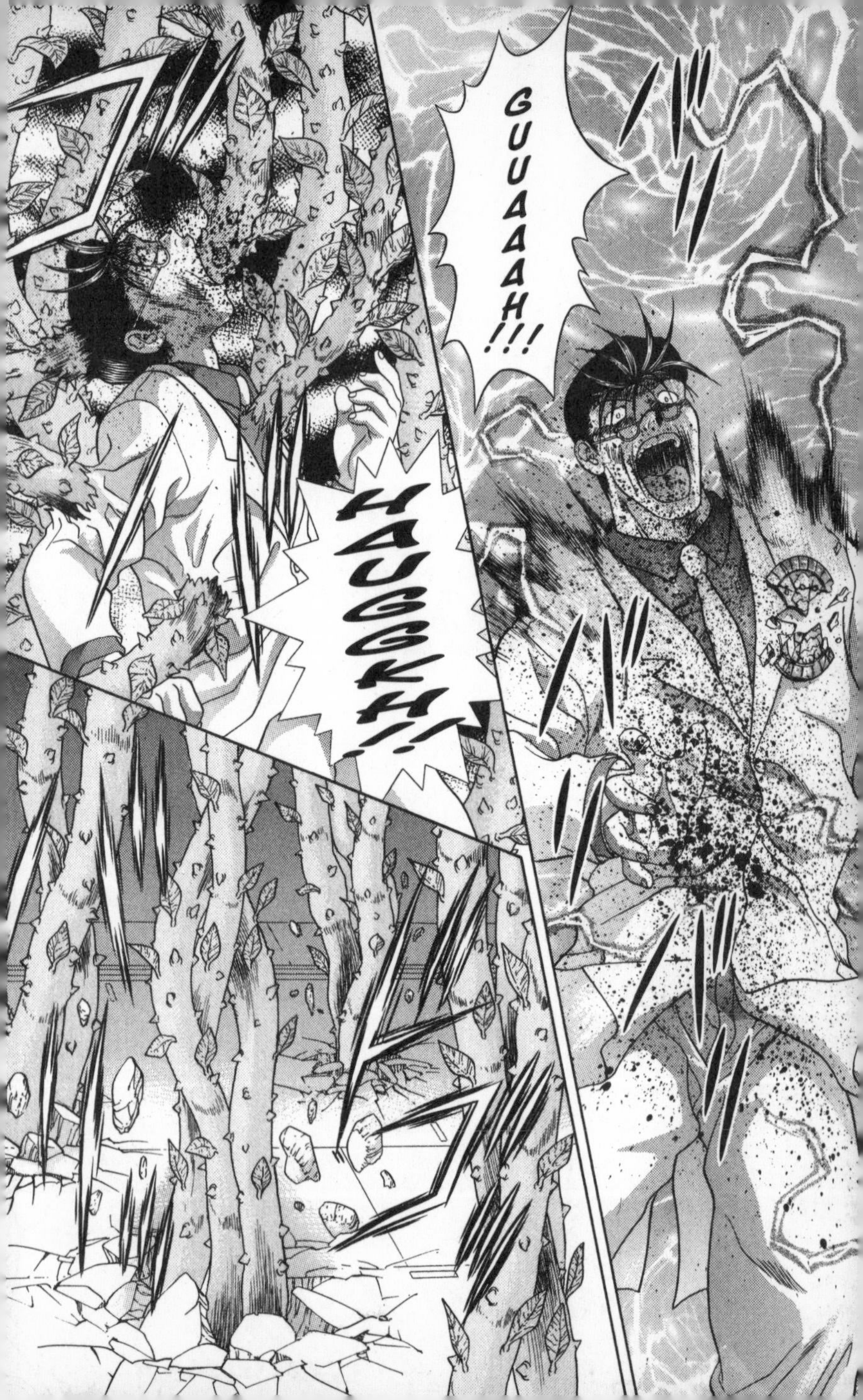
GUUAAAAH!!!
HAUGGKH!!

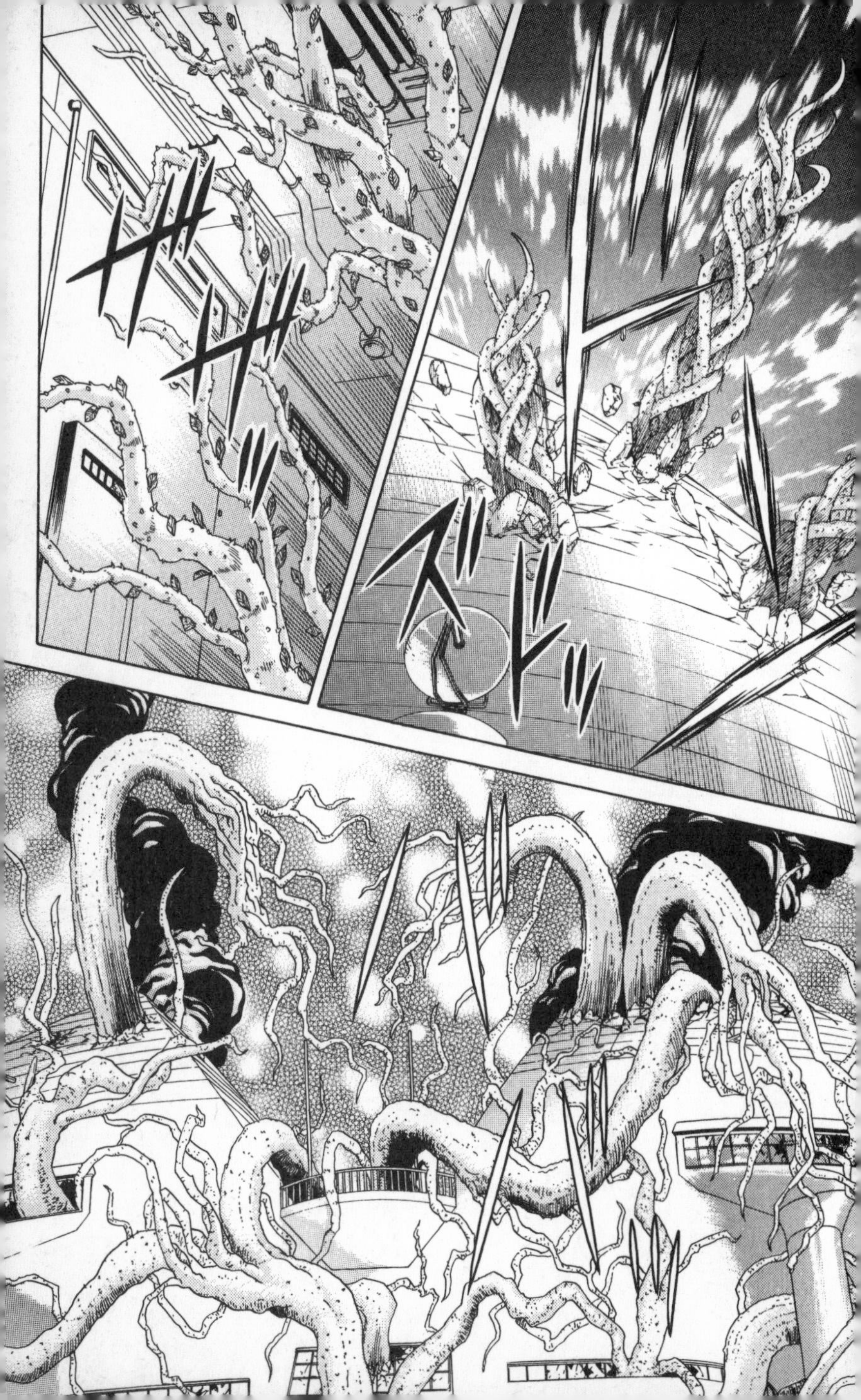
ズドッ
ザザッ

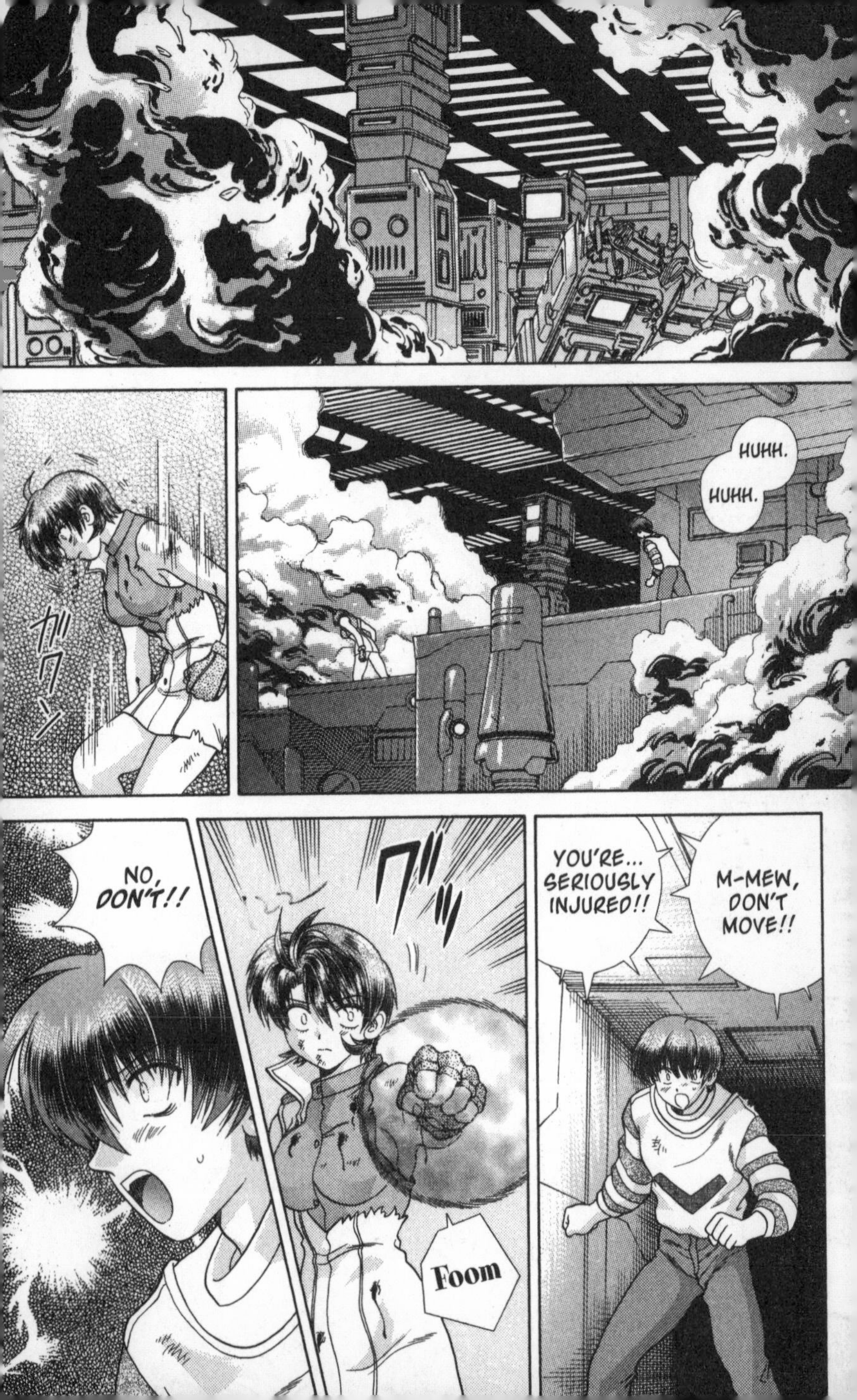
HUHH.
HUHH.
M-MEW, DON'T MOVE!!
YOU'RE... SERIOUSLY INJURED!!
Foom
NO, DON'T!!

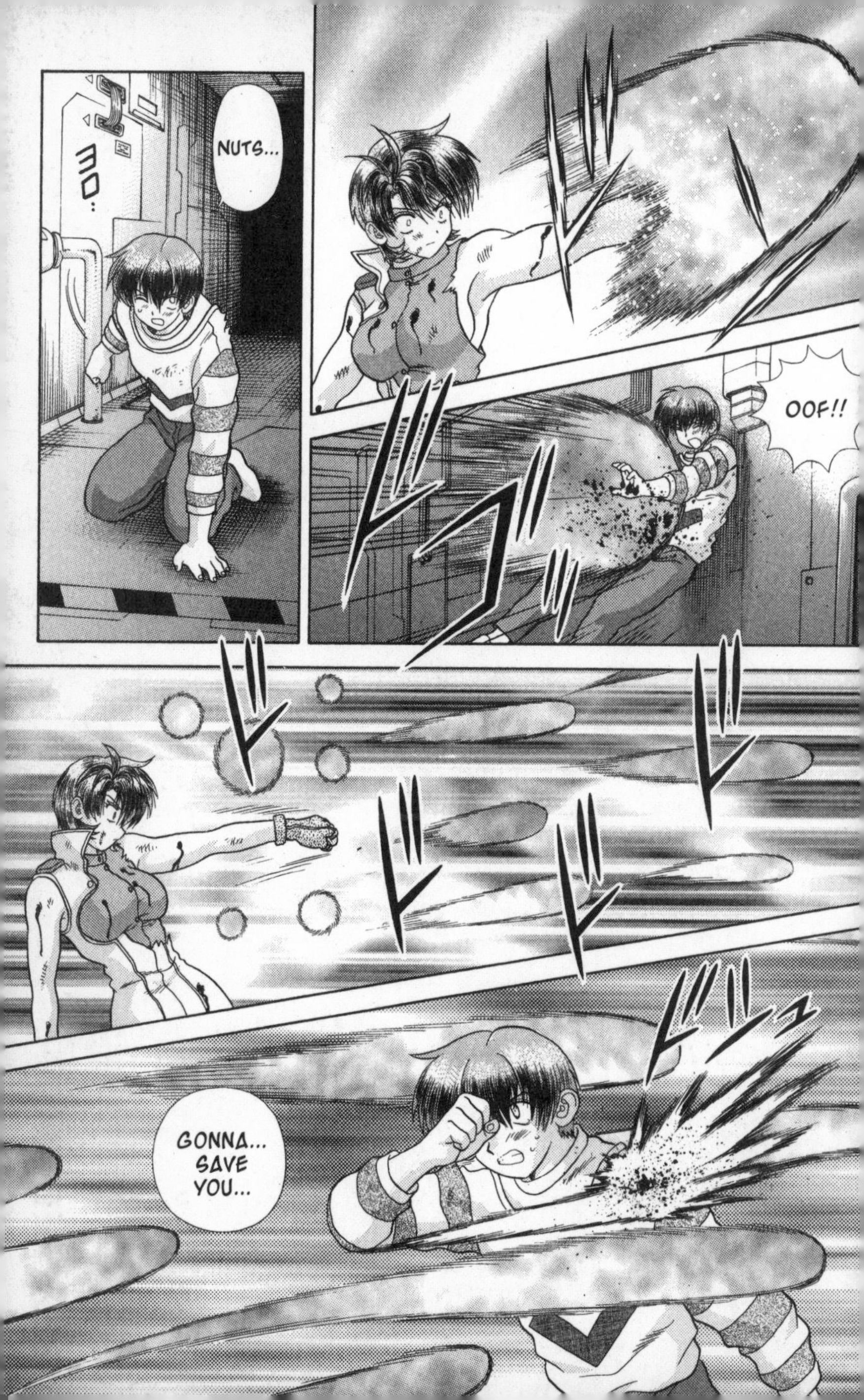
OOF!!
NUTS...
GONNA... SAVE YOU...

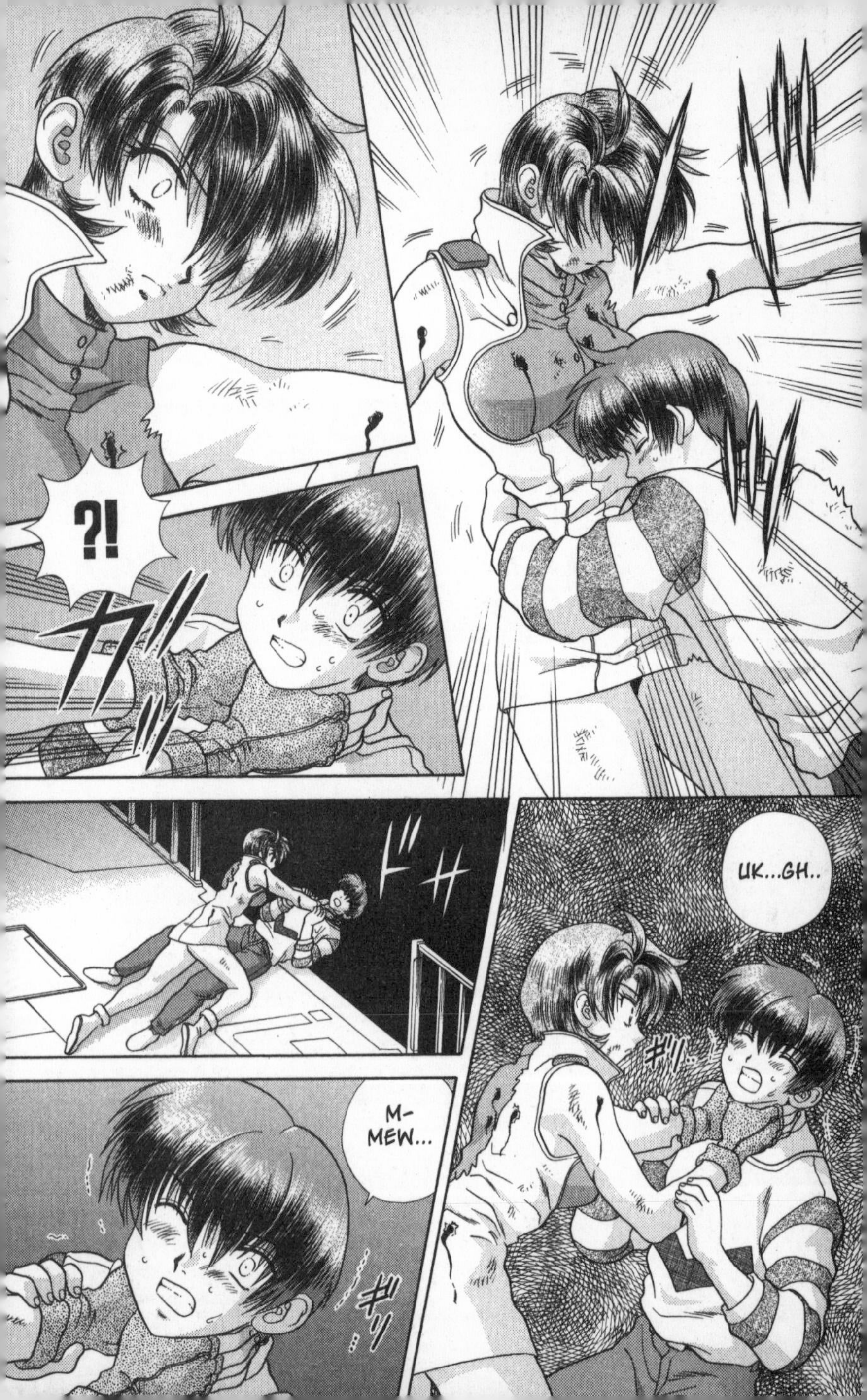
?!
UK...GH..
M-MEW...

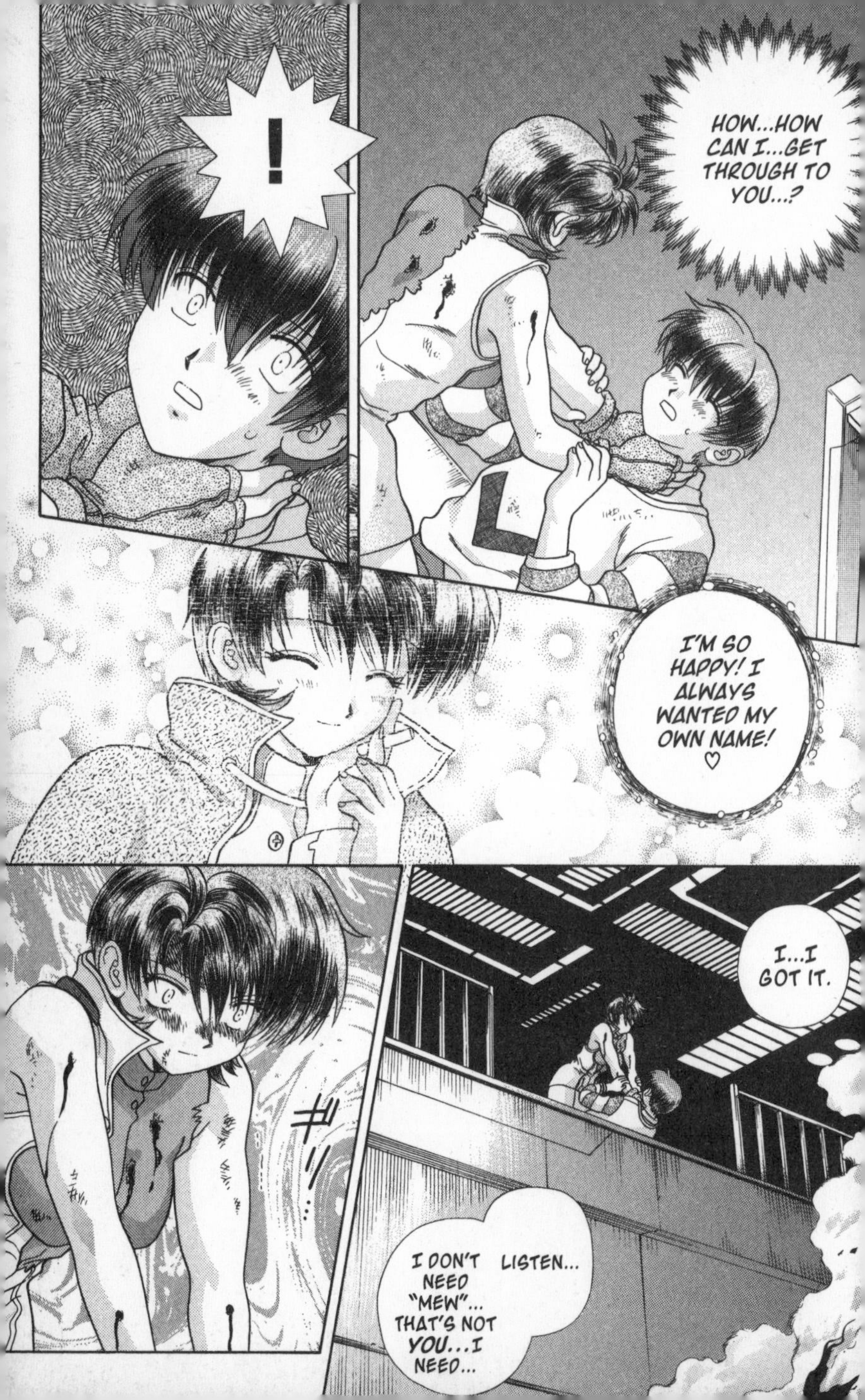
HOW...HOW CAN I...GET THROUGH TO YOU...?
!
I'M SO HAPPY! I ALWAYS WANTED MY OWN NAME! ♡
I...I GOT IT.
LISTEN...
I DON'T NEED "MEW"... THAT'S NOT YOU...I NEED...

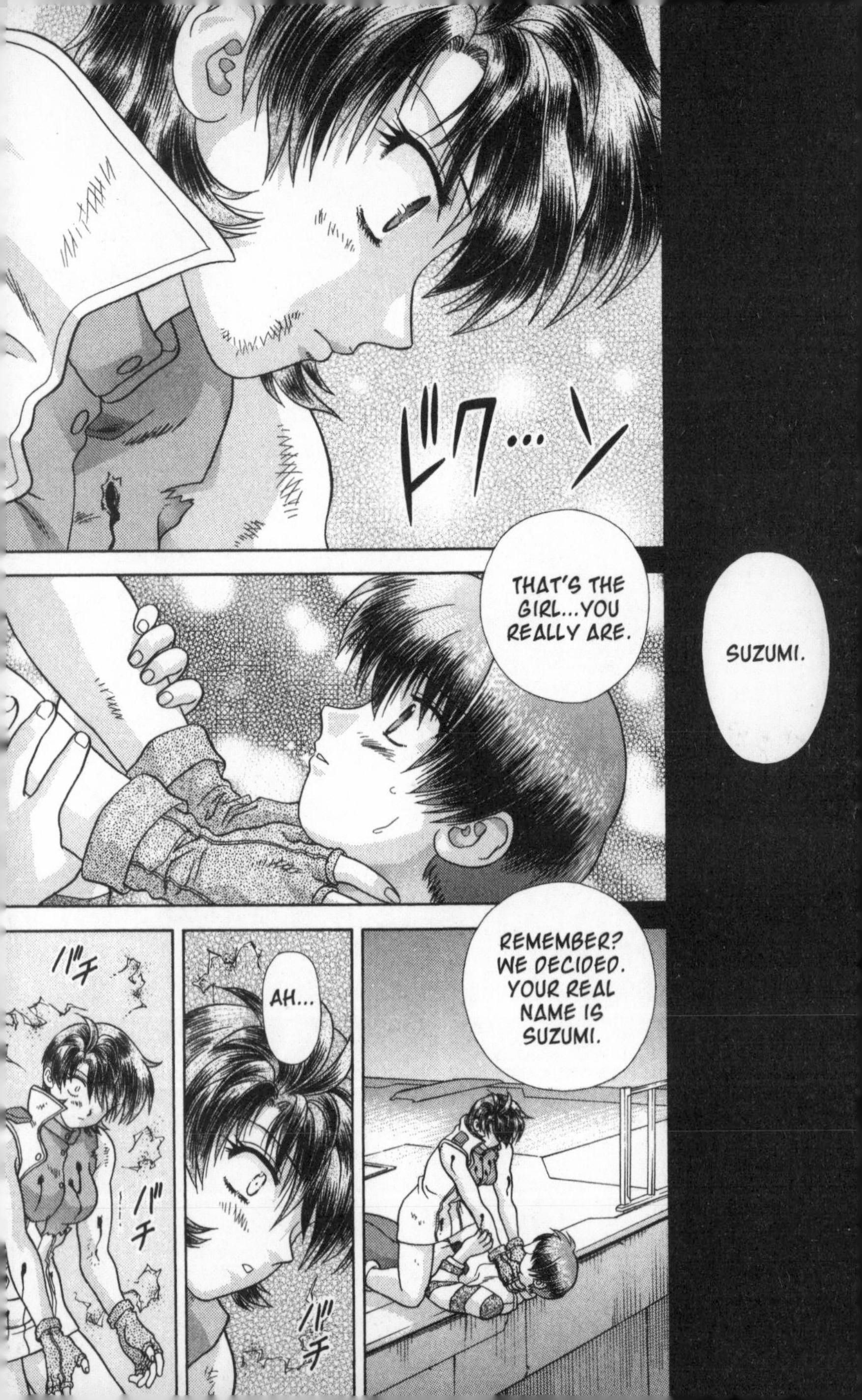
SUZUMI.
ドク…ン
THAT'S THE GIRL...YOU REALLY ARE.
REMEMBER? WE DECIDED. YOUR REAL NAME IS SUZUMI.
AH...
バチ
バチ
バチ

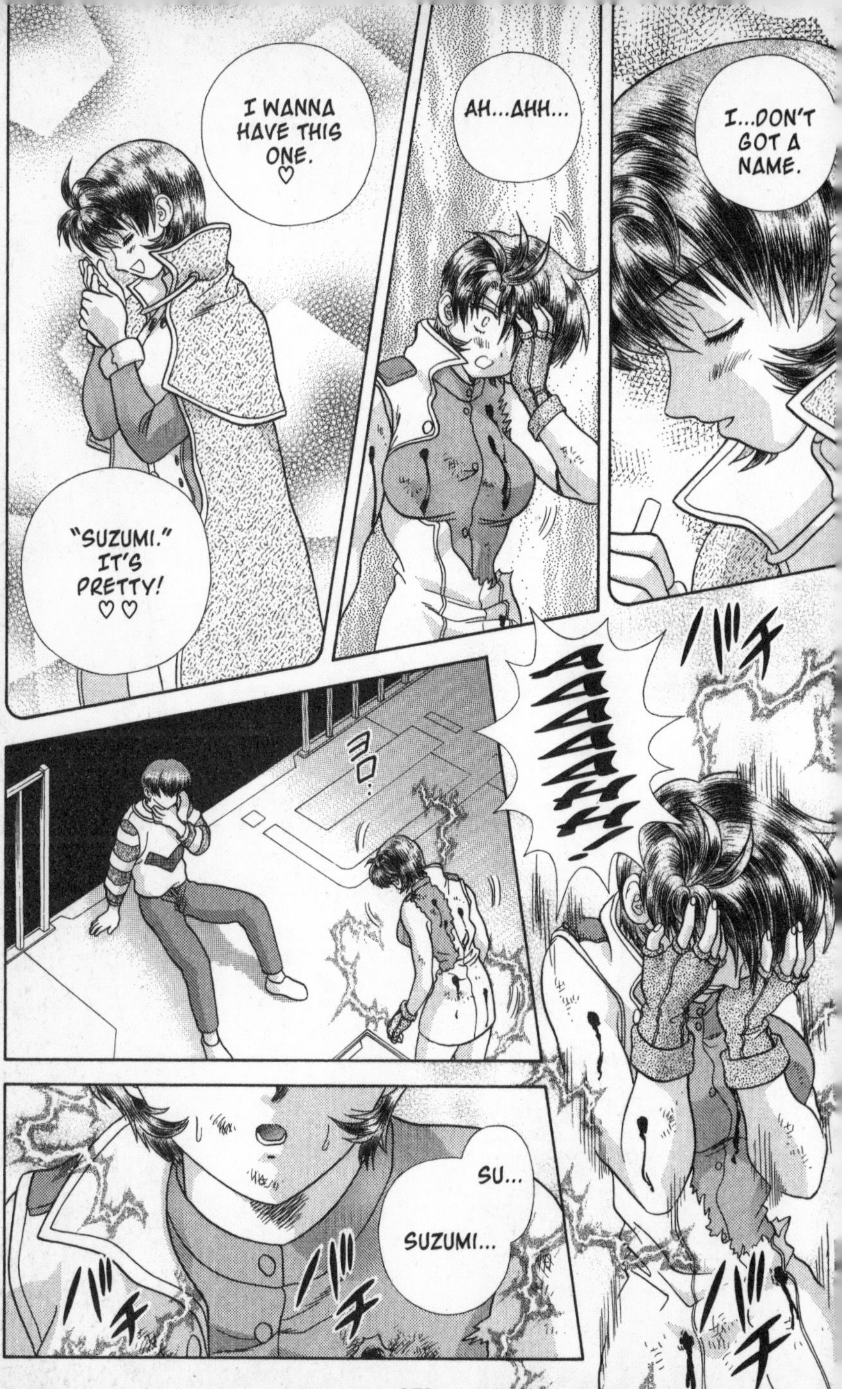
I...DON'T GOT A NAME.
AH...AHH...
I WANNA HAVE THIS ONE. ♡
"SUZUMI." IT'S PRETTY! ♡♡
バチ
AAAAAHH!
バチ
ヨロ...
SU...
SUZUMI...
バチ
バチ

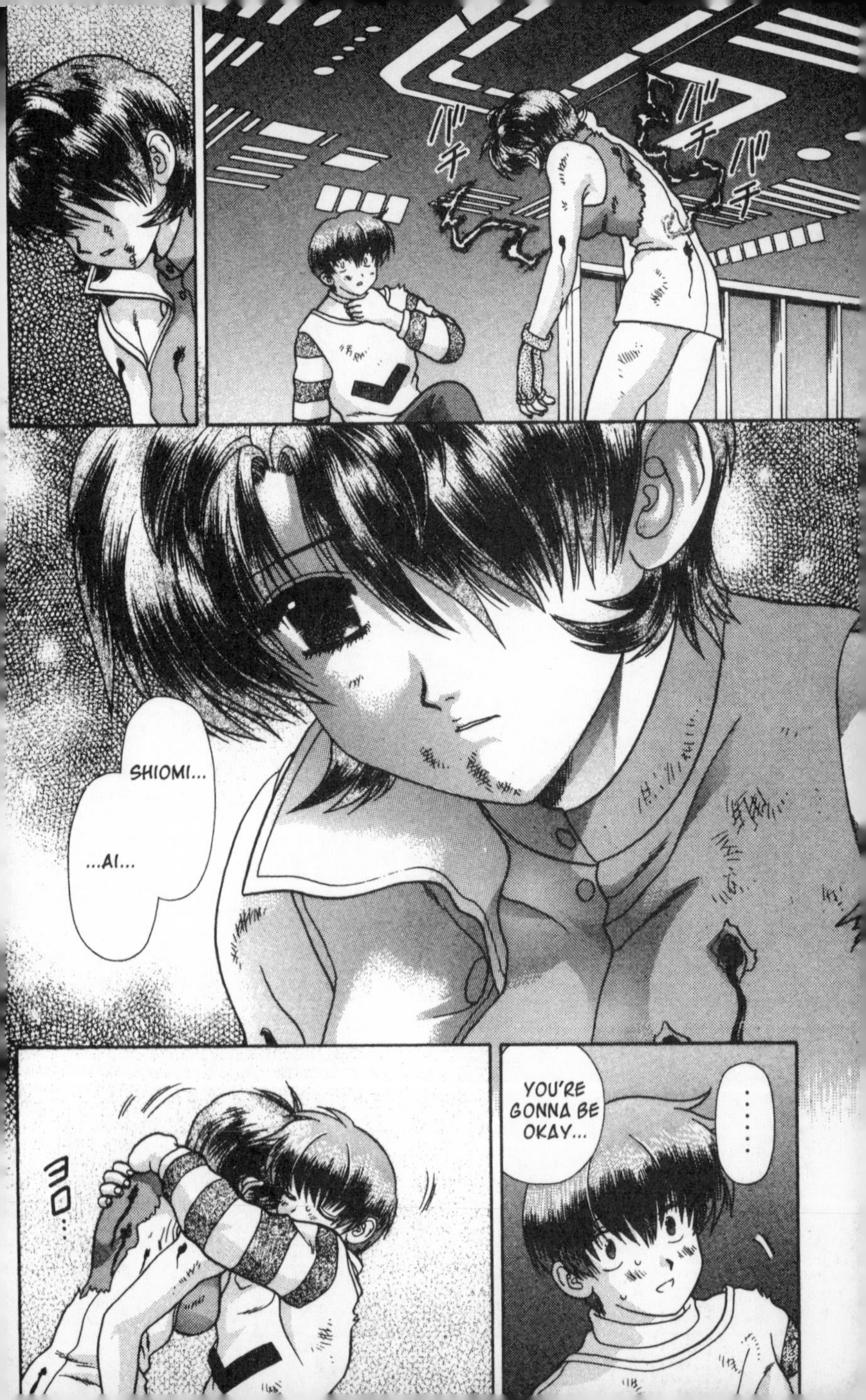

バチ
バチ
SHIOMI...
...AI...
YOU'RE GONNA BE OKAY...
......
ヨロ...

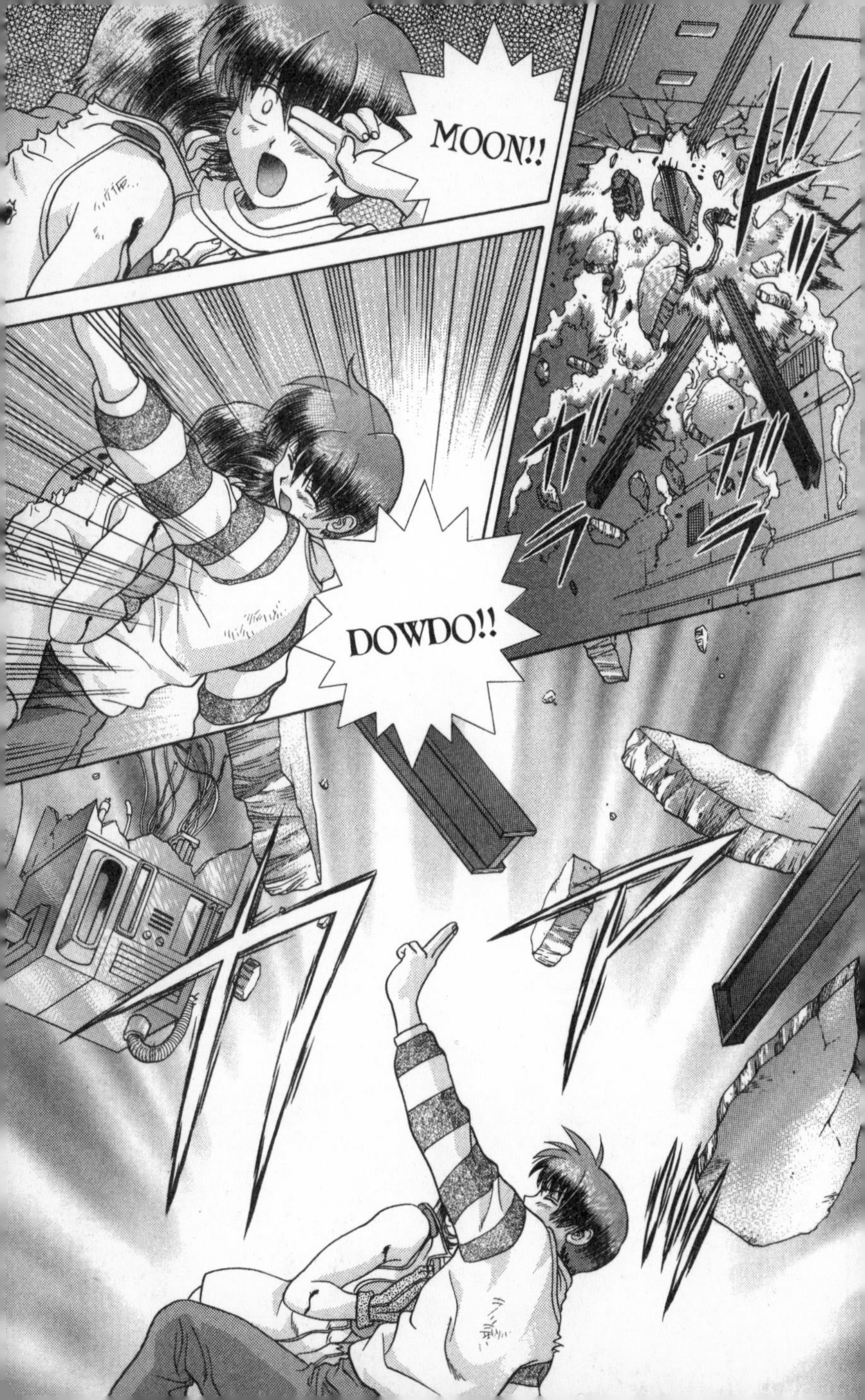
MOON!!
DOWDO!!

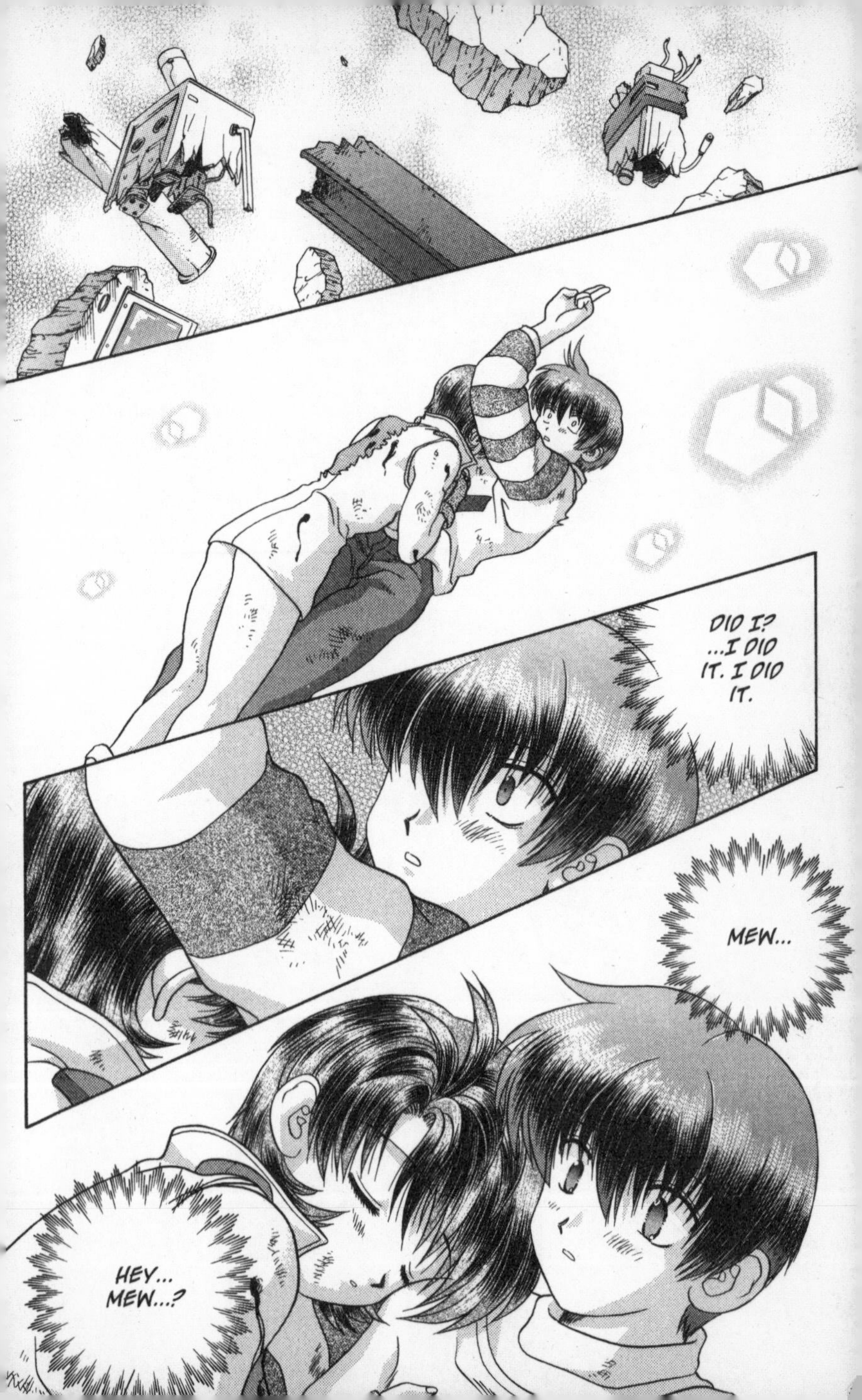
DID I? ...I DID IT. I DID IT.
MEW...
HEY... MEW...?

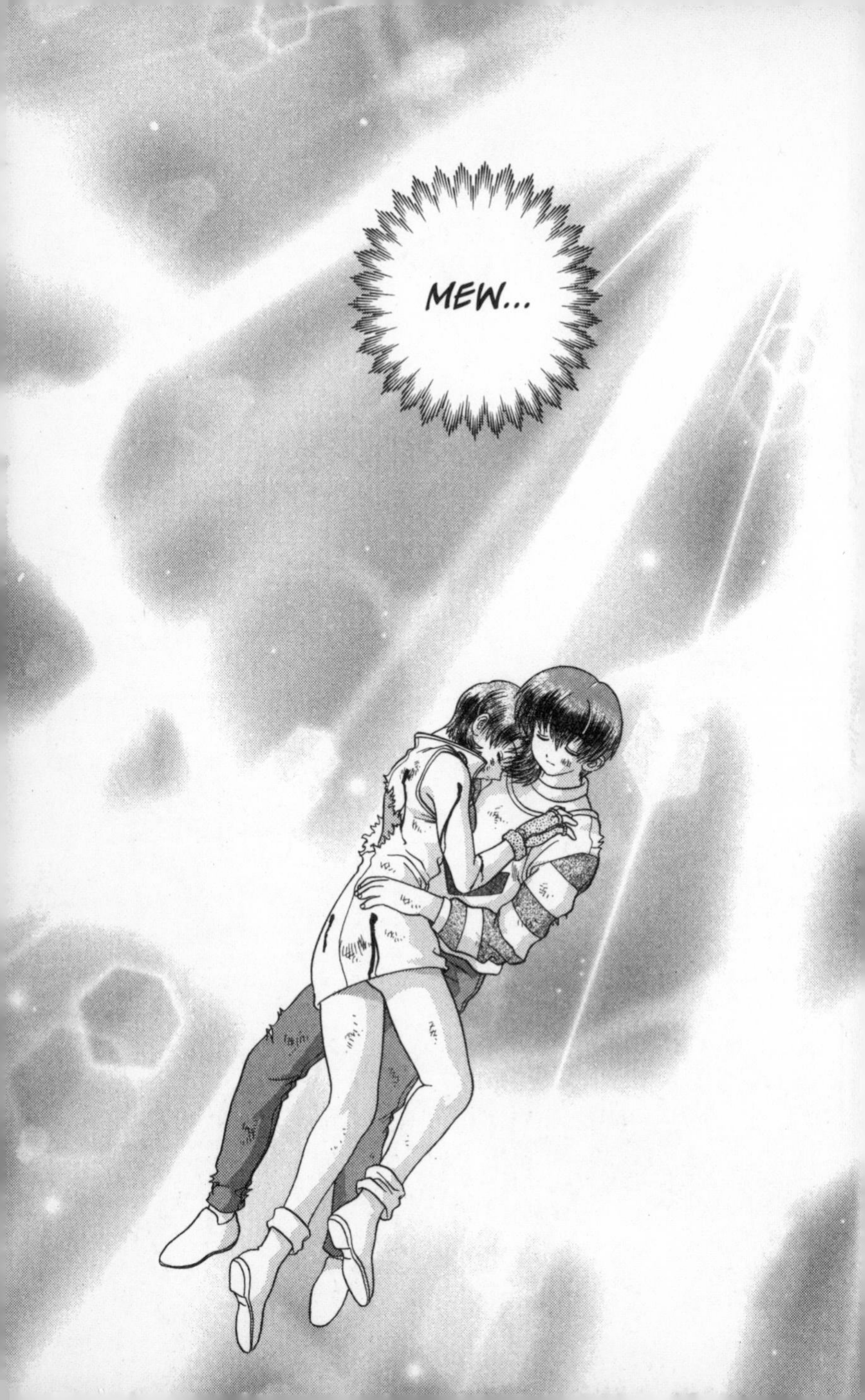
MEW...

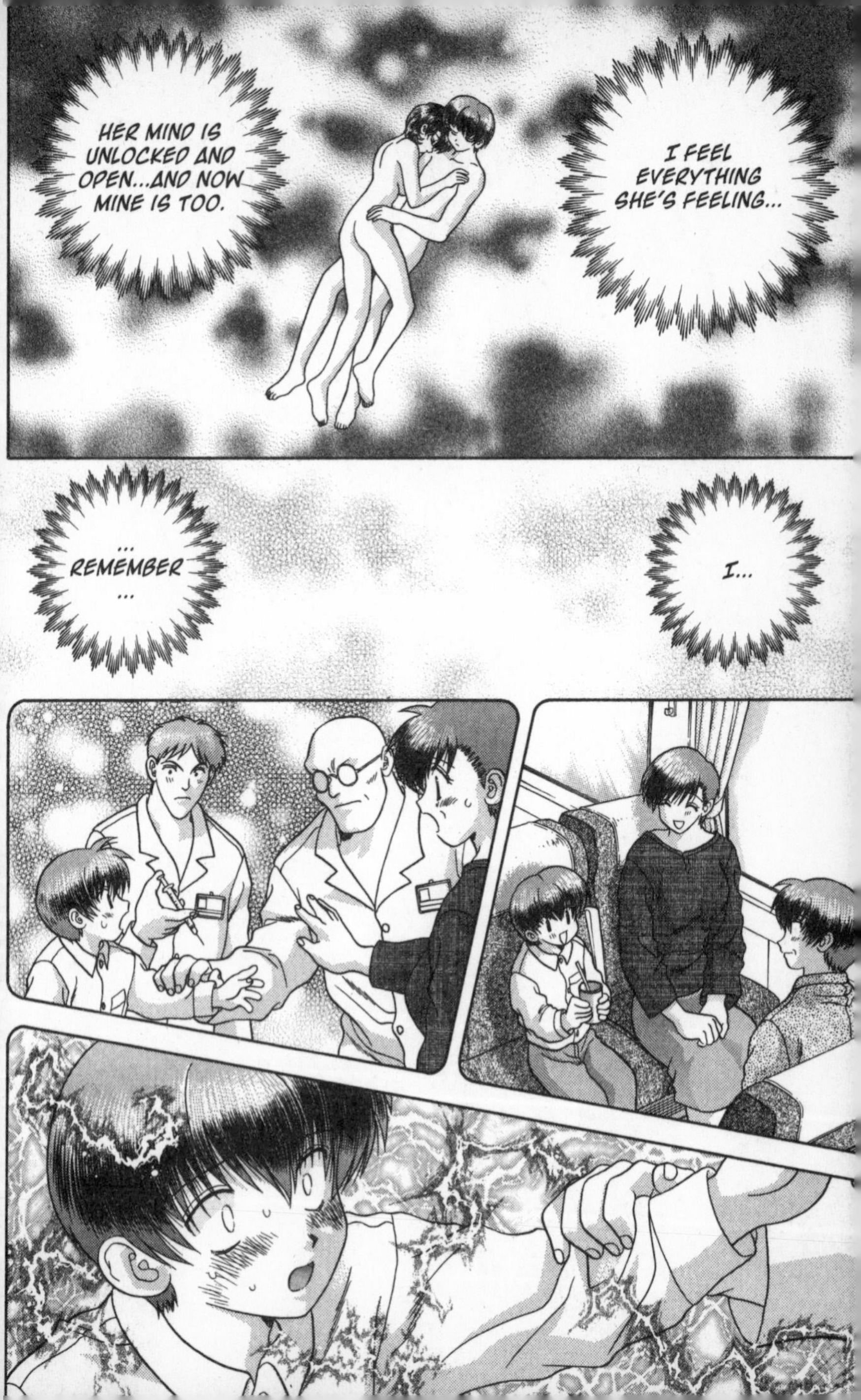
I FEEL EVERYTHING SHE'S FEELING...
HER MIND IS UNLOCKED AND OPEN...AND NOW MINE IS TOO.
I...
...REMEMBER...

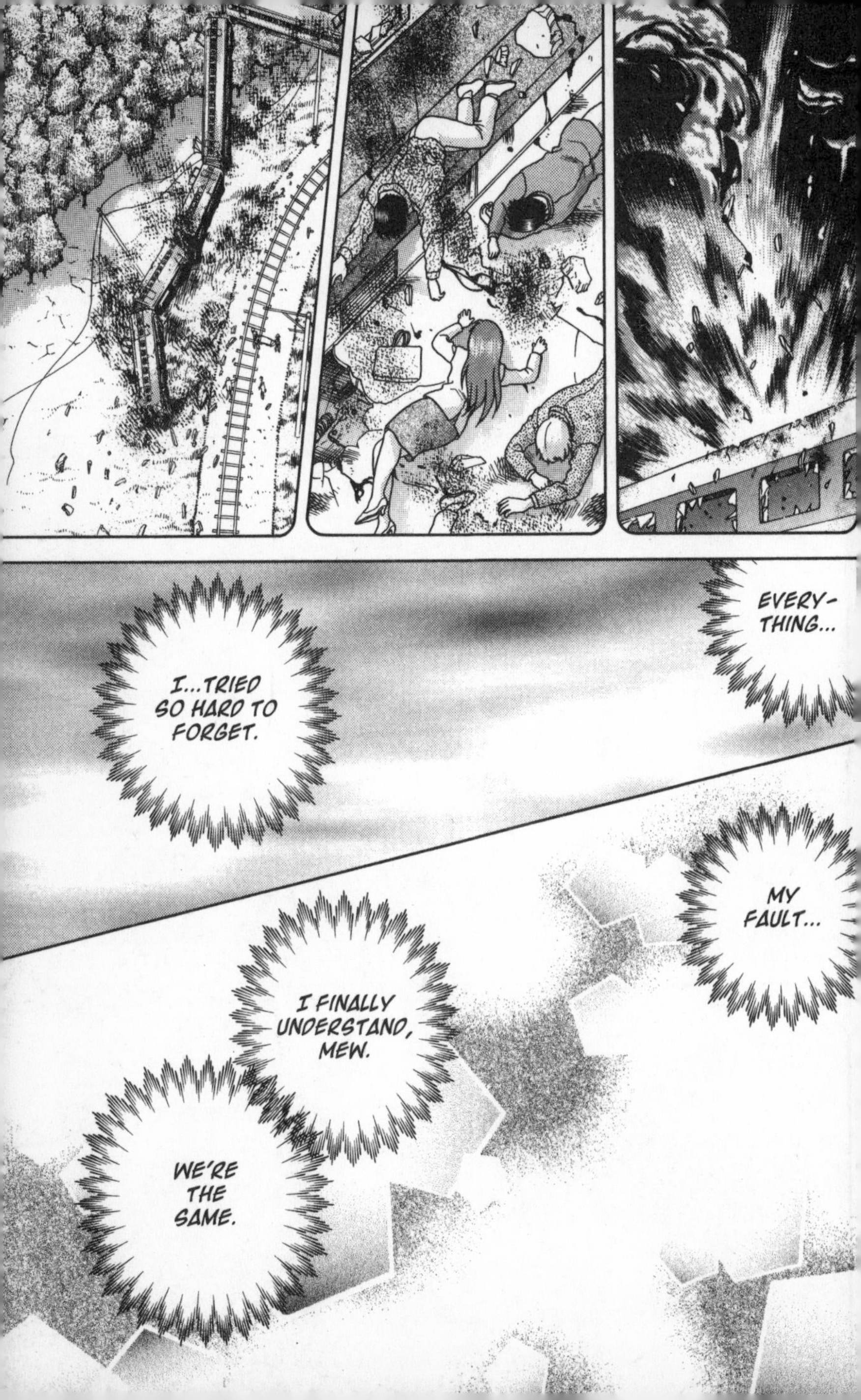
EVERY-THING...
I...TRIED SO HARD TO FORGET.
MY FAULT...
I FINALLY UNDERSTAND, MEW.
WE'RE THE SAME.

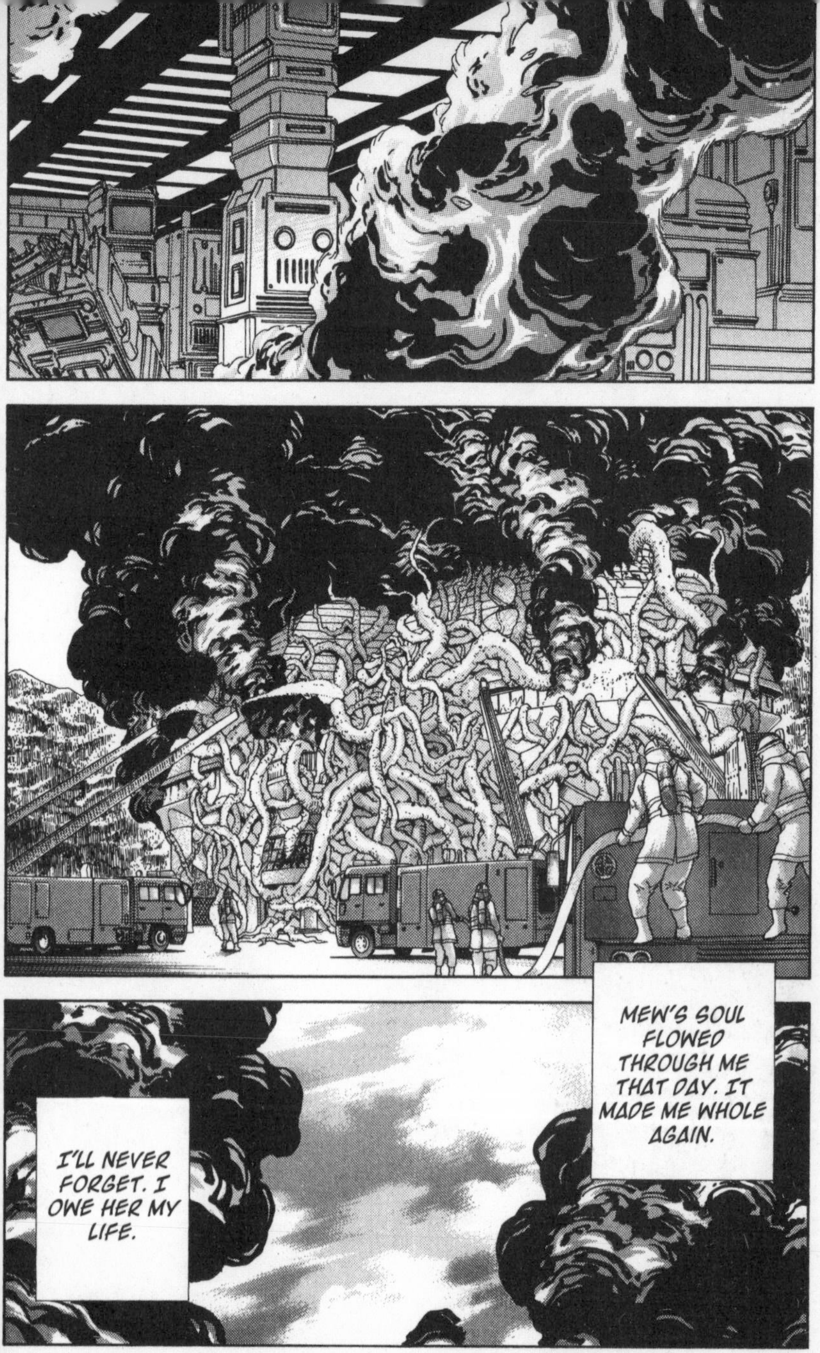
MEW'S SOUL FLOWED THROUGH ME THAT DAY. IT MADE ME WHOLE AGAIN.
I'LL NEVER FORGET. I OWE HER MY LIFE.

Past the Point of No Return **END**

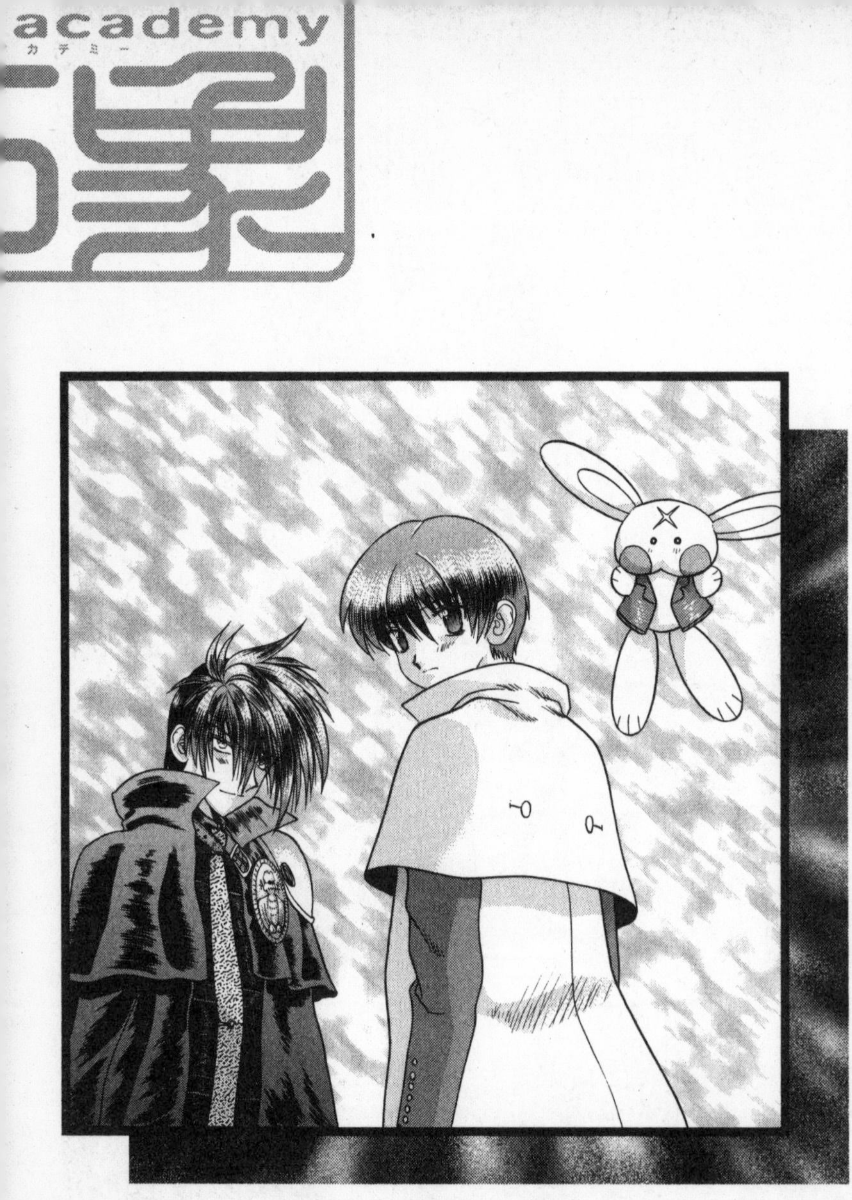

Final Chapter: Into a Brighter Future

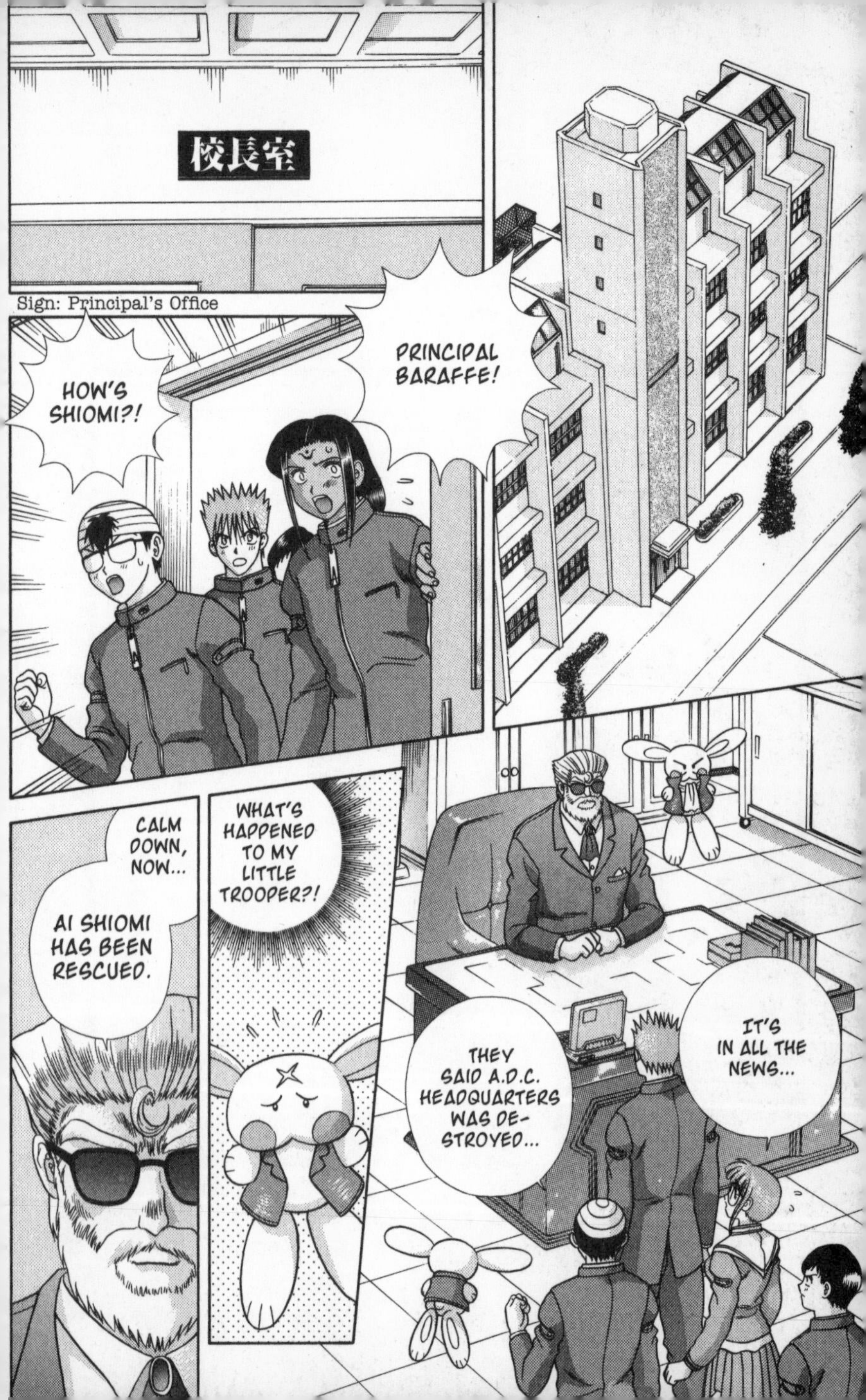

校長室
Sign: Principal's Office
PRINCIPAL BARAFFE!
HOW'S SHIOMI?!
IT'S IN ALL THE NEWS...
THEY SAID A.D.C. HEADQUARTERS WAS DE-STROYED...
WHAT'S HAPPENED TO MY LITTLE TROOPER?!
CALM DOWN, NOW...
AI SHIOMI HAS BEEN RESCUED.

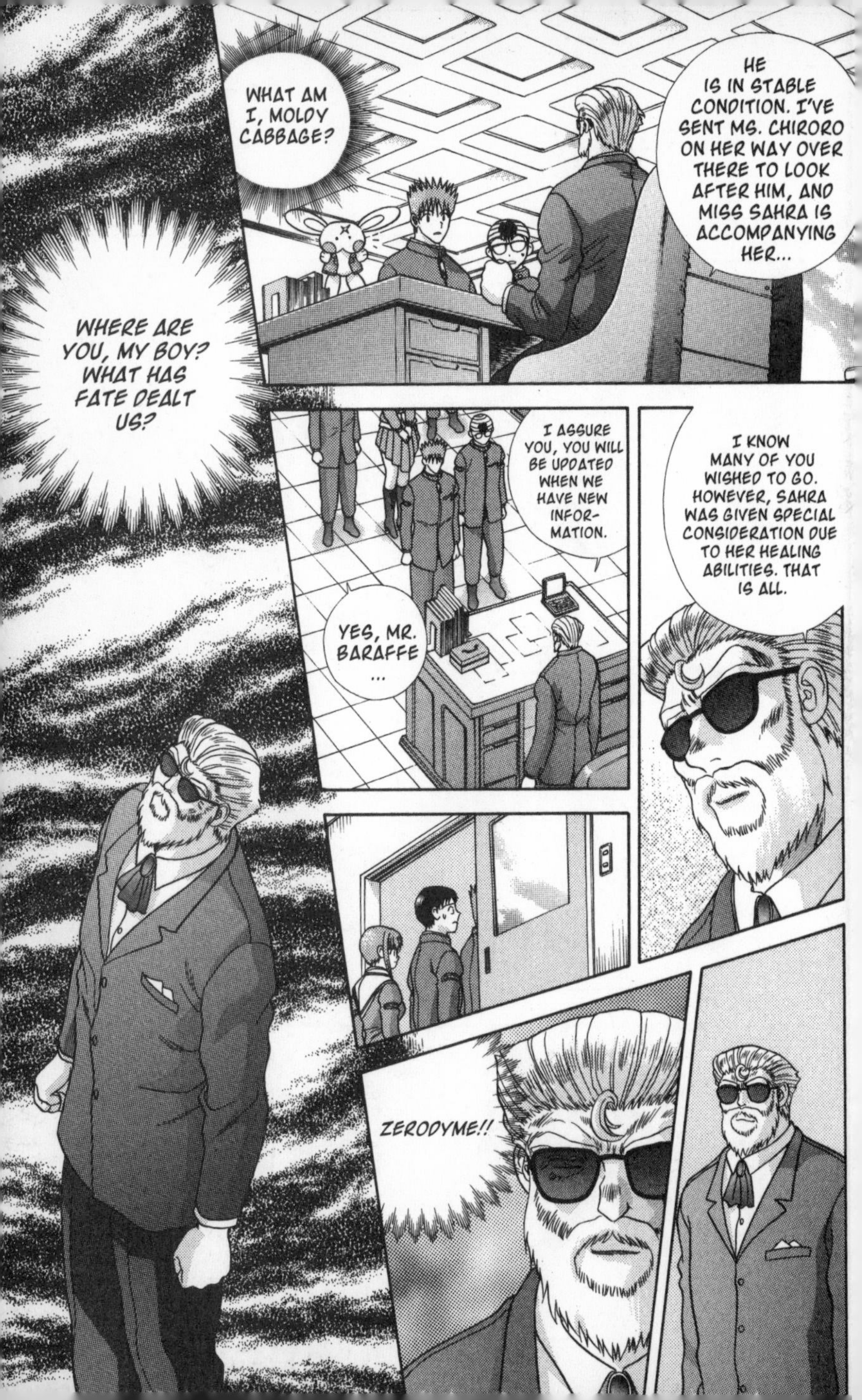
HE IS IN STABLE CONDITION. I'VE SENT MS. CHIRORO ON HER WAY OVER THERE TO LOOK AFTER HIM, AND MISS SAHRA IS ACCOMPANYING HER...
WHAT AM I, MOLDY CABBAGE?
I KNOW MANY OF YOU WISHED TO GO. HOWEVER, SAHRA WAS GIVEN SPECIAL CONSIDERATION DUE TO HER HEALING ABILITIES. THAT IS ALL.
I ASSURE YOU, YOU WILL BE UPDATED WHEN WE HAVE NEW INFOR-MATION.
YES, MR. BARAFFE ...
ZERODYME!!
WHERE ARE YOU, MY BOY? WHAT HAS FATE DEALT US?

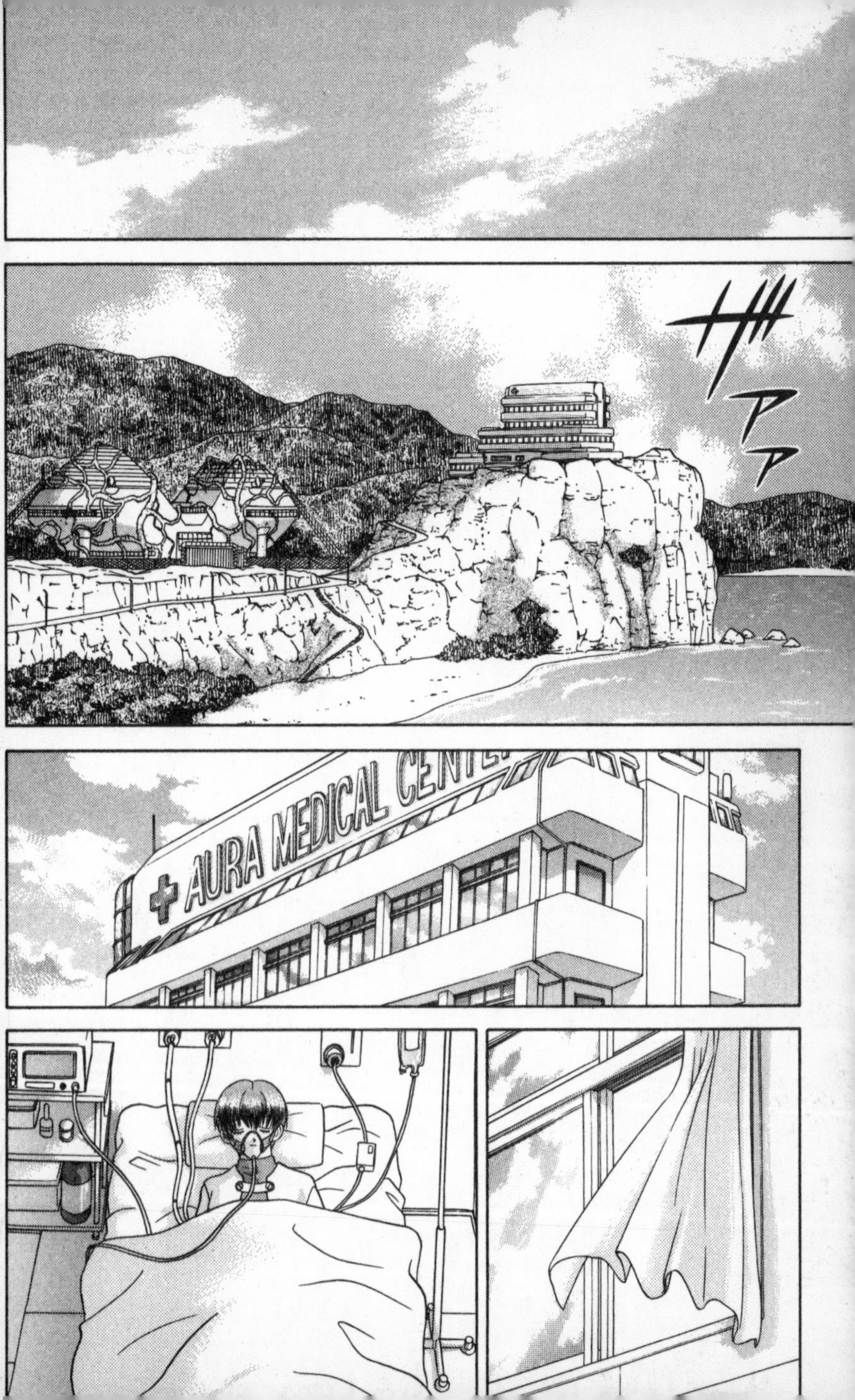
ザァァ
AURA MEDICAL CENTE

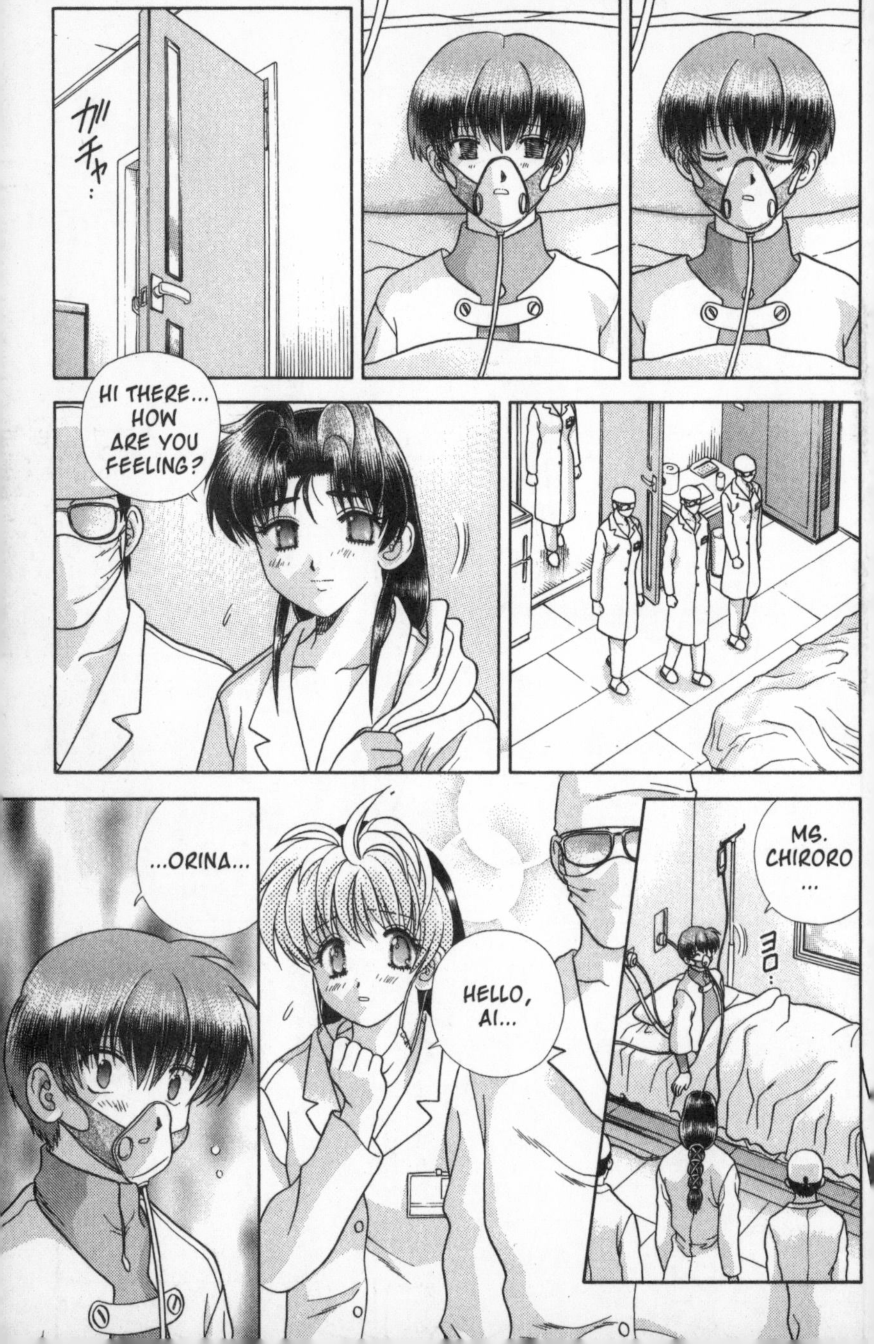
ガチャ…
HI THERE... HOW ARE YOU FEELING?
MS. CHIRORO ...
ヨロ…
HELLO, AI...
...ORINA...

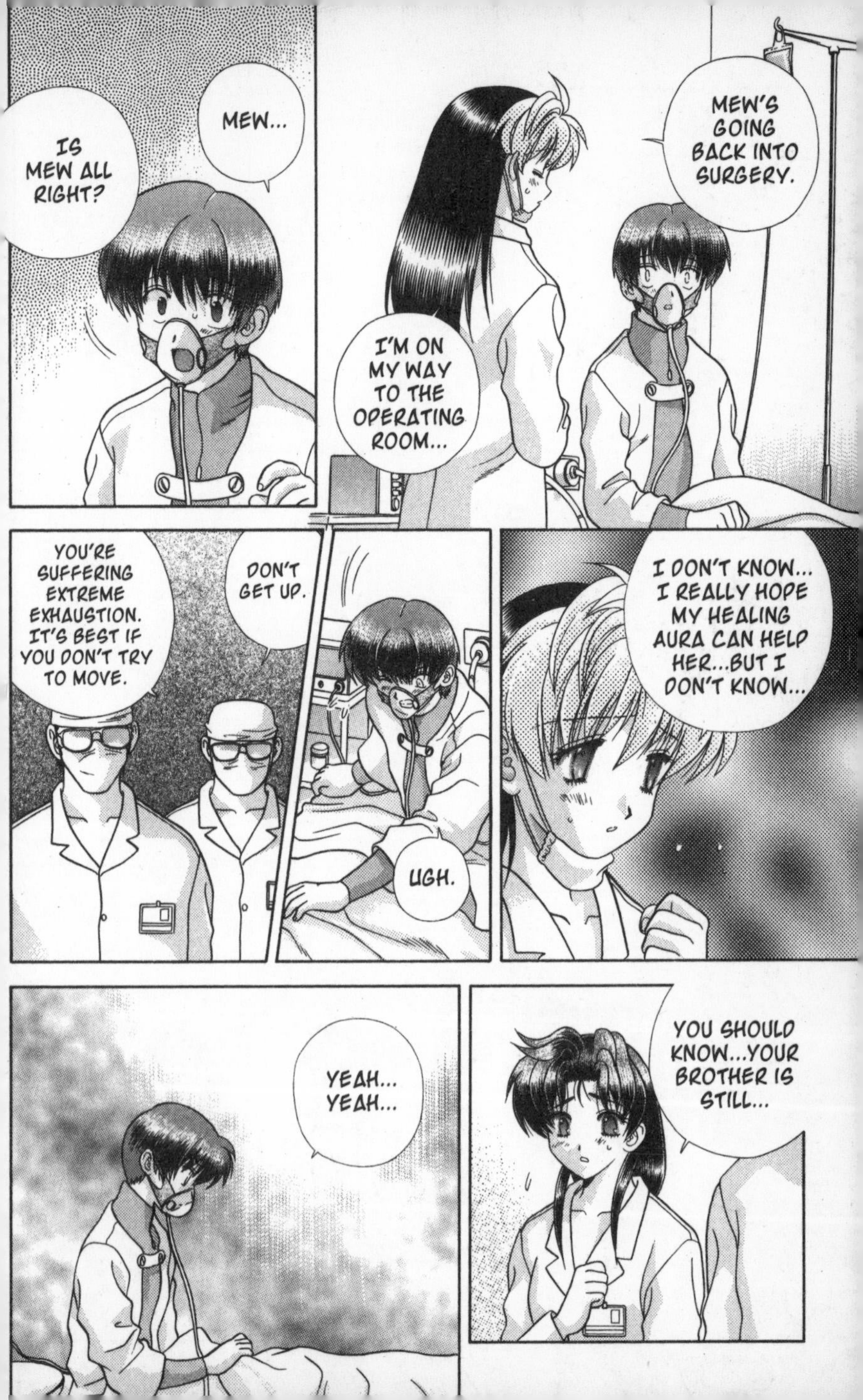
MEW'S GOING BACK INTO SURGERY.
I'M ON MY WAY TO THE OPERATING ROOM...
MEW...
IS MEW ALL RIGHT?
I DON'T KNOW... I REALLY HOPE MY HEALING AURA CAN HELP HER...BUT I DON'T KNOW...
UGH.
DON'T GET UP.
YOU'RE SUFFERING EXTREME EXHAUSTION. IT'S BEST IF YOU DON'T TRY TO MOVE.
YOU SHOULD KNOW...YOUR BROTHER IS STILL...
YEAH... YEAH...

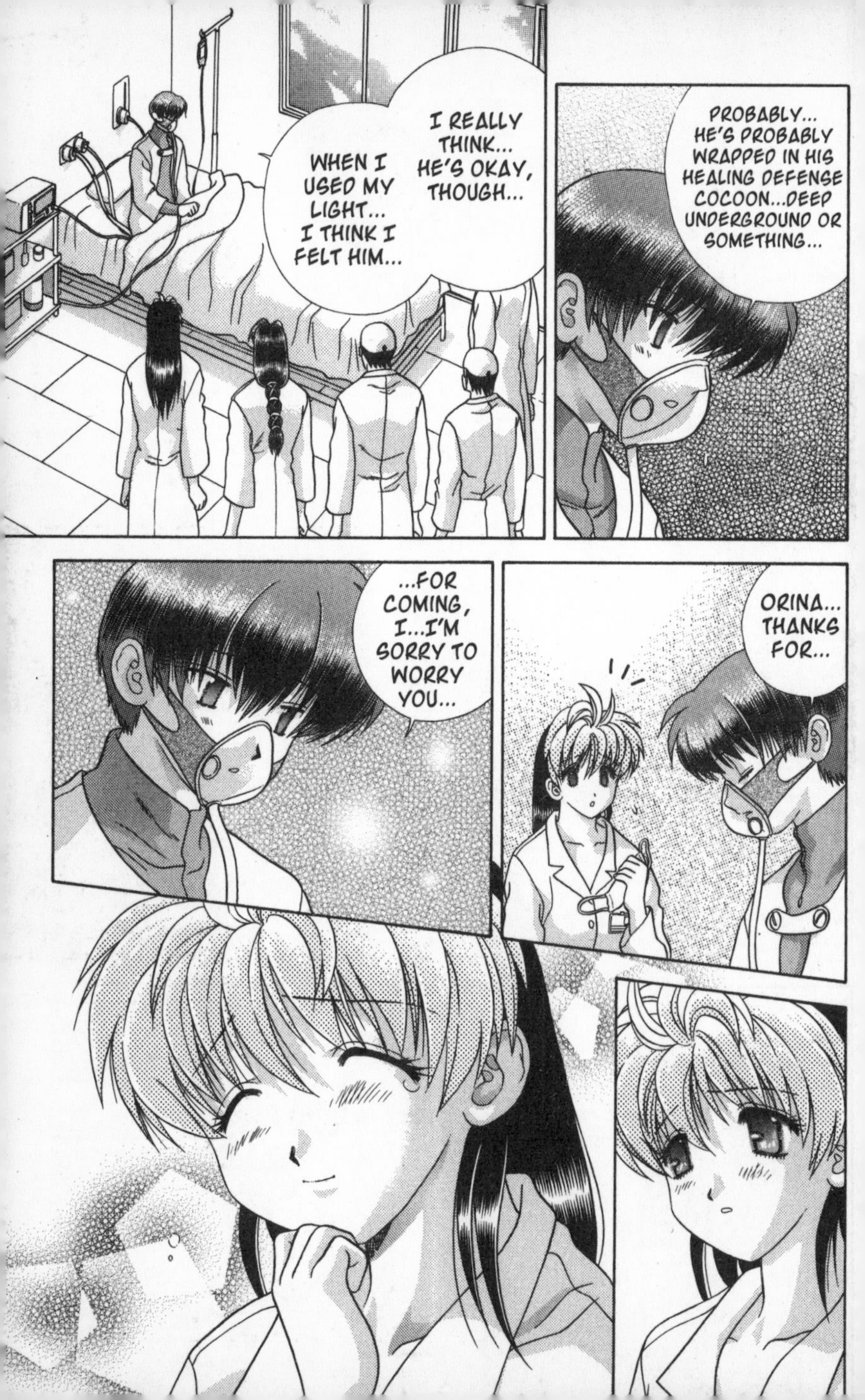
PROBABLY... HE'S PROBABLY WRAPPED IN HIS HEALING DEFENSE COCOON...DEEP UNDERGROUND OR SOMETHING...
I REALLY THINK... HE'S OKAY, THOUGH...
WHEN I USED MY LIGHT... I THINK I FELT HIM...
ORINA... THANKS FOR...
...FOR COMING, I...I'M SORRY TO WORRY YOU...

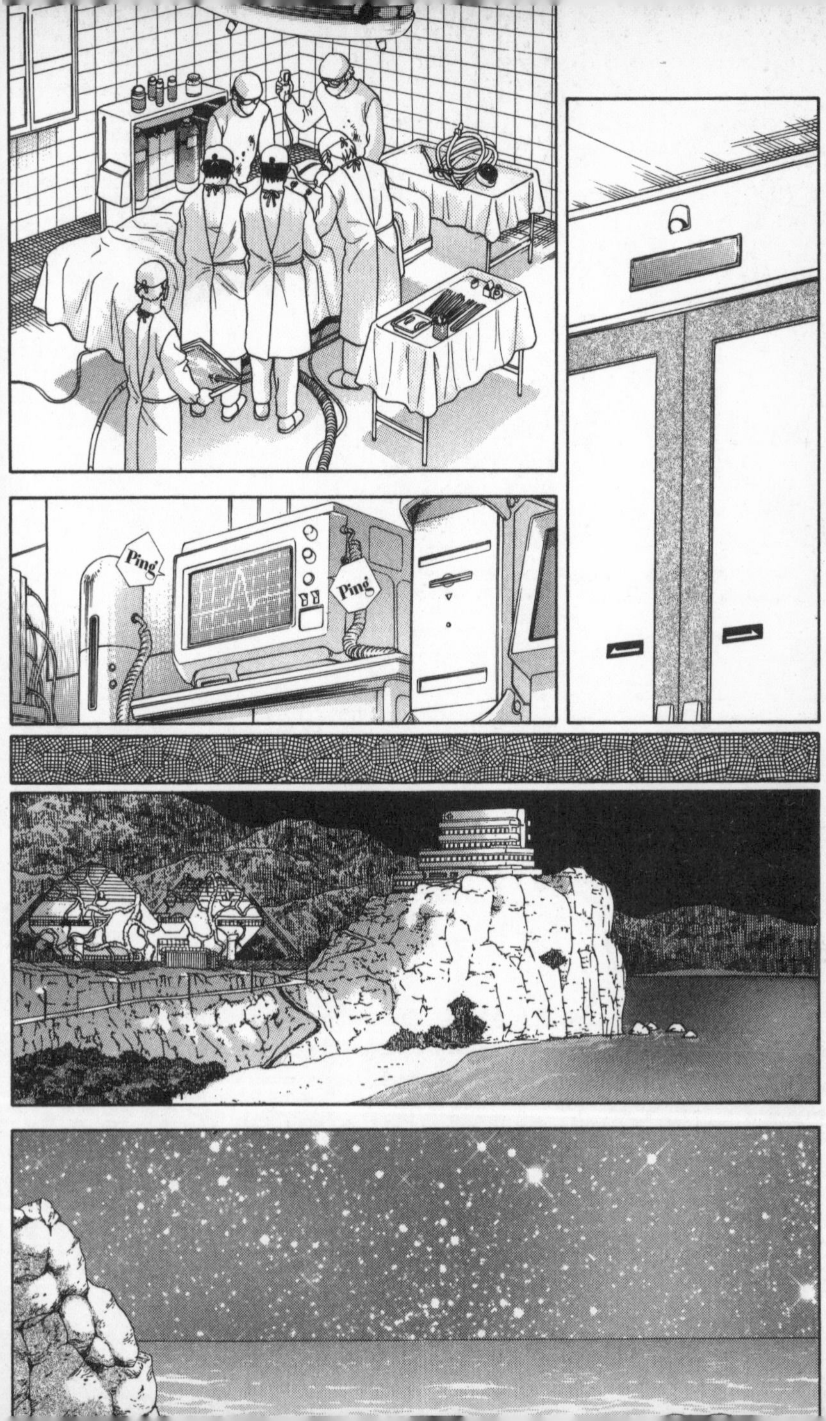
Ping
Ping

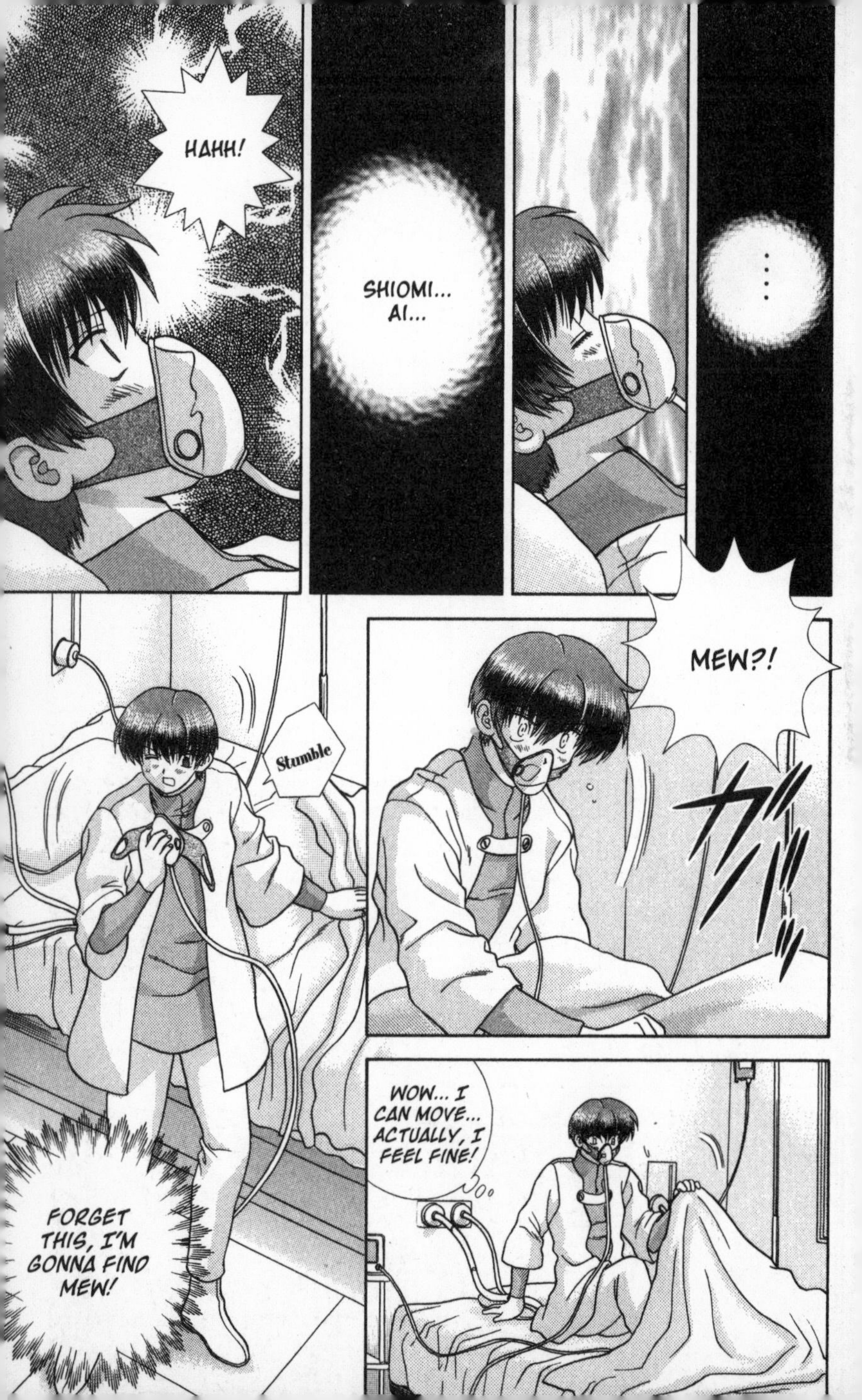
....
SHIOMI... AI...
HAHH!
MEW?!
WOW... I CAN MOVE... ACTUALLY, I FEEL FINE!
Stumble
FORGET THIS, I'M GONNA FIND MEW!

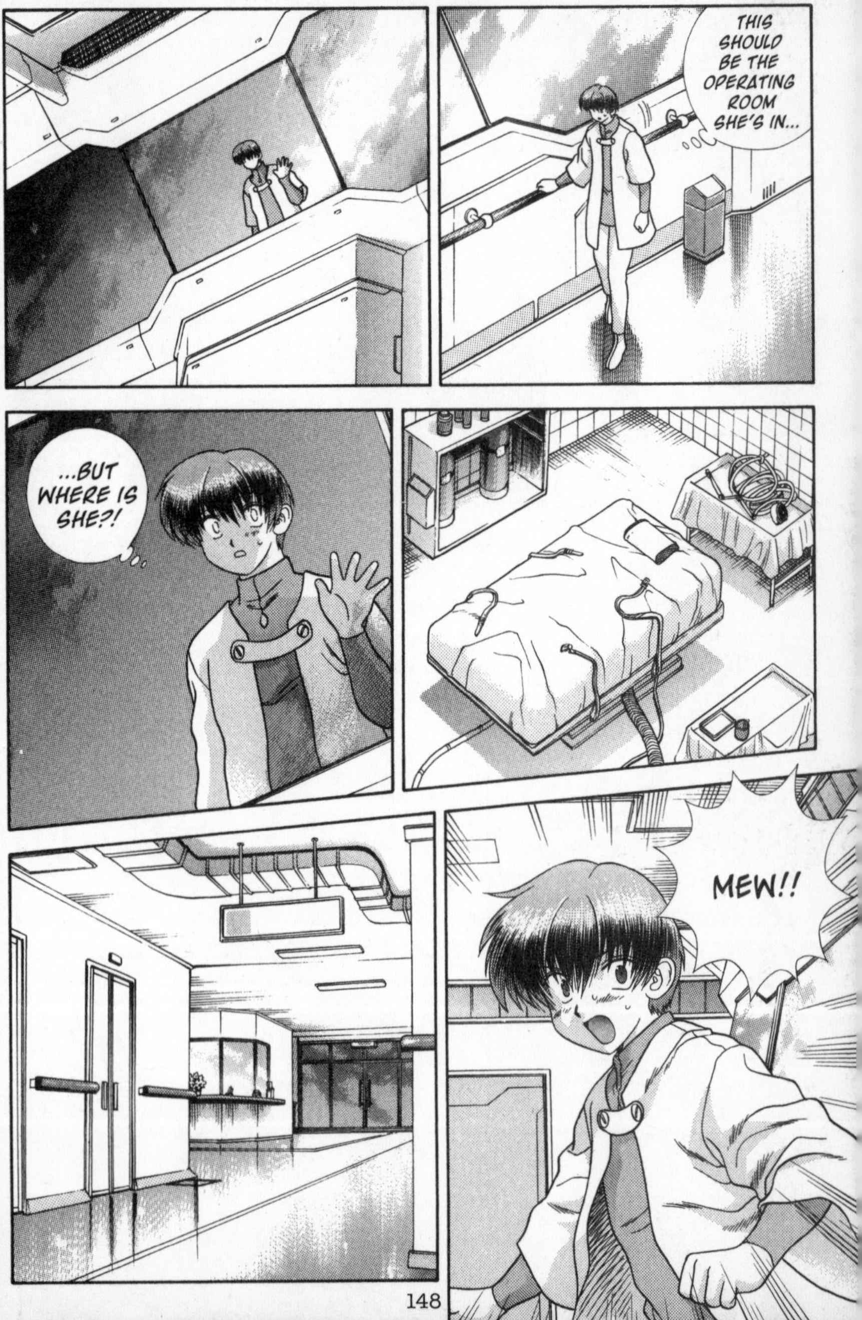
THIS SHOULD BE THE OPERATING ROOM SHE'S IN...
...BUT WHERE IS SHE?!
MEW!!

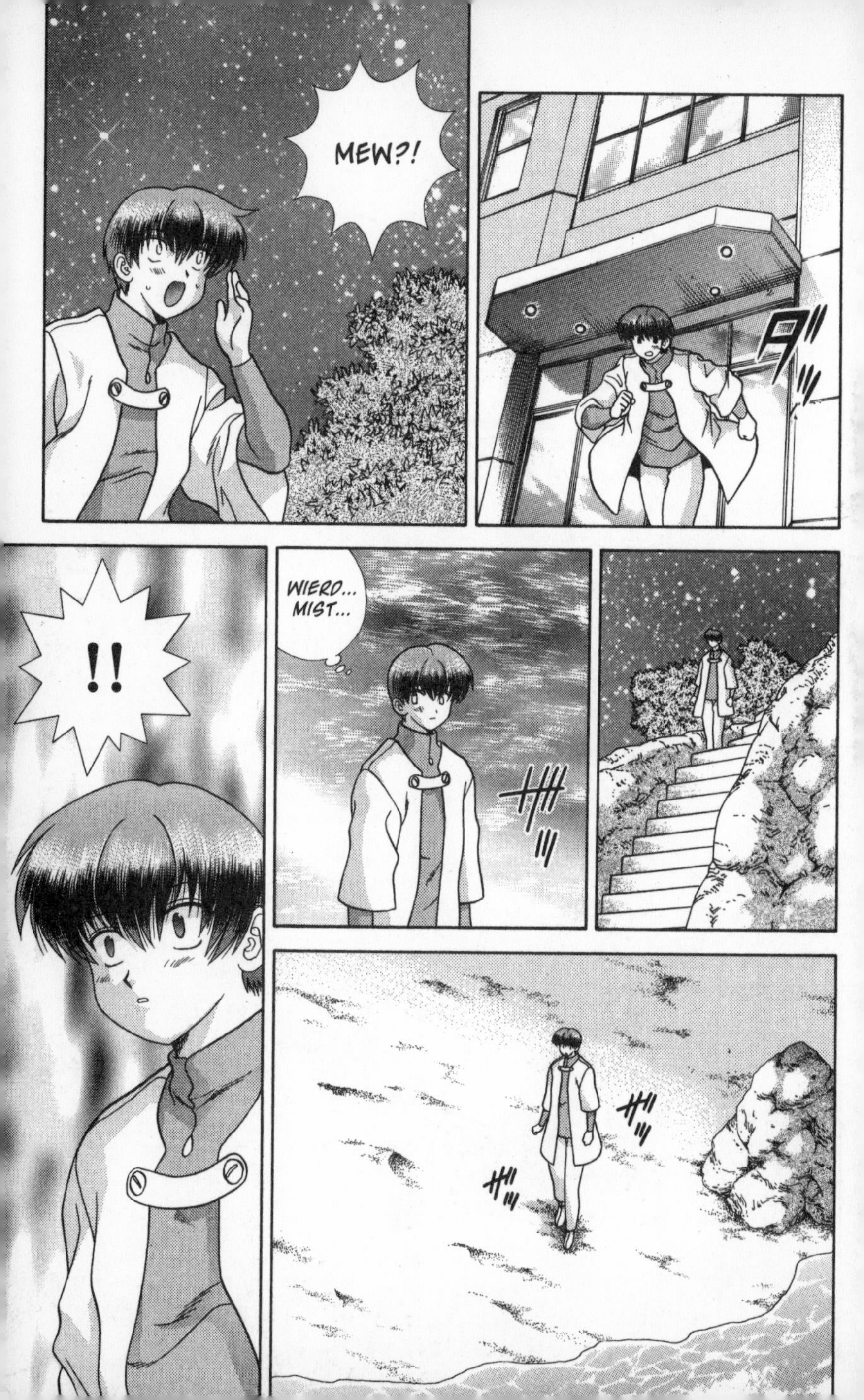
MEW?!
WIERD... MIST...
!!

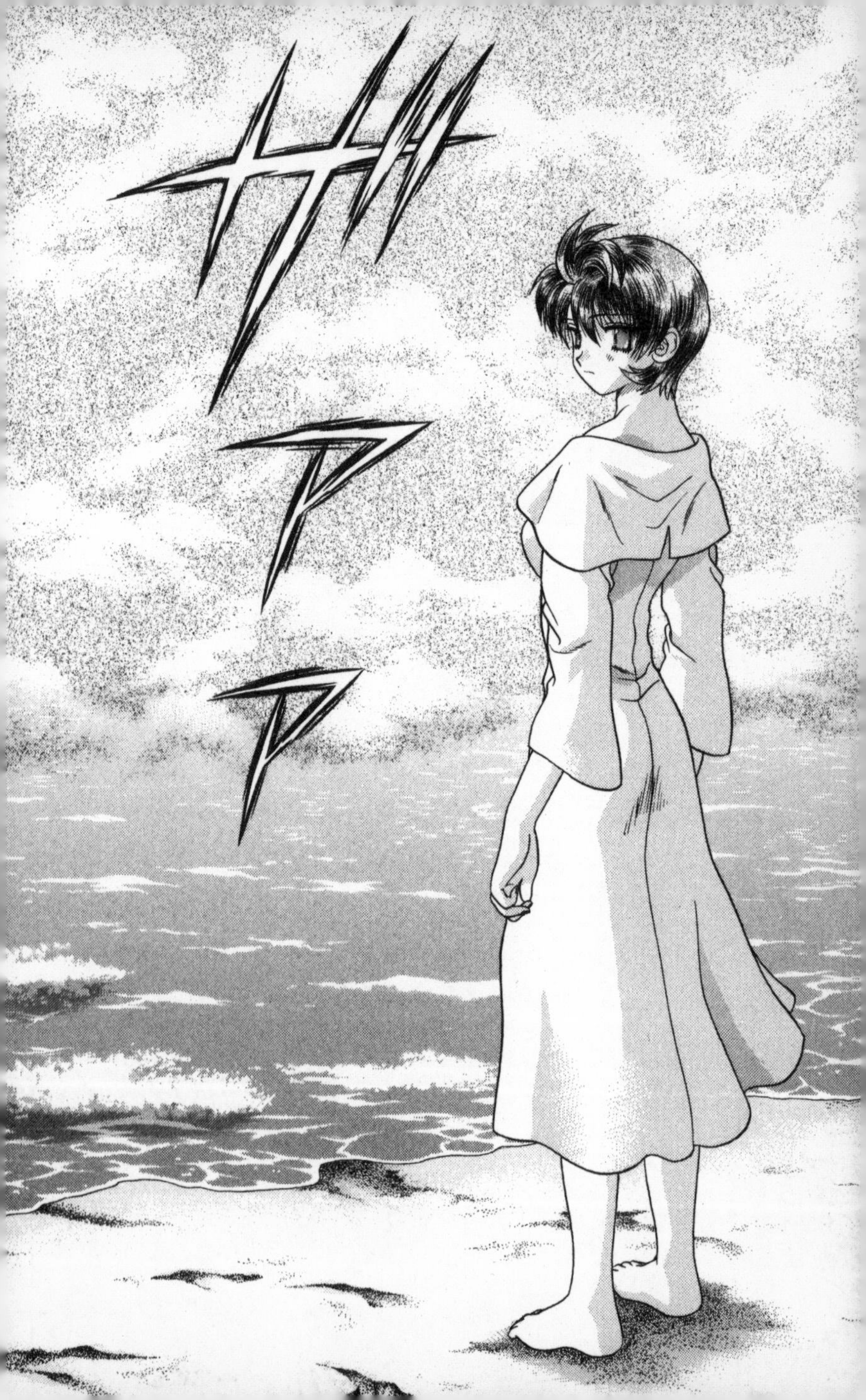
ザアア

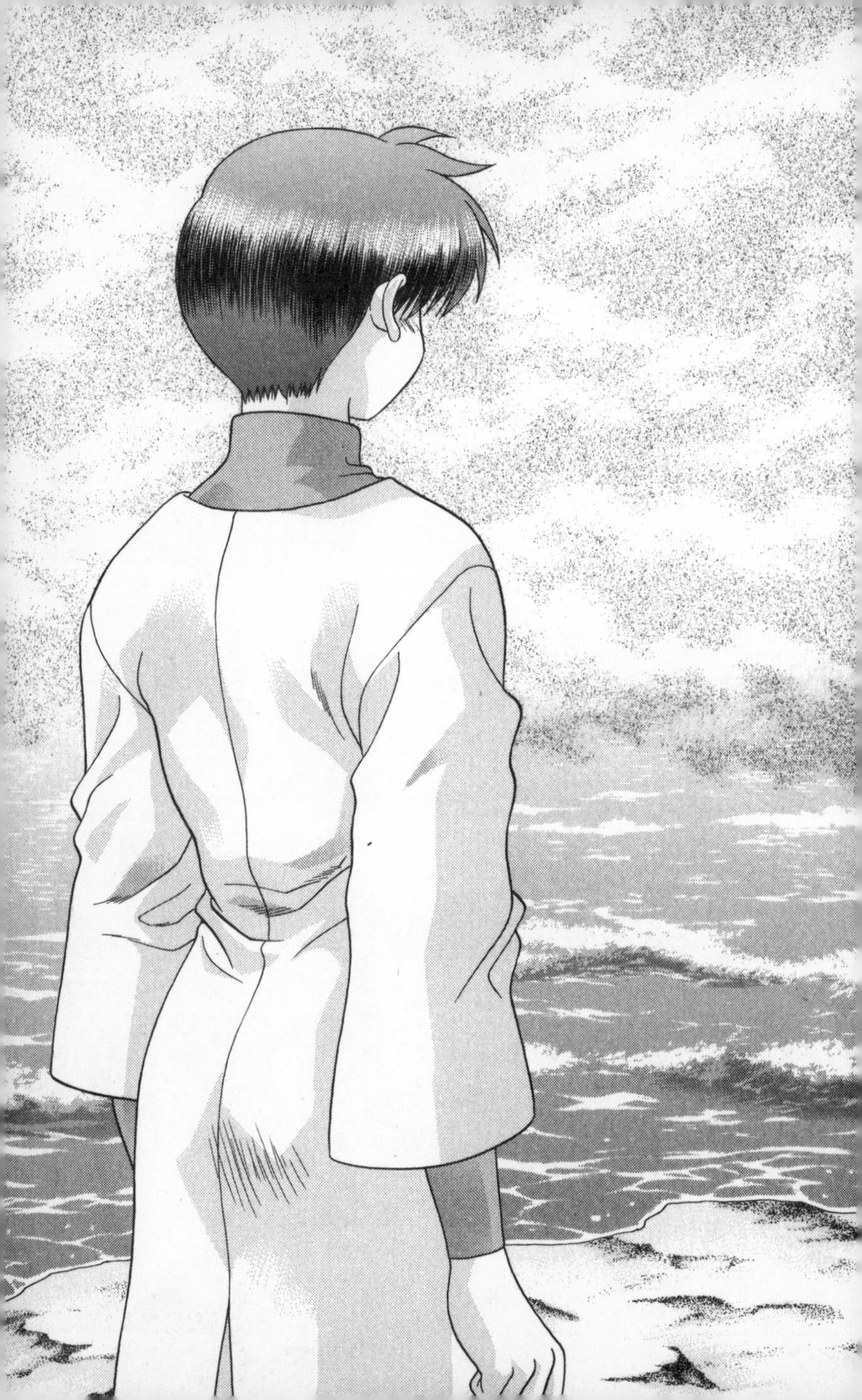

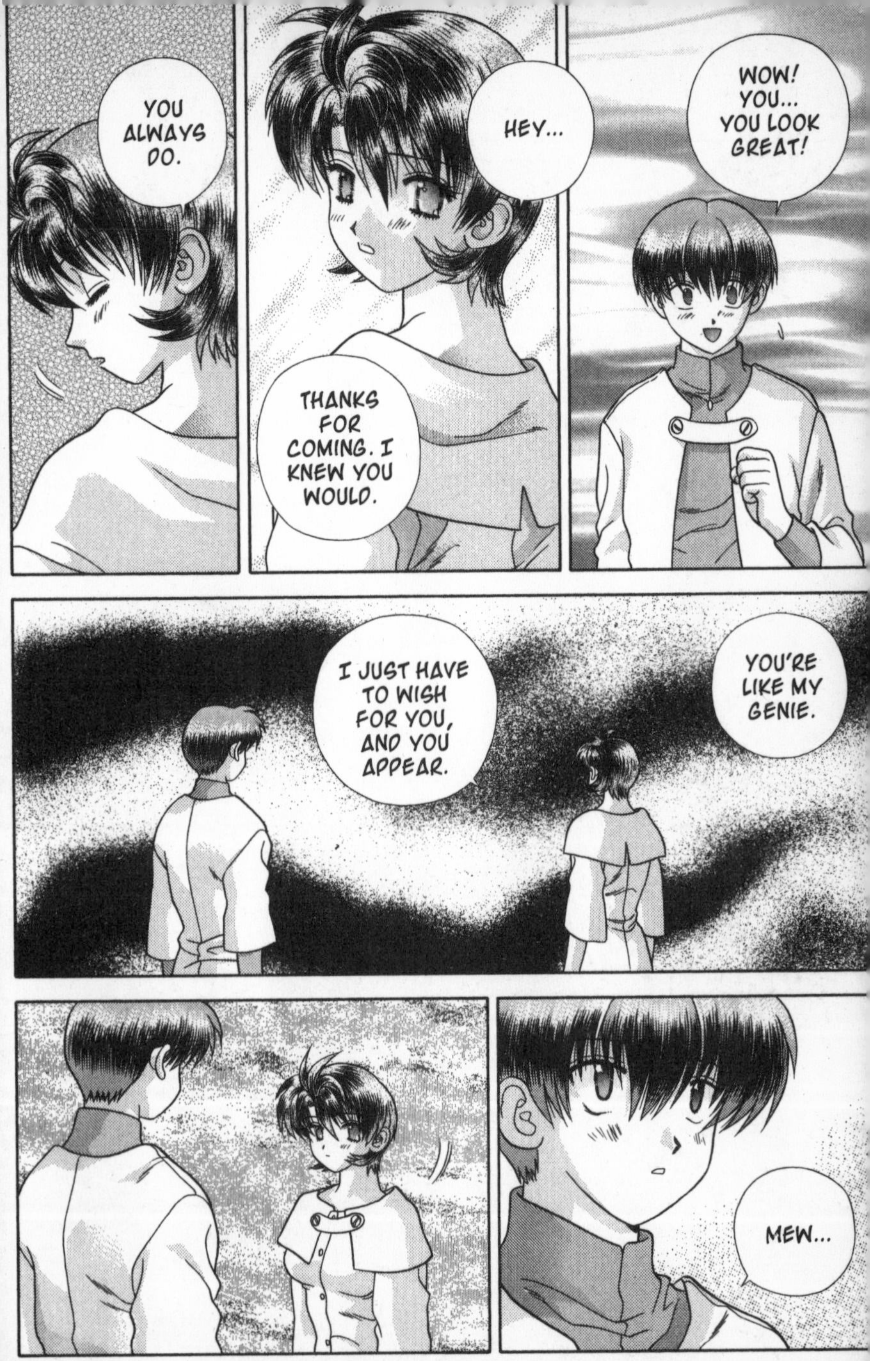
WOW! YOU... YOU LOOK GREAT!
HEY...
THANKS FOR COMING. I KNEW YOU WOULD.
YOU ALWAYS DO.
YOU'RE LIKE MY GENIE.
I JUST HAVE TO WISH FOR YOU, AND YOU APPEAR.
MEW...

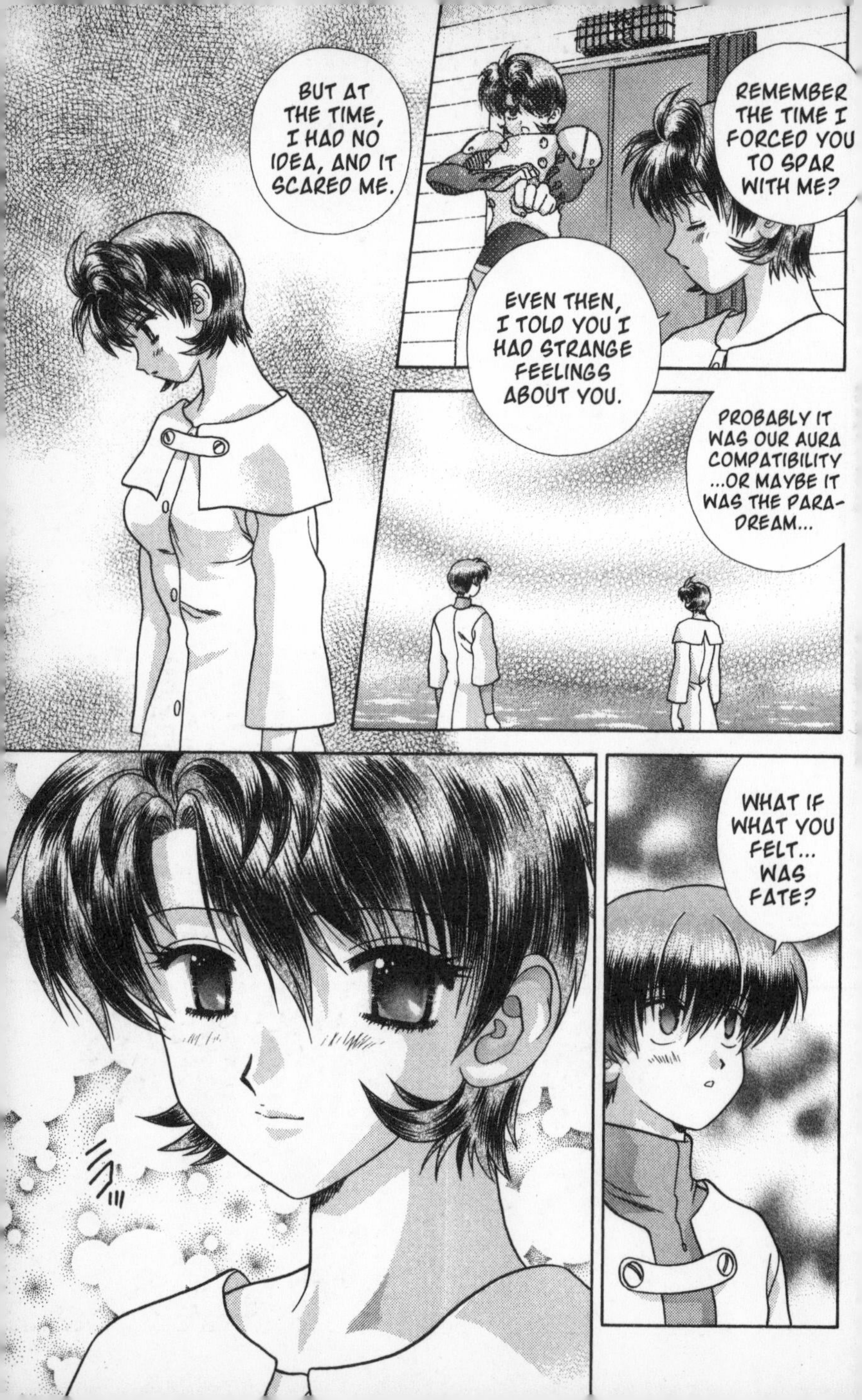
REMEMBER THE TIME I FORCED YOU TO SPAR WITH ME?
EVEN THEN, I TOLD YOU I HAD STRANGE FEELINGS ABOUT YOU.
PROBABLY IT WAS OUR AURA COMPATIBILITY ...OR MAYBE IT WAS THE PARA-DREAM...
BUT AT THE TIME, I HAD NO IDEA, AND IT SCARED ME.
WHAT IF WHAT YOU FELT... WAS FATE?

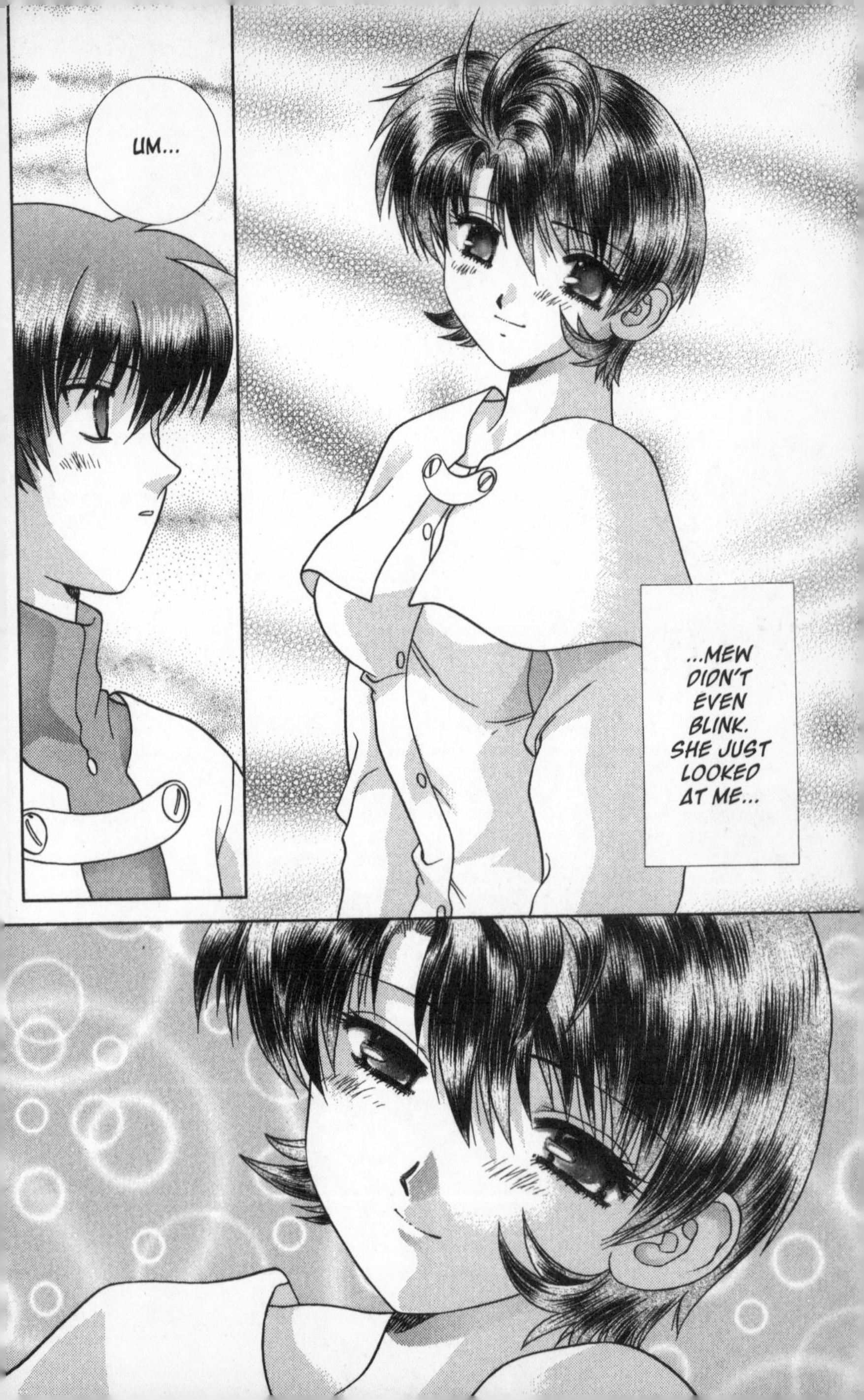
...MEW DIDN'T EVEN BLINK. SHE JUST LOOKED AT ME...
UM...

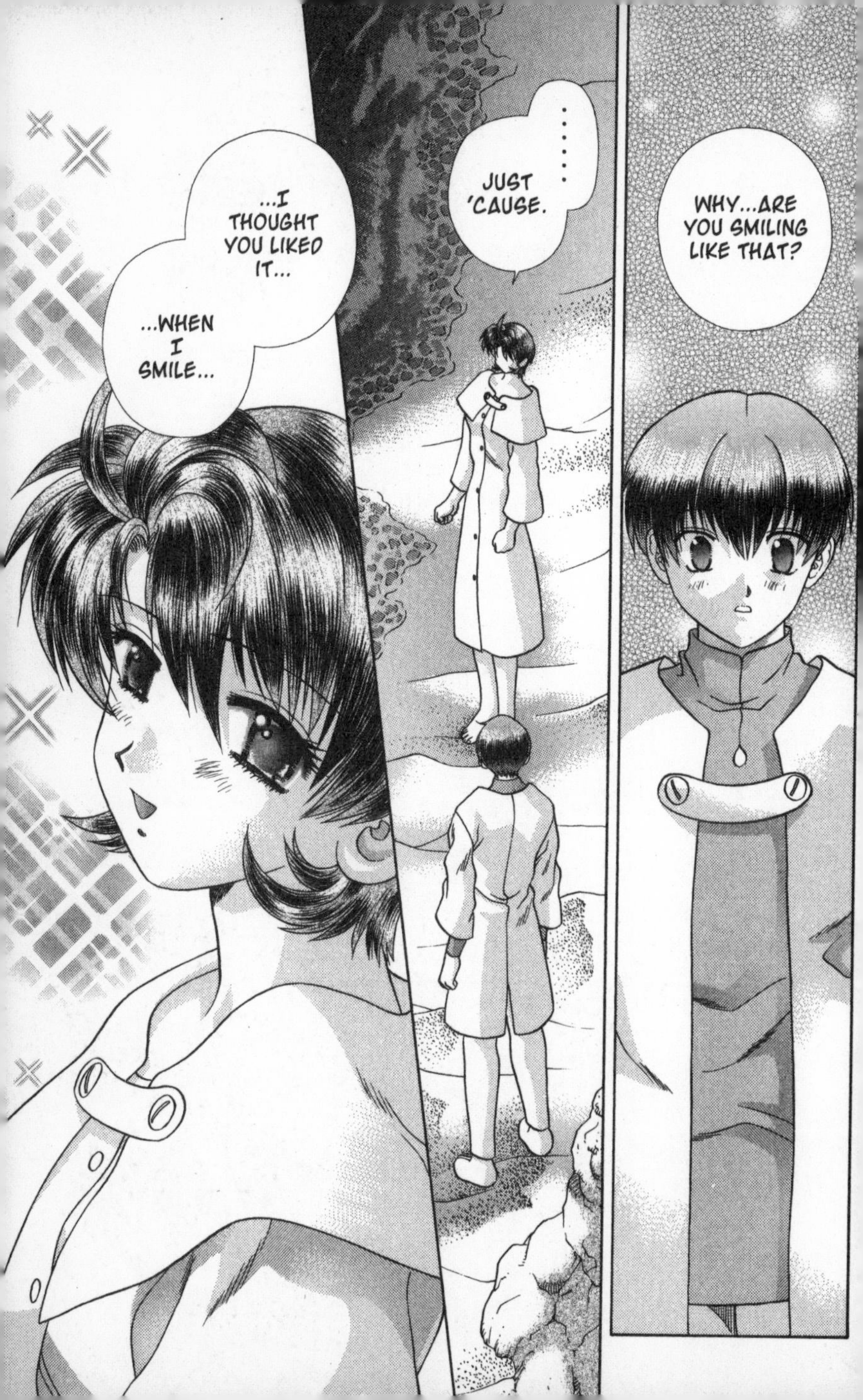
WHY...ARE YOU SMILING LIKE THAT?
......
JUST 'CAUSE.
...I THOUGHT YOU LIKED IT...
...WHEN I SMILE...

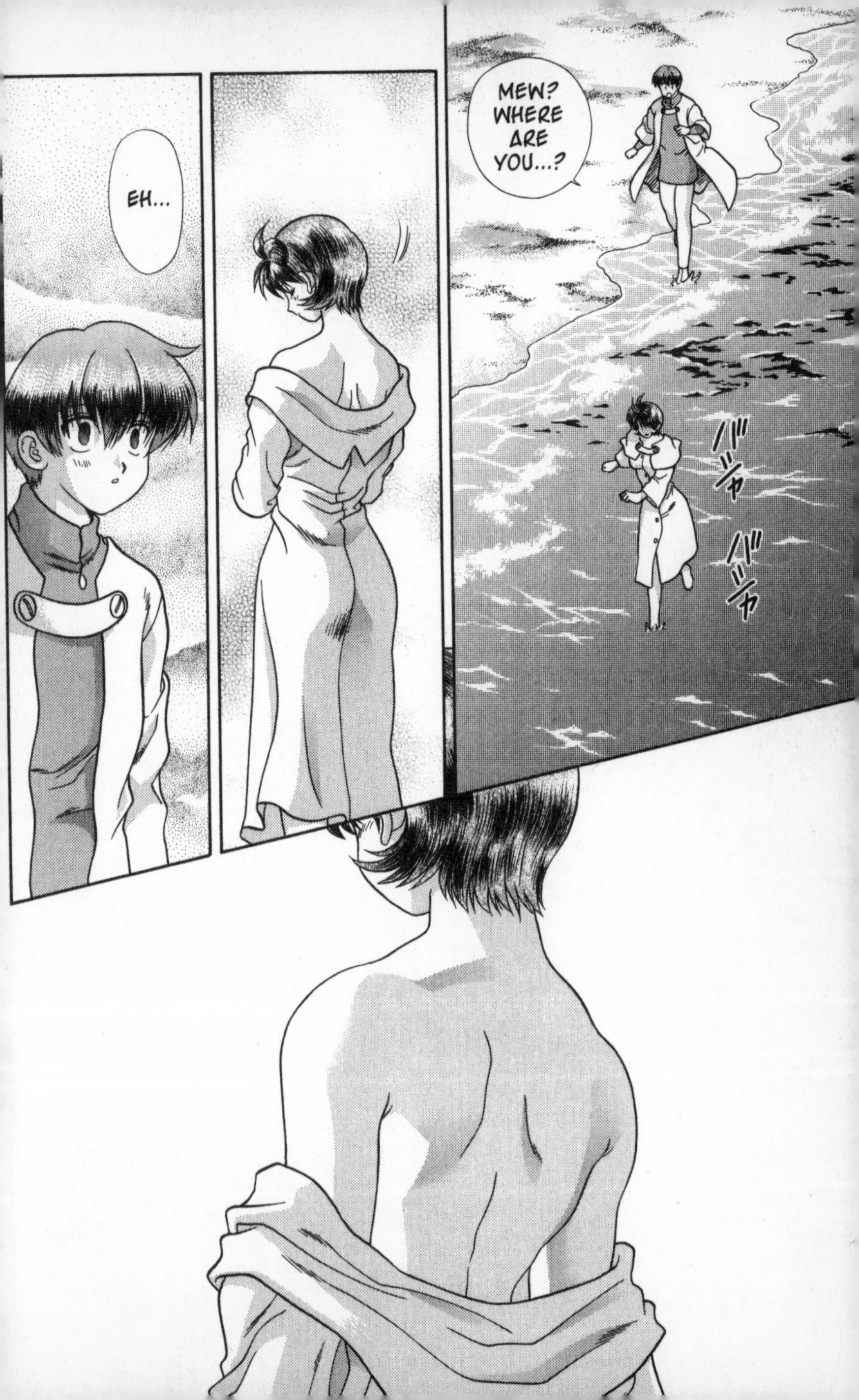
MEW? WHERE ARE YOU...?
バシャ
バシャ
EH...

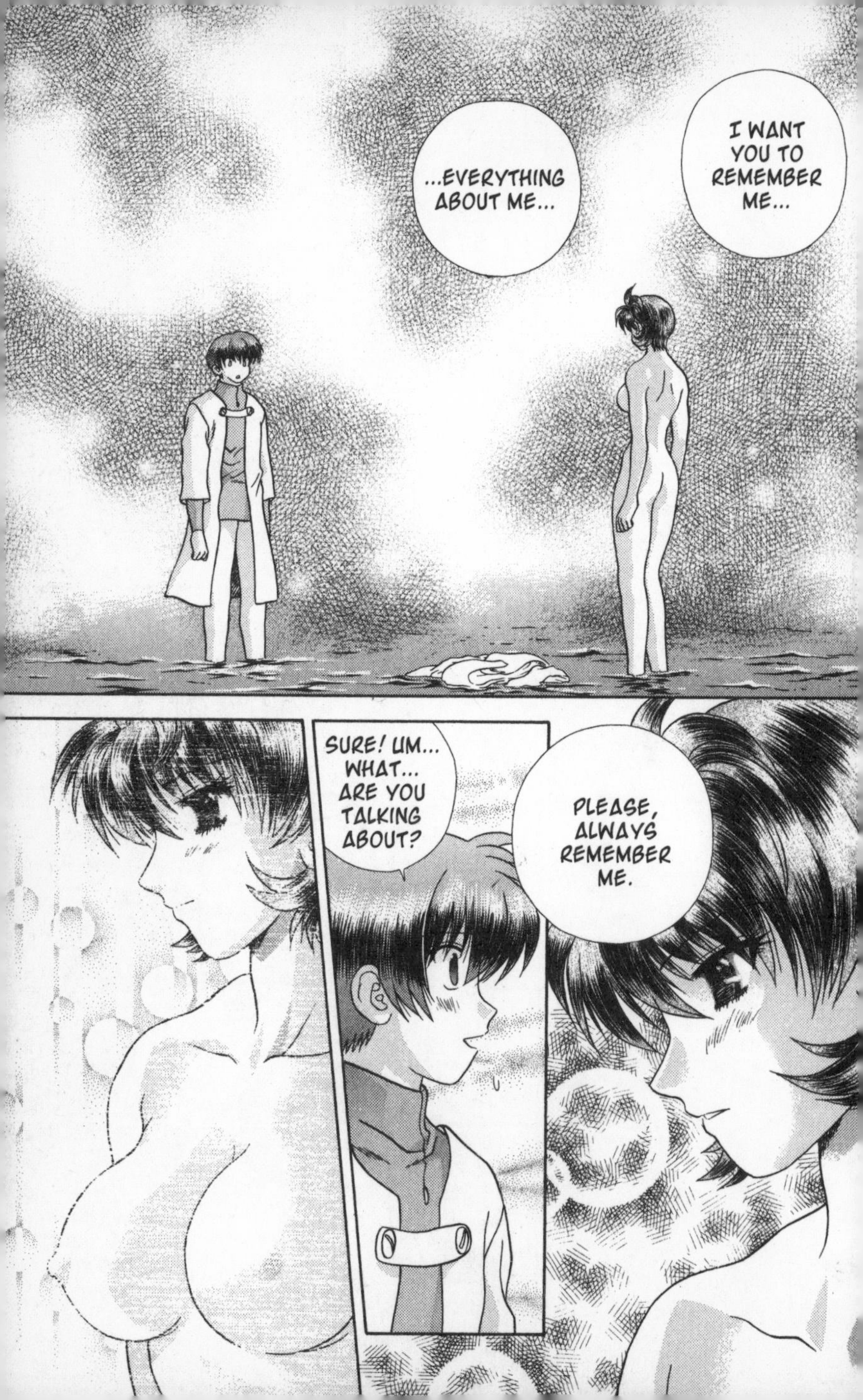
I WANT YOU TO REMEMBER ME...
...EVERYTHING ABOUT ME...
PLEASE, ALWAYS REMEMBER ME.
SURE! UM... WHAT... ARE YOU TALKING ABOUT?

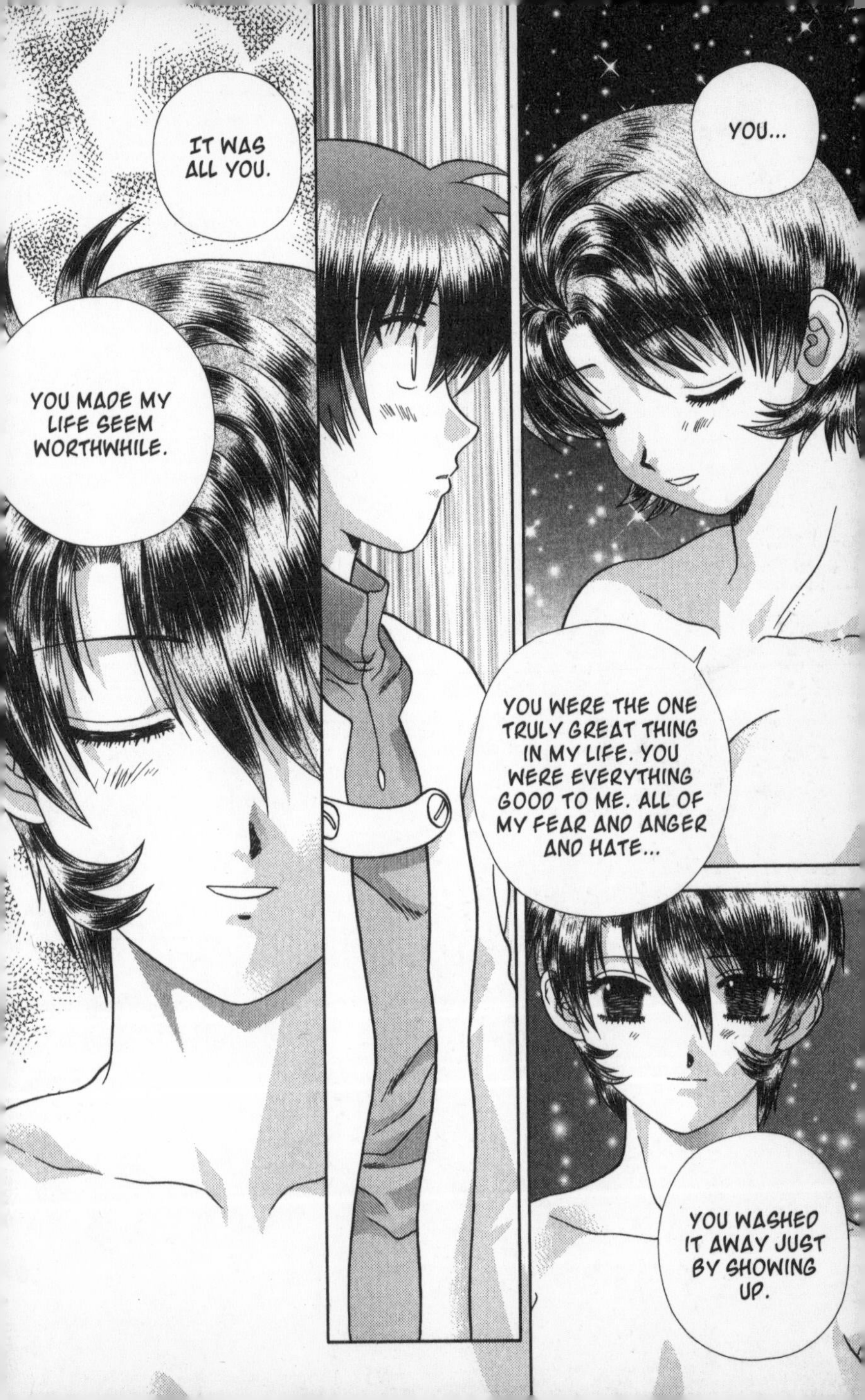
YOU...
YOU WERE THE ONE TRULY GREAT THING IN MY LIFE. YOU WERE EVERYTHING GOOD TO ME. ALL OF MY FEAR AND ANGER AND HATE...
YOU WASHED IT AWAY JUST BY SHOWING UP.
IT WAS ALL YOU.
YOU MADE MY LIFE SEEM WORTHWHILE.

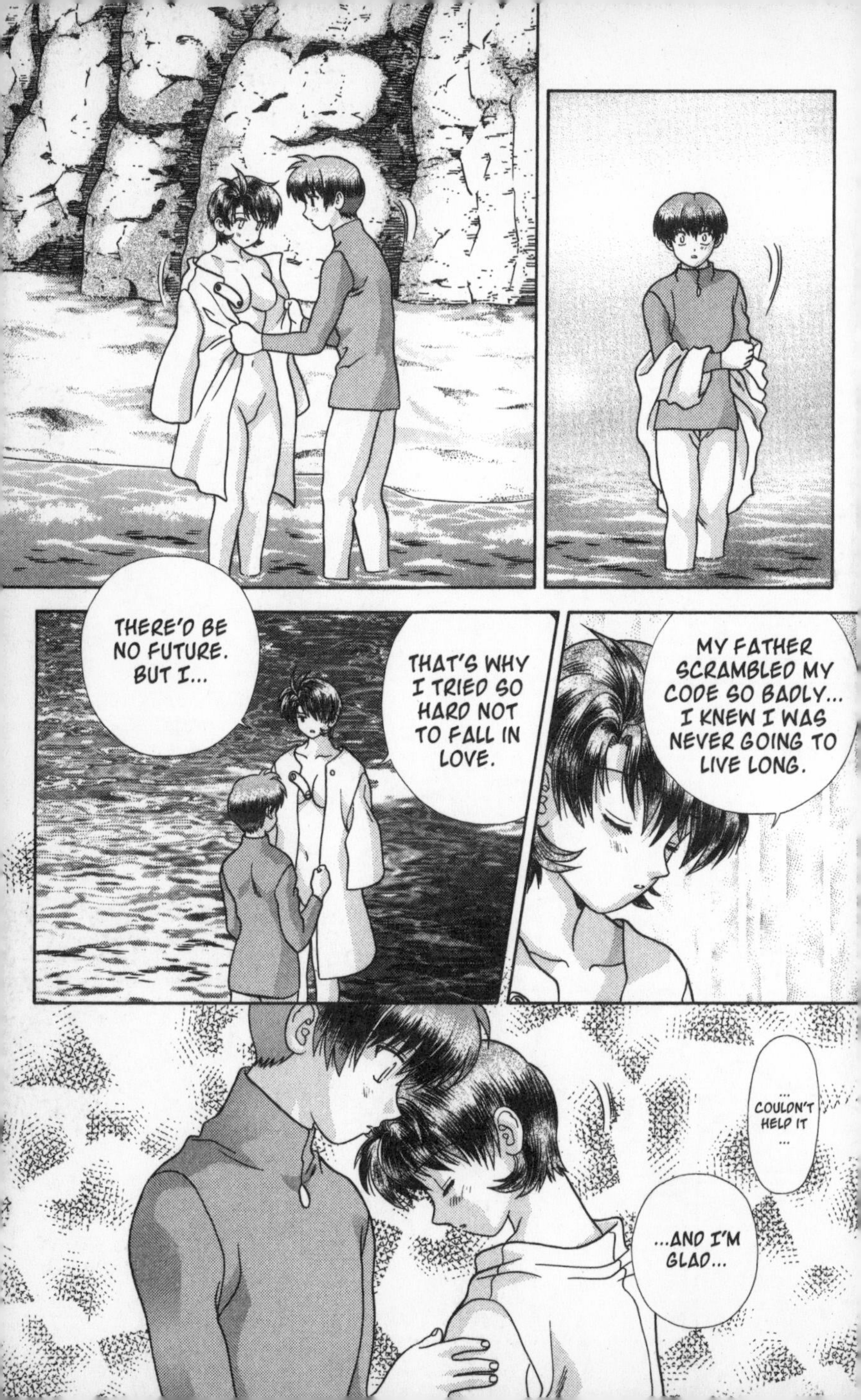
MY FATHER SCRAMBLED MY CODE SO BADLY... I KNEW I WAS NEVER GOING TO LIVE LONG.
THAT'S WHY I TRIED SO HARD NOT TO FALL IN LOVE.
THERE'D BE NO FUTURE. BUT I...
...COULDN'T HELP IT...
...AND I'M GLAD...

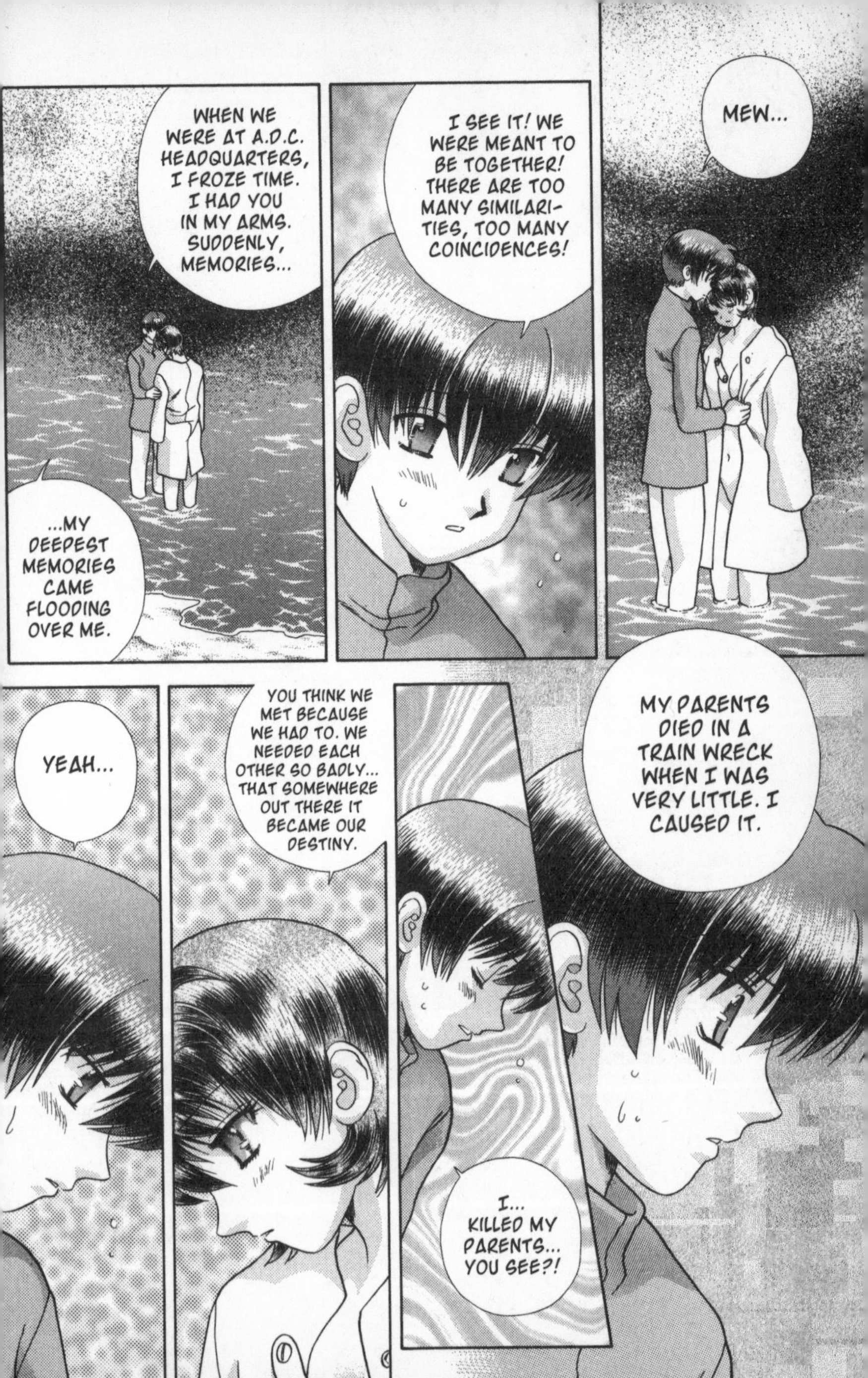
MEW...
I SEE IT! WE WERE MEANT TO BE TOGETHER! THERE ARE TOO MANY SIMILARI-TIES, TOO MANY COINCIDENCES!
WHEN WE WERE AT A.D.C. HEADQUARTERS, I FROZE TIME. I HAD YOU IN MY ARMS. SUDDENLY, MEMORIES...
...MY DEEPEST MEMORIES CAME FLOODING OVER ME.
MY PARENTS DIED IN A TRAIN WRECK WHEN I WAS VERY LITTLE. I CAUSED IT.
I... KILLED MY PARENTS... YOU SEE?!
YOU THINK WE MET BECAUSE WE HAD TO. WE NEEDED EACH OTHER SO BADLY... THAT SOMEWHERE OUT THERE IT BECAME OUR DESTINY.
YEAH...

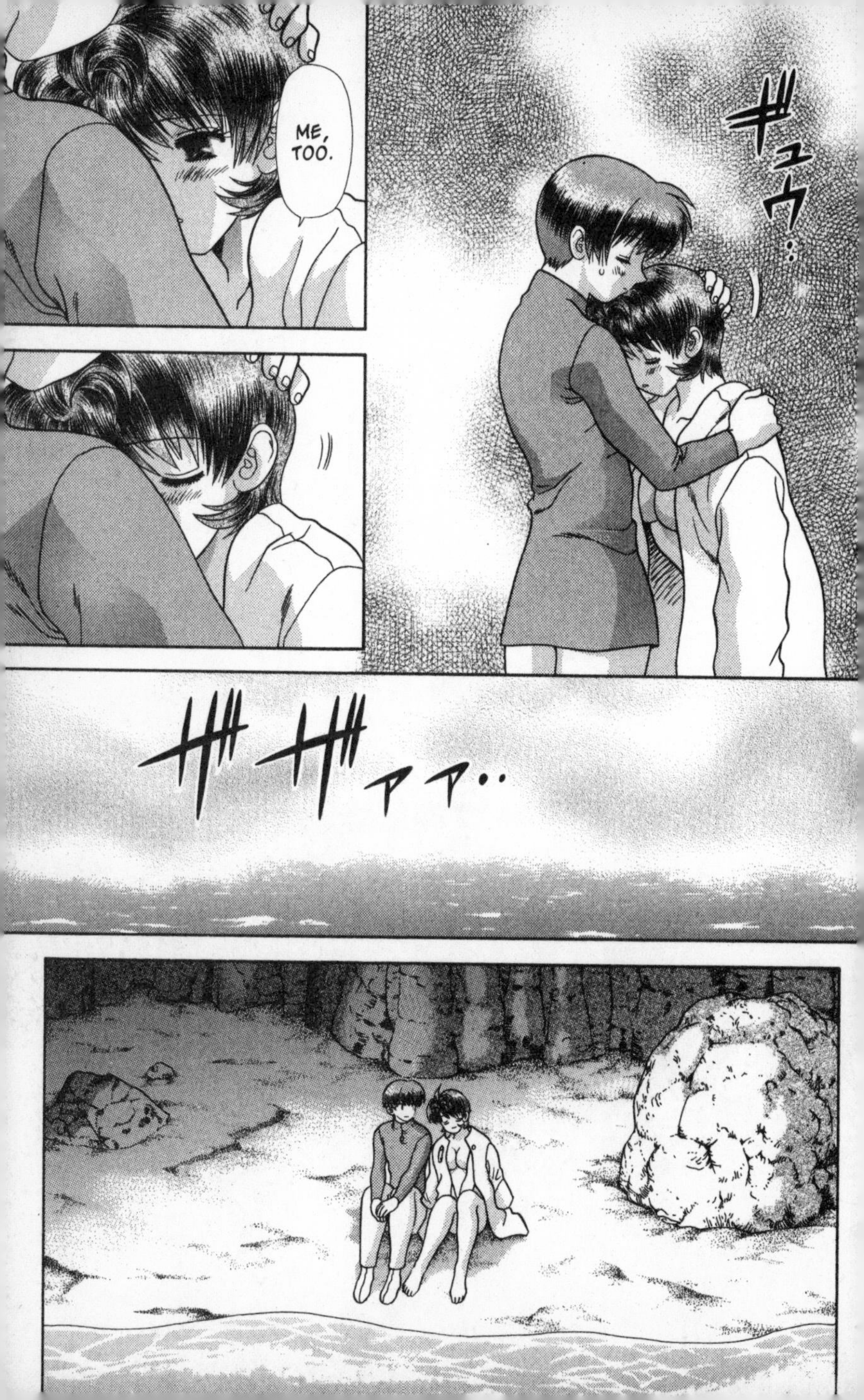
ギュウ..
ME, TOO.
ザザァァ..

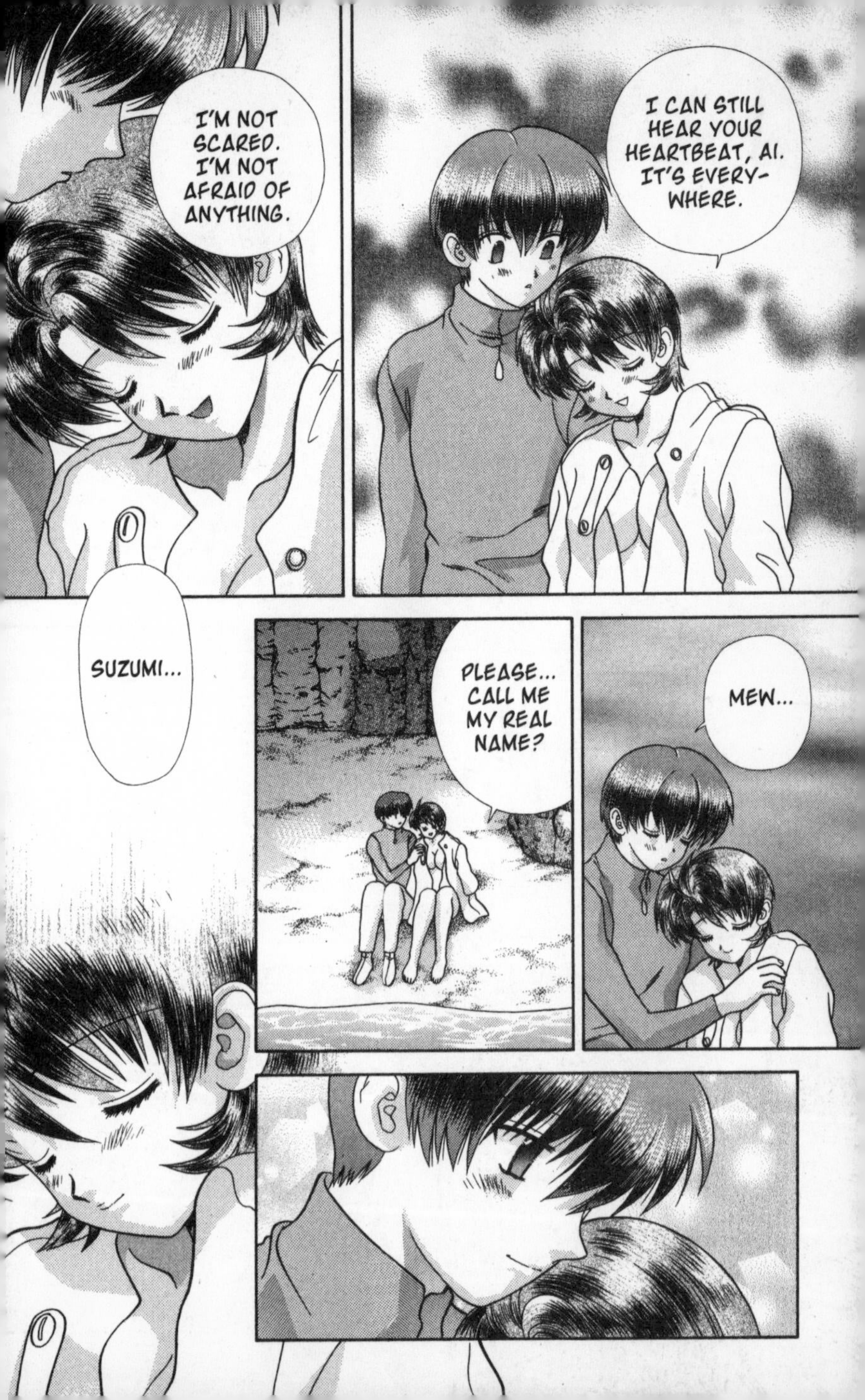
I CAN STILL HEAR YOUR HEARTBEAT, AI. IT'S EVERY-WHERE.
I'M NOT SCARED. I'M NOT AFRAID OF ANYTHING.
MEW...
PLEASE... CALL ME MY REAL NAME?
SUZUMI...

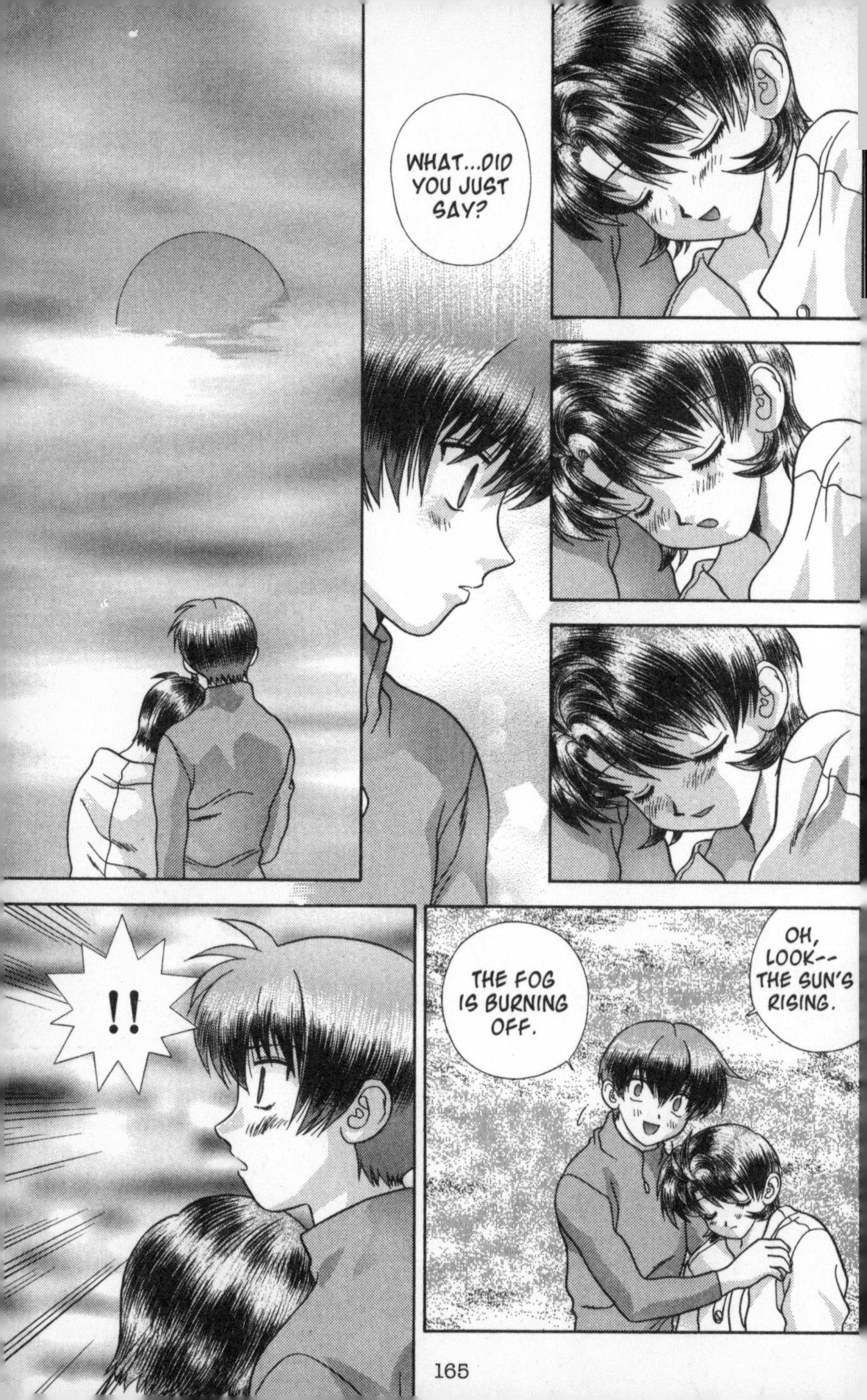
WHAT...DID YOU JUST SAY?
OH, LOOK-- THE SUN'S RISING.
THE FOG IS BURNING OFF.
!!

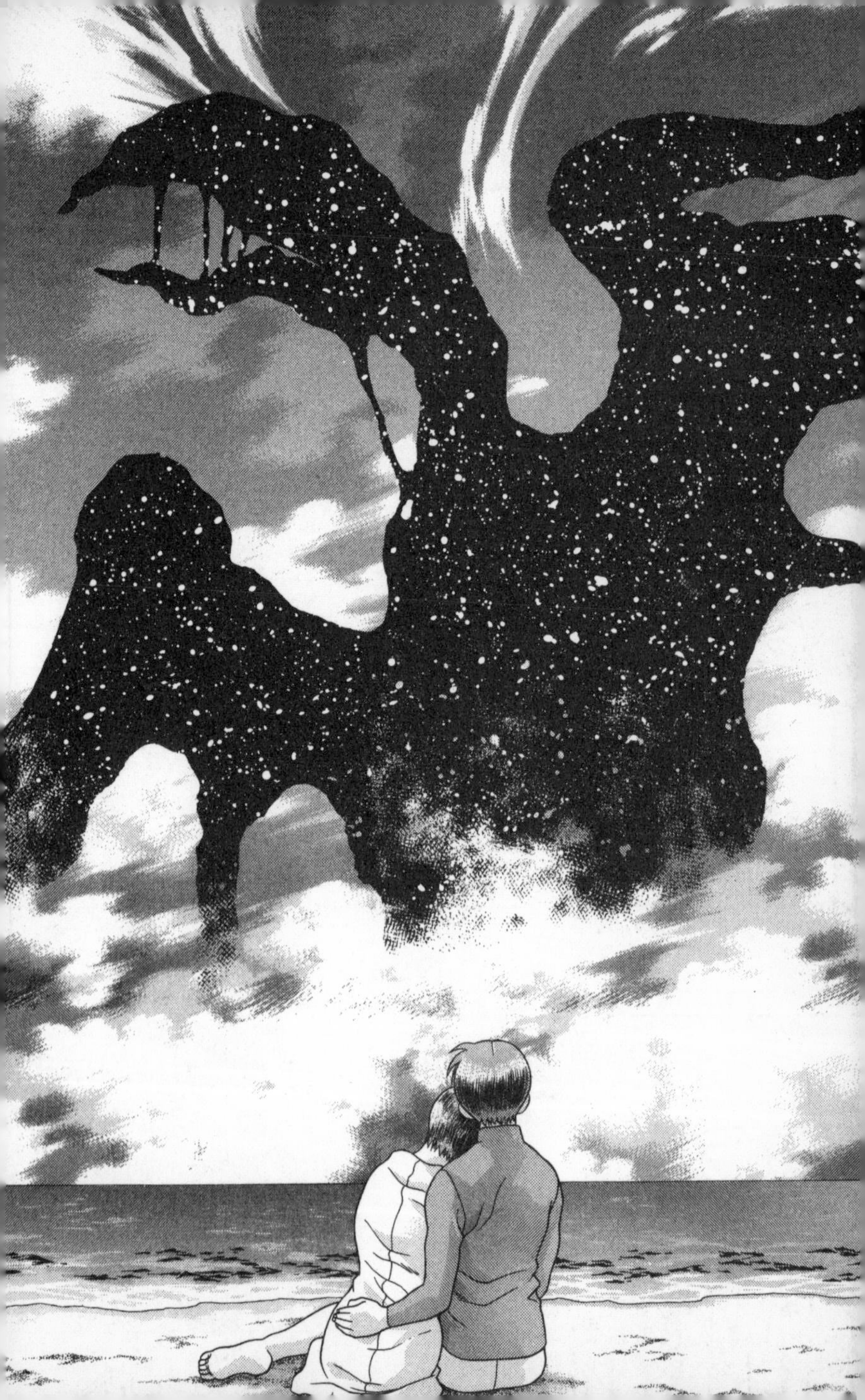

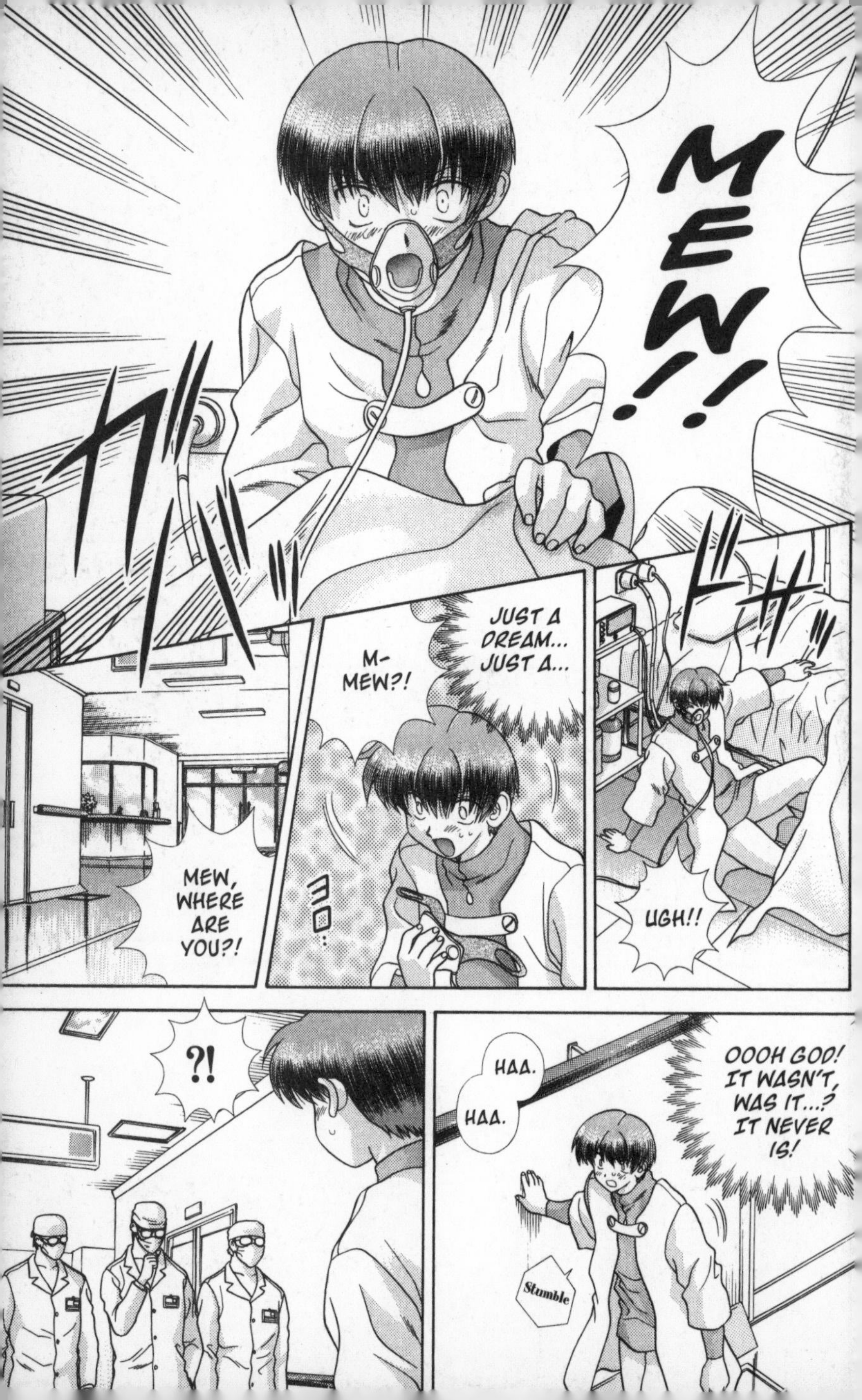
MEW!!
ガバッ
ドサッ!!
UGH!!
JUST A DREAM... JUST A...
M- MEW?!
ヨロ...
MEW, WHERE ARE YOU?!
OOOH GOD! IT WASN'T, WAS IT...? IT NEVER IS!
HAA.
HAA.
Stumble
?!

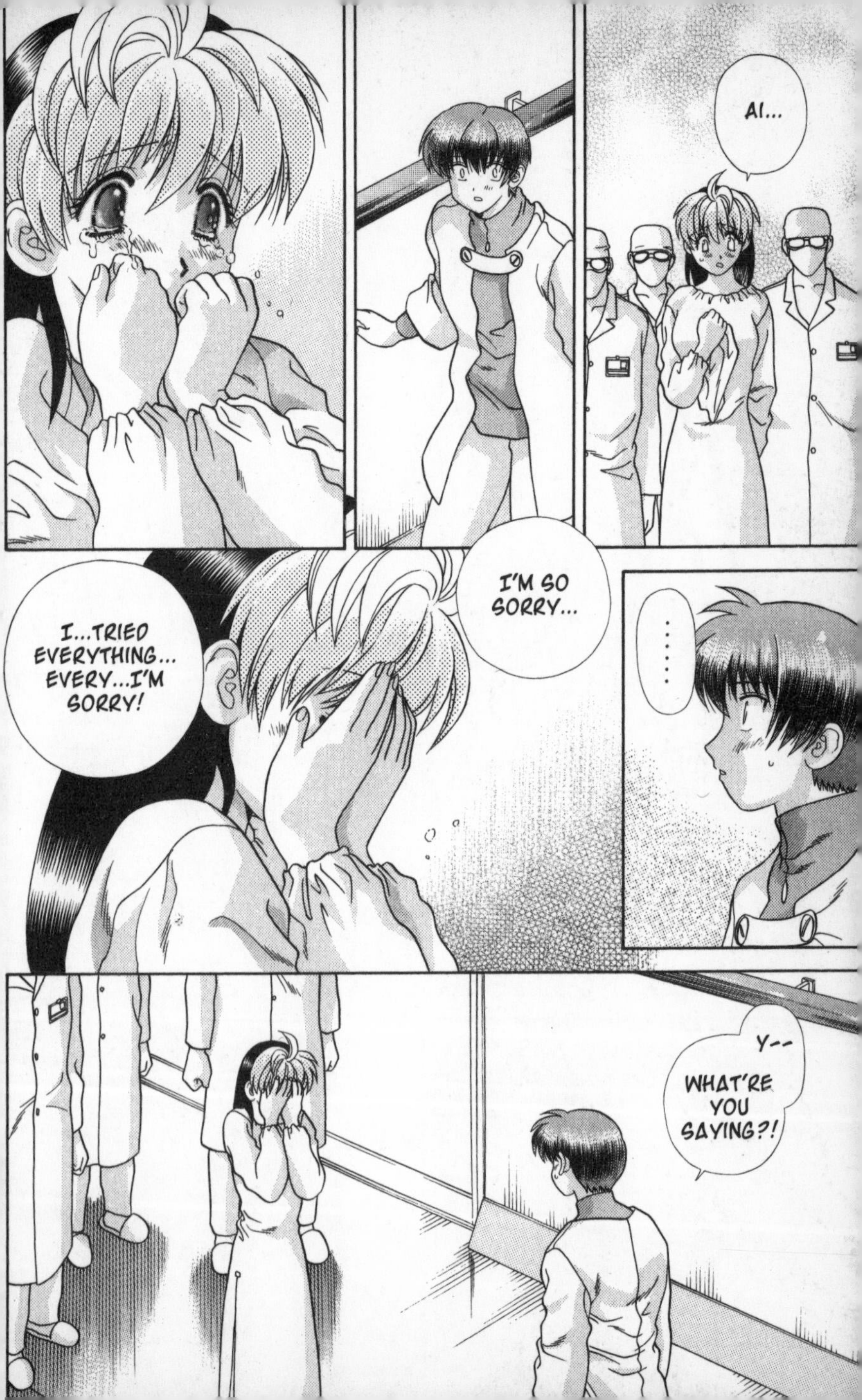
AI...
......
I'M SO SORRY...
I...TRIED EVERYTHING... EVERY...I'M SORRY!
Y-- WHAT'RE YOU SAYING?!

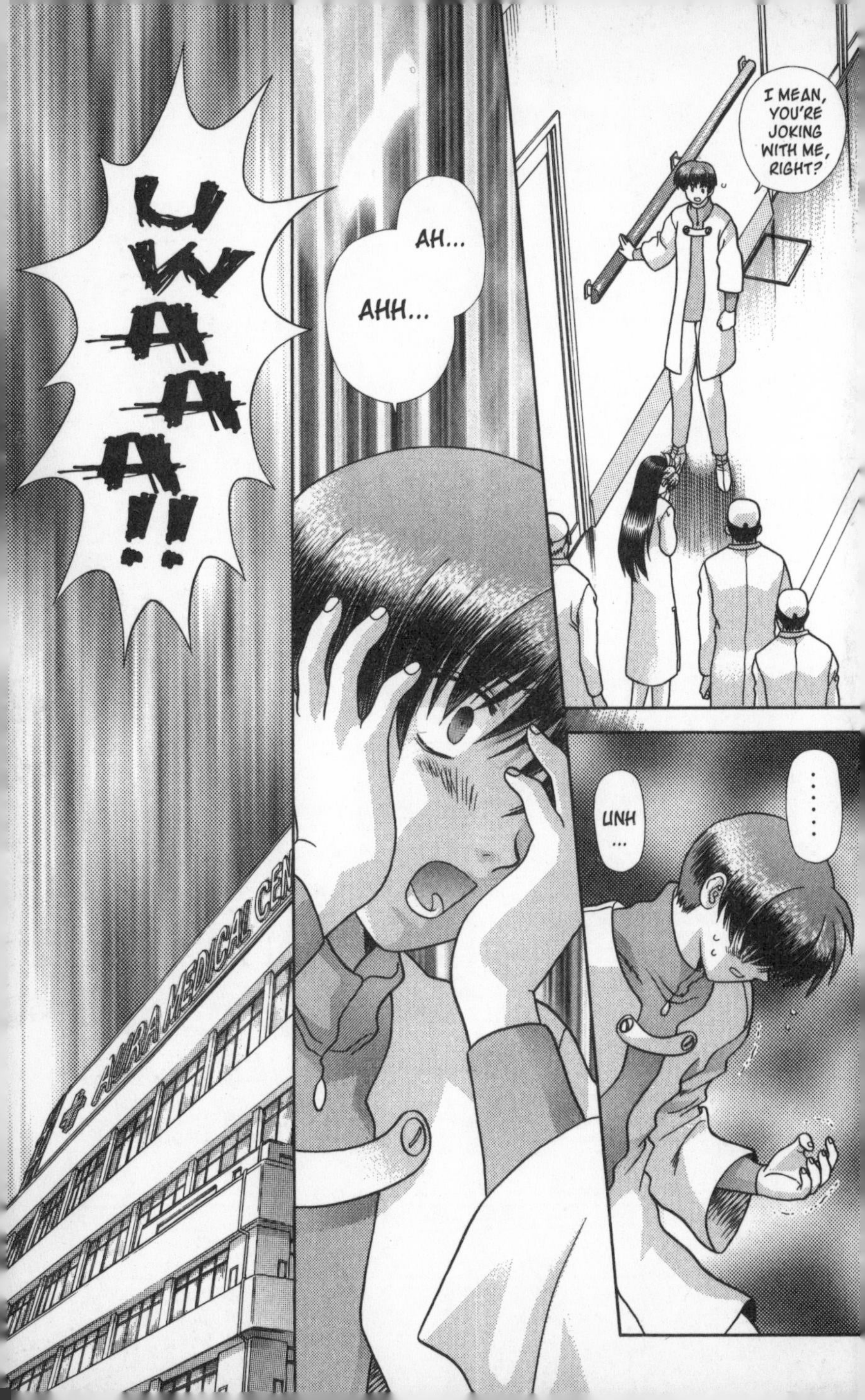
I MEAN, YOU'RE JOKING WITH ME, RIGHT?
......
UNH ...
AH...
AHH...
UWAAA!!

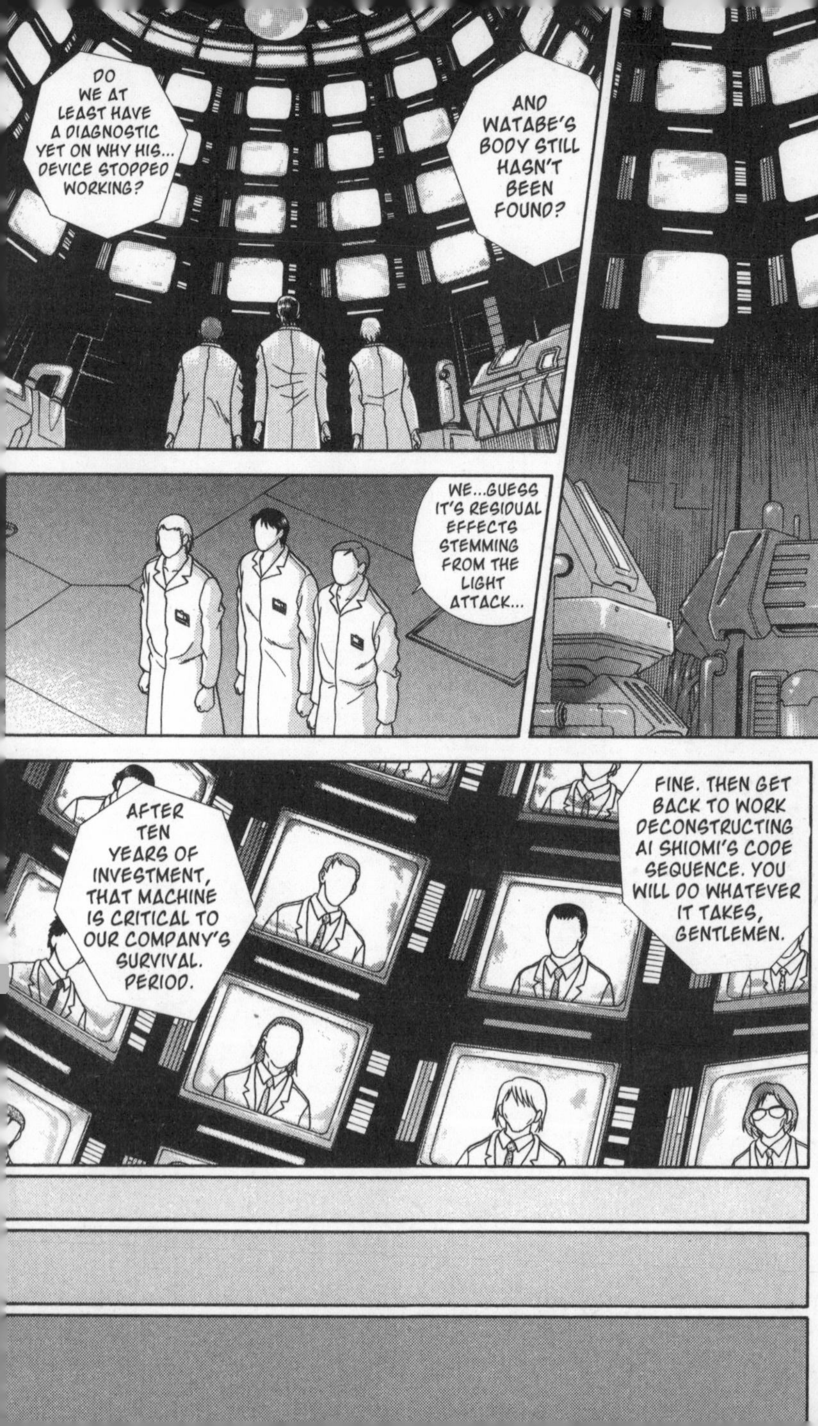
DO WE AT LEAST HAVE A DIAGNOSTIC YET ON WHY HIS... DEVICE STOPPED WORKING?
AND WATABE'S BODY STILL HASN'T BEEN FOUND?
WE...GUESS IT'S RESIDUAL EFFECTS STEMMING FROM THE LIGHT ATTACK...
AFTER TEN YEARS OF INVESTMENT, THAT MACHINE IS CRITICAL TO OUR COMPANY'S SURVIVAL. PERIOD.
FINE. THEN GET BACK TO WORK DECONSTRUCTING AI SHIOMI'S CODE SEQUENCE. YOU WILL DO WHATEVER IT TAKES, GENTLEMEN.

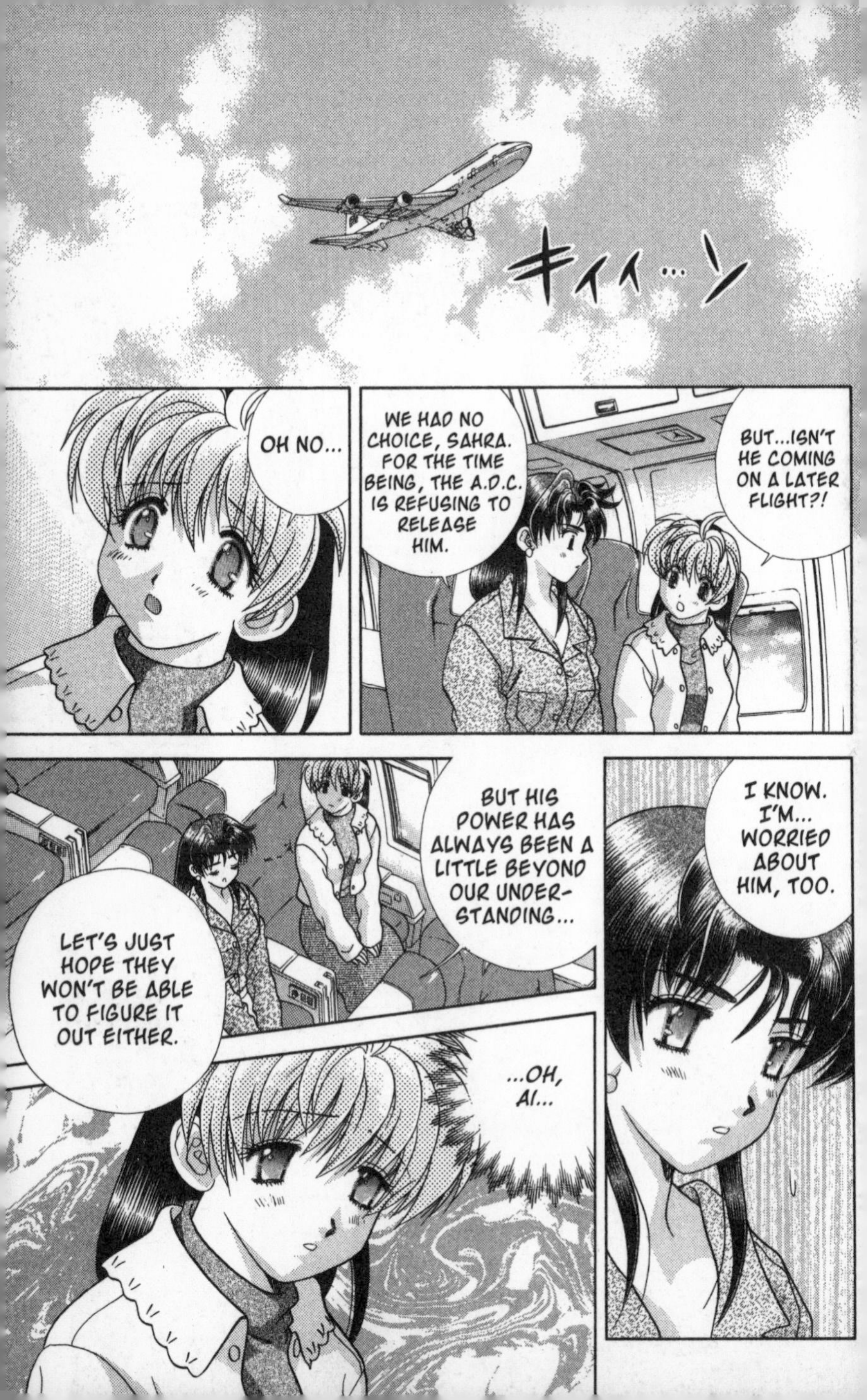
キィィ…ン
BUT...ISN'T HE COMING ON A LATER FLIGHT?!
WE HAD NO CHOICE, SAHRA. FOR THE TIME BEING, THE A.D.C. IS REFUSING TO RELEASE HIM.
OH NO...
I KNOW. I'M... WORRIED ABOUT HIM, TOO.
BUT HIS POWER HAS ALWAYS BEEN A LITTLE BEYOND OUR UNDER-STANDING...
LET'S JUST HOPE THEY WON'T BE ABLE TO FIGURE IT OUT EITHER.
...OH, AI...

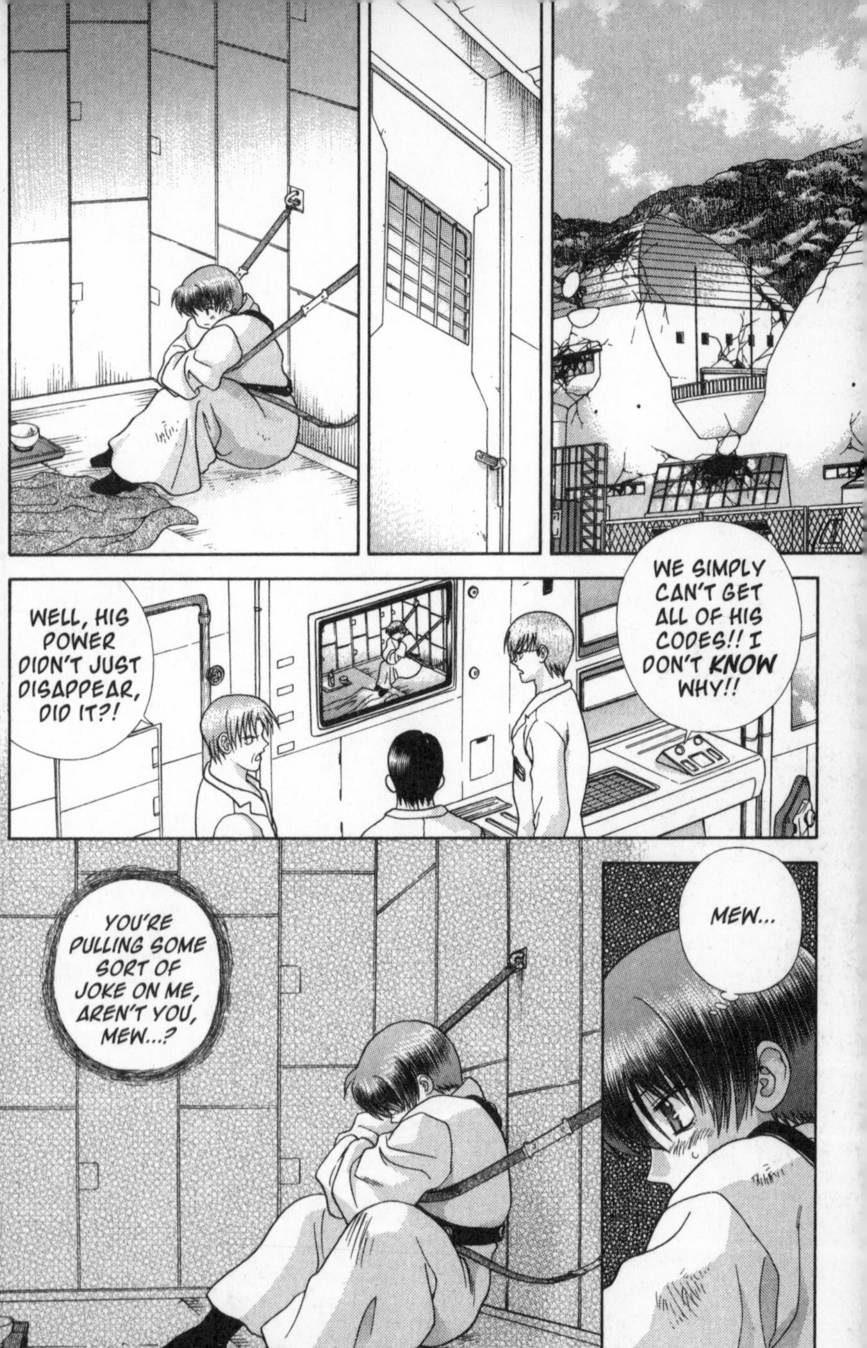
WE SIMPLY CAN'T GET ALL OF HIS CODES!! I DON'T KNOW WHY!!
WELL, HIS POWER DIDN'T JUST DISAPPEAR, DID IT?!
MEW...
YOU'RE PULLING SOME SORT OF JOKE ON ME, AREN'T YOU, MEW...?

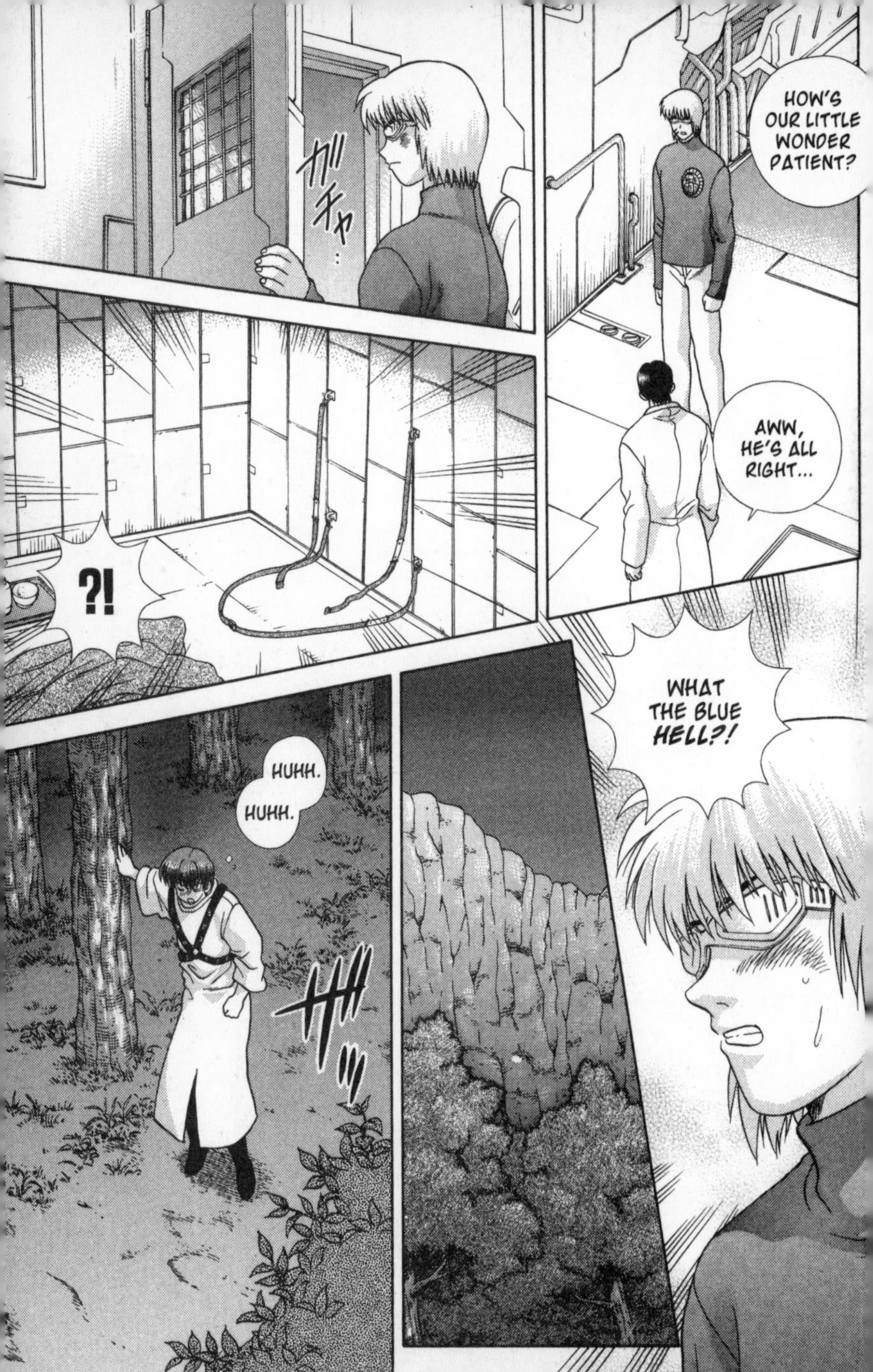
HOW'S OUR LITTLE WONDER PATIENT?
ガチャ
AWW, HE'S ALL RIGHT...
?!
WHAT THE BLUE HELL?!
HUHH.
HUHH.

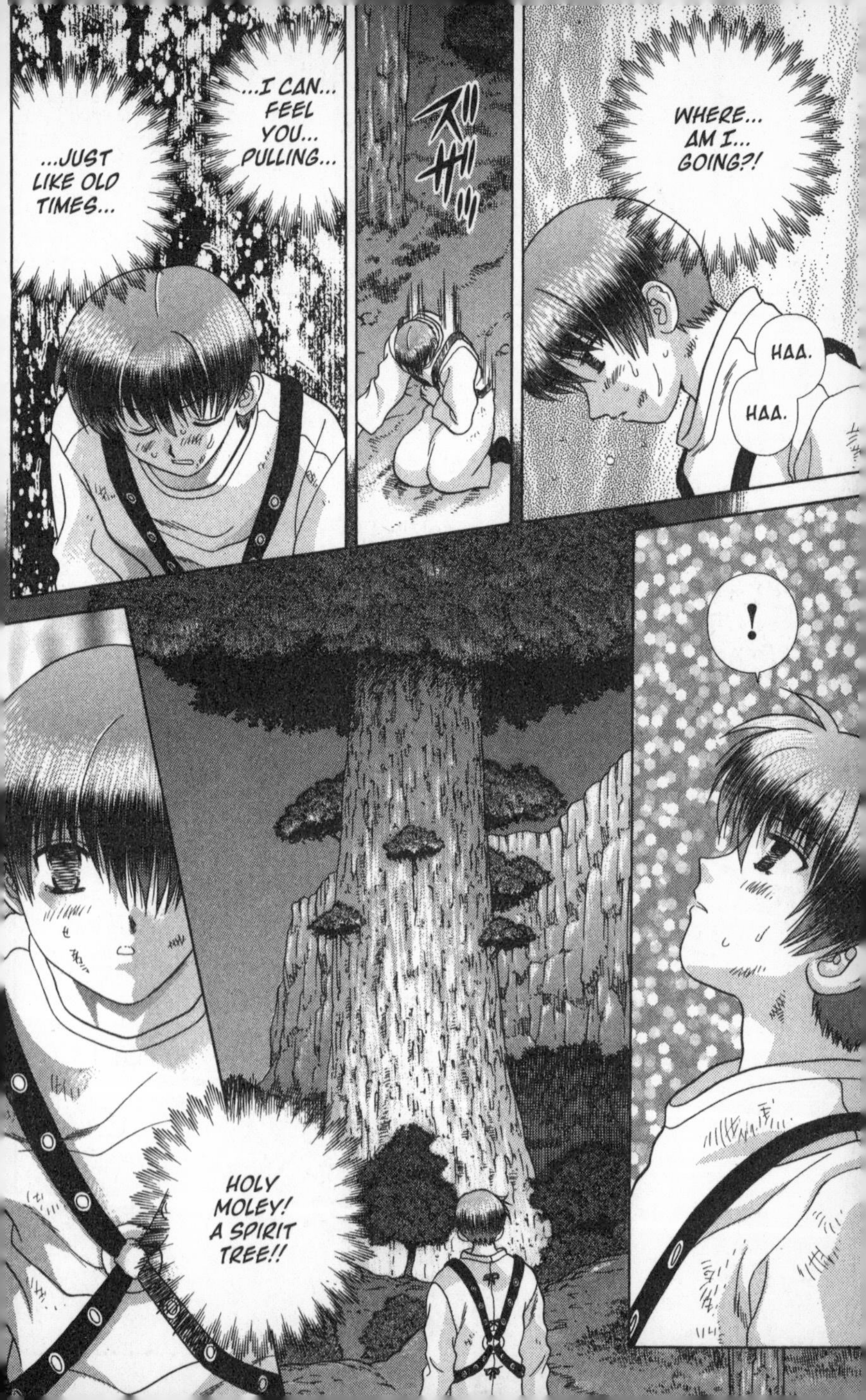
WHERE... AM I... GOING?!
HAA.
HAA.
...I CAN... FEEL YOU... PULLING...
...JUST LIKE OLD TIMES...
!
HOLY MOLEY! A SPIRIT TREE!!

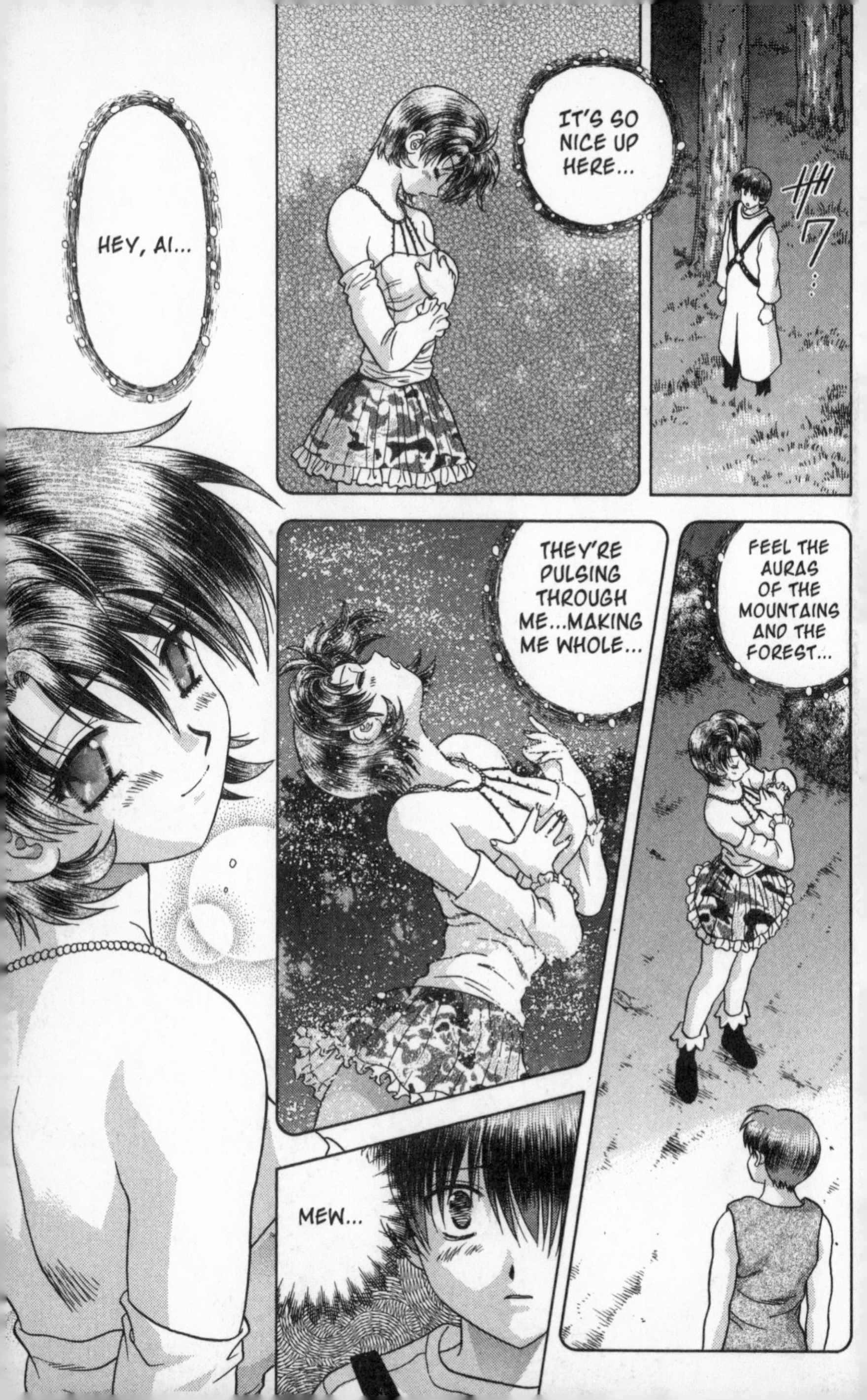
IT'S SO NICE UP HERE...
FEEL THE AURAS OF THE MOUNTAINS AND THE FOREST...
THEY'RE PULSING THROUGH ME...MAKING ME WHOLE...
MEW...
HEY, AI...

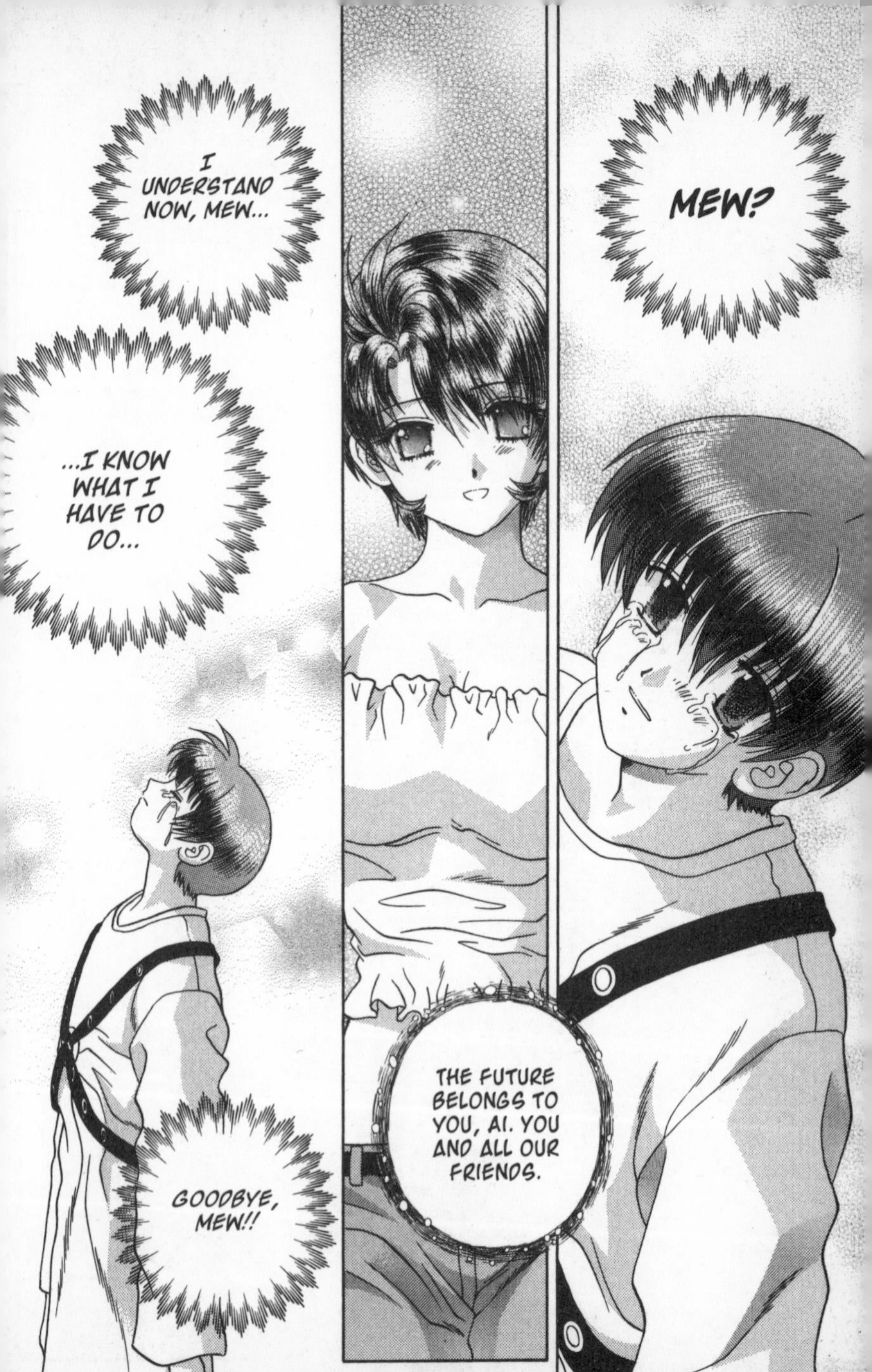
MEW?
THE FUTURE BELONGS TO YOU, AI. YOU AND ALL OUR FRIENDS.
I UNDERSTAND NOW, MEW...
...I KNOW WHAT I HAVE TO DO...
GOODBYE, MEW!!

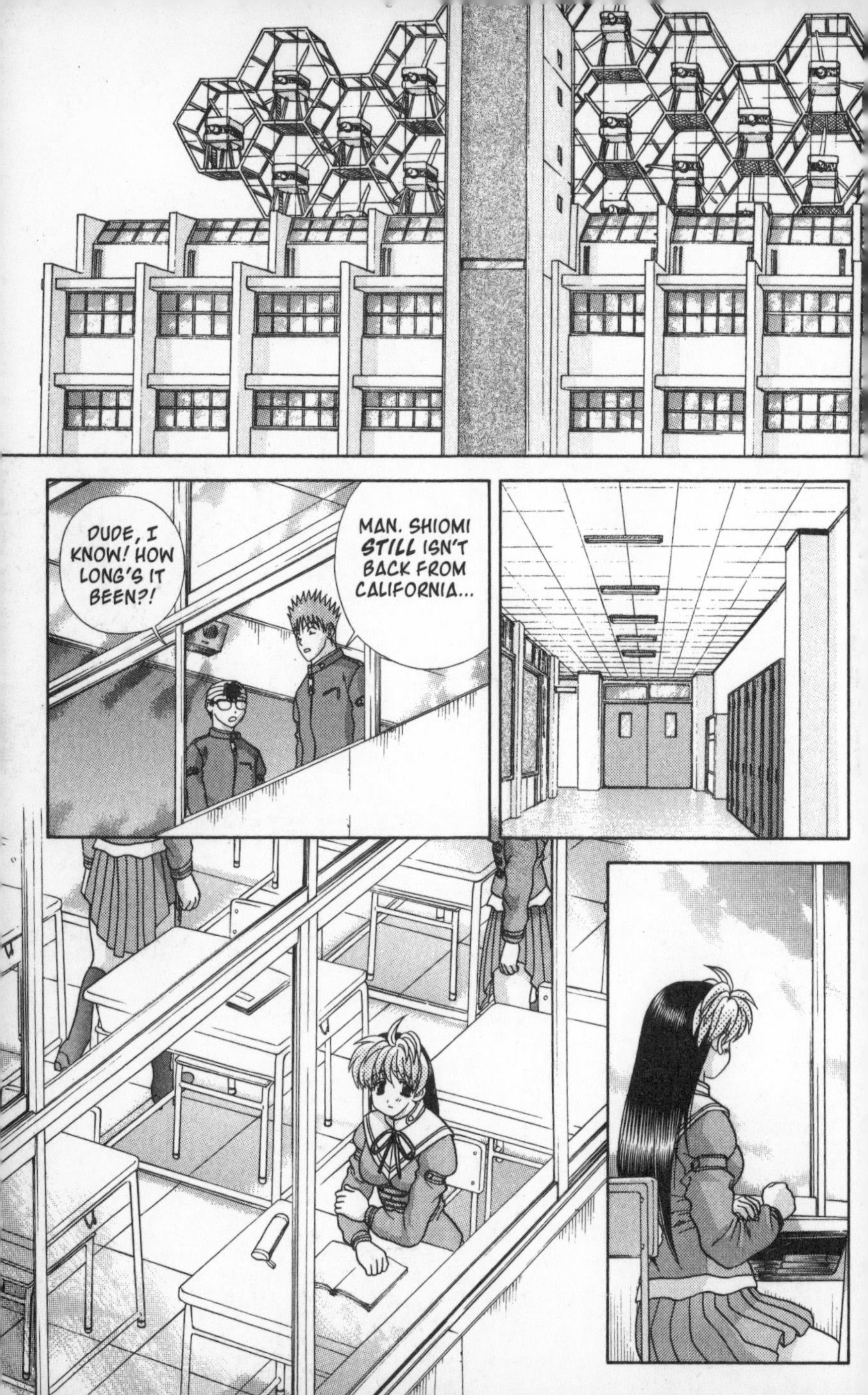
MAN. SHIOMI STILL ISN'T BACK FROM CALIFORNIA...
DUDE, I KNOW! HOW LONG'S IT BEEN?!

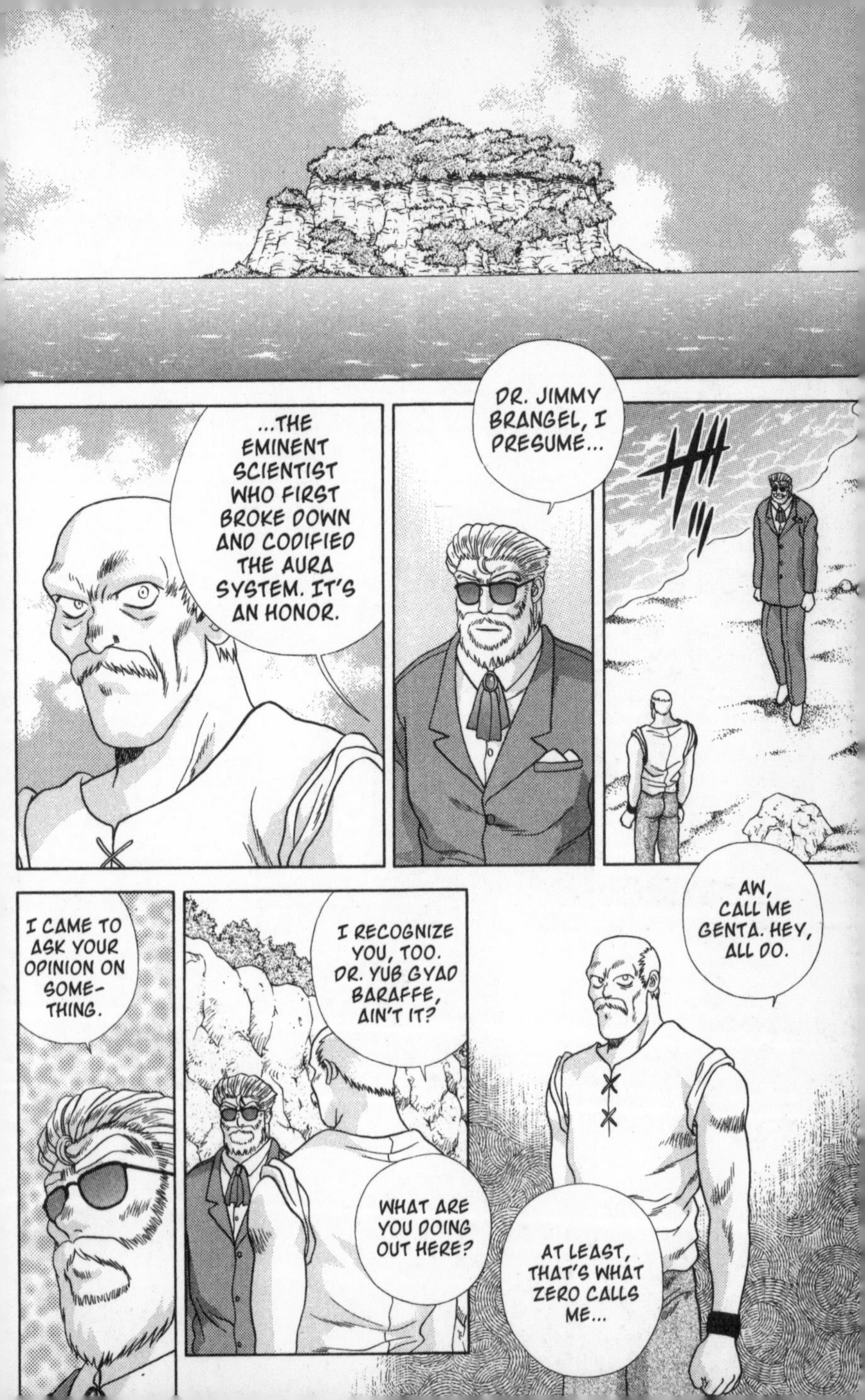
DR. JIMMY BRANGEL, I PRESUME...
...THE EMINENT SCIENTIST WHO FIRST BROKE DOWN AND CODIFIED THE AURA SYSTEM. IT'S AN HONOR.
AW, CALL ME GENTA. HEY, ALL DO.
AT LEAST, THAT'S WHAT ZERO CALLS ME...
I RECOGNIZE YOU, TOO. DR. YUB GYAD BARAFFE, AIN'T IT?
WHAT ARE YOU DOING OUT HERE?
I CAME TO ASK YOUR OPINION ON SOME-THING.

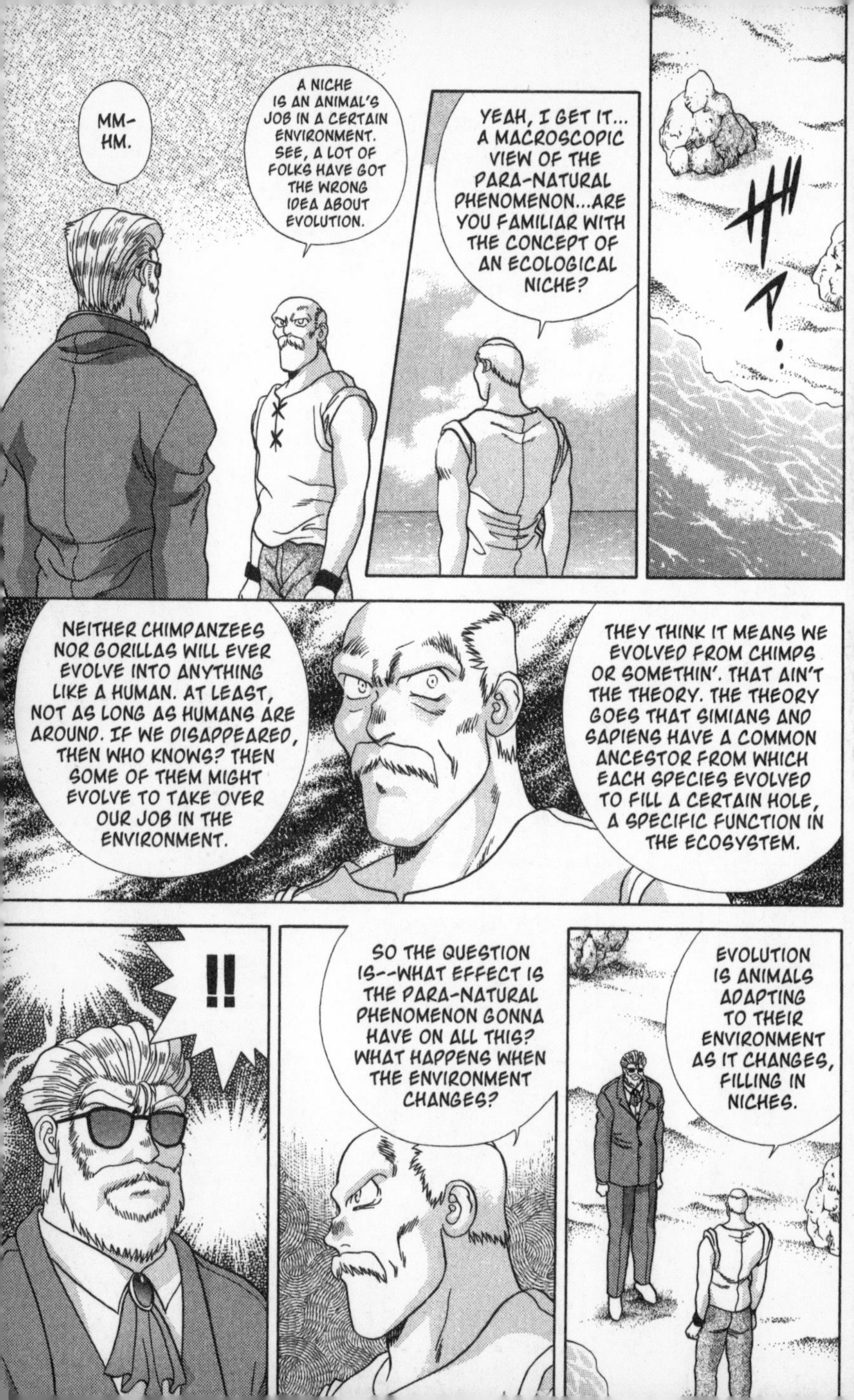

YEAH, I GET IT... A MACROSCOPIC VIEW OF THE PARA-NATURAL PHENOMENON...ARE YOU FAMILIAR WITH THE CONCEPT OF AN ECOLOGICAL NICHE?
MM-HM.
A NICHE IS AN ANIMAL'S JOB IN A CERTAIN ENVIRONMENT. SEE, A LOT OF FOLKS HAVE GOT THE WRONG IDEA ABOUT EVOLUTION.
THEY THINK IT MEANS WE EVOLVED FROM CHIMPS OR SOMETHIN'. THAT AIN'T THE THEORY. THE THEORY GOES THAT SIMIANS AND SAPIENS HAVE A COMMON ANCESTOR FROM WHICH EACH SPECIES EVOLVED TO FILL A CERTAIN HOLE, A SPECIFIC FUNCTION IN THE ECOSYSTEM.
NEITHER CHIMPANZEES NOR GORILLAS WILL EVER EVOLVE INTO ANYTHING LIKE A HUMAN. AT LEAST, NOT AS LONG AS HUMANS ARE AROUND. IF WE DISAPPEARED, THEN WHO KNOWS? THEN SOME OF THEM MIGHT EVOLVE TO TAKE OVER OUR JOB IN THE ENVIRONMENT.
EVOLUTION IS ANIMALS ADAPTING TO THEIR ENVIRONMENT AS IT CHANGES, FILLING IN NICHES.
SO THE QUESTION IS--WHAT EFFECT IS THE PARA-NATURAL PHENOMENON GONNA HAVE ON ALL THIS? WHAT HAPPENS WHEN THE ENVIRONMENT CHANGES?
!!

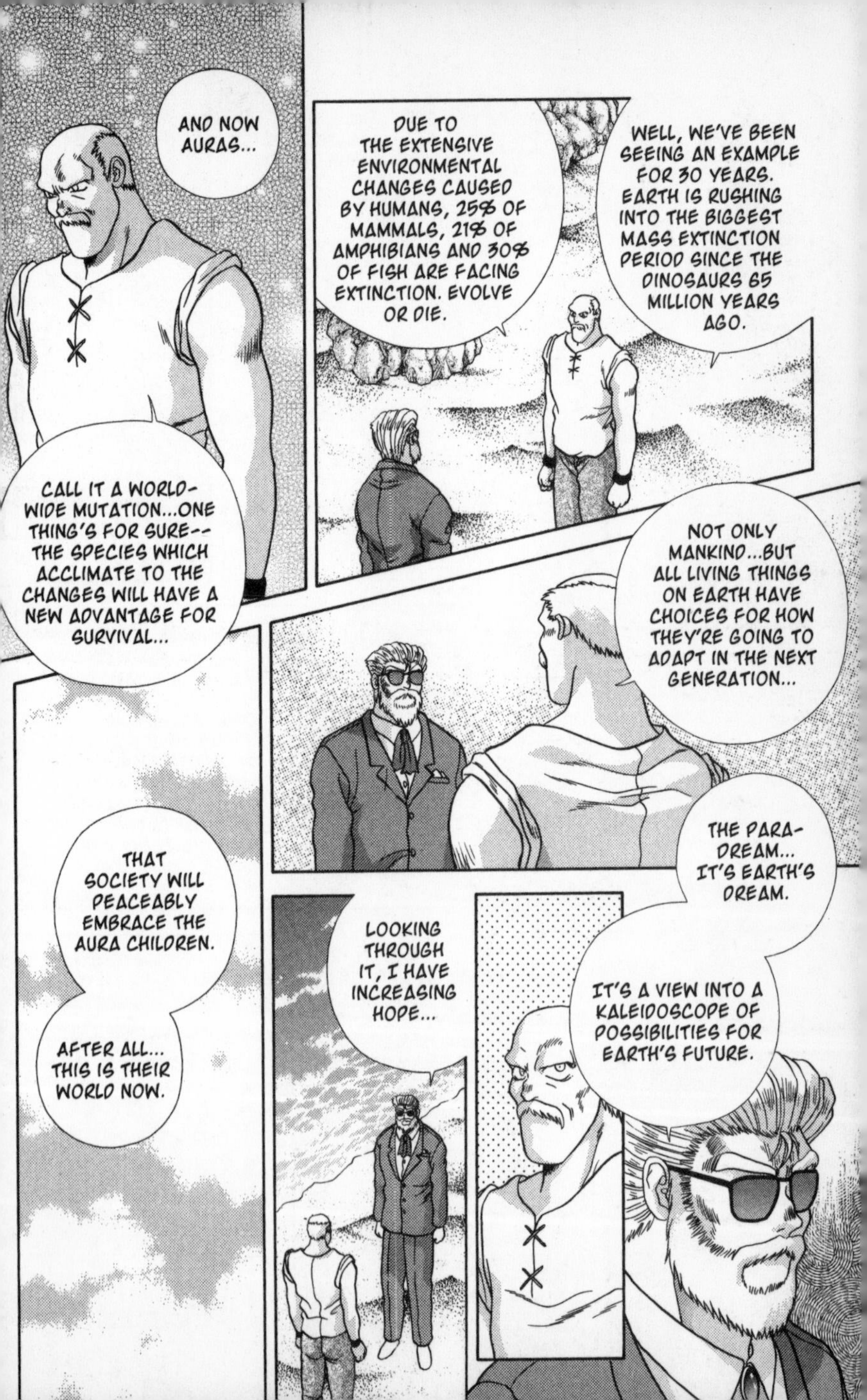
WELL, WE'VE BEEN SEEING AN EXAMPLE FOR 30 YEARS. EARTH IS RUSHING INTO THE BIGGEST MASS EXTINCTION PERIOD SINCE THE DINOSAURS 65 MILLION YEARS AGO.
DUE TO THE EXTENSIVE ENVIRONMENTAL CHANGES CAUSED BY HUMANS, 25% OF MAMMALS, 21% OF AMPHIBIANS AND 30% OF FISH ARE FACING EXTINCTION. EVOLVE OR DIE.
AND NOW AURAS...
CALL IT A WORLD-WIDE MUTATION...ONE THING'S FOR SURE--THE SPECIES WHICH ACCLIMATE TO THE CHANGES WILL HAVE A NEW ADVANTAGE FOR SURVIVAL...
NOT ONLY MANKIND...BUT ALL LIVING THINGS ON EARTH HAVE CHOICES FOR HOW THEY'RE GOING TO ADAPT IN THE NEXT GENERATION...
THE PARA-DREAM... IT'S EARTH'S DREAM.
IT'S A VIEW INTO A KALEIDOSCOPE OF POSSIBILITIES FOR EARTH'S FUTURE.
LOOKING THROUGH IT, I HAVE INCREASING HOPE...
THAT SOCIETY WILL PEACEABLY EMBRACE THE AURA CHILDREN.
AFTER ALL... THIS IS THEIR WORLD NOW.

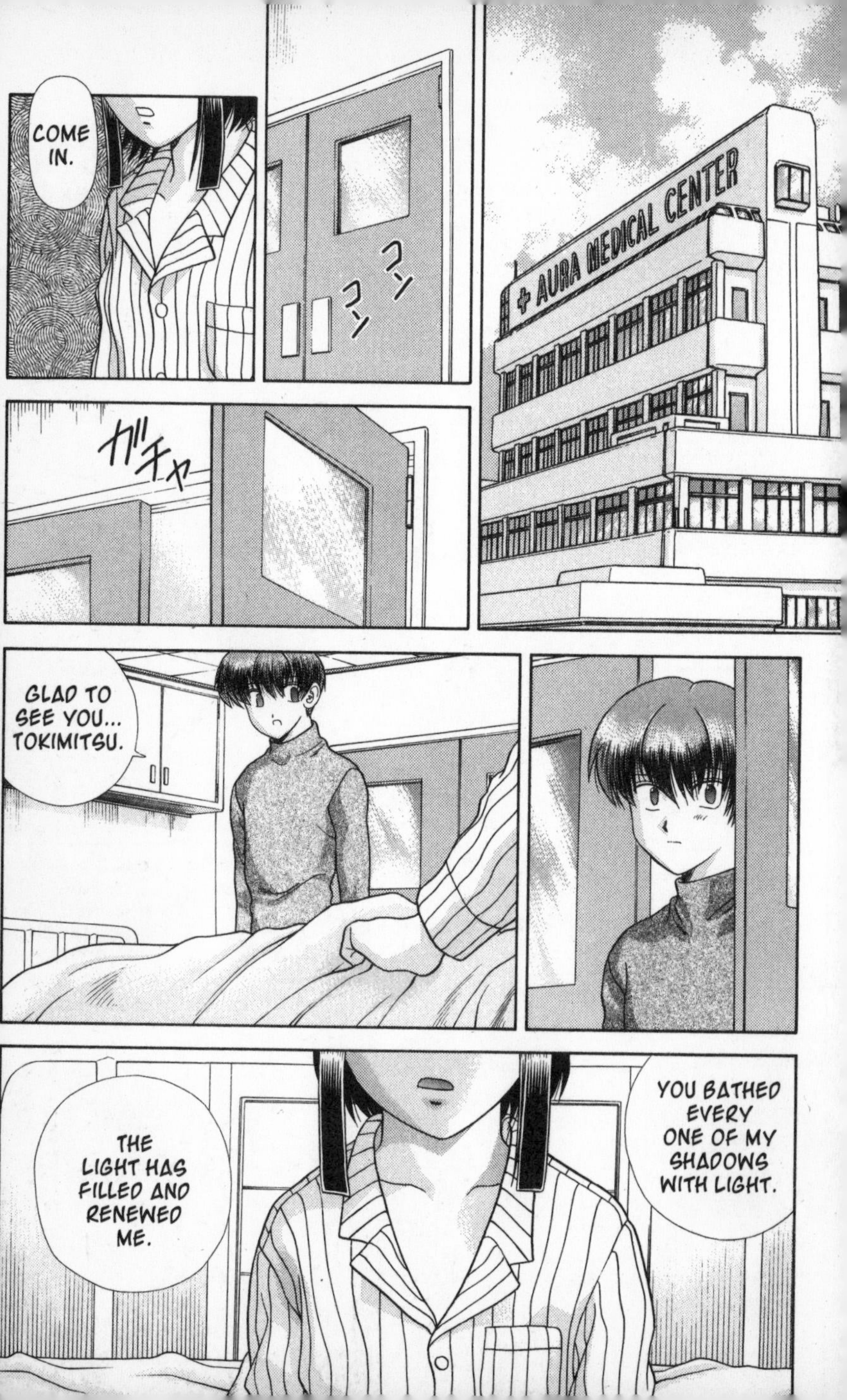
+ AURA MEDICAL CENTER
コン コン
COME IN.
ガチャ
GLAD TO SEE YOU... TOKIMITSU.
YOU BATHED EVERY ONE OF MY SHADOWS WITH LIGHT.
THE LIGHT HAS FILLED AND RENEWED ME.

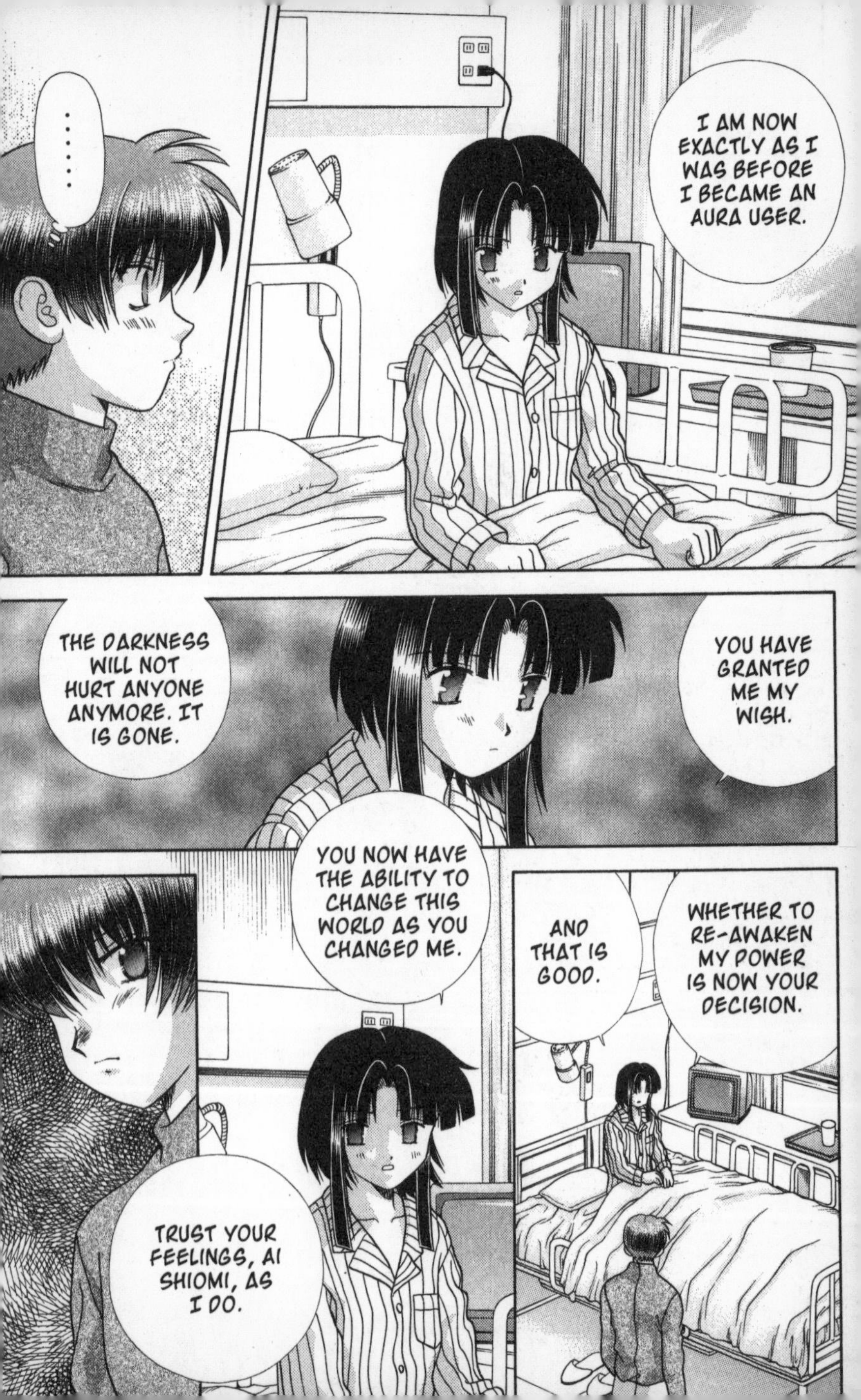
I AM NOW EXACTLY AS I WAS BEFORE I BECAME AN AURA USER.
......
YOU HAVE GRANTED ME MY WISH.
THE DARKNESS WILL NOT HURT ANYONE ANYMORE. IT IS GONE.
WHETHER TO RE-AWAKEN MY POWER IS NOW YOUR DECISION.
AND THAT IS GOOD.
YOU NOW HAVE THE ABILITY TO CHANGE THIS WORLD AS YOU CHANGED ME.
TRUST YOUR FEELINGS, AI SHIOMI, AS I DO.

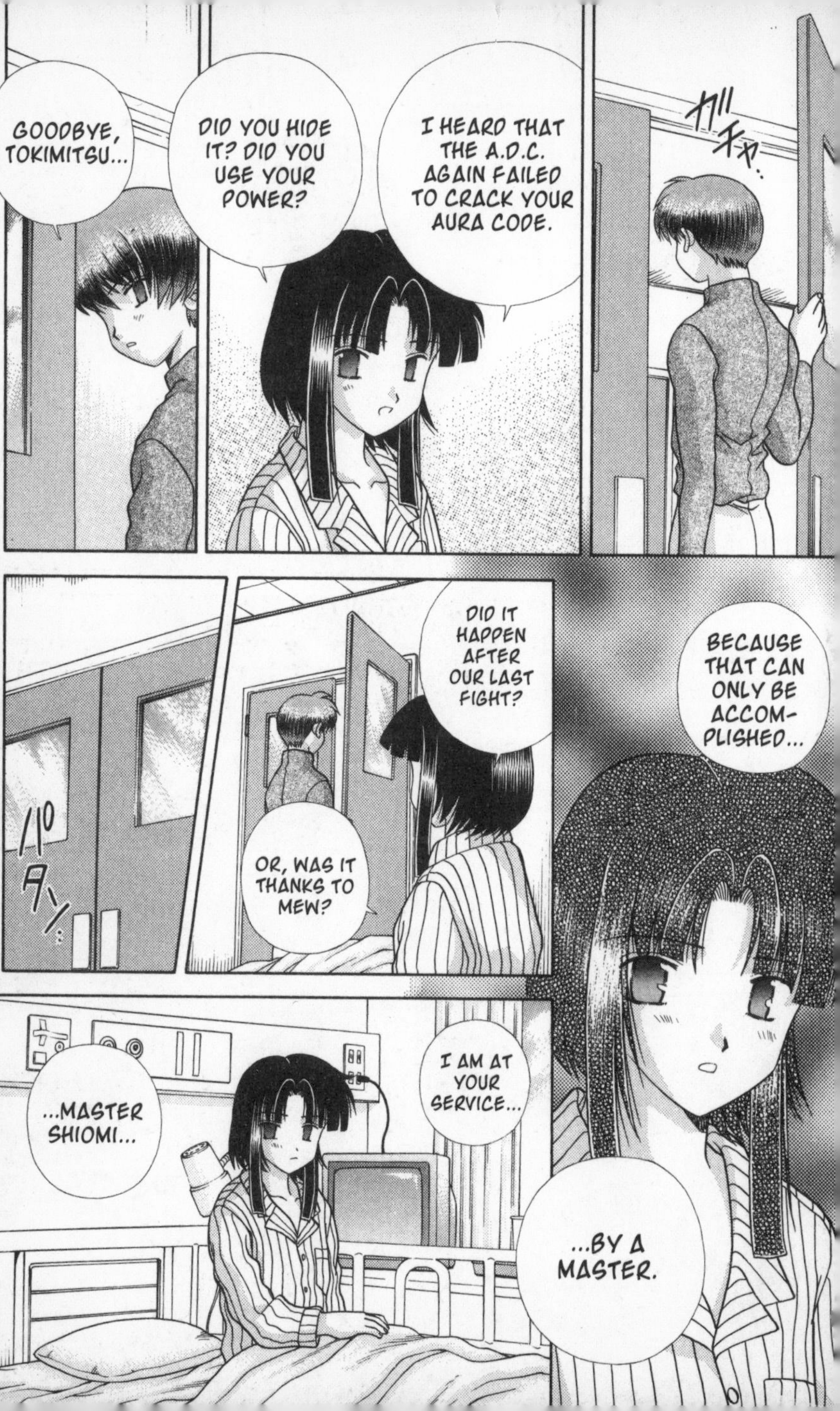
ガチャ..
I HEARD THAT THE A.D.C. AGAIN FAILED TO CRACK YOUR AURA CODE.
DID YOU HIDE IT? DID YOU USE YOUR POWER?
GOODBYE, TOKIMITSU...
BECAUSE THAT CAN ONLY BE ACCOM-PLISHED...
...BY A MASTER.
DID IT HAPPEN AFTER OUR LAST FIGHT?
OR, WAS IT THANKS TO MEW?
パタン..
I AM AT YOUR SERVICE...
...MASTER SHIOMI...

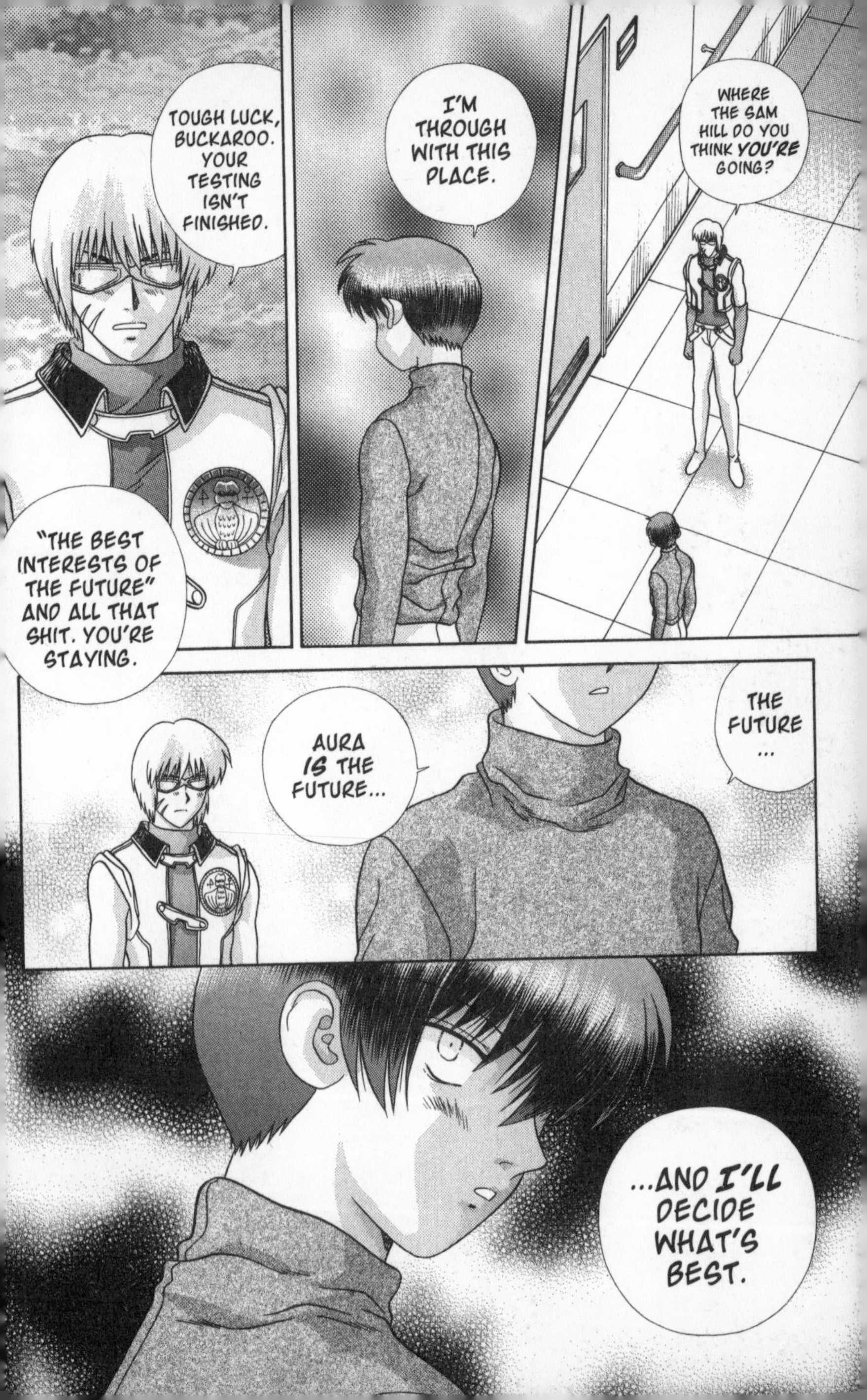
WHERE THE SAM HILL DO YOU THINK YOU'RE GOING?
I'M THROUGH WITH THIS PLACE.
TOUGH LUCK, BUCKAROO. YOUR TESTING ISN'T FINISHED.
"THE BEST INTERESTS OF THE FUTURE" AND ALL THAT SHIT. YOU'RE STAYING.
THE FUTURE ...
AURA IS THE FUTURE...
...AND I'LL DECIDE WHAT'S BEST.

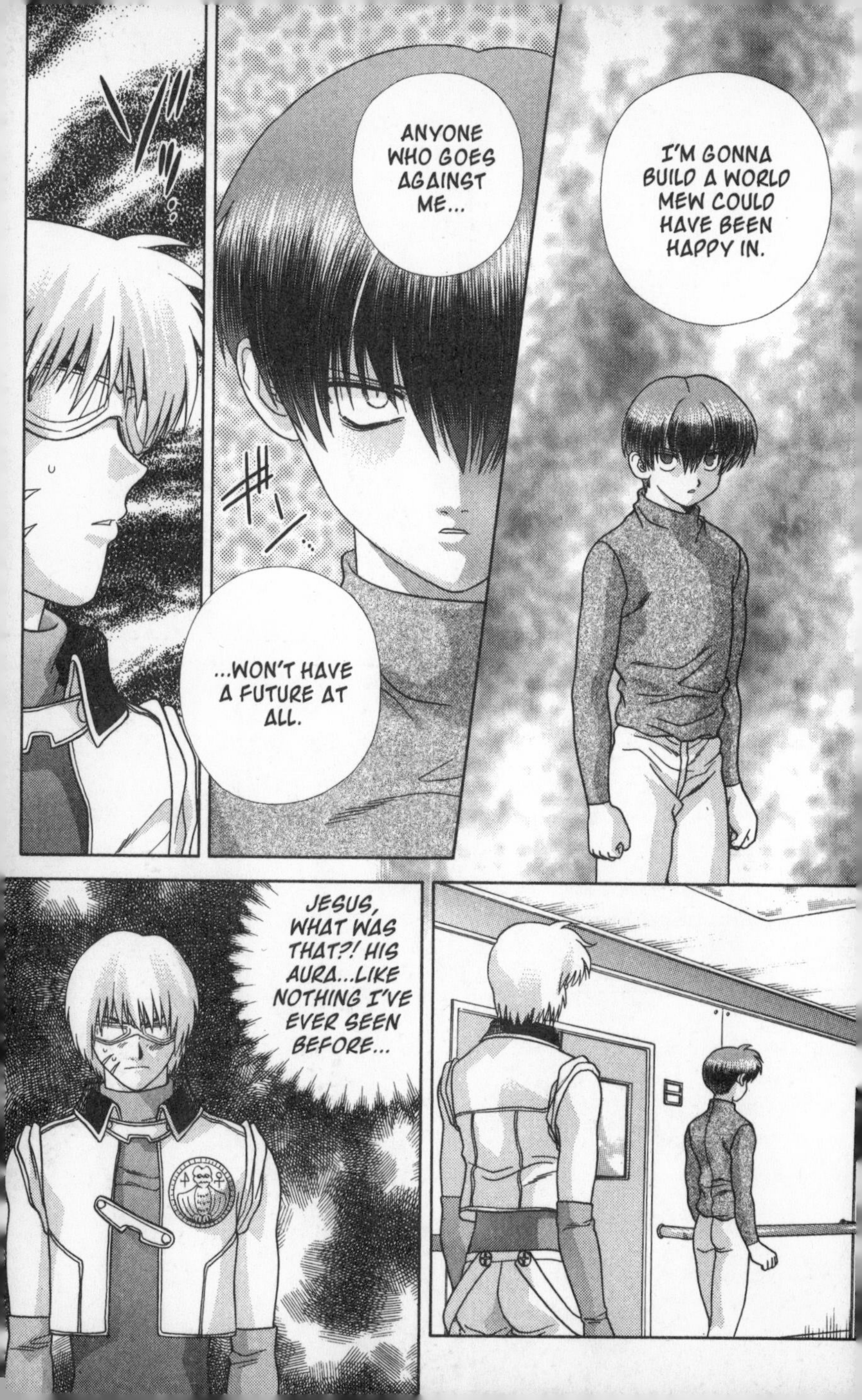
I'M GONNA BUILD A WORLD MEW COULD HAVE BEEN HAPPY IN.
ANYONE WHO GOES AGAINST ME...
...WON'T HAVE A FUTURE AT ALL.
JESUS, WHAT WAS THAT?! HIS AURA...LIKE NOTHING I'VE EVER SEEN BEFORE...

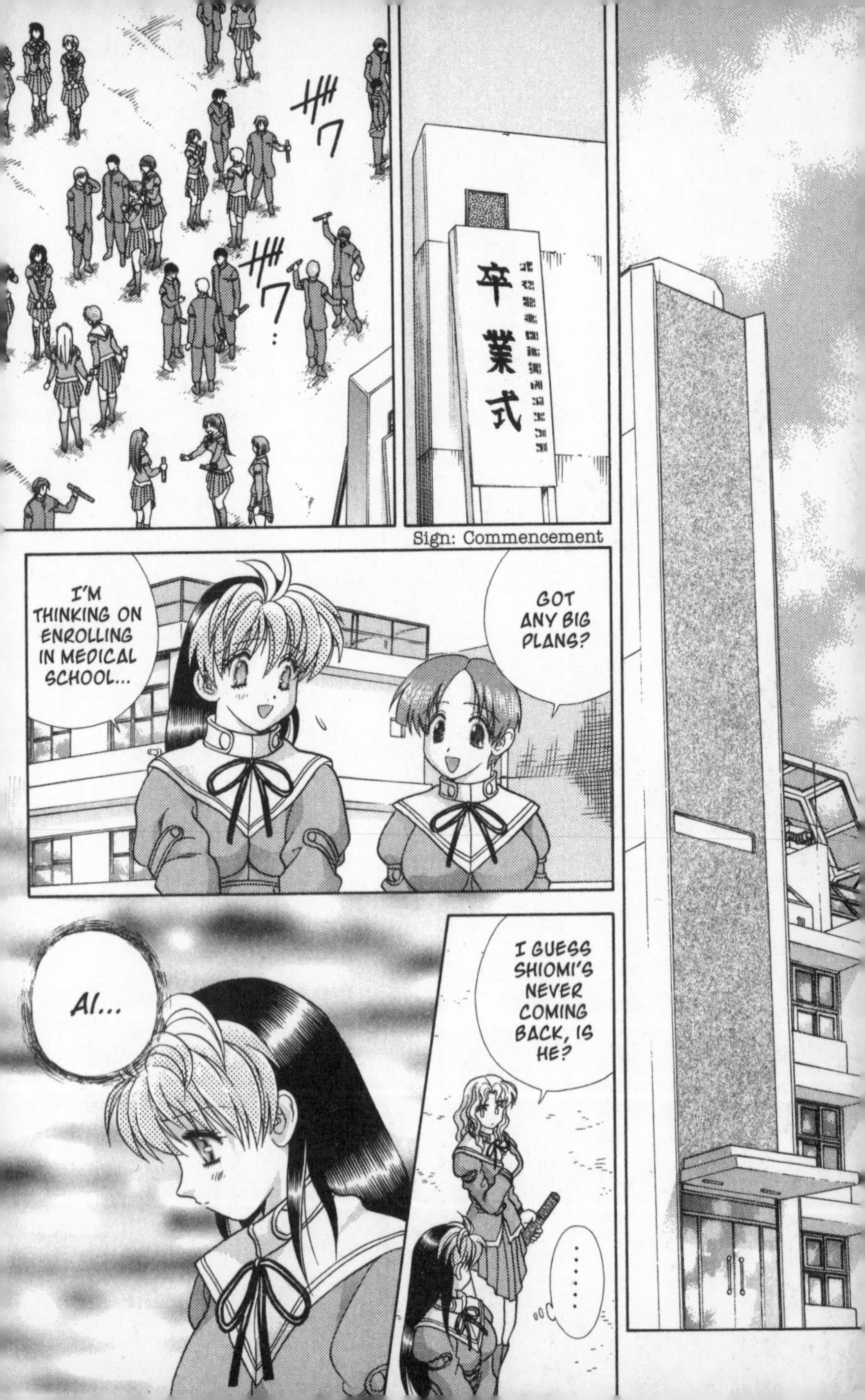
卒業式
Sign: Commencement
ザワ
ザワ…
GOT ANY BIG PLANS?
I'M THINKING ON ENROLLING IN MEDICAL SCHOOL...
I GUESS SHIOMI'S NEVER COMING BACK, IS HE?
......
AI...

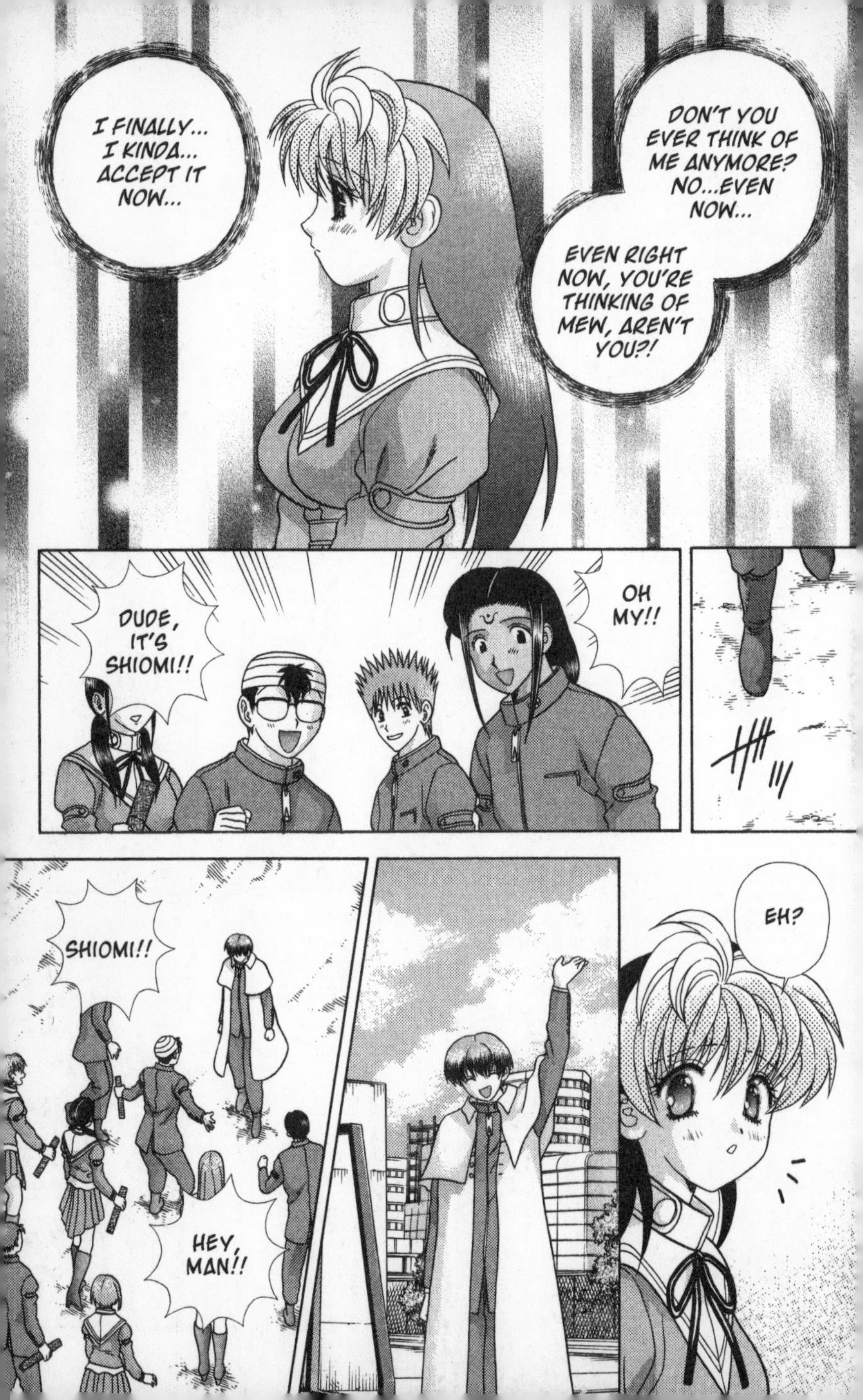
DON'T YOU EVER THINK OF ME ANYMORE? NO...EVEN NOW...
EVEN RIGHT NOW, YOU'RE THINKING OF MEW, AREN'T YOU?!
I FINALLY... I KINDA... ACCEPT IT NOW...
OH MY!!
DUDE, IT'S SHIOMI!!
EH?
SHIOMI!!
HEY, MAN!!

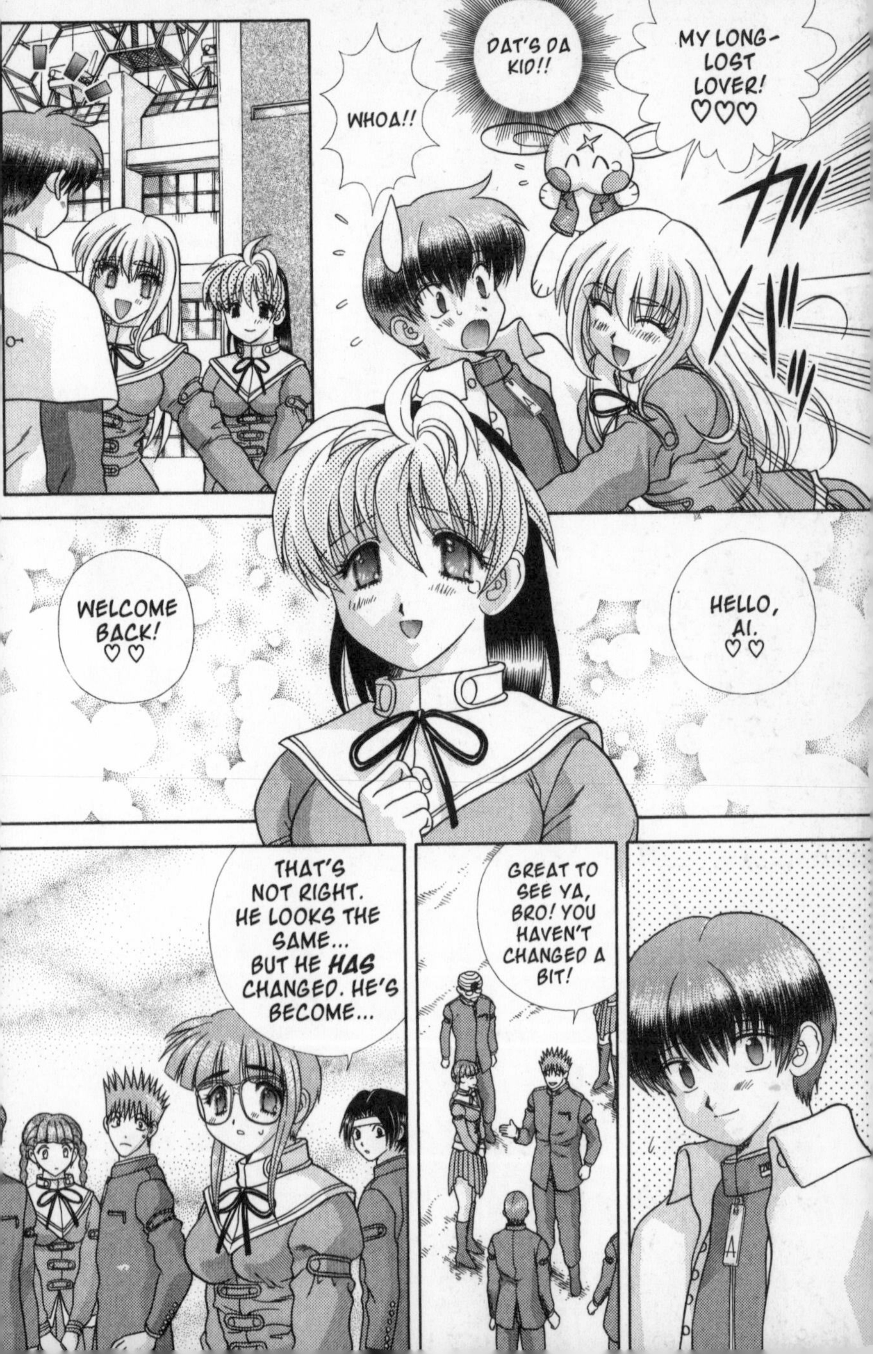
MY LONG-LOST LOVER! ♡♡♡
DAT'S DA KID!!
WHOA!!
HELLO, AI. ♡♡
WELCOME BACK! ♡♡
GREAT TO SEE YA, BRO! YOU HAVEN'T CHANGED A BIT!
THAT'S NOT RIGHT. HE LOOKS THE SAME... BUT HE *HAS* CHANGED. HE'S BECOME...

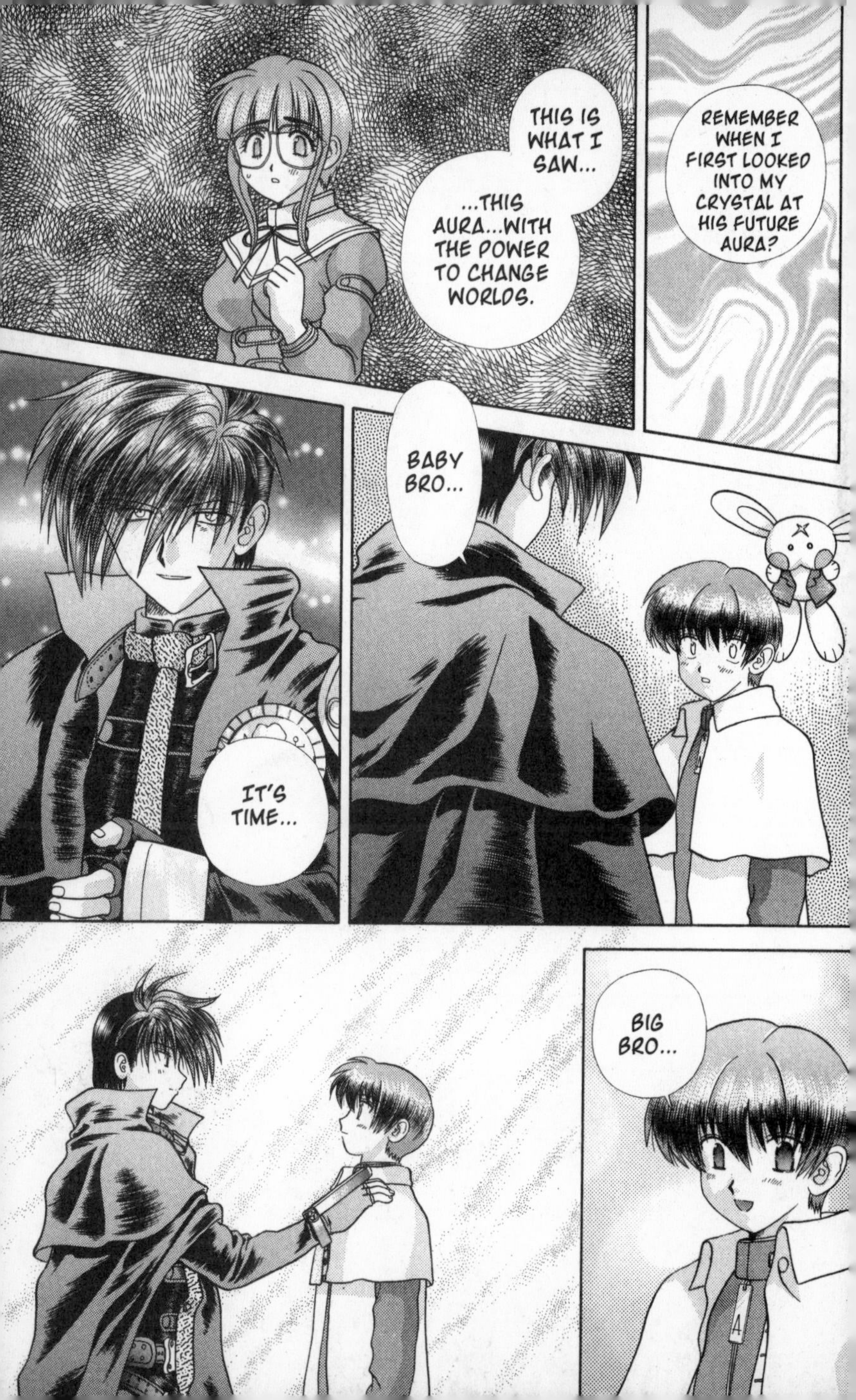
REMEMBER WHEN I FIRST LOOKED INTO MY CRYSTAL AT HIS FUTURE AURA?
THIS IS WHAT I SAW...
...THIS AURA...WITH THE POWER TO CHANGE WORLDS.
BABY BRO...
IT'S TIME...
BIG BRO...

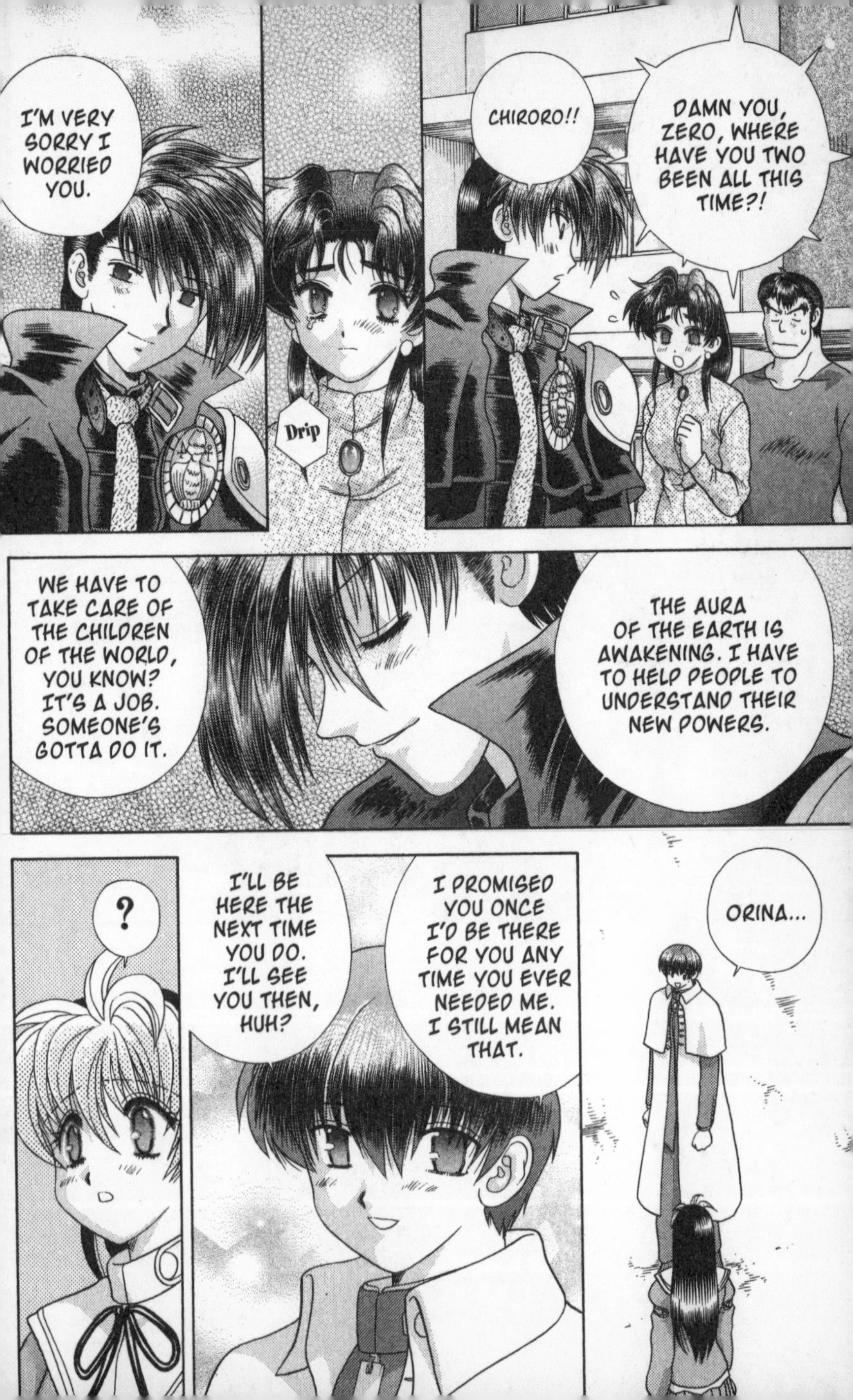
DAMN YOU, ZERO, WHERE HAVE YOU TWO BEEN ALL THIS TIME?!
CHIRORO!!
Drip
I'M VERY SORRY I WORRIED YOU.
THE AURA OF THE EARTH IS AWAKENING. I HAVE TO HELP PEOPLE TO UNDERSTAND THEIR NEW POWERS.
WE HAVE TO TAKE CARE OF THE CHILDREN OF THE WORLD, YOU KNOW? IT'S A JOB. SOMEONE'S GOTTA DO IT.
ORINA...
I PROMISED YOU ONCE I'D BE THERE FOR YOU ANY TIME YOU EVER NEEDED ME. I STILL MEAN THAT.
I'LL BE HERE THE NEXT TIME YOU DO. I'LL SEE YOU THEN, HUH?
?

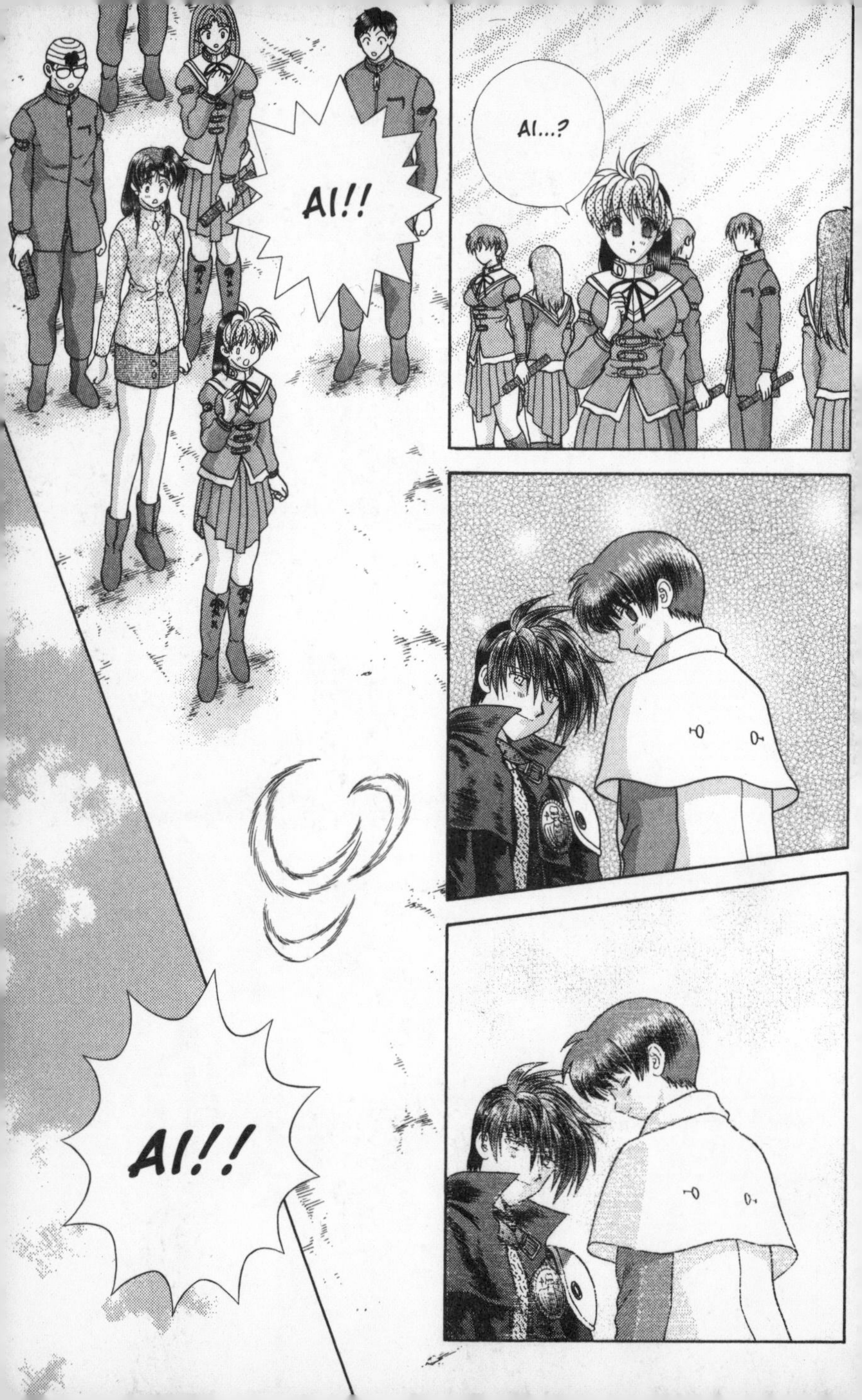
AI...?
AI!!
AI!!

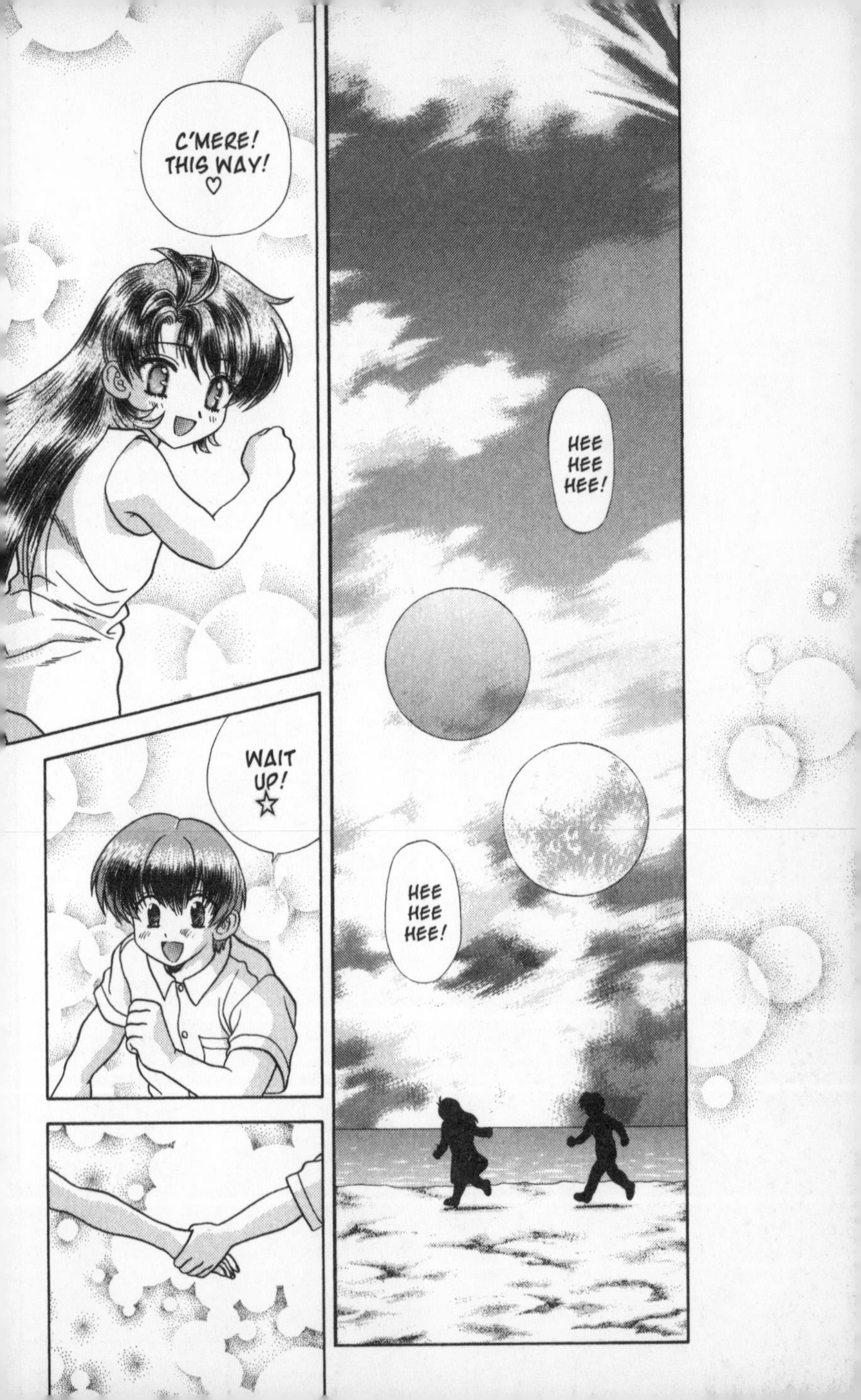
HEE HEE HEE!
HEE HEE HEE!
C'MERE! THIS WAY! ♡
WAIT UP! ☆

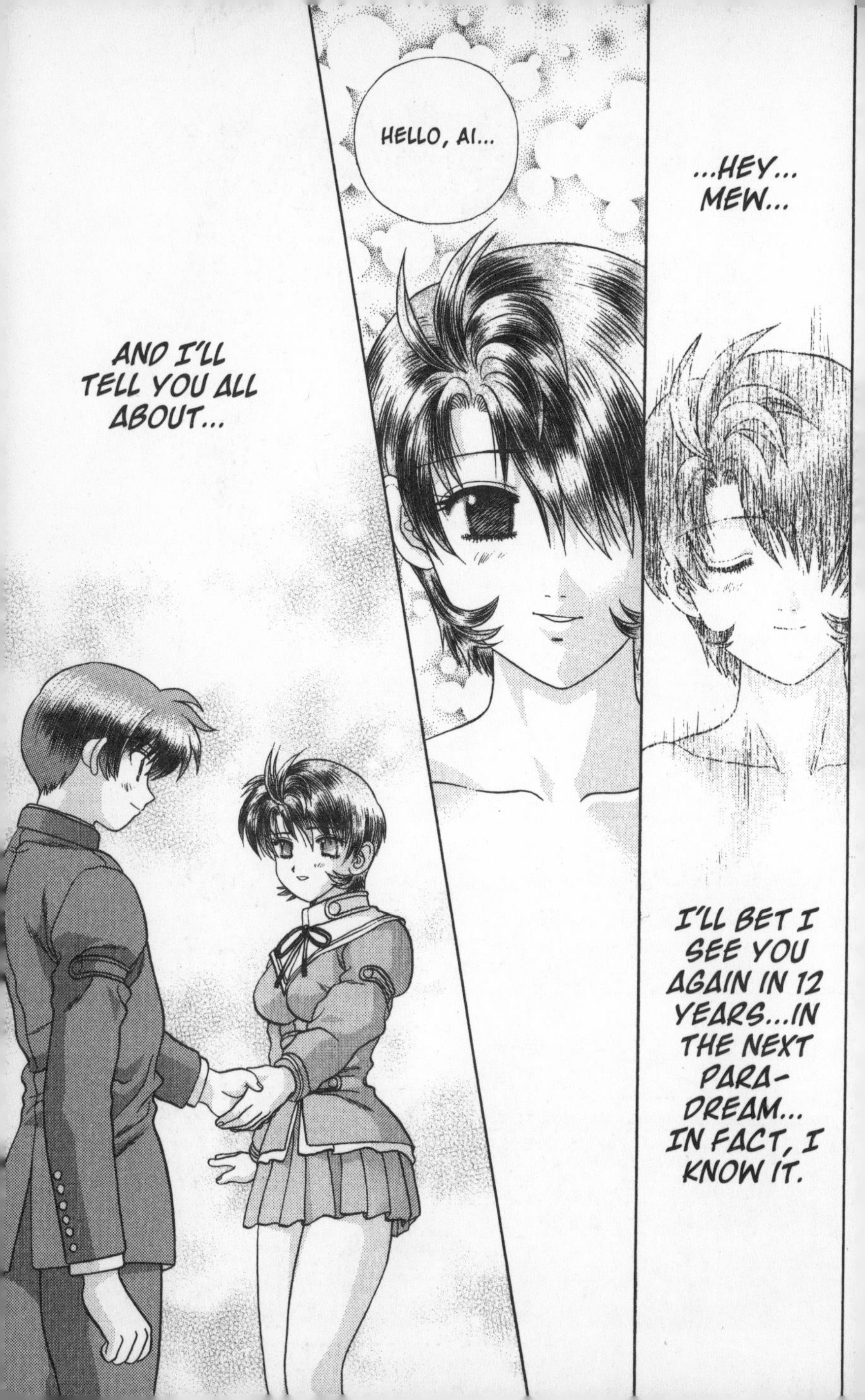
...HEY... MEW...
I'LL BET I SEE YOU AGAIN IN 12 YEARS...IN THE NEXT PARA-DREAM... IN FACT, I KNOW IT.
HELLO, AI...
AND I'LL TELL YOU ALL ABOUT...

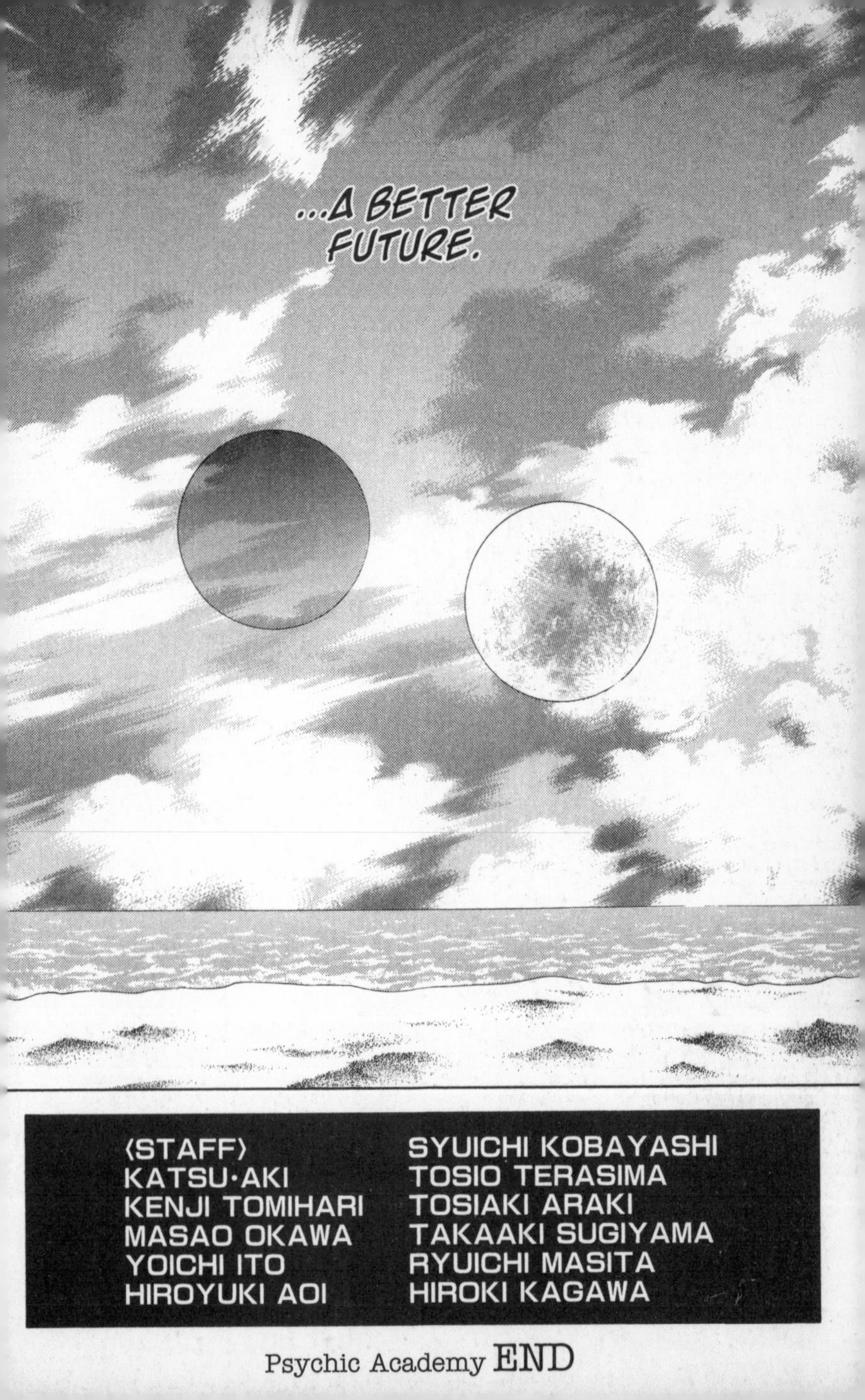
...A BETTER FUTURE.

⟨STAFF⟩

KATSU·AKI
KENJI TOMIHARI
MASAO OKAWA
YOICHI ITO
HIROYUKI AOI
SYUICHI KOBAYASHI
TOSIO TERASIMA
TOSIAKI ARAKI
TAKAAKI SUGIYAMA
RYUICHI MASITA
HIROKI KAGAWA

Psychic Academy END

TOKYOPOP SHOP

Ayumu struggles with her studies, and the all-important high school entrance exams are approaching. Fortunately, she has help from her best bud Shii-chan, who is at the top of the class. But when the test results come back, the friends are surprised: Ayumu surpasses Shii-chan's scores and gets into the school of her choice—without Shii-chan! Losing her friend is so painful for Ayumu that she starts cutting herself to ease her sorrow. Finally, Ayumu seeks comfort in a new friend, Manami. But will Manami prove to be the friend that Ayumu truly needs? Or will Ayumu continue down a dark path?

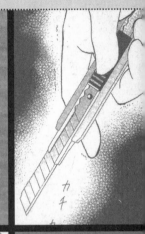

Volume 1

LIFE

Keiko Suenobu

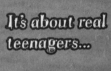

It's about real teenagers...

It's about real high school...

It's about real life.

LIFE
BY KEIKO SUENOBU

Ordinary high school teenagers...
Except that they're not.

READ THE ENTIRE FIRST CHAPTER ONLINE FOR FREE:

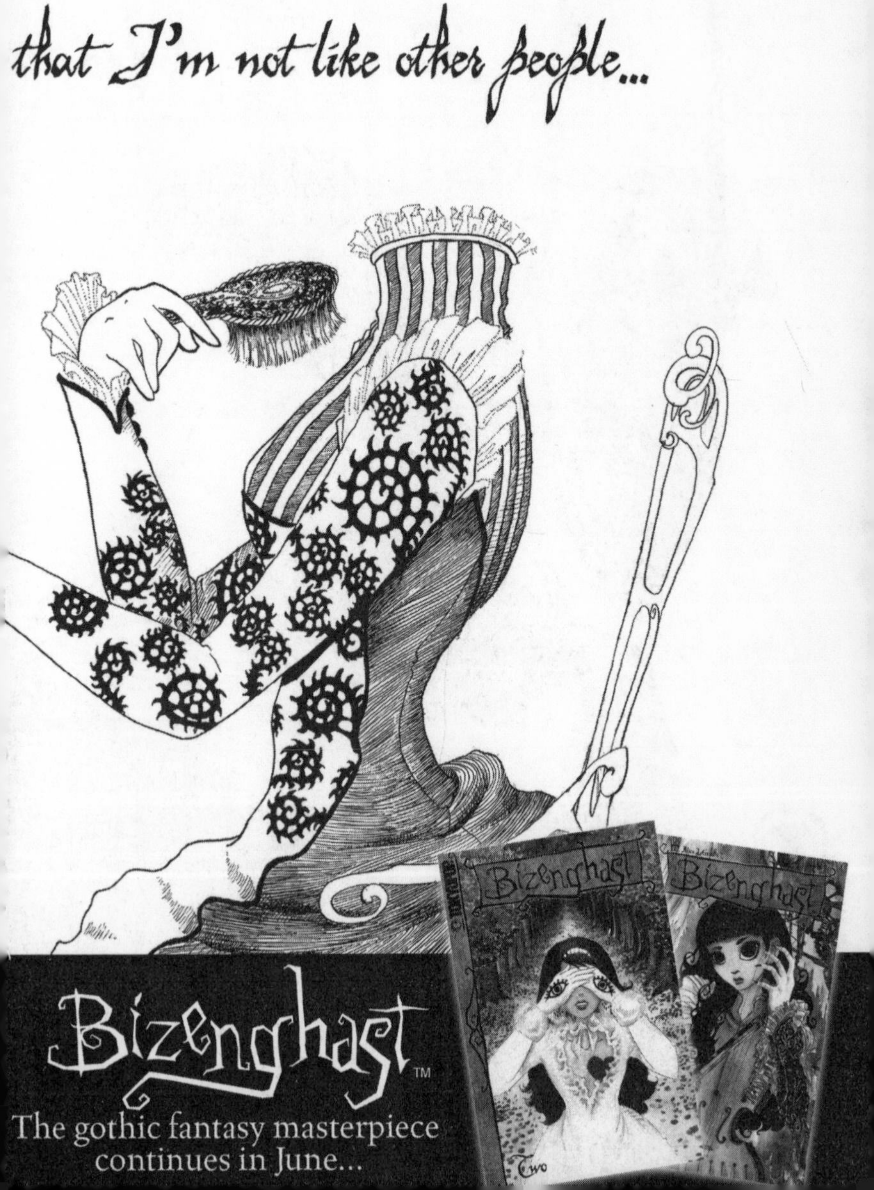
that I'm not like other people...
Bizenghast™
The gothic fantasy masterpiece
continues in June...
Bizenghast
Bizenghast
Two

STOP!

This is the back of the book.
You wouldn't want to spoil a great ending!

This book is printed "manga-style," in the authentic Japanese right-to-left format. Since none of the artwork has been flipped or altered, readers get to experience the story just as the creator intended. You've been asking for it, so TOKYOPOP® delivered: authentic, hot-off-the-press, and far more fun!

DIRECTIONS

If this is your first time reading manga-style, here's a quick guide to help you understand how it works.

It's easy... just start in the top right panel and follow the numbers. Have fun, and look for more 100% authentic manga from TOKYOPOP®!